Biblical Theology

Biblical Theology

Covenants and the Kingdom of God in Redemptive History

Jeong Koo Jeon

Foreword by Steve Baugh

WIPF & STOCK · Eugene, Oregon

BIBLICAL THEOLOGY
Covenants and the Kingdom of God in Redemptive History

Copyright © 2017 Jeong Koo Jeon. All rights reserved. Except for brief quotations in critical publications or reviews, no part of this book may be reproduced in any manner without prior written permission from the publisher. Write: Permissions, Wipf and Stock Publishers, 199 W. 8th Ave., Suite 3, Eugene, OR 97401.

Wipf & Stock
An Imprint of Wipf and Stock Publishers
199 W. 8th Ave., Suite 3
Eugene, OR 97401

www.wipfandstock.com

PAPERBACK ISBN: 978-1-5326-0580-2
HARDCOVER ISBN: 978-1-5326-0582-6
EBOOK ISBN: 978-1-5326-0581-9

Manufactured in the U.S.A.   JANUARY 26, 2017

In memory of the great biblical theologian Dr. Meredith G. Kline (1922–2007) and Reverend Won Sang Lee (1937–2016), who lived an exemplary life of care, humility, love, prayer, and passion for global mission in Christ

Contents

Foreword by Steve Baugh | *ix*
Preface | *xi*
Introduction | *xiii*

1	The Covenant of Creation and the Kingdom of God	1
2	The Noahic Covenants and the Kingdom of God	33
3	The Abrahamic Covenant and the Kingdom of God	58
4	The Mosaic Covenant and the Kingdom of God	85
5	The Davidic Covenant and the Kingdom of God	131
6	The New Covenant and the Kingdom of God	172

Conclusion | *220*
Appendix A   Covenant Theology and Old Testament Ethics | *225*
Appendix B   Redemptive Historical Poems | *246*
Bibliography | *251*
Names Index | *263*
Subject Index | *267*
Scripture Index | *279*

Foreword

THE BIBLE IS A story with a beginning, a middle, and an end. (And what an ending it has!) While this may seem to be an obvious and unnecessary observation, it is actually critical for the most accurate description of the Bible's contents in any one place and for grasping the message of the whole.

The discipline known in our circles as Biblical Theology traces the Bible's message historically in what is known as its "organic development." This phrase is very rich with meaning. The term "organic" reflects the fact that the Bible has a natural unity to it. It may have originated in sixty-six books composed over the course of well over a millennium; nevertheless, it displays a remarkable unity because it is an organic whole with one divine author originating it through a host of inspired human authors. Yet the second term, "development," acknowledges that the Bible's message is not static but unfolding; it grows. This growth is like how a story grows: with a unity of plot and characters. In the case of the Bible the main characters are the sovereign, divine King and his covenant people in Christ Jesus.

Geerhardus Vos, who is cited from time to time in this book, once gave the happy analogy for the organic development of Scripture in the image of an acorn growing into a stately oak tree. Like an acorn, God's revelation was originally given in seed form. But an acorn is an *oak* acorn, not a mulberry seed, a maple helicopter, or a magpie egg. As the oak acorn grows it becomes a tiny shoot with leaves that are identifiable as oak leaves, and it is *still* an oak, even though it is not the spreading oak tree yet. Throughout its life, the oak tree develops with an essential, organic unity to it. So also the message of the Bible from Genesis to Revelation: it is organically unified, but it develops.

The story of the Bible's organic development is the story traced in this book by Dr. Jeong Koo Jeon, centered on the Bible's twin themes of covenant and kingdom. Dr. Jeon both surveys the Bible's contents from one epoch to another and sketches out for the reader some of the main issues discussed over the years by Reformed scholars in our deliberations on the Bible's unified message, adding his own analysis. We don't believe our work is done, and we have sometimes debated various interpretive

Foreword

viewpoints rather strenuously, as you will see here; but Dr. Jeon expertly guides the reader through the main lines of interpretation of the whole of God's revelation from beginning to end. The scope of this work might seem breathtaking at first, but the reader will hopefully be aided by the focus upon covenant and kingdom presented here, which provide the Bible's own organizing center.

Dr. Steve Baugh
Professor of New Testament
Westminster Seminary California

Preface

It is my special privilege to publish *Biblical Theology* to celebrate and commemorate the quincentennial of the Protestant Reformation in Europe in 1517. I have had opportunities to visit the global mission field including Bolivia, Brazil, and parts of Northeast Asia to teach in the areas of biblical and systematic theology. In doing so, I was compelled to write a book on biblical theology that is understandable and accessible to lay leaders, seminarians, pastors, and missionaries on the global mission field. This is the reason I began to write and publish biblical theological articles in various journals.

I completed this writing project while I was a visiting scholar at Westminster Theological Seminary from September 2014 to May 2015. I give my special thanks to Dr. Jeffrey Jue, who sponsored and supported my visiting scholarship. Dr. Steve Park and his congregation, Jubilee Presbyterian Church, generously allowed me to use their beautiful guest house while I was staying in Philadelphia. The students, faculty, and the board members of Chesapeake Theological Seminary and Faith Theological Seminary have been a constant source of joy and encouragement to me in my teaching and writing ministry.

I have been greatly indebted to many godly individuals, churches, and various other organizations throughout my teaching and writing ministry. I would like to mention just a few names and give my special thanks for their prayers and financial assistance to complete this book: Dr. Jinmo Timothy Cho; Reverend Minki Hong and his former church, Hosanna Presbyterian Church; Dr. Chang-Wuk Kang; Dr. Sahng Yeon Kim; Revererend Owen Lee and his church, Christ Central Presbyterian Church; the Korean congregation at Chapelgate Presbyterian Church; and Way & Gate Foundation Inc.

Teaching and writing about biblical theology has been a constant joy and excitement. The fountainhead of my thought has been primarily through the illumination of the Holy Spirit. In addition, the ideas and examples of biblical and systematic theology by John Calvin, John Owen, Francis Turretin, Jonathan Edwards, Charles Hodge, Herman Bavinck, Geerhardus Vos, Cornelius Van Til, and Meredith G. Kline have been the backbone of my *Biblical Theology*. Because the Bible is the infallible and inerrant Word of God, I have tried to maintain a constant dialogue and harmony between biblical and systematic theology. In many ways, my book is the fruit of biblical, historical, and theological reflection.

The editors of different journals and magazines graciously gave me permission to republish those journal articles and redemptive historical poems in this book: "The Abrahamic Covenant and the Kingdom of God." *The Confessional Presbyterian* 7 (2011): 123–38, 249–50; "The Covenant of Creation and the Kingdom of God." *The Confessional Presbyterian* 9 (2013): 123–42; "Covenant Theology and Old Testament Ethics: Meredith G. Kline's Intrusion Ethics." *Kerux* 16/1 (2001): 3–32; "The Garden of Eden." *New Horizons* 23/7 (2002):21; "Glory in the Midst of Darkness." *Kerux* 17/1 (2002): 43–44; "The Noahic Covenants and the Kingdom of God." *Mid-America Journal of Theology* 22 (2013): 179–209. Dr. Jeffrey Waddington read my manuscript, and improved the quality of writing with careful proof reading. Mrs. Paige Britton provided an excellent work for copy editing. My former professor Dr. Steve Baugh encouraged me with his wonderful and insightful foreword despite his busy schedule. Nonetheless, for whatever shortcomings of the book remain, I am wholly responsible.

In the Spring of 2013, I experienced an unexpected sepsis due to appendicitis while I was on my teaching trip in Southern California. I lost consciousness for almost three weeks while I was hospitalized at Cedars-Sinai Medical Center. God miraculously healed me, and I recovered completely to even the doctors' surprise. I cannot forget all the people who fervently prayed and helped my family during that difficult period of time.

May the Lord richly bless all those who read my book. I praise the Lord for his grace, mercy, and provision to this undeserved sinner like me, giving me a second life even during the present pilgrimage. *Soli Deo Gloria!*

Introduction

The Bible and Redemptive History

GOD REVEALED HIMSELF IN his creation and the Bible. God's revelation in his creation, including man and the universe, is a general revelation. General revelation sufficiently reveals God's existence to all. Therefore, no one can question the existence of God because everyone inherently knows the existence of God as it is engraved in their hearts, as Paul writes to believers in Rome (Rom 1:18–21). However, general revelation does not reveal redemptive grace, the good news of the gospel and the dual aspect of God's final judgment between the eschatological Kingdom of God and the Kingdom of Satan. Because of the influence of sin and total depravity of the human mind and soul, man cannot inherently know the good news of the gospel and the essence of God's kingdom apart from Scripture. So God rejoices in revealing himself as Creator, Redeemer and Consummator in the Bible, which is also known as special revelation. In this regard, a proper understanding and distinction between general and special revelation is essential.[1] Herman Bavinck encapsulates the importance of a proper distinction between general and special revelation:

> It is the unanimous conviction of Christian theologians that general revelation is inadequate. Pelagians do assert the sufficiency of natural revelation, and they were followed in the eighteenth century by rationalists and deists. The defect of all general revelation is that it can supply us with no knowledge of Christ and divine grace and forgiveness. In addition, natural knowledge is not without error and its claims highly debated.[2]

---

1. Karl Barth as the architect of the existential hermeneutic and theology rejects the proper place of general revelation because his concept of revelation is unbiblically Christo-monistic. Cf. Brunner and Barth, *Natural Theology*, 67–128. For a balanced understanding of the distinction between general and special revelation, see Bavinck, *Reformed Dogmatics: Prolegomena*, 301–2; Berkhof, *Introduction to Systematic Theology*, 128–43.

2. Bavinck, *Reformed Dogmatics: Prolegomena*, 301–2.

Introduction

In so doing, Bavinck insightfully articulates that both general and special revelation finds "its fulfillment and meaning in Christ." Moreover, a proper understanding of general revelation not only connects "the kingdom of heaven and the kingdom of earth" but also integrates "creation and redemption together in one great eschatological cantata of praise." Likewise, grasping the eschatological goal in God's creation and redemption and the distinction between general and special revelation is essential:

> All revelation—general and special—finally finds its fulfillment and meaning in Christ. God's revelation in Scripture and in Christ provides the spectacles of faith that enables us to understand general revelation better, as well as a basis for encounters with non-Christians. In no way should the Christian faith be represented as otherworldly or anti-creation. Rather, grace and nature are united in the Christian faith, and general revelation links the kingdom of heaven and the kingdom of earth—it joins creation and redemption together in one great eschatological cantata of praise. Grace restores nature, a religious life is woven into the very fabric of ordinary human experience. Finally, God is one and the same loving God in creation and redemption; grace restores nature.[3]

The Bible as God's special revelation is composed of sixty-six books, including the Old and New Testaments from Genesis to Revelation. However, the followers of Judaism reject the New Testament as the part of the biblical canon. This is logical because they reject Jesus Christ as the Messiah who came as the fulfillment of the Messianic prophecy in the Old Testament, the Hebrew Bible. The Bible is characteristically the inspired Word of God and is the only infallible and inerrant guide to our faith, theology, and life in the present world.[4] Against "the mind of the modern theologian" who denies the Bible as the Word of God, Edward Young points out the crucial importance of believers presupposing the Bible as the infallible and inerrant Word of God:

> If, however, we do accept the teaching of the Bible, God grant that we may not be ashamed of that teaching! The Bible, in manifold ways, has proclaimed and asserted its divinity. It has emphatically declared that in a unique manner it has come to us from God. If, in professing to believe the Bible, we are going to be serious, let us accept its claims and not try to explain them away! Let us follow our God who cannot lie; and since He cannot lie, let us believe that His Word is truth itself. Those copies of Scripture which came forth from God Almighty were infallible and inerrant. No matter what men may say to the contrary, no matter how much they may seek to obscure the issue, in the very nature of the case it could not have been otherwise.[5]

---

3. Ibid., 302.

4. For a comprehensive description and analysis of the Bible as the infallible and inerrant Word of God from a biblical, historical, and theological perspective in light of the contemporary rejection of this, see Lillback and Gaffin, *Thy Word Is Still Truth*.

5. Edward J. Young, *Thy Word Is Truth*, 91–92.

Introduction

God wants to be glorified through his people, the elect who are chosen in his Son Jesus Christ. To live a life that is glorifying to God, we need to recover a worldview that is deeply rooted in the Bible. The present age is a pilgrimage for believers who eagerly anticipate the age to come. To recover the concrete biblical worldview, we need to understand the grand drama of redemptive history which flows throughout the Bible. The Bible reveals redemptive history from creation through fall, redemption, and consummation. History, revealed in the Bible, is not static. It is a dynamic and dramatic story that unravels according to the pattern of redemptive history, anticipated in the divine covenants.

Covenants and the Kingdom of God

History, as revealed in the Bible, is deeply concerned with redemption. From Abraham's calling in Genesis 11, the entire Old Testament deals with the ancient history of Israel in the cultural, religious, and political contexts of the ancient Near Eastern world. However, it is important to remember that the ancient history of Israel as revealed in the Old Testament is redemptive, foreshadowing the coming Messiah, the eschatological Kingdom of God and the final judgment. God used different covenants as a means to govern his creation, and to guide and accomplish redemption in the Son of God, Jesus Christ. Both world history and redemptive history are carefully planned and guided by God's diverse covenants. Kline observes the close relationship between divine covenants and the Kingdom of God as follows:

> It was stated earlier that there is a close connection between divine covenant and divine kingdom. Viewed as commitment transactions with their rituals, documents, and stipulated terms and procedures, covenants function as administrative instruments of God's kingly rule. Indeed, the connection is sometimes closer than this. As we have observed, *berith* in some passages denotes the actual historical realization of the arrangement defined in the covenantal stipulations and sanctions. Covenant thus becomes a particular administration of God's kingship, whether in the bestowal of his holy kingdom as a royal grant on a special covenant people as their peculiar inheritance or in the sovereign government of a temporal world order whose benefits are common to all alike (as in the postdiluvian common grace covenant of Gen 9). It is in this sense that covenant is used to designate the major divisions of covenant theology.[6]

God's covenants reveal his creation, providential care of the universe, world history, and redemption in Jesus Christ. The telos of the divine covenants is not the fulfillment of an earthly utopia in the present age, but the final judgment and visible realization of the everlasting Kingdom of God in Jesus Christ and eternal separation of the Kingdom of Satan.

---

6. Kline, *Kingdom Prologue*, 4.

INTRODUCTION

The Historical Critical Interpretation and Biblical Theology

Albert Schweitzer, as a New Testament scholar, medical doctor, and musician, was the most famous missionary in the twentieth century. He received the Nobel Peace Prize in 1952 for his service and sacrifice in Africa. In the introduction of his book, *The Quest of the Historical Jesus*, Schweitzer, reflecting on the historical critical interpretation of the life of Jesus by the German liberals in the nineteenth century, claims that "the greatest achievement of German theology is the critical investigation of the life of Jesus." He begins his book with the following remarks:

> When, at some future day, our period of civilization shall lie, closed and completed, before the eyes of later generations, German theology will stand out as a great, a unique phenomenon in the mental and spiritual life of our time. For nowhere save in the German temperament can there be found in the same perfection the living complex of conditions and factors—of philosophic thought, critical acumen, historical insight, and religious feeling—without which no deep theology is possible. And the greatest achievement of German theology is the critical investigation of the life of Jesus. What it has accomplished here has laid down the conditions and determined the course of the religious thinking of the future. In the history of doctrine its work has been negative; it has, so to speak, cleared the site for a new edifice of religious thought. In describing how the ideas of Jesus were taken possession of by the Greek spirit, it was tracing the growth of that which must necessarily become strange to us, and, as a matter of fact, has become strange to us.[7]

However, our assessment is that the most harmful influences to the church in modern days, especially in the Global Mission Age, come from the historical critical reading and interpretation of the life of Jesus and the Bible. The exponents and followers of the historical critical interpretation of the life of Jesus and the Bible arose due to unbelief, intellectual pride, and lack of humility in the face of the triune God, as Herman Bavinck correctly assessed nearly a century ago:

> Critical opposition to this view of inspiration [organic inspiration] remains strong. While objections—e.g., from historical criticism—should not be ignored, we must not overlook the spiritual-ethical hostility to Scripture from the forces of unbelief. While not all questioning of Scripture reveals hostile unbelief, it is important to underscore the duty of every person to be humble before Scripture. Holy Scripture must judge us, not the reverse. The Holy Spirit opens our heart to trust, believe, and obey God's Word in Scripture. Submission remains a struggle, also an intellectual one. We must acknowledge our limitations, the reality of mystery, our weakness of faith, without despairing of all knowledge and truth. Our hope is in Christ, the true man in whom

---

7. Schweitzer, *The Quest of the Historical Jesus*, 1.

Introduction

human nature is restored. That is the purpose of Scripture: to make us wise unto salvation (2 Tim 3:15).[8]

The rise of the historical critical interpretation has significantly influenced biblical hermeneutics and theology. Liberal theology in the nineteenth century was centered in and culminated in Germany. Hegel's idealistic philosophy of history, represented in *The Phenomenology of Spirit* in 1807 and *The Philosophy of History* in 1840 influenced the development of the historical critical interpretation of the Bible for liberal theologians.[9] The dialectical view of history, laid out by Hegel, was accepted and applied by political thinkers, biologists and theologians. For example, Darwin's biological evolutionism, portrayed in *On the Origin of Species* in 1859, was a biological application of Hegel's dialectical view of history.[10] Karl Marx's and Friedrich Engels' political philosophy, laid out in *The Communist Manifesto* in 1848, was the political and philosophical implication of Hegel's dialectical view of history. Liberal theologians, particularly liberal biblical scholars, adopted Hegel's dialectical view of history and applied it to their understanding and interpretation of history in the Bible and formation of the Bible.

If Hegel's dialectical understanding of the philosophy of history was the cornerstone of the rise of the historical critical school in Germany in the nineteenth century, then Kant was the father of the moralistic concept of God's kingdom in liberal theology. Liberal theologians did not believe in the good news of the gospel and the everlasting Kingdom of God. The proponents of liberal theology reinterpreted the Kingdom of God in light of optimistic moralism, in which human beings may accomplish and establish the optimistic moral kingdom of God on earth because people are morally capable to achieve this and do good. This realization of the moralistic kingdom of God is the goal of religious and political organizations. Likewise, liberal theologians thoroughly reinterpreted the biblical concept of the kingdom of God in light of the Kantian ideal of the optimistic moralistic kingdom of God.

The historical critical reading of the Bible had been represented by existential hermeneutics and theology in the twentieth century. Karl Barth and Rudolf Bultmann were the champions of existential hermeneutics and theology. They fused existential philosophy with hermeneutics and theology, interpreting the Bible in light of the lens of existentialism. Although they were critical of nineteenth century classical liberalism, they shared the basic presuppositions of classical liberalism that the Bible *is not* the inspired and inerrant Word of God with their acceptance of the historical critical reading of the Bible. In existential hermeneutics and theology, the Bible is not the inspired and inerrant Word of God, but it *becomes* the Word of God when people personally encounter the message of the Bible. Presupposing the historical critical

---

8. Bavinck, *Reformed Dogmatics: Prolegomena*, 389.
9. Hegel, *The Phenomenology of Spirit*; Hegel, *The Philosophy of History*.
10. Darwin, *The Origin of Species*.

Introduction

reading of the Bible, Barth insists that the recognition of "a biblical story" as "saga or legend" does not have to be considered as "an attack on the substance of the biblical witness." In doing so, Barth removes the solid backbone of biblical and systematic theology from the Bible:

> Thus the judgment that a biblical story is to be regarded either as a whole or in part as saga or legend does not have to be an attack on the substance of the biblical witness. All that might be said is that according to the standards by which "historical" truth is usually measured *elsewhere* or generally, this story is one that to some degree eludes any sure declaration that it happened as the narrative says. Saga or legend can only denote the more or less intrusive part of the story-tellers in the story told. There is no story in which we do not have to reckon with this aspect, and therefore with elements of saga or legend according to the general concept "historical" truth. This applies also to the stories told in the Bible. Otherwise they would have to be without temporal form. Yet this fundamental uncertainty in general historicity, and therefore the positive judgment that here and there saga or legend is actually present, does not have to be an attack on the substance of the biblical testimony.[11]

Although Bultmannn and Barth shared a common denominator, the historical critical reading of the Bible, Bultmann's emphasis lies in the demythologization of supernatural events in the Bible with existential implication. According to Bultmann, the Bible is full of mythological events, such as Jesus Christ's incarnation, bodily resurrection, and ascension. For example, Bultmann argues that Jesus' bodily resurrection, depicted in the four Gospels, was not a historical event but a mythological one, which reflects the faith of his original disciples and the early Christian community:

> Now, it is beyond question that the New Testament presents the event of Jesus Christ in mythical terms. The problem is whether that is the only possible presentation. . . . Now, it is clear from the outset that the event of Christ is of a wholly different order from the cult-myth of Greek or Hellenistic religion. Jesus Christ is certainly presented as the Son of God, a pre-existent divine being, and therefore to that extent a mythical figure. But he is also a concrete figure of history—Jesus of Nazareth. His life is more than a mythical event; it is a human life which ended in the tragedy of crucifixion. We have here a unique combination of history and myth. The New Testament claims that this Jesus of history, whose father and mother were well known to his contemporaries (John 6.42) is at the same time the pre-existent Son of God, and side by side with the historical event of the crucifixion it sets the definitely non-historical event of the resurrection.[12]

---

11. Barth, *Church Dogmatics*, 1/1: 327.

12. Bartsch, *Kerygma and Myth*, 34. For more information on Bultmann's existential hermeneutics and theology, see Bultmann, *History and Eschatology*; Bultmann, *History of the Synoptic Tradition*; Bultmann, *Jesus and the Word*.

Introduction

Nevertheless, when the Easter event is proclaimed as kerygma, we encounter the Word of God as the spiritual reality of believers just like the original disciples. In that sense, Bultmann argues that when we encounter the message of kerygma, then the Bible *is* the Word of God:

> It is so only when Scripture is heard as a word addressed personally to ourselves, as kerygma—i.e. when the experience consists in encounter and response to the address. That Scripture is the Word of God is something which happens only in the here and now of encounter; it is not a fact susceptible to objective proof. The Word of God is hidden in Scripture, just like any other act of his.[13]

Likewise, Bultmann's presupposition of the historical critical reading of the Bible and demythologization of the supernatural events in the Bible in light of existentialism removes not only the possibility of systematic theology, but also of biblical theology, which explores the creation, fall, redemption, and consummation from a redemptive historical perspective.

As we live in the Global Mission Age by God's grace, the evangelical church has to put to death the historical critical reading of the Bible, which has been one of the major sources of intellectual and spiritual poisons in the church.

Dispensational Interpretation and Biblical Theology

Since the middle of the nineteenth century, dispensational hermeneutics and theology has been the most influential hermeneutics and theology in evangelical theology both in England and North America, including the present day of the Global Mission Field. Grudem summarizes the general overview of dispensationalism as follows:

> A theological system that began in the nineteenth century with the writings of J. N. Darby. Among the general doctrines of this system are the distinction between Israel and the church as two groups in God's overall plan, the pretribulational rapture of the church, a future literal fulfillment of Old Testament prophecies concerning Israel, and the dividing of biblical history into seven periods, or "dispensations," of God's ways of relating to his people.[14]

Classical dispensationalism divided the Bible into seven different dispensations. The Scofield Reference Bible has played a major role in spreading dispensational hermeneutics and theology in the English-speaking world and beyond. The crucial problem with dispensationalism is its failure to interpret the Bible in light of redemptive historical continuity and progress. Receiving severe criticism, classical dispensationalism underwent revisions by different scholars within the dispensational school.

---

13. Bartsch, *Kerygma and Myth*, 101.
14. Grudem, *Systematic Theology*, 1240.

Introduction

Furthermore, classical dispensationalism has been rearranged as a modified dispensationalism. In recent years, progressive dispensationalism has played an important role in reshaping and representing dispensationalism.[15]

According to Ryrie, "the essence of dispensationalism" is "the distinction between Israel and the church":

> The essence of dispensationalism, then, is the distinction between Israel and the church. This grows out of the dispensationalist's consistent employment of normal or plain or historical-grammatical interpretation, and it reflects an understanding of the basic purpose of God in all His dealings with mankind as that of glorifying Himself through salvation and other purposes as well.[16]

The clear distinction between Israel and the church is the result of an unhealthy literal interpretation of the Bible. In addition, dispensational hermeneutics does not have the hermeneutical and theological vision of redemptive historical continuity between the Old and New Testaments, which is a vitally important concept for biblical hermeneutics and theology. As a result, dispensational theology makes an unbiblical distinction between Israel and the church, which creates both unhealthy theological and practical consequences.

Redemptive Historical Interpretation and Biblical Theology

As we briefly explored, biblical and systematic theology have been significantly marred by the historical critical school and the dispensational school. As we proclaim the good news of the gospel, the Church community in this eschatological age needs to restore a concrete biblical hermeneutics which can be a cornerstone of biblical and systematic theology. During the Protestant Reformation, Calvin exhibited redemptive historical hermeneutics in his writings, representatively in his *Institutes of the Christian Religion* in 1559. In his *magnum opus*, Calvin harmonized biblical and systematic theology, although he did not use this terminology. A wonderful harmony between biblical and systematic theology in Calvin's theology is a result of a redemptive historical interpretation, which was deeply embedded in Calvin's biblical hermeneutics and theology.[17] His redemptive historical hermeneutics is Christocentric, Christotelic,

---

15. For my comprehensive and critical analysis of classical, modified, and progressive dispensationalism, see Jeon, *Covenant Theology*, 231–57. Our presupposition in providing a critique of dispensationalism is that in general, dispensationalism is within the boundary of evangelical theology. For a critical examination of dispensationalism in light of redemptive historical hermeneutics, see Allis, *Prophecy & the Church*; Poythress, *Understanding Dispensationalists*.

For the intra-mural discussions within dispensationalism about biblical hermeneutics and theology, see Bateman, *Three Central issues in Contemporary Dispensationalism*; Blaising and Bock, *Dispensationalism, Israel and the Church*; Saucy, *The Case for Progressive Dispensationlaism*.

16. Ryrie, *Dispensationalism*, 48.

17. For a comprehensive analysis of Calvin's redemptive historical hermeneutics, see Jeon, *Calvin and the Federal Vision*, 43–92.

covenantal, and eschatological. Certainly, Calvin demonstrated his redemptive historical hermeneutics not only in his interpretation of the New Testament but also in the interpretation of the Old Testament:

> As such, Calvin demonstrated that he understood the Old Testament not only from a redemptive historical perspective, which can be identified as Christocentric but also a Christotelic perspective, which always directed "its end in Christ and in eternal life" (*eius finis in Christo et vita aeterna*). Calvin made a great theological point when he demonstrated that there is only one covenant of grace in all of God's redemptive history. For Calvin, it was not anachronistic to apply back the "promise of spiritual and eternal life" (*spiritualis aeternaeque vitae promissionem*) of redemptive grace in Christ to the Old Testament believers. So, even the Old Testament believers were justified by faith alone in Christ, in whom they had everlasting hope and spiritual life, while they enjoyed earthly blessings through obedience to God's law.[18]

Calvin's redemptive historical hermeneutics making a balance between biblical and systematic theology was further expounded and advanced by Reformed hermeneutics and theology after the Protestant Reformation.[19] Notably, Geerhardus Vos self-consciously expounded his biblical theology, having redemptive historical hermeneutics in mind, which Calvin laid as a concrete foundation during the Protestant Reformation and developed further in the Reformed tradition. In doing so, Vos was able to respond to the historical critical school's radical reinterpretation of redemptive history and the Kingdom of God. Vos harmonized the two theological disciplines of biblical and systematic theology in his own life and theological context, responding to the rise of the historical critical reading of the Bible and the *disharmony* of biblical and systematic theology.[20] Adopting Vosian biblical theology, Kline further advanced redemptive historical interpretation in his discussions of the divine covenants, the Kingdom of God, God's judgments, and other subject matter, properly and carefully utilizing the ancient Near Eastern documents to defend the antiquity and Mosaic authorship of the Pentateuch.[21]

---

18. Ibid., 65–66.

19. John Owen (1616–1683) represented redemptive historical hermeneutics among the English Puritans in the seventeenth century. Later, Jonathan Edwards (1703–1758) expounded the Bible in light of redemptive historical hermeneutics, representing the New England Puritans in the eighteenth-century historical context. See Edwards, *A History of Redemption*; Owen, *Biblical Theology*.

20. For Vos' insight on biblical theology in light of redemptive historical hermeneutics, see Olinger, *A Geerhardus Vos Anthology*; Vos, *Biblical Theology*; Vos, *The Eschatology of the Old Testament*; Vos, *Grace and Glory*; Vos, *The Pauline Eschatology*; Vos, *Redemptive History and Biblical Interpretation*; Vos, *Reformed Dogmatics*; Vos, *The Teaching of the Epistle to the Hebrews*; Vos, *The Teaching of Jesus*.

21. Kline, *Glory in Our Midst*; Kline, *God, Heaven and Har Magedon*; Kline, *Images of the Spirit*; Kline, *Kingdom Prologue*, 1–382; Kline, *By Oath Consigned*; Kline, *The Structure of Biblical Authority*; Kline, *Treaty of the Great King*. For a sympathetic and critical analysis on Kline's biblical theology, see Jeon, *Covenant Theology*, 191–334.

INTRODUCTION

Biblical theology, in a proper sense, is a theological discipline that explores redemptive history as it is revealed in the Bible, while systematic theology is a theological discipline which is a logical and topical exploration and understanding of biblical doctrines. Both biblical and systematic theology are based and drawn from the teachings of the Bible. In that sense, the two disciplines should come together harmoniously without contradiction. Vos comprehensively explains the harmonious relationship of biblical and systematic theology as follows:

> There is no difference in that one would be more closely bound to the Scriptures than the other. In this they are wholly alike. Nor does the difference lie in this, that the one transforms the Biblical material, whereas the other would leave it unmodified. Both equally make the truth deposited in the Bible undergo a transformation: but the difference arises from the fact the principles by which the transformation is effected differ. In Biblical Theology the principle is one of historical, in Systematic Theology it is one of logical construction. Biblical Theology draws a *line* of development. Systematic Theology draws a *circle*. Still, it should be remembered that on the line of historical progress there is at several points already a beginning of correlation among elements of truth in which the beginnings of the systematizing process can be discerned.[22]

As such, the redemptive drama, deeply embedded in the Bible, is *historical* which has an organic relationship and connection with the creation, fall, redemption, and consummation. Moreover, the proper understanding of redemptive history is deeply rooted in the grammatical-historical interpretation of the Bible, because the grammatical-historical interpretation presupposes the Bible as the infallible and inerrant Word of God. In other words, the redemptive historical interpretation of the Bible presupposes the grammatical-historical interpretation. Poythress comprehensively describes the importance of the presupposition of grammatical-historical interpretation for the proper interpretation and understanding of the Bible:

> Interpretation of the Bible involves both a linguistic side, focusing on the language of the Bible, and a historical side, focusing on the events and the contexts in which they occur. As the once-for-all perspective reminds us, the authority and holiness of God demand that we pay attention to the original context of God's speech, in both its linguistic and its historical aspects. Thus, we may speak of *grammatical-historical* interpretation. Grammatical-historical interpretation focuses on the original context. But, as we have shown, its reflections cohere with the later transmission, the modern reception, and the significance of events in the total plan of God. Thus, grammatical-historical interpretation, rightly understood, is a perspective on a total engagement with God . . . The grammatical aspect of the original context coheres with the speaking of God throughout history. The historical aspect of the original context coheres with

---

22. Vos, *Biblical Theology*, 15–16.

the action of God and the plan of God throughout history. And our understanding of both aspects undergoes progressive transformation in our own individual and corporate history in the church today.[23]

As we explore redemptive history in the Bible, we must be aware that God made different covenants with his people and creatures. God revealed a dynamic and wondrous redemptive drama in the Bible. However, that drama is not abstract but covenantal. God executes his sovereign redemptive drama in history by making and administering different and successive covenants, as Vos suggests:

> The Bible is, as it were, conscious of its own organism; it feels, what we cannot always say of ourselves, its own anatomy. The principle of successive *Berith*-makings (Covenant-makings), as marking the introduction of new periods, plays a large role in this, and should be carefully heeded. Alongside of this periodicity principle, the grouping and correlation of the several elements of truth within the limits of each period has to be attended to. Here again we should not proceed with arbitrary subjectivism.[24]

Exploring and understanding God's covenants are key to understanding redemptive history, which has the historical order of creation, fall, redemption, and consummation. Redemptive history has an eschatological goal, which is the final judgment where God will clearly and visibly separate between the eschatological Kingdom of God and the Kingdom of Satan. Likewise, an exploration and understanding of the covenant of creation, the covenant of grace and the covenant of common grace, the Noahic covenants, the Abrahamic covenant, the Mosaic covenant, the Davidic covenant and the New Covenant in light of the Kingdom of God and his judgment will provide us with a comprehensive picture of redemptive drama and biblical worldview, which are revealed in the Bible. Let us explore God's grand redemptive drama which is organically connected through the different covenants in the Bible.

---

23. Poythress, *God-Centered Biblical Interpretation*, 164.
24. Vos, *Biblical Theology*, 16.

1

The Covenant of Creation and the Kingdom of God

GOD DISPLAYED HIS POWER and glory through the creation of the heavens and the earth. In creation God revealed himself as the Creator, not as the Redeemer. Genesis 1–3 sum up the story of creation, the fall, the inauguration of redemption, the covenant of common grace, and the expulsion of Adam and Eve from the Garden of Eden.[1]

Historically, biblical commentators and theologians have debated whether Genesis 1–3 can be considered as covenantal accounts. We will argue that Genesis 1–3 should be interpreted in light of covenant because God is a personal and covenantal God, not an abstract God. In that sense, he does not execute his works of creation, redemption, and world history outside of his own covenants.

We will see that the Genesis creation accounts reveal indirectly that the triune God actively participated in the work of creation in both visible and invisible realms. We will confirm our thesis, noting that the triune God's participation in the work of creation is outwardly affirmed in the testimonies of the New Testament, although it is only implicitly present in the Genesis creation accounts.

Moreover, using the framework of the covenantal accounts, we will view and explore God's covenant in Genesis 1:1—2:25 in light of the covenant of creation. And under the umbrella of the covenant of creation, we will identify and explore God's covenant with Adam as the Edenic covenant of works. After Adam and Eve committed the original sin, breaking the covenant of works, God introduced another covenant, different from the covenant of works, namely the covenant of grace (Gen 3:15). Making the covenant of grace was not only the revelation of God's saving grace but also the inauguration of redemptive history. In that sense, we will argue that the

---

1. For divergent interpretations of the accounts of creation and the prelapsarian as well as the postlapsarian Adamic status, see Calvin, *Genesis*, 1:1—3:23; C. Collins, *Genesis 1—4*; J. Collins, *Introduction to the Hebrew Bible*; Dumbrell, *Covenant and Creation*, 33–39; Edwards, *A History of Redemption*, 2–46; Golding, *Covenant Theology*, 105–20; Horton, *Introducing Covenant Theology*, 83–104; Kline, *God, Heaven, and Har Magedon*, 78–92; Kline, *Kingdom Prologue*, 8–117; LaRondelle, *Our Creator Redeemer*, 3–10; Murray, *The Covenant of Grace*, 12–16; Robertson, *The Christ of the Covenants*, 67–87; Vos, *Biblical Theology*, 27–40; Waltke, *An Old Testament Theology*, 179–268; Wenham, *Genesis 1—15*, 1–91; Williams, *Far as the Curse Is Found*, 83–99.

proper historical order, covering creation, fall, and redemption, is law first and then gospel, or grace, not vice versa.

Reformed theologians have properly understood and interpreted Genesis 3:15 as the inauguration of redemptive history, identifying it as the covenant of grace. Nevertheless, by and large, scholars have not paid enough attention to the inauguration of the covenant of common grace in Genesis 3:16–19, which is essential to a proper understanding of the biblical worldview, as well as of redemptive history. In that sense, we will explore the importance of the covenant of common grace, which is the backbone of world history as we know it after Adam and Eve were expelled from the Garden of Eden.

The Covenant of Creation and the Edenic Covenant of Works

On the sixth day of creation, God created man as the *imago Dei*, which suggests that God clothed Adam and Eve with his wisdom, righteousness, and holiness. In doing so, he engraved the moral law on their hearts. In turn, they could glorify God through their obedient life in their worship and works in the holy Garden of Eden.

All the material and spiritual blessings that Adam and Eve enjoyed in the Garden of Eden were purely God's gifts. Nevertheless, they were not under the covenant of grace, but the covenant of works. While Adam and Eve were ruling and governing the holy Garden of Eden as vicegerents, God gave them a specific commandment not to eat from the tree of the knowledge of good and evil. The tree of the knowledge of good and evil alluded to the hellish judgment, while the tree of life was a symbol of the heavenly blessing in the Garden of Eden. In that sense, there were dual sanctions, such as blessings and curses, under the principle of the covenant of works, providing a vision of both the eschatological heavenly blessings and eschatological hellish curses.

The Creator and Six Days of Creation

The process of God's creation was a supernatural process. If we examine God's creation for six days from the perspective of the present providential world that we live in, we may fail to understand the exact nature of the six days of creation. Genesis 1:1 can be considered as the historical preamble, which identifies God as the Creator. It also summarizes creation as out of nothing (*creatio ex nihilo*). There is only one creation of the original universe in the beginning by the Creator, although there are two creation accounts (Gen 1:2—2:24). The first one is the chronological order and twenty-four hour day creation account, which covers six successive days with the seventh day being the Sabbath (Gen 1:2—2:3). The other is the account of the creation of Adam, the formation of the Garden of Eden, the making of the covenant of works with Adam,

The Covenant of Creation and the Kingdom of God

and the creation of Eve (Gen 2:4–25).[2] Genesis 1:1 is not the summary account of the heavens and the earth that God created in Genesis 1:2—2:3 for six consecutive days. Rather, it summarizes the absolute beginning in which God created space, waters, and angelic hosts. So, Genesis 1:2 describes the visible manifestation of the chaos, which was filled with waters before the creation of the original heavens and the earth.

Genesis 1:1 suggests that God is not only the Creator but also the Creator out of nothing (*ex nihilo*).[3] It sums up God's creation out of nothing (*ex nihilo*), which was the absolute beginning of time, space, water, and the heavenly hosts, also known as angels. In doing so, God revealed himself as the Creator out of nothing, over against the ancient Near Eastern worldview, which denied creation out of nothing and rejected the distinction between the Creator and creature.[4] God rejoiced, revealing through Moses that he created the heavens and the earth out of nothing in the beginning. In doing so, he safeguarded the Creator and creature distinction. Reflecting on God's cre-

---

2. Evangelical scholars disagree about the interpretation of "day" (יוֹם) in the Genesis creation account. Some hold the view that the creation days of Genesis 1—2 are twenty-four-hour days. Some view it from the perspective of the day-age interpretation, which reads the days of the Genesis creation as sequential long days or an epoch. And others hold the framework view which identifies the days of the creation account as neither chronological nor twenty-four-hour days. For the comprehensive and critical interaction among the proponents of the three different views, see Hagopian, *The Genesis Debate*, 15–307. For the comprehensive analysis of the framework view, see Futato, "Because It Had Rained," 1–21; Kline, "Because It Had Not Rained," 146–157; Kline, *God, Heaven and Har Magedon*, 223–250.

3. Calvin persuasively summarizes Genesis 1:1 as creation out of nothing (*creatio ex nihilo*) as follows: "To expound the term 'beginning,' of Christ, is altogether frivolous. For Moses simply intends to assert that the world was not perfected at its very commencement, in the manner in which it is now seen, but that it was created an empty chaos of heaven and earth. His language therefore may be thus explained. When God in the beginning created the heaven and the earth, the earth was empty and waste. He moreover teaches by the word 'created,' that what before did not exist was now made; for he has not used the term . . . (*yatsar,*) which signifies to frame or form, but . . . (*bara,*) which signifies to create. Therefore his meaning is, that the world was made out of nothing. Hence the folly of those is refuted who imagine that unformed matter existed from eternity; and who gather nothing else from the narration of Moses than that the world was furnished with new ornaments, and received a form of which it was before destitute. This indeed was formerly a common fable among heathens, who had received only the obscure report of creation, and who, according to custom, adulterated the truth of God with strange figments . . . Let this, then, be maintained in the first place, that the world is not eternal, but was created by God. There is no doubt that Moses gives the name of heaven and earth to that confused mass which he, shortly afterwards, (verse 2,) denominates *waters*. The reason of which is, that this matter was to be the seed of the whole world. Besides, this is the generally recognized division of the world." Calvin, *Genesis*, 1:1. However, Waltke interprets Genesis 1:1 as a summary account of the creation in Genesis 1:2–23. See Waltke, *An Old Testament Theology*, 179–80.

4. The ancient Near Eastern cosmogony embraces a polytheistic and pantheistic worldview, which is reflected in the several texts of creation and the flood myth in the ancient Near East. This view does not make any distinction between the Creator and creature, which is distinctive in the Genesis creation account. For the ancient Near Eastern cosmogony and the diverse texts of its mythological tradition, see Arnold and Beyer, *Readings from the Ancient Near East*, 13–70; Pritchard, *The Ancient Near East*, 1–100. The *Enuma Elish*, known as the Babylonian Genesis, represents and perhaps makes the closest parallel with the Genesis creation accounts. For a comparative analysis between the story of the *Enuma Elish* and the biblical creation account, see Heidel, *The Babylonian Genesis*; Millard, "A New Babylonian Genesis Story," 3–18; Waltke, *An Old Testament Theology*, 197–203.

ation in the beginning, the psalmist invites us to praise the steadfast love of Yahweh, which has been revealed through his creation of the heavens and the earth. Yahweh created the heavens and the earth, not through existing material, but out of nothing (*ex nihilo*) by his word:

> 4 For the word of the Lord is upright, and all his work is done in faithfulness. 5 He loves righteousness and justice; the earth is full of the steadfast love of the Lord. 6 *By the word of the Lord the heavens were made, and by the breath of his mouth all their host.* 7 He gathers the waters of the sea as a heap; he puts the deeps in storehouses. 8 Let all the earth fear the Lord; let all the inhabitants of the world stand in awe of him! 9 *For he spoke, and it came to be; he commanded, and it stood firm.* (Ps 33:4–9)[5]

Reflecting on the creation account of Genesis, the author of Hebrews declares that God created the universe out of nothing by his word, which was against the Greco-Roman worldview, a reflection of the Greek philosophical worldview which emphasized eternally existing matter, denying the personal Creator. And only believers may accept and comprehend by faith God's out-of-nothing creation: "Now faith is the assurance of things hoped for, the conviction of things not seen. For by it the people of old received their commendation. *By faith we understand that the universe was created by the word of God, so that what is seen was not made out of things that are visible*" (Heb 11:1–3).

Genesis 1:1–2 not only reveals God's creation of the heavens and the earth out of nothing (*ex nihilo*), but it also conveys implicitly the masterful work of the triune God. In fact, God exists eternally not only as a personal and covenantal God, but also as the triune God—as the Father, the Son, and the Spirit. The opening two verses of the Bible begin as follows:

> 1 In the beginning God created the heavens and the earth [בְּרֵאשִׁית בָּרָא אֱלֹהִים אֵת הַשָּׁמַיִם וְאֵת הָאָרֶץ]. 2 The earth was without form and void, and darkness was over the face of the deep. And the Spirit of God was hovering over the face of the waters [וְרוּחַ אֱלֹהִים מְרַחֶפֶת עַל־פְּנֵי הַמָּיִם]. (Gen 1:1–2)

The plural form of "God" (אֱלֹהִים) indirectly implies that the triune God as the Creator actively participated and was in the creation of the visible and invisible realms in the beginning. The visible presence of theophanic glory was present in the process of creation. It signifies that God himself was not only the eyewitness of his own creation but also the eyewitness of the covenant-making process in the covenant of creation. And the expression, "the Spirit of God was hovering over the face of the waters," identifies that the Holy Spirit as "the Spirit of God" actively participated in the work of creation along with God the Father. Likewise, the visible presence of "the Spirit of

---

5. All quotations from the Bible are cited from English Standard Version unless otherwise specified. In addition, all the italics within the quotation of the Bible are my emphases.

God" signifies that the Holy Spirit was the Creator, as well as the divine witness of the creational covenant account.[6] In fact, the psalmist reflects the creation account of Genesis, and affirms that the Holy Spirit played an active role as the Spirit of creation, who is the Creator:

> 19 He made the moon to mark the seasons; the sun knows its time for setting. 20 You made darkness, and it is night, when all the beasts of the forest creep about . . . 24 *O Lord, how manifold are your works! In wisdom have you made them all; the earth is full of your creatures.* 25 Here is the sea, great and wide, which teems with creatures innumerable, living things both small and great. 26 There go the ships, and Leviathan, which you formed to play in it. 27 These all look to you, to give them their food in due season. 28 When you give it to them, they gather it up; when you open your hand, they are filled with good things. 29 When you hide your face, they are dismayed; when you take away their breath, they die and return to their dust. 30 *When you send forth your spirit, they are created* [תְּשַׁלַּח רוּחֲךָ יִבָּרֵאוּן], *and you renew the face of the ground.* (Ps 104:19–30)

Moreover, "the Spirit of God" as the Holy Spirit was the divine source of light before God created light on the fourth day. And the shining glory of "the Spirit of God" became the source of the separation of day and night before the creation of the lights (Gen 1:14–19). Furthermore, God used the first person plural form in his creation command of man, saying "Let us make man in our image, after our likeness" (Gen 1:26a). This is indirect divine revelation that the triune God as the Creator actively and harmoniously participated in the creation of man.[7]

To perceive the pre-incarnate Messiah as the Creator was unthinkable for the first-century Jews who were committed to Judaism. In fact, Jesus as the Son of God was a blasphemous idea for Jews who followed the monotheistic concept of Judaism. It is the main reason why Paul before his conversion, along with his contemporary followers of Judaism, persecuted the church. However, after his Damascus Road conversion experience, Paul was not only transformed as the apostle for the gospel of Jesus Christ but also for the triune God through the revelation of the exalted Jesus Christ. Thereafter, he abandoned the monotheism of Judaism. In light of the creation account of Genesis and the revelation of the exalted Jesus Christ, Paul confirms that Jesus as the Son of God created the visible and invisible realms in the beginning. The Son is not only the Creator, but also the Sustainer, as well as the Redeemer:

---

6. For "the Spirit of God was hovering over the face of the waters" as the divine witness not only of creation but also of the making of the covenant of creation; see Kline, *Images of the Spirit*, 13–34; Kline, *Kingdom Prologue*, 30–33.

7. Explaining and interpreting Genesis 1:26, Calvin properly asserts that it is the divine revelation of "a plurality of Persons in the Godhead" and nuances that the creation account of Genesis indirectly suggests creation as the work of the triune God: "Christians, therefore, properly contend, from this testimony, that there exists a plurality of Persons in the Godhead. God summons no foreign counselor; hence we infer that he finds within himself something distinct; as, in truth, his eternal wisdom and power reside within him." Calvin, *Genesis*, 1:26.

15 He is the image of the invisible God, the firstborn of all creation. 16 *For by him all things were created, in heaven and on earth, visible and invisible, whether thrones or dominions or rulers or authorities—all things were created through him and for him* [ὅτι ἐν αὐτῷ ἐκτίσθη τὰ πάντα ἐν τοῖς οὐρανοῖς καὶ ἐπὶ τῆς γῆς, τὰ ὁρατὰ καὶ τὰ ἀόρατα, εἴτε θρόνοι εἴτε κυριότητες εἴτε ἀρχαὶ εἴτε ἐξουσίαι· τὰ πάντα δι' αὐτοῦ καὶ εἰς αὐτὸν ἔκτισται·]. 17 And he is before all things, and in him all things hold together. 18 And he is the head of the body, the church. He is the beginning, the firstborn from the dead, that in everything he might be preeminent. 19 For in him all the fullness of God was pleased to dwell, 20 and through him to reconcile to himself all things, whether on earth or in heaven, making peace by the blood of cross. (Col 1:15–20)

Similarly, John affirms that Jesus as the Son of God actively participated in the creation of the heavens and the earth, after the apostle witnessed and reflected on Jesus' life, death, resurrection, and ascension along with the ongoing divine revelation. The Hellenistic idea of *logos* perceived that an impersonal principle of reason provided natural order to the cosmos. Countering the Hellenistic world view and concept of *logos*, the apostle John explains that God created all things through "the Word" (*Logos*). And he identifies that "the Word" was the pre-incarnate Son of God[8]:

1 *In the beginning was the Word, and the Word was with God, and the Word was God. 2 He was in the beginning with God. 3 All things were made through him, and without him was not anything made that was made* [Ἐν ἀρχῇ ἦν ὁ λόγος, καὶ ὁ λόγος ἦν πρὸς τὸν θεόν, καὶ θεὸς ἦν ὁ λόγος. οὗτος ἦν ἐν ἀρχῇ πρὸς τὸν θεόν. πάντα δι' αὐτοῦ ἐγένετο, καὶ χωρὶς αὐτοῦ ἐγένετο οὐδὲ ἕν. ὃ γέγονεν]. 4 In him was life, and the life was the light of men. 5 The light shines in the darkness, and the darkness has not overcome it. 6 There was a man sent from God, whose name was John. 7 He came as a witness, to bear witness about the light, that all might believe through him. 8 He was not the light, but came to bear witness about the light. 9 The true light, which enlightens everyone, was coming into the world. 10 *He was in the world, and the world was made through him, yet the world did not know him* [ἐν τῷ κόσμῳ ἦν, καὶ ὁ κόσμος δι' αὐτοῦ ἐγένετο, καὶ ὁ κόσμος αὐτὸν οὐκ ἔγνω.]. 11 He came to his own, and his own people did not receive him . . . 14 And the Word became flesh and dwelt among us, and we have seen his glory, glory as of the only Son from the Father, full of grace and truth. (John 1:1–14)

The testimony in the prologue of the Gospel of John affirms that God the Father created the world in the beginning *through* the Logos, the Son. The pre-incarnate Son as the Logos is a metaphorical expression, which identifies the Son of God as the eternal divine being, as well as the Creator. It is a confirmation that the creation of the

---

8. Harris mistakenly argues that the concept of the Logos in the Gospel of John was borrowed from the Jewish theologian and philosopher Philo's idea of Logos. Harris, *Understanding the Bible*, 302–10.

cosmos in the beginning was the work of the triune God, which was already implicitly present in the Genesis creation accounts.

Some first-century Jewish Christians, even after their conversion to Christianity, questioned the true identity of Jesus Christ. They were confused about the Lord's identity even after his death, resurrection and ascension and the Pentecost event. Reflecting this ongoing confusion about the true identity of Jesus, the author of the book of Hebrews answers the question in the prologue. He states that God the Father created the cosmos *through* the Son, who sat down "at the right hand of the Majesty on high" after his death and resurrection. The exalted Son is now "the radiance of the glory of God" in the invisible heavenly realm, and his glorified body is enveloped in the invisible heaven. In providing this answer, the author of Hebrews identifies and confirms the Son as the Creator, Redeemer, and Sustainer of the cosmos:

> 1 Long ago, at many times and in many ways, God spoke to our fathers by the prophets, 2 *but in these last days he has spoken to us by his Son, whom he appointed the heir of all things, through whom also he created the world* [ἐπ' ἐσχάτου τῶν ἡμερῶν τούτων ἐλάλησεν ἡμῖν ἐν υἱῷ, ὃν ἔθηκεν κληρονόμον πάντων, δι' οὗ καὶ ἐποίησεν τοὺς αἰῶνας·]. 3 He is the radiance of the glory of God and the exact imprint of his nature, and he upholds the universe by the word of his power. After making purification for sins, he sat down at the right hand of the Majesty on high, 4 having become as much superior to angels as the name he has inherited is more excellent than theirs. (Heb 1:1–4)

Later on, the exalted Jesus showed to the apostle John through a vision the heavenly throne where he was enthroned after his ascension. He revealed himself as "the Lord God Almighty." And twenty-four elders worshipped him, falling down before him, seated on the heavenly throne. And they praised the enthroned Jesus as "our Lord and God" (ὁ κύριος καὶ ὁ θεὸς ἡμῶν), and acknowledged that he created "all things" (τὰ πάντα). As such, the enthroned Jesus in the heavenly Kingdom of God affirmed to the apostle John that he participated in the creation of all things in the beginning as the Creator:

> 8 And the four living creatures, each of them with six wings, are full of eyes all around and within, and day and night they never cease to say, "Holy, holy, holy, is the Lord God Almighty, who was and is and is to come!" 9 And whenever the living creatures give glory and honor and thanks to him who is seated on the throne, who lives forever and ever, 10 the twenty-four elders fall down before him who is seated on the throne and worship him who lives forever and ever. They cast their crowns before the throne, saying, 11 *"Worthy are you, our Lord and God, to receive glory and honor and power, for you created all things, and by your will they existed and were created* [ἄξιος εἶ, ὁ κύριος καὶ ὁ θεὸς ἡμῶν, λαβεῖν τὴν δόξαν καὶ τὴν τιμὴν καὶ τὴν δύναμιν, ὅτι σὺ ἔκτισας τὰ πάντα καὶ διὰ τὸ θέλημά σου ἦσαν καὶ ἐκτίσθησαν.]." (Rev 4:8–11)

When we closely examine the Genesis creation accounts, we can easily identify that God created a mature universe and creature. For example, God did not create an infant Adam and have him grow up to be a man; rather, he created a mature historical Adam who could immediately discern moral law, written in his heart, and carry out his creaturely duties as vicegerent toward God, the Great King. In that regard, all the contemporary scientific investigation to measure the age of the earth by examining the present cosmos will fail. In short, God did not create the heavens and the earth to reveal their exact age, but for His glory—He who is a masterful, mighty, awesome, glorious, and beautiful Creator. Nevertheless, the age of the universe should not be considered millions or billions of years old as some theologians and scientists have suggested. The age of the universe and the age of human history are almost identical, when we recall how the historical Adam was created by God at the sixth normal calendar day following his creation of the universe. So, we can estimate that about six thousand years has passed after God created the universe, as Calvin argues in the following:

> An obstinate person would be no less insolently puffed up on hearing that within the essence of God there are three persons than if he were told that God foresaw what would happen to man when he created him. And they will not refrain from guffaws when they are informed that but more than five thousand years have passed since the creation of the universe, for they ask why God's power was idle and asleep for so long.[9]

The incomprehensible beauty and glory of God was revealed and manifested through the wonderful beauty and glory of "the heavens and the earth" that God created in the beginning. The creation of "the heavens and the earth" was God's visible display of His invisible beauty and glory. In fact, God saw himself in his magnificent work of creation through the six days. When God saw his creation in Genesis 1, "it was good" (כִּי־טוֹב:; vv. 10, 12, 18, 21, 25). Moreover, when the process of creation was completed after six successive days, God saw everything that he had made in the heavens and the earth, and "it was very good" (טוֹב מְאֹד; v. 31). Thus, the original heavens and earth were so beautiful and glorious because they were the reflection and projection of goodness, holiness, beauty, and glory of the heavenly Kingdom of God, which is an invisible realm in the present age. God is a beautiful and glorious God par excellence. In fact, God is Beauty itself, which is why the present heavens and earth are so beautiful and glorious. Although we do not gaze upon the original universe, which was recreated during the universal judgment of the Noahic Flood, God has revealed his beauty in other ways. For instance, his beauty was revealed in the sanctuary of the tabernacle and in the temple of the covenant community of Israel in the Old Testament. Indeed, the glory of the

---

9. Calvin, *Institutes*, 3.21.4. Some theologians who are committed to theistic evolution see the age of the universe as millions or billions of years. And some evangelicals, trying to harmonize the Bible and science, view the age of the universe as millions or billions of years. But, as I have already argued, the contemporary scientific measurement of the age of the earth will not work because God created the mature universe.

Lord was visibly manifested in the sanctuary of the tabernacle and temple as a shining glory. And it was not earthly glory and beauty, but a heavenly glory and beauty. The psalmist invites the covenant community to praise Yahweh, who is the Creator and the Redeemer. And he recognizes that "strength and beauty are in his sanctuary," because heavenly beauty was revealed in the sanctuary of the tabernacle:

> 1 Oh sing to the Lord a new song; sing to the Lord, all the earth! 2 Sing to the Lord, bless his name; tell of his salvation from day to day. Declare his glory among the nations, his marvelous works among all the peoples! 4 For great is the Lord, and greatly to be praised; he is to be feared above all gods. 5 For all the gods of the peoples are worthless idols, but the Lord made the heavens. 6 *Splendor and majesty are before him; strength and beauty are in his sanctuary* [הוֹד־וְהָדָר לְפָנָיו עֹז וְתִפְאֶרֶת בְּמִקְדָּשׁוֹ׃]. (Ps 96:1–6)

David beheld the visible glory and beauty of the Lord, which shined splendidly as theophanic glory in the sanctuary of the tabernacle. He sought and yearned to dwell "in the house of the Lord" so that he could see in his lifetime "the beauty of the Lord," which was intruded into the earthly sanctuary of the tabernacle:

> 1 The Lord is my light and my salvation; whom shall I fear? The Lord is the stronghold of my life; of whom shall I be afraid? 2 When evildoers assail me to eat up my flesh, my adversaries and foes, it is they who stumble and fall. 3 Though an army encamp against me, my heart shall not fear; though war arise against me, yet I will be confident. 4 One thing have I asked of the Lord, that will I seek after: that I may dwell in the house of the Lord all the days of my life, *to gaze upon the beauty of the Lord and to inquire in his temple* [לַחֲזוֹת בְּנֹעַם־יְהוָה וּלְבַקֵּר בְּהֵיכָלוֹ׃]. (Ps 27:1–4)

The beauty of the Lord was visibly reflected in his creation of the original universe. So when God saw the original universe after he created it for six successive days, "it was very good" (Gen 1:31). In fact, the beauty of the Lord was present before Adam and Eve in the holy Garden of Eden as theophanic glory. Although the original heavens and earth were very good, beautiful and glorious, it was not yet heavenly glory and beauty. It was the earthly reflection of heavenly glory and beauty. The culmination of the beauty of the Lord was projected in the Garden of Eden. The heavenly glory and beauty will ultimately be realized and consummated in the heavenly Kingdom of God for the elect alone when the Parousia comes.

The chronological order of day and night in the process of six days creation was God's covenant making process with his own creature. As we know, we do not see the word 'covenant' in Genesis 1—3, which covers the creation, the fall, the inauguration of redemption and common grace, and the expulsion from the holy Garden of Eden. However, Yahweh confirms later that the process of his creation was, in fact, a covenant making process (Jer 33:14–26). Retrospective of his creation in the Genesis creation accounts, Yahweh reveals that the Davidic covenant is unbreakable as was his covenant with day and night when he first created the universe:

> 19 The word of the Lord came to Jeremiah: 20 "Thus says the Lord: If you can break my covenant with the day and my covenant with the night, so that day and night will not come at their appointed time, 21 then also my covenant with David my servant may be broken, so that he shall not have a son to reign on his throne, and my covenant with the Levitical priests my ministers. 22 As the host of heaven cannot be numbered and the sands of the sea cannot be measured, so I will multiply the offspring of David my servant, and the Levitical priests who minister to me." 23 The word of the Lord came to Jeremiah: 24 "Have you not observed these people are saying, 'The Lord has rejected the two clans that he chose'? Thus they have despised my people so that they are no longer a nation in their sight. 25 Thus says the Lord If I have not established my covenant with day and night and the fixed order of heaven and earth, then I will reject the offspring of Jacob and David my servant and will not choose one of his offspring to rule over the offspring of Abraham, Isaac, and Jacob. For I will restore their fortunes and will have mercy on them." (Jer 33:19–26)

Yahweh affirms that the process of his creation was a covenant making process. In that sense, the Genesis creation accounts can be rightly designated as the covenant of creation; like the Davidic covenant, it is unbreakable.

Sabbath and Creation Eschatology

After the completion of the creation, God rested the seventh day, and he sanctified it. He commanded Adam and Eve to keep the Sabbath, sanctifying it in the holy Garden of Eden. The original Sabbath rest pointed to everlasting rest in the heavenly Kingdom of God for the Edenic covenant community. Thus, Adam and Eve yearned for the impending eternal rest and joy of the heavenly Kingdom of God as they kept the Sabbath holy in the Garden of Eden as the Edenic covenant community.

The chronological account of God's creation ends with the seventh day. He rested from his work, which displayed the magnificent original cosmos according to his sovereign design and purpose: "And on the seventh day God finished his work that he had done, and he rested on the seventh day from all his work that he had done. So God blessed the seventh day and made it holy, because on it God rested from all his work that he had done in creation" (Gen 2:2–3).

God's rest on the seventh day was the archetypal pattern of man's Sabbath rest. Keeping the Sabbath day as holy was not only a creation ordinance but also the sign of the Edenic covenant of works, which was covenantally binding on the Edenic covenant community. As Adam and Eve observed the Sabbath rest in the holy Garden of Eden, they meditated and anticipated the coming of the heavenly Sabbath rest. Likewise, the ultimate goal and vision of the Edenic covenant of works was to fully

The Covenant of Creation and the Kingdom of God

realize the Sabbath rest in the heavenly Kingdom of God. It is remarkable to know that keeping the Sabbath day as holy was covenantally binding on the covenant community of Israel as we read it in Exodus 20:8–11:

> 8 Remember the Sabbath day, to keep it holy. 9 Six days you shall labor, and do all your work, 10 but the seventh day is a Sabbath to the Lord your God. On it you shall not do any work, you, or your son, or your daughter, your male servant, or your female servant, or your live stock, or sojourner who is within your gates. 11 For in six days the Lord made heaven and earth, the sea, and all that is in them, and rested on the seventh day. Therefore the Lord blessed the Sabbath day and made it holy. (Ex 20:8–11)

Keeping the Sabbath day in the Garden of Eden was strictly applied, because the Edenic covenant community was a theocratic kingdom, obligated to keep all the commandments of God. Genesis 2:1–3 indicates that God commanded Adam and Eve to keep the Sabbath day holy. And the requirements of the moral law were written in Adam and Eve's hearts (Rom 2:12–15). Similarly, the covenant community of Israel was obligated to keep the Sabbath as holy with the cessation of daily works, because they were the theocratic community under the Sinaitic covenant of law as the descendants of Abraham. God further elaborated his commandment to keep the Sabbath as holy to the covenant community of Israel within the historical context of the Deuteronomic covenant renewal at the plain of Moab (Deut 5:12–15):

> 12 "Observe the Sabbath day, to keep it holy, as the Lord your God commanded you. 13 Six days you shall labor and do all your work, 14 but the seventh day is a Sabbath to the Lord your God. On it you shall not do any work, you or your son or your daughter or your male servant or your female servant, or your ox or your donkey or any of your livestock, or the sojourner who is within your gates, that your male servant and your female servant may rest as well as you. 15 You shall remember that you were a slave in the land of Egypt, and the Lord your God brought you out from there with a mighty hand and an outstretched arm. Therefore the Lord your God commanded you to keep the Sabbath day." (Deut 5:12–15)

When God made the Sinaitic covenant with Israel, keeping the Sabbath day holy was the *sign* of the covenant. The entire nation of Israel was obligated to keep the Sabbath holy. Otherwise, God would execute the judgment of death for those who violated the commandment of the Sabbath as he revealed to Israel through Moses, the mediator of the covenant:

> 12 And the Lord said to Moses, 13 "You are to speak to the people of Israel and say, 'Above all you shall keep my Sabbaths, *for this is a sign between me and you throughout your generations, that you may know that I, the Lord sanctify you.* 14 You shall keep the Sabbath, because it is holy for you. Everyone who profanes it shall be put to death. Whoever does any work on it, that soul shall be

cut off from among his people. 15 Six days shall work be done, but the seventh day is a Sabbath of solemn rest, holy to the Lord. Whoever does any work on the Sabbath day shall be put to death. 16 Therefore the people of Israel shall keep the Sabbath, observing the Sabbath throughout their generations, as a covenant forever. 17 *It is a sign forever between me and the people of Israel* that in six days the Lord made heaven and earth, on the seventh day he rested and was refreshed.'" (Ex 31:12–17)

As such, keeping the Sabbath holy symbolized the Sinaitic covenant between God and Israel. Similarly, keeping the Sabbath holy was the *sign* of the covenant of works between God and the Edenic covenant community, represented by the first Adam. Sabbath as the symbol of the covenant of works suggests that God's ultimate intention for the people of God was not to live in the Garden of Eden endlessly. It is true that the Garden of Eden was an earthly paradise and a symbolic projection of the heavenly paradise where there was no sin. Nevertheless, the Edenic covenant community was, in a sense, an eschatological covenant community, which awaited the coming consummation of the heavenly Kingdom of God. So, keeping the Sabbath holy in the Garden of Eden was the sign of the Edenic covenant of works, where obeying the law was the means of fulfilling the heavenly Kingdom of God.

The Covenant of Works

There were two different types of international treaties in the ancient Near East: One is the treaty of royal grant, and the other is the suzerainty treaty. Remarkably, biblical covenants reflect the two different types of the ancient Near Eastern treaties. The representative example of the treaty of royal grant is beautifully reflected in the Prediluvian Noahic covenant, the Abrahamic covenant, the Davidic covenant, and the New Covenant. In that sense, the Abrahamic covenant, made before the Sinaitic covenant, may be rightly called the covenant of royal grant, and was a representative example of promissory covenant in the Old Testament. Meanwhile, the Sinaitic covenant is a good example of the reflection of the suzerainty treaty, in which dual sanctions in terms of blessings and curses are clearly stated. We may designate the Sinaitic covenant as the suzerainty covenant. A suzerainty treaty held to a general pattern of order in the treaty making process, such as a historical preamble, historical prologue, stipulations, and dual sanctions. This ancient Near Eastern typical order is well-reflected in the covenant making process of the Sinaitic covenant (Ex 19—24). In light of the ancient Near Eastern treaties, we can categorize the Adamic covenant of works as a suzerainty covenant where we can identify historical preamble, historical prologue, stipulations, and dual sanctions.[10]

10. The two different types of covenants in the Old Testament with comparative analysis of the ancient Near Eastern treaties have been found in Hegg, *The Abrahamic Covenant and the Covenant of Grant in the Ancient Near East*; Hillers, *Covenant: The History of a Biblical Idea*; Jeon, "The Abrahamic

The Covenant of Creation and the Kingdom of God

God appointed Adam as the representative covenantal head in which he represented his descendents. At the same time, he was under the covenant of works. So, if he did not eat the fruit of the tree of the knowledge of the good and evil during the probation period, God could have granted the heavenly Kingdom of God which was promised. Not only Adam, but also his descendents would have also inherited eternal life and the heavenly Kingdom of God, which was the ultimate goal of the triune God's creation. In that sense, the fulfillment of the eschatological blessings was very real in the Garden of Eden.

We do not find the word *covenant* in the depiction of God's relationship with Adam before the fall in Genesis 2:4–25. Historically, many scholars have denied that God had any covenantal relationship with Adam in the Garden of Eden.[11] However, Hosea affirms that Yahweh had a covenantal relationship with Adam before the fall. But Adam broke this covenant. Reflecting Adam's breach of the covenant, Hosea claims that the covenant community of Israel broke the Sinaitic covenant of law as Adam had done:

> 4 What shall I do with you, O Ephraim? What shall I do with you, O Judah? Your love is like a morning cloud, like the dew that goes early away. 5 Therefore I have hewn them by the prophets; I have slain them by the words of my mouth, and my judgment goes forth as the light. 6 For I desire steadfast love and not sacrifice, the knowledge of God rather than burnt offerings. 7 *But like Adam they transgressed the covenant; there they dealt faithlessly with me* [וְהֵמָּה כְּאָדָם עָבְרוּ בְרִית שָׁם בָּגְדוּ בִי]. 8 Gilead is a city of evildoers, tracked with blood. 9 As robbers lie in wait for a man, so the priests band together; they murder on the way to Shechem; they commit villainy. 10 In the house of Israel I have seen a horrible thing; Ephraim's whoredom is there; Israel is defiled. 11 For you also, O Judah, a harvest is appointed, when I restore the fortunes of my people. (Hos 6:4–11)

God pronounced his covenant lawsuit against the idolatrous covenant community of Israel, and cursed them mercilessly based upon the Sinaitic covenant. Hosea 6:4–11 testifies that Israel broke the Sinaitic covenant of law like Adam in the Garden of Eden. Indeed, the Israelites already knew through the testimony of Genesis 3 that Adam broke the covenant made with God in the Garden of Eden. The proper

---

Covenant and the Kingdom of God," 127–33; Kline, *The Structure of Biblical Authority*; McCarthy, *Old Testament Covenant*; Mendenhall, *Law and Covenant*; Weinfeld, "The Covenant of Grant in the Old Testament and the Ancient Near East," 184–203.

11. John Stek has represented scholars who deny covenant idea in Genesis 1—2. See Stek, "'Covenant' Overload in Reformed Theology," 12–41. In doing so, he limits the idea of covenant only in redemptive category. For critical response to Stek's argument, see Bartholomew, "Covenant and Creation: Covenant Overload or Covenantal Deconstruction," 11–33. Although Bartholomew recognizes the creational covenant in Genesis 1—2 over against Stek, he fails to affirm the Adamic covenant of works in the Garden of Eden.

interpretation of Hosea 6:7 is crucial because it provides a definitive biblical and historical background for God's covenantal relationship with Adam.

Interpreting Genesis 2:15–17, C. John Collins affirms that God's arrangement with Adam was a covenant. He supports the covenantal arrangement by rightly citing Hosea 6:7. Nevertheless, he plainly rejects the concept of the covenant of works. In doing so, he asserts that he does not find an antithesis between the covenant of works and the covenant of grace in "the analogy of Adam and Christ" in Romans 5:12–21:

> If we are secure in calling this a covenant, shall we call it a "covenant of works"? Christians have insisted on this, thinking that the analogy of Adam and Christ in Romans 5:12–21 requires it. By this argument, the two covenant heads must be equivalent: just as Jesus *earned* life for those he represents, so Adam must have been able to *earn* life for those he represented. The trouble with this is the fact that Romans 5 depends more on *disanalogy* between Adam and Christ than it does on pure analogy; as Wright points out, Romans 5:15 "denies that there is a direct balance or equivalence between Adam's trespass and God's gift in Christ."[12]

However, it is important to note that the Edenic covenant before the fall was not the covenant of grace or promise, but the covenant of works.[13] We need to maintain the proper historical order of the covenant of works and the covenant of grace, as Turretin properly recognizes:

> As to order, the covenant of works precedes and the covenant of grace follows. From this to that, there is granted an appeal from the throne of justice to the throne of mercy. Hence the violator of the covenant of nature has a remedy in

---

12. Collins, *Genesis 1—4*, 114. For the biblical theological affirmation of the covenant of works, see Beale, *A New Testament Biblical Theology*, 916–20; Kline, *Kingdom Prologue*, 8–117; Waltke, *An Old Testament Theology*, 259–60, 287–88. Theological elaborations in respect to the covenant of works have been found in Grudem, *Systematic Theology*, 516–18; Reymond, *A New Systematic Theology of the Christian Faith*, 430–40; Francis Turretin, *Institutes of Elenctic Theology*, 1:569–89; 2:189–92.

13. Karl Barth, the great architect of the neo-orthodox theology of the twentieth century, plainly denies the prelapsarian covenant of works, categorizing it as "an original universalism." Following the footsteps of the historical critical school, he denies the biblical accounts of creation and fall as historical accounts, leveling them as "creation sagas." In doing so, he bases his concept of the divine covenant upon monocovenantalism, which destroys the historical and logical orders of law and gospel, or grace: "In this case it is not impossible or illegitimate to believe that properly, in some inner depth of His being behind the covenant of grace, He might not be able to do this. It is only on the historical level that the theologumenon of the *foedus naturae* or *operum* can be explained by the compact of the Federal theology with contemporary humanism. In fact it derives from anxiety lest there might be an essence in God in which, in spite of that contract, His righteousness and His mercy are secretly and at bottom two separate things . . . This anxiety and therefore this proposition of a covenant of works could obviously never have arisen if there had been a loyal hearing of the Gospel and a strict looking to Jesus Christ as the full and final revelation of the being of God. In the eternal decree of God revealed in Jesus Christ the being of God would have been seen as righteous mercy and merciful righteousness from the very first. It would have been quite impossible therefore to conceive of any special plan of a God who is righteous *in abstracto*, and the whole idea of an original covenant of works would have fallen to the ground." Barth, *Church Dogmatics*, 4:65.

the covenant of grace, but the violator of the covenant of grace has no further remedy or hope of pardon because there is no other by which he can be reconciled to God. On this account, the sin against the Holy Ghost is unpardonable because it is committed against the covenant of grace.[14]

Thus, God's covenant with Adam was breakable because the covenantal blessings or curses depended upon Adam's obedience or disobedience, in the same way that the Sinaitic covenant of law was breakable. This is the main reason why Hosea makes a comparison between Adam's breach of the Edenic covenant of works and Israel's breach of the Sinaitic covenant of law.[15]

Dual Sanctions

In the midst of the Garden of Eden, the Lord God planted the tree of life and the tree of the knowledge of good and evil. The Garden of Eden was the original paradise which symbolized and anticipated an eschatological Garden of Eden, the heavenly Kingdom of God, the ultimate goal and direction of his magnificent creation of the original universe. God formed the first Adam out of "dust from the ground." And he became "a living creature" made in the image of God. Moses clearly describes the formation of the first Adam, the Garden of Eden, the tree of life, and the tree of the knowledge of good and evil as follows:

> 7 [T]hen the Lord God formed the man of dust from the ground and breathed into his nostrils the breath of life, and the man became a living creature. 8 And the Lord God planted a garden in Eden, in the east, and there he put the man whom he had formed. 9 And out of the ground the Lord God made to spring up every tree that is pleasant to the sight and good for food. The tree of life was in the midst of garden, and the tree of the knowledge of good and evil. (Gen 2:7–9)

The two trees in the Garden of Eden visually demonstrated that the Adamic covenant of works had dual sanctions, such as blessings and curses. The principle of the Edenic covenant of works was not grace but law, which required perfect obedience. And the reward of perfect obedience was the blessing of the heavenly Kingdom of God, but the result of disobedience was the curse of hellish judgment. When Yahweh made the Sinaitic covenant of law with the covenant community of Israel, he also revealed the dual sanctions of the covenant. He revealed the dual sanctions through the mediator of the Sinaitic covenant of law, Moses, as follows:

---

14. Turretin, *Institutes of Elenctic Theology*, 2:191.
15. The KJV translation of Hosea 6:7 loses Hosea's comparative analysis between Adam's breach to the covenant of works and Israel's breaking of the Sinaitic covenant of law when it translates "like Adam" to "like men": "But they like men have transgressed the covenant: there have they dealt treacherously against me."

> 1 And the Lord spoke to Moses, saying, 2 "Speak to the people of Israel and say to them, I am the Lord your God. 3 You shall not do as they do in the land of Egypt, where you lived, and you shall not do as they do in the land of Canaan, to which I am bringing you. You shall not walk in their statutes. 4 You shall follow my rules and keep my statutes and walk in them. I am the Lord your God. 5 You shall therefore keep my statutes and my rules; if a person does them, he shall live by them: I am the Lord." (Lev 18:1–5)

Leviticus 18:5 is the principle of the Sinaitic covenant of law which was applied to the covenant community of Israel in the Old Testament. When the covenant community of Israel was faithful to the Mosaic law, Yahweh blessed them, especially in the Promised Land. However, Yahweh executed his covenant lawsuit against his people when they disobeyed the Mosaic law. In doing so, Yahweh demonstrated the reality of the blessings of heaven and the curses of hell in a typological manner throughout the history of Old Testament Israel. We identify this as the Old Covenant eschatology.

Strikingly, the commandment in Leviticus 18:5, "Do this, and you shall live or you shall die," was the principle of the Edenic covenant of works. And the dual sanctions such as heavenly blessings and curses were visibly and symbolically represented by the tree of life and the tree of the knowledge of good and evil in the Garden of Eden. The implication of Leviticus 18:5 suggests that the principle of the inheritance of the heavenly Kingdom of God in the Edemic covenant of works was not grace or gospel but law. Therefore, the proper historical order of the divine revelation and eschatological heavenly blessings is law and gospel, or grace, not vice versa.[16]

The tree of life was a sacramental tree which symbolized eternal life, while the tree of the knowledge of good and evil symbolized death and eternal punishment. Vos beautifully summarizes the eschatological meaning and character of the tree of life in the Garden of Eden as follows:

> From the significance of the tree in general its specific use may be distinguished. It appears from Gen. 3.22, that man before his fall had not eaten of it, while yet nothing is recorded concerning any prohibition which seems to point to the understanding that the use of the tree was reserved for the future, quite in agreement with the eschatological significance attributed to it later. The tree was associated with the higher, the unchangeable, the eternal life to be secured by obedience throughout his probation. Anticipating the result by a present enjoyment of the fruit would have been out of keeping with its sacramental character. After man should have been made sure of the attainment of the highest life, the tree would appropriately have been the sacramental means for communicating the highest life. After the fall God attributes to man the inclination of snatching the fruit against the divine purpose. But this very desire implies the

---

16. Reflecting the principle of law in Leviticus 18:5, Paul makes a distinction between law and gospel. And he applies the hermeneutical and theological principle to note justification by faith and salvation by grace alone in his epistles. Cf. Rom 10:1–8; Gal 3:10–14.

> understanding that it somehow was the specific life-sacrament for the time after the probation. According to Rev. 2.7 it is to 'him that overcometh' that God promises to give of the tree of life in the midst of his paradise. The effort to obtain the fruit after the fall would have meant a desperate attempt to steal the fruit where the title to it had been lost [cp. Gen. 3.22].[17]

Adam and Eve were banned from the tree of life after the fall (Gen 3:22–24). However, the tree of life will be restored in "the paradise of God," which will be consummated in the heavenly Kingdom of God. And God will grant glorified believers "to eat of tree of life" (Rev 2:7). Moreover, in the New Jerusalem, God will not only restore "the tree of life" but also "the river of the water of life," as the angel showed John through a vision. But the tree of the knowledge of good and evil will not be restored because it symbolized death and eternal curse in the Garden of Eden as the opposite of life and everlasting blessing:

> 1 *Then the angel showed me the river of the water of life*, bright as crystal, flowing from the throne of God and of the Lamb 2 through the middle of the street of the city; also, on either side of the river, *the tree of life with its twelve kinds of fruit, yielding its fruit each month*. The leaves of the tree were for the healing of the nations. (Rev 22:1–2)

Likewise, the tree of life in the Garden of Eden was sacramental, and pointed to eternal life and everlasting blessings in the heavenly Kingdom of God. It suggests that the purpose and goal for the Adamic covenant of works and creation itself was thoroughly eschatological.

As the *imago Dei*, God engraved his moral law on man's heart from the beginning of man's creation. The moral law was given to the covenant community of Israel on Mount Sinai in the written form of the Ten Commandments (Ex 20). In addition to the moral law, written on man's heart, God gave the specific command not to eat the fruit of the knowledge of good and evil. The Lord God gave all the freedom and right to Adam to enjoy the fruits of "every tree of the garden." But he banned eating the fruit of the knowledge of good and evil. God threatened Adam that he would surely die if he violated God's specific command: "And the Lord God commanded the man, saying, 'You may surely eat of every tree of the garden, but of the tree of the knowledge of good and evil you shall not eat, for in the day that you eat of it you shall surely die'" (Gen 2:16–17).

God's specific command suggests that Adam was under probation as the representative covenantal head. If he had passed the intensified probation period, he would have confirmed his righteousness, holiness, and wisdom endowed by God as the *imago Dei*. He would have been granted by God eternal life and the heavenly Kingdom of God along with his descendents that he represented. However, Adam failed to accomplish his covenantal duty. And the original eschatological vision was destroyed.

---

17. Vos, *Biblical Theology*, 28–29.

Contrast between Adam and Christ

Recently, growing numbers of scholars within the evangelical community are beginning to reject the historical Adam in their interpretation of the creation accounts of Genesis 1—2. For example, Peter Enns argues that there was no historical Adam in the Garden of Eden. In doing so, he insists that Paul's comparison and contrast between Adam and Christ in Romans 5:12–21 does not require us to believe in the existence of the historical Adam:

> In making his case, Paul does not *begin* with Adam and move to Christ. Rather, the reality of the risen Christ drives Paul to mine Scripture for ways of explicating the wholly unexpected in-breaking of the age to come in the crucifixion and resurrection of the Son of God. Adam read as "the first human," *supports* Paul's argument about the universal plight and remedy of humanity, but it is not a *necessary* component for that argument. In other words, attributing the cause of universal sin and death to a historical Adam is not necessary for the gospel of Jesus Christ to be a fully historical solution to that problem. To put it positively, as Paul says, we all need the Savior to deliver us from sin and death. That core Christian truth, as I see it, it is unaffected by this entire discussion.[18]

However, we need to remind ourselves that the historical Adam was foundational for Paul's soteriology as well as his understanding of redemptive history. For Paul, if there was no historical Adam in the Garden of Eden, then the historical account of Christ's life, death, and resurrection are false as well. In other words, the historical Adam and the historical Christ's life, death, and resurrection stand and fall together in Paul's understanding of redemptive history and soteriology.

---

18. Enns, *The Evolution of Adam*, 82. Growing numbers of so-called evangelicals have begun to question the historicity of Adam. Enns tries to harmonize science and Scripture, as well as evolution and creation, and denies the historical Adam. In doing so, he assumes the theory of evolution as scientific truth, which is fundamentally a false presupposition. Sadly, Enns' theological hero is not the apostle Paul but Wellhausen, the great architect of documentary hypothesis. And his presupposition is not the Creator of the Bible, but naturalistic evolution, laid out by Charles Darwin. It is my assessment that his rejection of the historical Adam and adaptation of naturalistic evolution is hermeneutically and theologically consistent with his previous book, which provoked and divided the evangelical community. Cf. Enns, *Inspiration and Incarnation*; Enns, "Preliminary Observations on an Incarnational Model of Scripture," 219–36. Waltke, a leading Old Testament scholars, also adopts the viewpoint of theistic evolution, trying to harmonize between the Bible and science, creation and evolution: "The best harmonious synthesis of the special revelation of the Bible, of the general revelation of human nature that distinguishes between right and wrong and consciously or unconsciously craves God, and of science is the theory of theistic evolution . . . There is a synergistic *modus Vivendi* in recognizing that both science and theology have a contribution to make to our understanding of the origins of the creation. A scientific cosmogony contributes to answering the questions of how and when, and the rhetorical biblical cosmogony answers the more important questions of who and why." Waltke, *An Old Testament Theology*, 202–3. A similar argument, also denying the historical Adam, has been found in Carlson and Longman, *Science, Creation and the Bible*. For the affirmation of the historical Adam and Eve in light of the contemporary discussion of the origin of human beings, see C. Collins, "Adam and Eve as Historical People, and Why It Matters," 147–65; Collins, *Did Adam and Eve Really Exist?*

Before Paul's Damascus Road conversion experience, he was not aware of redemptive historical hermeneutics, in which redemptive history could be read in light of literal creation, fall, redemption, and consummation. However, after his conversion experience, Paul began to read the Hebrew scriptures according to redemptive history. He identified that one of the definitive tools to reading these texts from the perspective of redemptive history is comparing and contrasting between the historical Adam and Christ. This was a breakthrough for Paul in his understanding of redemptive history and soteriology as well. Likewise, Paul makes a profound contrast between the historical Adam and Christ to explain redemptive history, as well as redemptive blessings for the elect, in his letter to the Romans as follows:

> 12 Therefore, just as sin came into the world through one man, and death through sin, and so death spread to all men because all sinned—13 for sin indeed was in the world before the law was given, but sin is not counted where there is no law. 14 Yet death reigned from Adam to Moses, even over those whose sinning was not like the transgression of Adam, who was a type of the one who was to come. 15 But the free gift is not like the trespass. For if many died through one man's trespass, much more have the grace of God and the free gift by the grace of that one man Jesus Christ abounded for many. 16 And the free gift is not like the result of that one man's sin. For the judgment following one trespass brought condemnation, but the free gift following many trespasses brought justification. 17 For if, because *one man's trespass*, death reigned through that one man, much more will those who receive the abundance of grace and the free gift of righteousness reign in life through the one man Jesus Christ. 18 Therefore, as one trespass led to condemnation for all men, *so one act of righteousness leads to justification and life for all men. 19 For as by the one man's disobedience the many were made sinners, so by the one man's obedience the many will be made righteous.* 20 Now the law came in to increase the trespass, but where sin increased, grace abounded all the more, 21 so that, as sin reigned in death, grace also might reign through righteousness leading to eternal life through Jesus Christ our Lord. (Rom 5:12–21)

It is important to recognize that Paul presupposes the historicity of Adam and Christ when he makes a contrast between Adam and Christ. His contrast between Adam and Christ summarizes the miserable conditions of "all men" in the historical Adam and the abundant redemptive blessings in the historical Jesus Christ. Adam's original sin was imputed to all men when he broke the covenant of works as the representative covenantal head for the rest of humanity in the Garden of Eden. Thus, all men have been condemned to "death through sin" in Adam. However, Christ fulfilled the requirement of the covenant of works through his life and death. Paul expresses it as "one act of righteousness." God bestows all the promised blessings of the covenant of grace to his elect in Jesus Christ, the mediator of the covenant of grace. Likewise, all the elect may receive the redemptive blessings "through righteousness leading to eternal life through Jesus Christ our Lord." As Paul makes the contrast between Adam and Christ, he makes a contrast between Adam's disobedience to the covenant of works and Christ's obedience to it. And he expresses it antithetically as "one man's disobedience" and "one man's obedience."

Reflecting on Jesus' life, death, resurrection, and ascension to heaven, Paul integrates the resurrection of Christ, the resurrection of believers, and the bodily resurrection (1 Cor 15:1–58). In doing so, Paul distinguishes "a natural body" and "a spiritual body." He examines how a natural body is the present earthly form of human body, whereas a spiritual body is a transformed and glorified body which could dwell in the heavenly Kingdom of God. Paul signifies that a natural body is inherited from "the first man Adam" whereas a spiritual body will be given to believers in "the last Adam." It is significant to know that Paul uses the word, "the last Adam" to note that all the soteriological and eschatological blessings, given by God to believers, will be given in Christ, "the last Adam." Thus, Paul beautifully establishes this contrast between the first and last Adam as follows:

> 42 So is it with the resurrection of the dead. What is sown is perishable; what is raised is imperishable. 43 It is sown in dishonor; it is raised in glory. It is sown in weakness; it is raised in power. 44 *It is sown a natural body; it is raised a spiritual body*. If there is a natural body, there is also a spiritual body. 45 Thus it is written, *"The first man Adam became a living being"; the last Adam became a life-giving spirit*. 46 But it is not the spiritual that is first but the natural, and then the spiritual. 47 The first man was from the earth, a man of dust; the second man is from heaven. 48 As was the man of dust, so also are those who are of heaven. 49 Just as we have borne the image of the man of dust, we shall also bear the image of the man of heaven." (1 Cor 15:42–49)

Paul conceives that Adam in the Garden of Eden was the first man, created by God in his own image. Viewing Adam as the first human, Paul makes a contrast between Adam and Christ. The first Adam failed to pass the probation period under the Edenic covenant of works. He failed to obey perfectly the requirement of the law as the representative covenantal head. But Christ as the last Adam fulfilled all the requirements of the law through his incarnation, life, and death; he paid the penalty of sin to save the elect and grant the redemptive blessings of the heavenly Kingdom of God.

The Inauguration of the Covenant of Grace and the Covenant of Common Grace

After the fall, God inaugurated redemptive history through his successive speeches to Satan, Eve, and Adam (Gen 3:14–19). Examining this passage, Robertson claims that Genesis 3:14–19 demonstrates "the provisions of the Adamic administration of the covenant of redemption":

Genesis 3:14–19 records the provisions of the Adamic administration of the covenant of redemption. God speaks to Satan, to the woman, and to the man, following the order of their defection from loyalty to the Creator. Elements of curse and blessing are found in each address, thus serving structurally to bind inseparably the covenant of creation with the covenant of redemption.[19]

However, the proper reading of God's successive speeches in Genesis 3:14–19 should not be read as one single covenantal account, but as a twofold covenantal account. God's speech to Satan is the divine proclamation of the inauguration of covenant of grace (Gen 3:14–15). The following speech to Eve and Adam should not be interpreted as part of the covenant of grace but as part of the covenant of common grace.

The Inauguration of the Covenant of Grace

Adam and Eve had a joyful and intimate spiritual relationship with God in the Garden of Eden. They walked with God daily under his presence of visible glory which was manifested in the Garden of Eden. The presence of theophanic glory was a visible sign that the Garden of Eden was the earthly projection of the eternal heavenly Kingdom of God.[20] The visible presence of theophanic glory was the divine means of protection, guidance, intimate covenant relationship, and blessing for the Edenic covenant community.

However, by committing the original sin, Adam and Eve lost their original wisdom, righteousness, and holiness with which God endowed them as the *imago Dei*. At the same time, the presence of theophanic glory became an object of fear or curse after they broke the law in which God forbade them to eat the fruit of the tree of the knowledge of good and evil. The joyous covenantal marriage relationship between Adam and Eve immediately disappeared as well.

Satan, the principal deceiver, intruded the Garden of Eden, and used the serpent to deceive Eve. Eve was unable to guard against the deceptive challenge of the serpent and failed to drive out the serpent of the holy Garden of Eden. Instead, she ate the fruit of knowledge of good and evil. Moreover, she gave the fruit to Adam and he ate it as well. As soon as they consumed the fruit, their eyes opened, and they realized that they were naked. Sewing fig leaves together, they covered their naked bodies with loincloths (Gen 3:1–7).

As such, Adam and Eve failed to keep their priestly duty, which was to guard the Edenic sanctuary as holy while they executed the kingly duty to rule over God's creation as faithful stewards. By eating the fruit of the knowledge of good and evil, they were stripped of righteousness and holiness, which had clothed them as the *imago Dei*. As a result, they were unable to stand any longer before the visible presence of theophanic glory, because they lost the original righteousness and holiness due to the

---

19. Robertson, *The Christ of the Covenants*, 93.

20. For the biblical theological elaboration on the holy Garden of Eden as the Edenic theocratic kingdom, see Kline, *Kingdom Prologue*, 42–90.

breach of the Edenic covenant of works and original sin. Instead, they were terrified and hid themselves when they heard the sound of the Lord and faced the visible presence of theophanic glory, although they clothed themselves with loincloths to cover their outer nakedness and inner shame. Hearing "the sound of the Lord God," Adam and Eve were terrified, because it was a thunderous sound to sinners. The sound was reminiscent of the thunderous sound of the Lord on Mount Sinai when the covenant community made the Sinaitic covenant with Yahweh. Israel trembled and was terrified (Ex 19:16–20). Kline beautifully visualizes "the sound of the Lord God" as the approaching sound of original judgment as follows:

> It also describes God himself engaged in surveillance. Similarly, the purpose of the coming of the Lord denoted by this verb in Genesis 3:8 was to execute judgment. And the "voice" of Yahweh that signalized this coming was a terror going before him, driving the guilty pair into hiding from the Face of their Maker (Gen. 3:8b). This advent recorded in Genesis 3:8 thus corresponds fully in its purpose and effect to the awesome approach of the Glory met with elsewhere in Scripture, the approach with which a thunderous voice of Yahweh is regularly associated. There is every reason, therefore, to perceive God's movement through the garden in Genesis 3 as an advent in the terrible judicial majesty of his Glory theophany and to hear "the voice" that heralded this advent as the characteristic theophanic thunder.[21]

The visible appearance of theophanic glory before Adam and Eve after their breach of the Edenic covenant of works was the primal coming of the day of the Lord. As the Lord God appeared to Adam and Eve with the visible presence of theophanic glory, they were terrified and trembled because they heard "the sound of the Lord God" in the Garden of Eden, which was approaching them as the sound of judgment. Although they tried to hide themselves from the visible presence of theophanic glory, they were unable to do so.

> 8 *and they heard the sound of the Lord God walking in the garden as the Spirit of the day* [וַיִּשְׁמְעוּ אֶת־קוֹל יְהוָה אֱלֹהִים מִתְהַלֵּךְ בַּגָּן לְרוּחַ הַיּוֹם], and the man and his wife hid themselves from the presence of the Lord God among the trees of the garden. 9 But the Lord God called to the man and said to him, "Where are you?" 10 And he said, "I heard the sound of you in the garden, and I was afraid, because I was naked, and I hid myself." 11 He said, "Who told you that you were naked? Have you eaten of the tree of which I commanded you not to eat?" 12 The man said, "The woman whom you gave to be with me, she gave me fruit of the tree, and I ate." 13 Then the Lord God said to the woman, "What is this that you have done?" The woman said, "The serpent deceived me, and I ate." (Gen 3:8–13)

---

21. Kline, *Images of the Spirit*, 102.

Traditionally, Bible translators have translated "as the Spirit of the day" (לְרוּחַ הַיּוֹם) as "in the cool of the day."[22] However, it should be translated "as the Spirit of the day." "In the cool of the day" does not carry the meaning of the prophetic announcement of eschatological judgment, depicted by the term, "the day of the Lord." The visible appearance of theophanic glory after Adam's fall was the primal coming of the Lord to announce a prophetic judgment against Adam and Eve and Satan.[23] The visible coming of the Lord revealed the prophetic announcement of redemptive judgment in the Garden of Eden. Redemptive judgment is divine judgment, ultimately separating the Kingdom of Satan and the Kingdom of God. When God executes his redemptive judgment, he bases the judgment upon his covenant. God manifested the first universal implication of redemptive judgment in the episode of the Noahic flood in the historical context of the Prediluvian Noahic covenant (Gen 6:5—8:19). Although the Noahic flood was the first universal implication of redemptive judgment, separating covenant community and non-covenant community, God did not reveal the formula of eschatological judgment, "the day of the Lord."

Later, the prophets used "the day of the Lord" as the formula of eschatological judgment day. The earliest prophetic expression of "the day of the Lord" is found in Amos 5:18–27:

> 18 *Woe to you who desire the day of the Lord! Why would you have the day of the Lord? It is darkness, and not light* [הוֹי הַמִּתְאַוִּים אֶת־יוֹם יְהוָה לָמָּה־זֶּה לָכֶם יוֹם יְהוָה הוּא־חֹשֶׁךְ וְלֹא־אוֹר:], 19 as if a man fled from a lion, and a bear met him, or went into the house and leaned his hand against the wall, and a serpent bit him. 20

---

22. ESV, KJV, and NIV translate "לְרוּחַ הַיּוֹם" as "in the cool of the day." In doing so, the translation loses its eschatological connotation, which is significant in the literal and historical contexts. Young represents the traditional interpretation of Genesis 3:8. In doing so, he loses the significance of the primeval day of the Lord, which suggests the day of judgment: "Scripture employs an interesting phrase to designate the time at which God was walking. In the English versions we read of the cool of the day. The word which these versions have rendered 'cool' is better translated by 'wind' or 'spirit.' Some think that the reference is to the morning wind, but this seems to be contrary to the word's usage. The phrase 'wind of the day' would be the time when a cool wind blew, toward evening. The definite article which appears in the phrase 'the day' suggests that the phenomenon was a familiar one. It is a beautiful description. Toward evening, late in the afternoon, the cool wind blows. Then it was that the Lord God was walking in the garden. But where are the ones whom he had created? They want no part of the scene, for they hear His voice and they hear it as His enemies." Young, *Genesis 3*, 75.

23. For an insightful discussion of Genesis 3:8 as the primal *parousia* of the day of the Lord, see Kline, *Images of the Spirit*, 97–121. Kline observes that the appearance of theophanic glory in Genesis 3:8 symbolizes the day of the Lord, foreshadowing the judgment day of the Lord later, especially highlighted in the Old Testament prophetic age: "We may then translate Genesis 3:8a: 'They heard the sound of Yahweh God traversing the garden as the Spirit of the day.' The frightening noise of the approaching Glory theophany told them that God was coming to enter into judgment with them. The sound of judgment day preceded the awesome sight of the *parousia* of their Judge. It was evidently heard from afar before the searching, exposing beams of the theophanic light pierced through the trees in the midst of the garden. Momentarily, then, it seemed to them possible to hide from the eyes of Glory among the shadows of the foliage. Thus, inadvertently, they positioned themselves at the place of judgment in the garden, at the site of the tree of judicial discernment between good and evil." Ibid., 106.

> *Is not the day of the Lord darkness, not light, and gloom with no brightness in it?*
> ... 23 Take away from me the noise of your songs; to the melody of your harps I will not listen. 24 But let justice roll down like waters, and righteousness like an ever-flowing stream. 25 "Did you bring to me sacrifices and offerings during the forty years in the wilderness, O house of Israel? 26 You shall take up Sikkuth your king, and Kiyyun your star-god—your images that you made for your selves, 27 and I will send you into exile beyond Damascus," says the Lord, whose name is the God of hosts. (Amos 5:18–27)

Surprisingly, the prophetic judgment of the day of the Lord was against the Northern Kingdom of Israel, the covenant community of Israel who disobeyed the Sinaitic covenant of law, radically falling into idolatry. God announced his judgment upon the unfaithful covenant community, using a pagan Assyrian kingdom. It was precisely fulfilled in 722 B.C. according to the prophetic announcement of judgment. Ever since the prophetic announcement of judgment upon the Northern kingdom of Israel through Amos, "the day of the Lord" became a standard prophetic formula of divine judgment upon his own unfaithful covenant community and pagan kingdoms (cf. Isa 13:6, 9; Jer 46:10; Joel 3:14; Mal 4:5; Obad 15). In that sense, it is proper to observe that the origin of the prophetic announcement of the coming divine judgment as the day of the Lord in the Old Testament is God's prophetic announcement of judgment after Adam's fall as "the Spirit of the day" in Genesis 3:8.

Jesus in his famous discourse on the Mount of Olives, known as the Olivet Discourse, reveals that his Second Coming will be "the coming of the Son of Man," which will be the ultimate fulfillment of the day of the Lord when he will visibly separate between the elect and reprobate, and between the heavenly Kingdom of God and the Kingdom of Satan as the righteous and final judge:

> 36 "But concerning that day and hour no one knows, not even the angels of heaven, nor the Son, but the Father only. 37 *For as were the days of Noah, so will be the coming of the Son of Man* ["Ὥσπερ γὰρ αἱ ἡμέραι τοῦ Νῶε, οὕτως ἔσται ἡ παρουσία τοῦ υἱοῦ τοῦ ἀνθρώπου]. 38 For as in those days before the flood they were eating and drinking, marrying and giving in marriage, until the day when Noah entered the ark, 39 *and they were unaware until the flood came and swept them all away, so will be the coming of the Son of Man* [καὶ οὐκ ἔγνωσαν ἕως ἦλθεν ὁ κατακλυσμὸς καὶ ἦρεν ἅπαντας, οὕτως ἔσται [καὶ] ἡ παρουσία τοῦ υἱοῦ τοῦ ἀνθρώπου]. 40 Then two men will be in the field; one will be taken and one left. 41 Two women will be grinding at the mill; one will be taken and one left ... 44 Therefore you also must be ready, for the Son of Man is coming at an hour you do not expect." (Matt 24:36–44)

Likewise, Jesus revealed his second coming as "the coming of the Son of Man" (ἡ παρουσία τοῦ υἱοῦ τοῦ ἀνθρώπου). After his Damascus Road conversion experience, Paul began to proclaim the second coming of Jesus as "the day of the Lord (ἡμέρα κυρίου)," reflecting the prophetic announcement of the day of the Lord in the Old Testament and Jesus' self proclamation of "the coming of the Son of Man." He identifies the day of the Lord with "the coming of the Lord (τὴν παρουσίαν τοῦ κυρίου)," and "the coming of our Lord Jesus Christ (τῆς παρουσίας τοῦ κυρίου ἡμῶν Ἰησοῦ Χριστοῦ)" (cf. 1 Cor 5:3–5; 1 Thess 4:13—5:11; 2 Thess 2:1–4).

When Adam broke the covenant of works by eating the forbidden fruit of the knowledge of good and evil with Eve, he deserved immediate death and punishment. Nevertheless, God introduced his saving grace which will be offered in the woman's offspring. The proclamation of saving grace in the woman's offspring was the divine proclamation of the inauguration of redemptive history. The Lord God pronounced holy war against the power of the Kingdom of Satan. And the woman's offspring will wage holy war through his redemptive suffering against the power of the Kingdom of Satan. And that is the irony of redemptive grace and the power of the gospel. As such, the Lord God proclaimed the grace of the gospel to save his elect after Adam and Eve broke the Edenic covenant of works:

> 14 The Lord God said to the serpent, "Because you have done this, cursed are you above all livestock and above all beasts of the field; on your belly you shall go, and dust you shall eat all the days of your life. 15 I will put enmity between you and the woman, and between your offspring and her offspring; he shall bruise your head, and you shall bruise his heel." (Gen 3:14–15)

Genesis 3:15 can be considered *protoevangelium*, which is the first divine revelation of the gospel. In this way, the Messianic prophecy was inaugurated as well as redemptive history with the announcement of saving grace in the coming Messiah, the woman's offspring. In that sense, it is rightly considered the primitive gospel.

Having received the grace of *protoevangelium*, Adam believed God's promise in the woman's offspring, the coming Messiah, and had overwhelming joy and thanks for gift of salvation and eternal life, even though he deserved immediate death and eternal punishment in hell due to his transgression of God's commandment. As a token of the expression of his faith and thanks to God, he named his wife Eve, which carries the meaning of "life-giver." At the same time, the broken covenantal marriage relationship between Adam and Eve was restored under God's saving grace. Responding to Adam's faith in his saving grace, the Lord God killed an animal and clothed Adam and Eve with garments of animal skin: "20 The man called his wife's name Eve, because she was the mother of all living. 21 And the Lord God made for Adam and for his wife garments of skins and clothed them" (Gen 3:20–21). The Lord God's act of clothing was a symbolic act of covering Adam and Eve with his righteousness and holiness, which were stripped off due to original sin. In addition, it anticipated the system of animal sacrifices to atone for sin, instituted as ceremonial system and law under the Sinaitic covenant. It was a prophetic act foreshadowing the time when the woman's offspring

BIBLICAL THEOLOGY

would be slaughtered as an atonement for the sins of the elect.[24] Young properly reads Genesis 3:21 in light of redemptive history, affirming that God's clothing of Adam and Eve was clothing them "in the righteousness of Jesus Christ," as follows:

> As physical nakedness after the fall becomes a symbol of shame and shame is a sign of man's spiritually fallen nature, so also the clothing of that nakedness has a spiritual import. Man cannot clothe his nakedness, for man cannot deliver himself from the spiritual bondage into which sin has plunged him. To be properly clothed, he must possess a clothing that is acceptable with God, and such clothing must be furnished him by God. When he is properly clothed God will look upon him with favour, regarding him as standing in a right relationship with Himself. The mere skins of animals, however, in themselves cannot clothe the sinful condition of man; they cannot hide his nakedness. Only the righteousness of Christ can do that. If man therefore, is properly clothed he is in Christ. God would behold him properly clothed, clothed with a righteousness which is not his own, but the righteousness of another. God would behold man clothed in the righteousness of Jesus Christ. No, we have not read into the text when we see Christ here, for only in Christ is man properly clothed.[25]

In that sense, Genesis 3:21 can be the first indirect revelation that God declares sinners as righteous with the imputation of the righteousness of Jesus Christ. In fact, God clothes us with the righteousness of Jesus Christ when sinners are justified by faith.

The original Garden of Eden was a holy sanctuary of God where Adam and Eve could enjoy their lives as the vicegerents of God, the Great King. As long as they were faithful to their kingly and priestly duties, they could have enjoyed the blessings of their earthly paradise, anticipating the heavenly paradise. But to be sure, the Garden of Eden was not a place for sinners. Therefore, Adam and Eve lost their special privilege to live in the Garden of Eden when they committed the original sin. Their sins were certainly forgiven, and they received saving grace through the announcement of the *protoevengelium*. In the end, however, God expelled them from the Garden of Eden because they lost the privilege to live there:

---

24. Von Rad recognizes that the clothing act of God in Genesis 3:21 is the demonstration of "divine compassion" to Adam and Eve. However, he does not see the typological aspect of God's clothing act, which has a soteriological implication of the forensic aspect of justification, which is bestowed in Jesus Christ: "The clothing of the first pair appears in two different aspects; initially it is traced back to their spontaneous covering of themselves, but it is afterwards regarded as an arrangement made by the divine compassion, which will not have them naked and ashamed in each other's presence (Gen. III. 7, 21). It was God himself who covered their shame, thereby giving a new possibility to their togetherness as well as at the same time establishing by his own instrumentality a basic element in human culture." Von Rad, *Old Testament Theology*, 159.

25. Young, *Genesis 3*, 147–48. For the biblical theological exploration of the clothing in Genesis 3:7 and 21 in relation to Paul's clothing metaphors in his epistles, see Beale, *A New Testament Biblical Theology*, 452–55.

> 22 Then the Lord God said, "Behold, the man had become like one of us in knowing good and evil. Now, lest he reach out his hand and take also of the tree of life and eat, and live forever—23 therefore the Lord God sent him out from the garden of Eden to work the ground from which he was taken. 24 He drove out the man, and at the east of the garden of Eden he placed the cherubim and a flaming sword that turned every way to guard the way to the tree of life. (Gen 3:22–24)

Originally, God endowed to Adam and Eve the priestly duty of keeping the Edenic sanctuary and guarding against the intrusion of Satan. As they were expelled from the Garden of Eden, God placed the cherubim to keep the Edenic sanctuary. Also, "a flaming sword" guarded "the way to the tree of life," which was a sacramental tree and the symbol of everlasting life. It is remarkable to observe that reentering the holy Garden of Eden is only possible through the curse of "a flaming sword." Indeed, the curse of a flaming sword would fall upon the woman's offspring, the Messiah, so that all the elect may enter the heavenly Kingdom of God through God's grace alone when the Parousia comes.

The Covenant of Common Grace

God revealed his redemptive historical paradigm, by which he will save his elect through the woman's offspring who will be coming as the Messiah (Gen 3:15). So, Genesis 3:15 is not only the first proclamation of the gospel, but also the first revelation of the coming Messiah as the woman's offspring.

The triune God made the covenant of redemption eternally to save the elect after the fall. To save the elect, however, God must establish a world in which the elect and the reprobate may live together harmoniously, promoting common cultural endeavors over the course of history. In pursuit of this historical vision, in which believers and nonbelievers live together, God introduced the covenant of common grace as the backbone of redemptive history:

> 16 To the woman he said, "I will surely multiply your pain in childbearing; in pain you shall bring forth children. Your desire shall be for your husband, and he shall rule over you. 17 And to Adam he said, "Because you have listened to the voice of your wife and have eaten of the tree of which I commanded you, 'you shall not eat of it,' cursed is the ground because of you; in pain you shall eat of it all the days of your life; 18 thorns and thistles it shall bring forth for you; and you shall eat the plants of the field. 19 By the sweat of your face you shall eat bread, till you return to the ground, for out of it you were taken; for you are dust, and to dust you shall return. (Gen 3:16–19)[26]

---

26. Vos rightly interprets Genesis 3:16–19 as God's speech which cursed Eve and Adam "with the element of grace." Nevertheless, he does not observe that the passage is simultaneously the inauguration of the covenant of common grace, which is vital to a successive world history, as well as to

After Adam and Eve committed the original sin, God cursed his image bearers. As a result, childbearing for Eve would be painful. God cursed the natural realm, represented as "the ground," because of the first Adam's fall. God pronounced his curse that Adam would eat "the plants of the field" through painful labor. In addition, God cursed the ground so that "thorns and thistles" will be a constant problem for Adam, though he does not desire to deal with it. At the end of painful labor, Adam will return to the ground through death, which is the result of God's curse due to the fall. God's pronouncement of curses on Adam and Eve after their committal of their transgression was the representative curse, which will be directly passed on to their descendents because Adam's breach of the covenant of works was a representative breach.

Nevertheless, childbearing for Eve and consumption of "the plants of the field" through painful labor for Adam are God's gracious blessings. God promised Adam and Eve those gracious blessings which their descendants can share together between the elect and the reprobate after Adam and Eve were expelled from the Garden of Eden. In that sense, the benefits of God's grace, summarized in Genesis 3:16–19 are not the benefits of saving grace but common grace. They are temporary blessings which will be given without discrimination, as long as world history continues. They are the common blessings that form the family, community, state, and international or global society, and that allow human beings to develop science and technology. In that sense, Genesis 3:16–19 can be appropriately considered as the covenant of common grace. God promised unilaterally the continuity of human life through childbearing and the provision of habitable environment of the earth despite painful childbearing and labor.

After Adam and Eve were expelled from the Garden of Eden, they began a life of pilgrimage that was radically different from their life in the paradise of the Garden of Eden. They began their pilgrimage in the fallen world which God had cursed due to their sin, as God pronounced his judgment upon human beings and also the earth itself (Gen 3:16–19). Although the original Adamic covenant community was expelled from the Garden of Eden, they began their lives as a worshipping community in the midst of their pilgrim life in the cursed original world.

Meanwhile, God gave two sons, Cain and Abel, to Adam and Eve with his blessing. Abel was "a keeper of sheep" while Cain was "a worker of the ground." Later, Cain dedicated "an offering of the fruit of the ground," and Abel brought "the firstborn of his flock and of their fat portions" to the Lord. Yahweh was pleased with Abel's offering.

---

redemptive history: "Finally, we note the revelation of justice in the curses upon the woman and the man. The woman is condemned to suffer in what constitutes her nature as woman . . . The element of grace interwoven with this consists in the implication that, notwithstanding the penalty of death, the human race will be enabled to propagate itself . . . Cursed is the ground for man's sake; it brings forth thorns and thistles; here the element of grace mingling with the curse consists in that the bread will after all be bread; it will sustain life. As the woman is enabled to bring new life into the world, so the man will be enabled to support life by his toil." Vos, *Biblical Theology*, 44. For Genesis 3:16–19 as the inauguration of the covenant of common grace, see Kline, *Kingdom Prologue*, 153–60.

However, he did not accept Cain's offering. Out of anger, Cain killed his brother Abel when they were together in the field (Gen 4:1–8). The episode of Cain and Abel is the first divine revelation of predestination, which distinguishes between election and reprobation. Indeed, Cain and Abel were the members of the Adamic covenant community. Both of them participated in covenant worship, bringing offerings to the Lord outside the Garden of Eden. Yet God rejected Cain's offering and worship, whereas he accepted Abel's offering and worship. In doing so, God indirectly revealed that Cain was a reprobate while Abel was elect. The apostle John demonstrates that Cain was the first murderer and did not have "eternal life abiding in him." In doing so, John affirms that Cain was a reprobate, even though he was a member of the covenant family, and he emphasizes the importance of loving one another within the covenant community:

> 11 For this is the message that you have heard from the beginning, that we should love one another. 12 We should not be like Cain, who was of the evil one and murdered his brother. And why did he murder him? Because his own deeds were evil and his brother's righteous. 13 Do not be surprised, brothers, that the world hates you. 14 We know that we have passed out of death into life, because we love the brothers. Whoever does not love abides in death. 15 Everyone who hates his brother is a murderer, and you know that no murderer has eternal life abiding in him. (1 John 3:11–15)

Looking back on redemptive history, the apostle John goes back to the first murder of world history within the Adamic covenant community. He describes how Cain, who killed his own brother, would abide in eternal death. However, Cain's brother, Abel, demonstrated his righteousness and received the blessing of eternal life. In these words, the apostle John demonstrates that Cain was the first historical example of a reprobate, while Abel was a good example of an elect who demonstrated his saving faith with love and sacrifice. Similarly, the author of Hebrews affirms that Abel offered his sacrifice to God through his saving faith, bestowed on the elect alone (Heb 11:4; cf. Matt 23:35).

Meanwhile, the Garden of Eden before the fall was not the origin of the state. Rather, it was an earthly projection or symbol of the heavenly Kingdom of God. Moreover, the Edenic paradise was a theocratic kingdom. As the Adamic covenant community began their journey as pilgrims outside of the Garden of Eden, God allowed them to build a city under his common grace. Interestingly, the city was the origin of the state in which the elect and the reprobate lived together harmoniously, developing and sharing all facets of life, including science, technology, arts, music, and so on:

> 17 Cain knew his wife, and she conceived and bore Enoch. When he built a city, he called the name of the city after the name of his son, Enoch. 18 To Enoch was born Irad, and Irad fathered Mehujael, and Mehujael fathered Methushael, and Methushael fathered Lamech. 19 And Lamech took two wives. The name of the one was Adah, and the name of the other Zillah. 20 Adah bore Jabal; he was the father of those who dwell in tents and have livestock. 21

> His brother's name was Jubal; he was the father of all those who play the lyre and pipe. 22 Zillah also bore Tubal-cain; he was the forger of all instruments of bronze and iron. The sister of Tubal-cain was Naamah. (Gen 4:17–22)

As Cain built the city of Enoch, the city under God's common grace began to emerge as a visible realm, which was the origin of the state. People began to develop the benefits of common grace such as tents, musical instruments, and mechanical tools made of bronze and iron, all of which God had already envisioned as the rich and divergent benefits of the covenant of common grace in Genesis 3:16–19. However, as civilization emerged under God's common grace, developing culture, science, technology, and community, mankind did not glorify God through cultural endeavors, with the exception of the remnants within the covenant community.

At the time of Noah, mankind became increasingly arrogant and sinful despite God's gift of common grace in the original world. So God executed his redemptive judgment against mankind and the original world, and through the Prediluvian Noahic covenant only saved the Noahic covenant community, who entered the Ark (Gen 6:5—8:19). God restored and renewed his common grace after a redemptive judgment of a universal scale through the Postdiluvian Noahic covenant (Gen 8:20—9:17). After destroying his original creation through the flood judgment, God recreated it in the form of the present world. Afterward, Noah's children scattered to the different regions and developed the nations and kingdoms under God's common grace (Gen 10:1–32).

Meanwhile, Noah's descendents initially spoke in the same language and built a new city and tower, reaching "its top in the heavens." When people migrated to "a plain in the land of Shinar," they made a new city and the Tower of Babel with one aim. In doing so, they did not glorify the name of Yahweh. Rather, they claimed their own glory and ignored him, although they were able to build the city under the benefits and blessings of his common grace. So Yahweh confused their language so that they could no longer communicate and complete building the city. Then he scattered them "from there over the face of all the earth."

> 1 Now the whole earth had one language and the same words. 2 And as people migrated from the east, they found a plain in the land of Shinar and settled there. 3 And they said to one another, "Come, let us make bricks, and burn them thoroughly." And they had brick for stone, and bitumen for mortar. 4 Then they said, "Come, let us build ourselves a city and a tower with its top in the heavens, and let us make a name for ourselves, lest we be dispersed over the face of the whole earth." 5 And the Lord came down to see the city and the tower, which the children of man had built. 6 And the Lord said, "Behold, they are one people, and they have all one language, and this is only the beginning of what they will do. And nothing that they propose to do will now be impossible for them. 7 Come, let us go down and there confuse their language, so that they may not understand one another's speech." 8 So the Lord dispersed them from there over the face of all the earth, and they left off building the

city. 9 Therefore its name was called Babel, because there the Lord confused the language of all the earth. And from there the Lord dispersed them over the face of all the earth. (Gen 11:1–9)[27]

Although mankind began to develop the new city through the enormous benefits of God's common grace after the flood, they did not give glory and honor to their Creator. Rather, they tried to dethrone his power and glory and did not want to rule over the world as vicegerent under the Great King, Yahweh. They did not want to be faithful stewards in building the city and governing the world. Of course, the central focus in the process of building the new city should have been Yahweh and for his name to be glorified. However, the major focus of the Babel community was the Tower of Babel, the symbol of human arrogance, idolatry, apostasy, and desecration of Yahweh. It demonstrates humanity's total depravity in the highest degree and manner. At the peak of the apostasy of the Babel community, Yahweh came down to the city and confused their language and dispersed them throughout "the face of all the earth." In doing so, the triune God actively involved himself and cursed the community of Babel city, confusing their language.[28] Certainly, Yahweh's curse did not destroy the city of Babel, as he did Sodom and Gomorrah later, but only confused their language and scattered them. Yahweh confused the language of the community of Babel because of their sinful action and scattered them across the earth. Later, this order was reversed at the Pentecost event which was a remarkable turning point of redemptive history. At Pentecost, people who lived the life of diaspora gathered together and God united the gathered people in Jesus Christ through the gift of tongues (Acts 2:1–13). It was the visible and audible sign of the beginning of world mission to all nations. The beginning of the global mission was sealed by the Holy Spirit with the remarkable gift of tongues. Indeed, this is a remarkable redemptive historical reversal. When the Parousia comes, the Babel-like cities and nations, no matter how spectacular and magnificent to man's eyes and perspectives, will be unable to stand and face the catastrophic judgment, even though they are built under the benefits of God's common grace, inaugurated

---

27. The ancient Near Eastern parallel with the episode of the Tower of Babel has been found in the Sumerian epic "Enmerkar and the Lord of Aratta." See Arnold and Beyer, *Readings from the Ancient Near East*, 71.

28. Interpreting Genesis 11:7, Calvin rightly argues that the confusion of language against the community of the city of Babel was the work of the triune God. So the episode of the Tower of Babel indirectly or implicitly reveals the existence and work of the triune God already in the book of Genesis, as we observe the first time the triune God's work in his creation of man as his own image in Genesis 1:26: "The Jews think that he addresses himself to the angels. But since no mention is made of the angels, and God places those to whom he speaks in the same rank with himself, this exposition is harsh, and deservedly rejected. This passage rather answers to the former, which occurs in the account of man's creation, when the Lord said, 'Let us make man after our image.' For God aptly and wisely opposes his own eternal wisdom and power to this great multitude; as if he had said, that he had no need of foreign auxiliaries, but possessed within himself what would suffice for their destruction. Wherefore, this passage is not improperly adduced in proof that Three Persons subsist in One Essence of Deity. Moreover, this example of Divine vengeance belongs to all ages: for men are always inflamed with the desires of daring to attempt what is unlawful." Calvin, *Genesis*, 11:7.

in Genesis 3:16–19. God will gather his saved people throughout all the nations, and there will no longer be racial, cultural, and linguistic barriers among the people of God who were saved by God's grace in Jesus Christ, the mediator of the New Covenant.

Summary

God is a covenantal and personal being in the nature of his existence. Therefore, the process of creation in the beginning was also a covenant making process between the Creator and his creatures.

We endeavored to explore how Genesis 1—3 can be interpreted and seen from the perspective of covenantal accounts. In doing so, we have seen Genesis 1:1—2:25 in light of the covenant of creation. We also traced how Adam had a covenantal relationship with God in the Garden of Eden before the fall. It was not the covenant of grace, but the covenant of works, which has the form and pattern of a suzerainty treaty in the ancient Near East, having the dual sanctions of blessings and curses. The proper historical order is not grace (or gospel) and law. Rather, it is law and grace (or gospel).

We affirmed that after the breach of the Edenic covenant of works, God introduced another covenant, namely the covenant of grace, which is a redemptive covenant in Genesis 3:15. After Adam and Eve sinned by eating the forbidden fruit of the knowledge and good and evil, Yahweh appeared to them. They tried to hide and cover their sin and guilt by wearing loincloths made of fig leaves. We have interpreted Genesis 3:8 as the primal episode of "the day of the Lord," which signifies the eschatological judgment against sinful mankind and world.

The announcement of the primitive gospel with the inauguration of the covenant of grace in Genesis 3:15 is the announcement of God's plan to save the elect in the woman's offspring. In these words, God revealed his plan to provide a habitable environment to Adam's descendents on the earth (Gen 3:16–19). In that sense, we observed that Genesis 3:16–19 is the inauguration of the covenant of common grace, in which God unilaterally promised to execute his common grace without discrimination between the elect and reprobate until the Parousia.

2

The Noahic Covenants and the Kingdom of God

MANKIND AND THE OLD world faced catastrophic and universal judgment for the first time after Adam and Eve were expelled from the Garden of Eden, committing the original sin. The readers of the Bible recognize that both God's Flood judgment and the Postdiluvian promise were based upon his covenants.

Biblical commentators, interpreters, and theologians by and large neglect to note the *difference* between the Prediluvian and Postdiluvian Noahic covenants. Representatively, Robertson suggests that there is no distinction between the Prediluvian and Postdiluvian Noahic covenants. In doing so, he argues that the Noahic covenant should be considered as "the covenant of preservation" without making a proper distinction:

> The pre-diluvian and post-diluvian covenantal commitments of God to Noah fit the frequent pattern of covenantal administration in Scripture. It is not necessary to posit two covenants with Noah, one preceding the flood and one following the flood. Preliminary dealings precede formal inauguration procedures. God's commitment to "preserve" Noah and his family prior to the flood relates integrally to the "preservation" principle, which forms the heart of God's covenantal commitment after the flood.[1]

Having that in mind, we will examine the Noahic covenant (Gen 6:5—9:17) from the perspective of redemptive history and the Kingdom of God. On the one hand, we will explore and argue that the Prediluvian Noahic covenant (Gen 6:5—8:19) should be interpreted from the perspective of the covenant of grace. On the other hand, we will suggest that the Postdiluvian Noahic covenant (Gen 8:20—9:17) may be viewed from the perspective of the renewal or recovery of the covenant of common grace.[2]

---

1. Robertson, *The Christ of the Covenants*, 110.

2. For the comprehensive and critical interpretation of the Noahic covenant from divergent perspectives, see Busenitz, "Introduction to the Biblical Covenants," 173–89; J. Collins, *Introducing to the Hebrew Bible*, 79–80; Dumbrell, *Covenant and Creation*, 11–46; Edwards, *A History of Redemption*, 46–54; Horton, *Introducing Covenant Theology*, 111–28; Kline, *God, Heaven, and Har Magedon*, 78–92; Kline, *Kingdom Prologue*, 212–62; LaRondelle, *Our Creator Redeemer*, 18–22; Lunn, "Patterns in the Old Testament Metanarrative," 237–49; Murray, *The Covenant of Grace*, 12–16; Robertson, *The*

In the exploration of the Prediluvian Noahic covenant, we will identify it as the covenant of royal grant in the milieu of the ancient Near East treaties. And the covenant of royal grant is a harmonious concept with the covenant of grace, which is an inherently redemptive covenant.

Historically, there has been no consensus among Bible interpreters and theologians whether the Noahic Flood was universal or local. Keeping this in mind, we will seek to demonstrate that the Noahic Flood was universal. The redemptive historical understanding of the Flood judgment makes us conclude that it was not local, but universal. And the universal Flood judgment was the precursor of the final redemptive judgment, which will be universal as well.

As we view the Postdiluvian Noahic covenant as the renewal of the covenant of common grace, we will explore the biblical theological significance of the distinction between clean and unclean animals. Through the formation of the Noahic theocratic kingdom before the Flood judgment, God made a distinction between clean and unclean animals. And after the Flood judgment, God recovered the covenant of common grace and abrogated the distinction between clean and unclean animals, allowing the consumption of animal meats without any distinction.

And we will examine the divine institution of capital punishment under the authority of state, which is the institution of God's common grace. Furthermore, we will argue that capital punishment is warranted as long as world history continues until the Parousia. We will examine it in the light of the state as a divinely ordained institution under God's common grace.

The Prediluvian Noahic Covenant

God saw that the world was corrupt, and decided to execute his judgment upon the earth he created. In doing so, God commanded Noah to build the Ark so that the Noahic covenant community will enter the Ark when the catastrophic judgment falls on the wicked and corrupt world outside of the covenant community.

Covenant of Royal Grant and Universal Judgment

At the time of Noah, human beings had wicked hearts and lived wickedly, as citizens of the Kingdom of Satan. And God revealed his intention to wipe out human beings "from the face of the earth," including animals and "birds of the heavens" (Gen 6:5–7). In the midst of the corruption, God bestowed his special grace on Noah: "But Noah found *grace* in the eyes of the Lord" [וְנֹחַ מָצָא חֵן בְּעֵינֵי יְהוָה:] (Gen 6:8).[3] It is true that

---

Christ of the Covenants, 109–25; Vos, *Biblical Theology*, 45–55; Waltke, *An Old Testament Theology*, 284–304; Wenham, *Genesis 1—15*, 148–208; Williams, *Far as the Curse Is Found*, 83–99.

3. Here, I adopt the translation of the KJV. The Septuagint translates Genesis 6:8 as follows: "Νωε δὲ εὗρεν χάριν ἐναντίον κυρίου τοῦ θεοῦ." In doing so, it translates "חֵן" as "χάριν" which carries the

the principle of redemptive grace in the coming Messiah as the "woman's offspring" was already revealed in Genesis 3:15, which was the inauguration of the covenant of grace. Nevertheless, we can consider Genesis 6:8 as the first explicit divine revelation that sinners will be saved by God's grace alone. In addition, it revealed the principle of saving grace, sovereignly initiated by God and applied to sinners.

Before the Flood judgment, God made a covenant with Noah and commanded that Noah and his family, as the covenant community, enter the Ark and bring into the Ark all the living creatures, both male and female.

> 17 For behold, I will bring a flood of waters upon the earth to destroy all flesh in which is the breath of life under heaven. Everything that is on the earth shall die. 18 *But I will establish my covenant with you* [וַהֲקִמֹתִי אֶת־בְּרִיתִי אִתָּךְ], and you shall come into the ark, you, your sons, your wife, and your sons' wives with you. 19 And of every living thing of all flesh, you shall bring two of every sort into the ark to keep them alive with you. They shall be male and female. 20 Of the birds according to their kinds, and of the animals according to their kinds, of every creeping thing of the ground, according to its kind, two of every sort shall come in to you to keep them alive. 21 Also take with you every sort of food that is eaten, and store it up. It shall serve as food for you and for them." 22 Noah did this, he did all that God commanded him. (Gen 6:17–22)

Noah began to build the Ark according to God's architectural plan. It took about 120 years to complete the Ark. In the process of building the Ark, people followed the wicked lifestyle of the Kingdom of Satan, and mocked Noah's apparent stupidity. However, representing the Kingdom of God in the original world, Noah did not back down. He persistently built the Ark until it was completed according to God's master plan. Completing the Ark was Noah's victory against the people who mocked him and represented the Kingdom of Satan. In that sense, Noah was a victorious warrior who constantly fought against the power of the Kingdom of Satan on behalf of the Kingdom of God and the Great King. In the end, God as the Great King granted to Noah and his covenant family a special privilege to enter the Ark, which represented the heavenly Kingdom of God and a safe haven in the midst of the Flood judgment. In this sense, the Prediluvian Noahic covenant may be viewed and understood as the covenant of royal grant, as Kline summarizes in the following:

> As in all other administration in the Covenant of Grace series, the blessings of the covenant with Noah were a gift of grace to ill-deserving sinners, fallen in the first Adam. Yet there was a principle of works in this covenant in connection with the messianic aspect of the typology of the ark-salvation event. The covenant was a covenant of grant, bestowing kingdom benefits as a reward for faithful service rendered to the Lord of the covenant. Noah was a type of

---

meaning of *saving grace* so clearly.

Christ, the faithful Servant of the Lord, and as such he was the grantee of the ark covenant.[4]

Indeed, Noah's faithful obedience was a type of Christ's perfect and meritorious obedience as the mediator of the New Covenant. God used Noah's obedience to grant the Kingdom of God to Noah and his covenant family in the Ark. Although Noah faithfully obeyed God in completing the construction of the Ark, his obedience was *not meritorious* because his obedience at best was imperfect and not a sinless obedience as Jesus demonstrated through his life and death as the mediator of the New Covenant. Nevertheless, Kline considers Noah's obedience as meritorious in which God used his obedience to bestow the typological Kingdom in the Ark.

> The Genesis 6:18 covenant with Noah might be identified more precisely as a covenant of grant. That is the kind of covenant that ancient rulers gave to meritorious individuals for faithful service to the crown. Such grants had the character of a royal charter or prebend. They might guarantee to the grantee his special status, or bestow on him title over cities or lands with their revenues, or grant to territory under his authority exemptions from customary obligations.[5]

However, I suggest that meritorious obedience should be limited to the first and last Adam, although the first Adam, before the fall, failed to fulfill his meritorious obedience as the representative covenantal head in the Garden of Eden.

Meanwhile, through the prophetic words, God revealed to Noah that the Flood judgment would be universal, not local.[6] Although God did not say to Noah directly that the Flood judgment would be universal, his prophetic message in itself suggests that it would be indeed universal when he said that the Flood would cover "the earth to destroy all flesh in which is the breath of life under heaven" (v. 17).[7]

---

4. Kline, *God, Heaven and Har Magedon*, 78. I will use the term 'the covenant of royal grant' instead of simply 'the covenant of grant,' because the covenant of royal grant more effectively summarizes the idea of a king's grant to the faithful vassal after the vassal has completed his mission on behalf of the Great King.

5. Kline, *Kingdom Prologue*, 234. It is true that Kline limits Noah's obedience to grant the typological kingdom in the Ark as the reward to the faithful servant, avoiding legalism. However, it is better not to use the word 'merit,' because Noah's obedience, at best, was a faithful servant's obedience under God's saving grace. Waltke's comment is helpful here: "Our refusal to trust in the triune God's grace through the gospel of Jesus Christ and not to trust in ourselves mires us in the muck of our depravity. Our depravity keeps us from learning truth. The virtue of faith is God's gift to those whom he chooses as covenant partners (Eph. 2:8). 'It is God who works in you to will and to act according to his good purpose' (Phil. 2:13). In other words, Noah's righteousness is not a work to gain merit with God but the outcome of his faith in God, as seen in his building and provisioning the ark." Waltke, "An Old Testament Theology," 290.

6. The Epic of Gilgamesh in the ancient Near East, as the Old Babylonian flood myth account, represents and depicts a close parallel account to the Noahic Flood narrative. Cf. Arnold and Beyer, *Readings from the Ancient Near East*, 66–70; Pritchard, *The Ancient Near East*, 39–72. For a brief comparative analysis between the Noahic Flood narrative and the Mesopotamian flood myths, see Waltke, *An Old Testament Theology*, 291.

7. Interpreting Genesis 7:17, Calvin demonstrates that the Noahic Flood was universal, covering

God's prophetic word to Noah in respect to the universal Flood judgment was realized during Noah's lifetime. Noah completed the Ark according to God's architectural design, and entered the Ark with his covenant family members along with all the living birds and animals. And the flood began and continued forty days "on the earth," which was the fulfillment of God's prophetic word. The Flood judgment covered "so mightily on the earth that all the high mountains under the whole heaven were covered." Likewise, the Flood judgment covered the earth, blotting out every living flesh "from the earth." Most importantly, the name of the specific area was not mentioned to note and signify the local area of the Flood judgment. Rather, general terms were used such as "on the earth," "above the earth," "from the earth," and "under the whole heaven" to reveal that the scope of the Flood judgment covered the entire earth on a global scale:

> 17 The flood continued forty days *on the earth* [עַל־הָאָרֶץ]. The waters increased and bore up the ark, and it rose high *above the earth* [מֵעַל הָאָרֶץ]. 18 The waters prevailed and increased greatly *on the earth* [עַל־הָאָרֶץ], and the ark floated on the face of the waters. 19 And the waters prevailed so mightily *on the earth* [עַל־הָאָרֶץ] that all the high mountains *under the whole heaven* [תַּחַת כָּל־הַשָּׁמָיִם] were covered. 20 The waters prevailed above the mountains, covering them fifteen cubits deep. 21 And all flesh died that moved *on the earth* [עַל־הָאָרֶץ], birds, livestock, beasts, all swarming creatures that swarm *on the earth* [עַל־הָאָרֶץ], and all mankind. 22 Everything on the dry land in whose nostrils was the breath of life died. 23 He blotted out every living thing that was on the face of ground, man and animals and creeping things and birds of the heavens. They were blotted out *from the earth* [מִן־הָאָרֶץ]. Only Noah was left, and those who were in the Ark. 24 And the waters prevailed on the earth 150 days. (Gen 7:17–24)

---

the whole world: "Moses copiously insists upon this fact, in order to show that the whole world was immersed in the waters . . . But seeing it is plainly declared, that whatever was flourishing on the earth was destroyed, we hence infer, that it was an indisputable and signal judgment of God; especially since Noah alone remained secure, because he had embraced, by faith, the word in which salvation was contained. He then recalls to memory what we before have said; namely, how desperate had been the impiety, and how enormous the crimes of men, by which God was induced to destroy the whole world . . . These two things, directly opposed to each other, he connects together; that the whole human race was destroyed, but that Noah and his family safely escaped. Hence we learn how profitable it was for Noah, disregarding the world, to obey God alone: which Moses states, not so much for the sake of praising the man, as for that of inviting us to imitate his example . . . In this sense, Peter teaches that Noah's deliverance from the universal deluge was a figure of baptism (1 Pet. Iii. 21), as if he had said, the method of salvation, which we receive through baptism, agrees with the deliverance of Noah." Calvin, *The Book of Genesis*, 7:17. For scholars and commentators who view the Noahic Flood as universal or global, see Calvin, *The Book of Genesis*, 6:18—7:17; Owen, *Biblical Theology*, 202–4; Waltke, *An Old Testament Theology*, 284–300; Whitcomb and Morris, *The Genesis Flood*. Scholars who promote the Noahic Flood as local are as follows: Harrison, *Introduction to the Old Testament*, 98–104; Ramm, *The Christian View of Science and Scripture*; Young, *The Biblical Flood*.

Biblical Theology

Throughout redemptive history, God specified when his judgment was limited to the specific local area. The representative example was the judgment upon Sodom and Gomorrah, when God indicated the specified local area (Gen 18:22—19:19). And the vivid description of God's judgment upon Sodom and Gomorrah suggests that the local area was identified when God's judgment was limited to the specific local area: "23 The sun had risen on the earth when Lot came to Zoar. 24 Then the Lord rained on Sodom and Gomorrah sulfur and fire from the Lord out of heaven. 25 And he overthrew those cities, and all the valley, and all the inhabitants of the cities, and what grew on the ground" (Gen 19:23–25).

Peter, reflecting the Flood judgment and judgment upon Sodom and Gomorrah, specifies the local areas of Sodom and Gomorrah while he indirectly denotes the universal Flood judgment at the time of Noah, not identifying the local areas. So, Peter uses general words such as "the ancient world" (ἀρχαίου κόσμου), and "a flood upon the world of the ungodly" (κατακλυσμὸν κόσμῳ ἀσεβῶν) which allude to the Flood judgment as universal, covering the world:

> 4 If God did not spare angels when they sinned, but cast them into hell and committed them to chains of gloomy darkness to be kept until the judgment; 5 if he did not spare *the ancient world* [ἀρχαίου κόσμου], but preserved Noah, a herald of righteousness, with seven others, when he brought *a flood upon the world of the ungodly* [κατακλυσμὸν κόσμῳ ἀσεβῶν]; 6 if by turning *the cities of Sodom and Gomorrah* [πόλεις Σοδόμων καὶ Γομόρρας] to ashes he condemned them to extinction, making them an example of what is going to happen to the ungodly . . . (2 Pet 2:4–6)

Furthermore, Peter explains that the present world, described as "the present heavens and earth," will go through the recreating process by fiery judgment. And "ungodly men" will receive the final judgment just like the ungodly people outside the Noahic covenant community received judgment through the Flood. But the old and original earth was "formed out of water and by water" during the process of God's original creation. And the original earth as "the world of that time" (ὁ τότε κόσμος) was destroyed by the Flood judgment at the time of Noah. And we anticipate the universal fiery judgment upon "the present heavens and the earth" (οἱ νῦν οὐρανοὶ καὶ ἡ γῆ) at the day of judgment through God's intrusion:

> 5 But they deliberately forget that long ago by God's word the heavens existed and *the earth was formed out of water and by water*. 6 By these waters also *the world of that time* [ὁ τότε κόσμος] was deluged and destroyed. 7 By the same word *the present heavens and earth* [οἱ δὲ νῦν οὐρανοὶ καὶ ἡ γῆ] are reserved for fire, being kept for the day of judgment and destruction of ungodly men. (2 Pet 3:5–7)

Peter carefully chooses to say "the world of that time" to indicate that the original earth was destroyed globally and universally by the Flood judgment. In Peter's mind, the Flood judgment destroyed the original earth and recreated the present earth. However, when the final judgment comes, not only will the present earth face God's final judgment but also the present heavens. That is why Peter uses a carefully chosen word "the present heavens and earth" to note that the present world will face God's fiery judgment when "the day of judgment" comes.

The Flood and Redemptive Judgment

God revealed that the Noahic covenant community and "every living thing of all flesh" both "male and female" would be saved after they entered the Ark. In that sense, the Ark was the Ark of salvation. However, those who did not enter the Ark were faced with the Flood judgment. In doing so, God demonstrated the overall pattern of final judgment which will radically separate the elect from the reprobate with the heavenly blessings on the one hand and hellish curses on the other.[8]

Noah, as the mediator of the Prediluvian Noahic covenant, obeyed God's command in the process of building the Ark. In this sense, as we already discussed, Noah's obedience may be considered as typological of the perfect obedience of Jesus Christ in his life and death as the mediator of the New Covenant (Gen 6:22—7:5). God used Noah's obedience as a means to save the Noahic covenant community and every living thing when the Flood judgment came. Similarly, God will save only the elect because of Jesus' perfect and meritorious obedience unto the crucifixion when the final judgment comes.

Meanwhile, the Ark was the Ark of salvation. The Noahic covenant community, which entered the Ark, was saved when God displayed the Flood judgment upon the original world, including the people outside of the covenant community. In that sense, the Ark was a type of the eschatological heavenly Kingdom of God where the saved covenant community dwells eternally in heaven while the reprobate will be condemned forever in hell.

The Apostle Peter testifies that Christ proclaimed the gospel message through Noah to the people who did not listen to Noah's prophetic message, whose souls are now in hell. Through Noah's mouth, "the Spirit of Christ" went and proclaimed the message of repentance "to the spirits" (τοῖς πνεύμασιν) who are now in hell, which Peter describes as "in the prison" (ἐν φυλακῇ). This is the clear testimony that the Noahic covenant community was saved by the principle of grace and faith in the same way as believers under the New Covenant:

---

8. Gage is correct to note that the Flood judgment set a classical paradigm of recurring judgment in redemptive history, culminating in the final judgment: "This chapter proposes first to demonstrate that the flood of Noah establishes the fundamental paradigm of biblical judgment recurring in the destructions of Sodom, Egypt, Canaan, Jerusalem (both the first and second temples), and the present cosmos. This pattern of judgment is reducible to three elements: the 'days of Noah,' the 'flood' of judgment, and the deliverance of the remnant from wrath." Gage, *The Gospel of Genesis*, 63.

> 18 For Christ also suffered once for sins, the righteous for the unrighteous, that he might bring us to God, being put to death in the flesh but made alive in the spirit, 19 in which *he went and proclaimed to the spirits in the prison* [τοῖς ἐν φυλακῇ πνεύμασιν πορευθεὶς ἐκήρυξεν], 20 because they formerly did not obey, when God's patience waited in the days of Noah, while the ark was being prepared, in which a few, that is, eight persons, were brought safely through water. 21 Baptism, which corresponds to this, now saves you, not as a removal of dirt from the body but as an appeal to God for a good conscience, through the resurrection of Jesus Christ, 22 who has gone into heaven and is at the right hand of God, with angels, authorities, and powers having been subjected to him. (1 Pet 3:18–22)

Likewise, Peter understood and interpreted the history of the Old Testament in light of redemptive history, inaugurated in Genesis 3:15. Peter used to live by the principles of a legalistic Jewish worldview before he was called by Jesus. But, as a disciple of Jesus, Peter abandoned Jewish legalism, and was transformed into a redemptive historical theologian, witnessing the death, resurrection, and ascension of Jesus and the Pentecost event. Remarkably, Peter interpreted the Noahic Flood episode from the redemptive historical perspective. Noah, as the mediator of the Prediluvian Noahic covenant, obeyed God's command to build the Ark exactly as God designed. In addition to building the Ark, Noah was faithful to his prophetic mission as "a preacher of righteousness" (δικαιοσύνης κήρυκα), proclaiming the good news of the gospel before the incarnation of the Son of God (2 Pet 2:5).

God executed his judgment when Adam and Eve committed the original sin. Ultimately, Adam and Eve were expelled from the holy Garden of Eden because sinful human beings were not allowed to stay in the original holy land, although they were saved by the grace of God and clothed with the righteousness of Christ, which was typologically and symbolically manifested by God's clothing them with animal skins (Gen 3:21–24).

In the proclamation of the primitive gospel in Genesis 3:15, God prophetically proclaimed the battle between the Kingdom of God and the Kingdom of Satan. The deluge was the first visible example of holy war against the Kingdom of Satan. And God won the first universal holy war against the Kingdom of Satan by means of the Flood. In that sense, God set the stage. It is this redemptive historical paradigm which set the exemplary paradigm for the ongoing pattern of redemptive judgment. In fact, redemptive judgment will come to an end with the final judgment through the intrusion of heavenly fire. Edwards beautifully captures and demonstrates that the Flood judgment set the redemptive historical paradigm for the ongoing redemptive judgment, which will culminate in the final judgment:

> And therefore, God's destroying those enemies of the church by the flood, belongs to this affair of redemption: for it was one thing that was done in fulfillment of the covenant of grace, as it was revealed to Adam: "I will put enmity

between thee and the woman, and between thy seed and her seed; it shall bruise thy head." This destruction was only a destruction of the seed of the serpent in the midst of their most violent rage against the seed of woman, and so delivering the seed of woman from them, when in utmost peril by them . . . We read, that just before the world shall be destroyed by fire, the nations that are in the four quarters of the earth, shall gather together against the church as the sand of the sea, and shall go up on the breadth of the earth, and compass the camp of the saints about, and the beloved city; and then fire shall come down from God out of heaven, and devour them, Rev. xx. 8, 9. And it seems as though there was that which was very parallel to it, just before the world was destroyed by water. And therefore their destruction was a work of God that did as much belong to the work of redemption, as the destruction of the Egyptians belonged to the redemption of the children of Israel out of Egypt, or as the destruction of Sennacherib's mighty army, that had compassed about Jerusalem to destroy it, belonged to God's redemption of that city from them.[9]

Similarly, the Flood judgment is a distinctive divine judgment when we examine it from the perspective of redemptive history. In a word, it is a redemptive judgment, which is a typological manifestation of the final judgment. The final judgment will be revealed when the Parousia comes, and it will be the ultimate eschatological judgment where the elect and reprobate will be clearly and visibly manifested and distinguished between the everlasting heaven and hell. God demonstrated his redemptive judgment through the historical episode of the Flood judgment, separating between the Noahic covenant community and the rest of humanity (Gen 7:21–23).[10]

To be sure, God did not use man-made weapons, although they are some of the benefits of his common grace, inaugurated in Genesis 3:16–19. Rather, he used the Flood to execute his redemptive judgment during the time of Noah, which was the eschatological age of the original world. Interestingly, God will not use the means of the Flood to execute the final judgment against the present world when Jesus comes back again. Rather, he will use the means of heavenly fire, which is the sign of the manifestation of heavenly glory (2 Pet 3:6–13).

---

9. Edwards, *A History of the Work of Redemption*, 47–48.

10. In our contemporary world, a growing numbers of evangelicals deny the existence of hell. The denial of hell and the eternal punishment of the reprobate in hell is the result of failure to read the Bible from the perspective of redemptive history, in which God revealed unambiguously the hellish punishment and the existence of hell. For those who deny the existence of hell and the reality of eternal hellish punishment among so-called evangelicals, see Edwards and Stott, *Evangelical Essentials*, 313 –20; Hughes, *The True Image*, chap. 37; Pinnock, "The Destruction of the Finally Impenitent," 243–59; Wenham, *Facing Hell*; Wright, *Surprised by Hope*, 175–82. For the defense of the classical biblical doctrine of hell, responding to contemporary annihilationism and the denial of the existence of hell from diverse perspectives, see Morgan and Peterson, *Hell under Fire*; Peterson, *Hell on Trial*.

Ark as the Kingdom of God

After Noah, his covenant family, and all the living flesh according to God's command entered the Ark, God shut the door of the Ark. This indicates that the Kingdom of God in the Ark was inaugurated while those outside of the Ark faced the Flood judgment: "15 They went into the Ark with Noah, two and two of all flesh in which there was the breath of life. 16 And those that entered, male and female of all flesh, went in as God had commanded him. And the Lord shut him in" (Gen 7:15–16).

The Kingdom of God in the Ark was a foreshadowing of the everlasting Kingdom of God in heaven, as we already discussed. It is not difficult to imagine that the visible glory of the Lord was present in the Ark ever since God shut Noah inside. The visible presence of the glory of God was an indication that the Ark was a type of the coming of the Kingdom of God in heaven. In the consummated Kingdom of God, the glory of God will give its light so that there will be no need of light or a lamp, as the apostle John saw in his vision of the beautiful glory of God in the New Jerusalem, which will be the consummated heaven:

> 22 And I saw no temple in the city, for its temple is the Lord the Almighty and the Lamb. 23 And the city has no need of sun or moon to shine on it, for the glory of God gives its light, and its lamp is the Lamb. 24 By its light will the nations walk, and the kings of the earth will bring their glory into it, 25 and its gates will never be shut by day—and there will be no night there. 26 They will bring into it the glory and the honor of the nations. 27 But nothing unclean will ever enter it, nor anyone who does what is detestable or false, but only those who are written in the Lamb's book of life. (Rev 21:22–27)

God's shutting Noah into the Ark was the turning point of redemption in the original world. It was the turning point of the separation of heaven and hell in a typological manner in that original world. In the Ark, the glory of God was fully present and began to shine inside of the Ark. In this way, the Noahic covenant community foretasted the Kingdom of God in heaven with the presence of visible glory. Meanwhile, God cursed the original world outside of the Ark with Flood judgment after he shut Noah into the Ark. He cursed people and all the living things outside of the Ark with a hellish curse and judgment. In doing so, God demonstrated that the final judgment will separate elect and reprobate.

The separation between the Noahic covenant community and non-covenant community outside of the Ark revealed the existence of heaven and hell. Jesus in his famous Olivet Discourse explained the visible realization of the Kingdom of God in his Second Coming, which will be fulfilled with "the coming of the Son of Man" (ἡ παρουσία τοῦ υἱοῦ τοῦ ἀνθρώπου). Notably, he explained it in light of the Flood judgment at the time of Noah which was the eschatological age in the original world:

> 36 But concerning that day and hour no one knows, not even the angels of heaven, nor the Son, but the Father only. 37 For as were the days of Noah, so will be *the coming of the Son of Man*. 38 For as in those days before the flood they were eating and drinking, marrying and giving in marriage, until the day when Noah entered the ark, 39 and they were unaware until the flood came and swept them all away, so will be *the coming of the Son of Man* [ἡ παρουσία τοῦ υἱοῦ τοῦ ἀνθρώπου]. 40 Then two men will be in the field; one will be taken and one left. 41 Two women will be grinding at the mill; one will be taken and one left. 42 Therefore, stay awake, for you do not know on what day your Lord is coming. (Matt 24:36–42)

In the original world, the Flood judgment was the realization of the separation between the Noahic covenant community and non-covenant community. For the Noahic covenant community, it foreshadowed the heavenly Kingdom of God in the Ark. Meanwhile, it was the day of hellish judgment for those who were outside of the Noahic covenant community. So, the day of Noah's entrance into the Ark was the day of judgment in the original world, visibly separating the Kingdom of God and the Kingdom of Satan. In the Olivet Discourse, Jesus clearly explained that no one knows the day of "the coming of the Son of Man" (ἡ παρουσία τοῦ υἱοῦ τοῦ ἀνθρώπου), except the heavenly Father. And it will be the day of the final judgment, separating the redeemed elect and non-redeemed reprobate. Furthermore, it will be the day of separation of the fully realized Kingdom of God and the Kingdom of Satan.

The Postdiluvian Noahic Covenant

After the Flood judgment, God blessed the Noahic covenant community to live in the newly created world so that world history may continue until the Parousia. Having that in mind, God recovered and renewed the covenant of common grace, inaugurated in Genesis 3:16–19, which was temporarily lifted when he executed the universal Flood judgment upon the earth (Gen 8:20—9:17).[11]

The Recovery of the Covenant of Common Grace

God revealed the primitive gospel, which is the good news of the gospel through the woman's offspring (Gen 3:15). And then he revealed the covenant of common grace as the backbone of redemptive history to save his elect through the process of world history (Gen 3:16–19). The Flood judgment was not the final judgment. Rather, it

---

11. For representative scholars who read the Postdiluvian Noahic covenant as a covenant of common grace, see Horton, *Introducing Covenant Theology*, 111–19; Kline, *God Heaven and Har Magedon*, 81; Kline, *Kingdom Prologue*, 244–62; VanDrunen, *A Biblical Case for Natural Law*, 26–35; Waltke, *An Old Testament Theology*, 284–304. Horton and VanDrunen basically follow and adopt Kline's biblical theological exposition of the Noahic covenant of common grace.

was a precursor of the final judgment. In that sense, a stable world environment and natural world order were recovered and shared by both the elect and reprobate under God's providential care and protection without any discrimination. God recovered and renewed the blessings of the covenant of common grace after the Flood judgment, so he may continuously save his elect, expanding the spiritual kingdom throughout all the nations. And this was the divine plan for the last days (Gen 9:1,7).

After the earth had dried out, Noah and his covenant family went out from the Ark, including every living thing. And then Noah built an altar and worshipped the Lord with burnt offerings. The Lord accepted the burnt offerings as "the pleasing aroma" [רֵיחַ הַנִּיחֹחַ]. And Yahweh promised not to "curse the ground" anymore on a global scale. In addition to that, he promised that he would not again "strike down every living creature" as he did in the universal Flood judgment. In the following, Yahweh promised that he would bless the present world with his provisional care and protection:

> 20 Then Noah built an altar to the Lord and took some of every clean animal and some of every clean bird and burnt offerings on the altar. 21 And when the Lord smelled *the pleasing aroma* [רֵיחַ הַנִּיחֹחַ], the Lord said in his heart, "I will never again curse the ground because of man, for the intention of man's heart is evil from his youth. Never will I ever again strike down every living creature as I have done. 22 While the earth remains, seedtime and harvest, cold and heat, summer and winter, day and night, shall not cease." (Gen 8:20–22)

As Noah and his covenant community restored their worship with burnt offerings after they came out from the Ark, their pilgrimage was renewed in the present world, which was recreated by God through the Flood judgment. Certainly, the burnt offerings in the altar foreshadowed the final sacrifice, fulfilled in the coming Messiah. It signified that the grant of the new world order and blessings was granted by God to the Noahic covenant community and his descendents in the milieu of Messiah's sacrificial work and ministry to redeem his elect.

As we already explored and examined, the Prediluvian Noahic covenant was the covenant of grace directly related to personal salvation and redemption, providing the vision of the Kingdom of God in heaven through a typological picture. So, God made the covenant with Noah who was the head of the covenant family. However, the Postdiluvian Noahic covenant was very distinctive because God made it not only with Noah but also with his family, descendants, all the living things upon the earth, and the earth itself. These distinctive characteristics give an indication that the Postdiluvian Noahic covenant was not directly related to personal salvation and redemption along with the bestowment of the heavenly Kingdom of God, which is the essence of the covenant of grace, but was the covenant of common grace. And this provides the possibility of human history on the earth:

> 8 Then God said to Noah and to his sons with him, 9 "Behold, I establish my covenant with you and your offspring after you, 10 and with every living

creature that is with you, the birds, the livestock, and every beast of the earth with you, as many as came out of the ark; it is for every beast of the earth. 11 I establish my covenant with you, that never again shall all flesh be cut off by the waters of the flood, and never again shall there be a flood to destroy the earth." 12 And God said, "This is the sign of the covenant that I make between me and you and every living creature that is with you, for all future generations: 13 I have set my bow in the cloud, and it shall be a sign of the covenant between me and the earth." (Gen 9:8–13)

Interestingly, God showed a rainbow as the sign of the Postdiluvian Noahic covenant. Meanwhile, he instituted circumcision as the sign of the covenant of grace when he made the Abrahamic covenant later on. The sacramental practice of circumcision was continued throughout the history of the Old Covenant Israelites, even under the Sinaitic covenant. Jesus, as the mediator of the New Covenant, instituted water baptism as the sign of the New Covenant, replacing the sign of circumcision. The distinctive characters of circumcision and water baptism, as the signs of the covenant, lie in the fact that they apply to the body of the covenant community members. However, the sign of the Postdiluvian Noahic covenant was not applied to the body of the covenant community because the Postdiluvoan Noahic covenant was not directly related to salvation and redemption. In that sense, the rainbow can be rightly viewed as the sign of the covenant of common grace after the Flood judgment.

In addition, the rainbow represented a battle bow in the ancient Near East. In fact, the bow was a representative symbol of war in the ancient Near East. When a battle bow pointed to a target vertically, the images of battle and wrath were involved. However, when the battle was over, warriors laid down and took aside the battle bow, loosening it. The rainbow in the air, as the sign of the covenant, was like a loosened battle bow after God's holy war against the old world. So, the rainbow signifies that God laid down the battle bow he used to curse and condemn the old world through the Flood.[12]

12. For divergent interpretations of the symbolical meaning of rainbow in the Noahic covenant, see Robertson, *The Christ of the Covenants*, 123–25; von Rad, *Genesis: A Commentary*, 133–34; Williams, *Far As the Curse Is Found*, 96–98. Kline comprehensively summarizes the biblical theological meaning of rainbow as the sign of the covenant of common grace in relation to the battle bow in the ancient Near East as follows: "This arching color-spectrum in the heavens is designated by the word for the archer's bow. The war-bow is mentioned in God's arsenal of wrath, particularly when he is viewed as advancing in the judgment-storm, dispatching his arrows of lightning (cf., e.g., Deut 32:42; Pss 7:12[13]; 18:14[15]; 64:7[8]; 77:17[18]; 144:6; Hab 3:11; Zech 9:14). However, in the sign of the rainbow is not raised vertically and drawn taut in the face of the foe but is suspended in the relaxed horizontal position. There are Near Eastern representations of kings, first seen engaged in battle, then returning in peace, with the state-god of the storm depicted above in stance identical to the king's in each case. In the battle scene king and god hold bows fitted with arrows and full drawn, while in the peace scene their bows hang at their side, loosened. Accordingly, the designation of the rainbow as a battle-bow may best be interpreted as suggesting the picture of the divine warrior with his weapons laid aside, turning from the path of judgment against rebellious mankind, prepared now to govern them with forbearance for a season." Kline, *Kingdom Prologue*, 247–48. Von Rad's analysis in respect to the rainbow in relation to "the bow of war" in the literary context of Genesis 9:8–17 is helpful, although he stands in the tradition of the historical-critical school: "The Hebrew word that we translate

The rainbow, as the sign of the covenant of common grace, means that God would not wage holy war on a global scale until the Parousia. Throughout redemptive history after the Flood judgment, God used holy war to curse the world. But it was not on a global scale but local as we see in the judgments of Sodom and Gomorah, Exodus, conquest of Canaan, and others. In that sense, a rainbow, as the sign of the Postdiluvian Noahic covenant, was a sign of the peace treaty between God and the present world signifying he would not curse the world on a global scale until the Parousia. The Postdiluvian Noahic covenant is a unilateral covenant of common grace in which God promised to provide a relatively stable living environment on the earth, executing his common grace to both the elect and reprobate alike.

God's remarkable provision in the Postdiluvian Noahic covenant demonstrates that the present world will not end with the catastrophic disasters of earthquake, hurricanes, famine, global warming, pollution and nuclear wars. The covenant of common grace warranties that God, as the sovereign Lord of world history and the universe, will take care of the present world until the final judgment comes. Waltke comprehensively summarizes God's providential care to the present world in light of the covenant of common grace until the final judgment, as follows:

> His unconditional covenant takes into account the universal and inevitable reality of human sinfulness. This earth will not be torn down until it is ultimately consumed by fire, whereupon it will be replaced by a new cosmos (2 Peter 3:10–13). God's providential preservation of all life throughout the span of human life until the final eschaton is known as God's "common grace"—the Creator's indiscriminate goodwill by which "he causes his sun to rise on the evil and the good, and sends rain on the righteous and the unrighteous" (Matt. 5:45).
>
> Many people waste time and emotional energy worrying about the earth's destruction from various disasters, such as a recurrent big bang, and an asteroid disturbing the earth's orbit, or a life-annihilating thermonuclear war. They should not. The earth will be here until Jesus comes again.[13]

Meanwhile, the covenant of grace is bilateral because it requires believers' obedience while God executes sovereignly his saving grace only to the elect. However, the covenant of common grace is unilateral where God promises his provision to provide a stable environment for both the elect and reprobate until the final judgment comes. As such, when God recovered and renewed the covenant of common grace after the Flood judgment, he promised *unilaterally* that he would not use the Flood to judge the present world (Gen 9:11–15).

'rainbow' usually means in the Old Testament 'the bow of war.' The beauty of the ancient conception thus becomes apparent: God shows the world that he has put aside his bow. Man knows of the blessing of this new gracious relationship in the stability of the orders of nature, i.e., first of all in the sphere of the impersonal elements only." Von Rad, *Genesis*, 134.

13. Waltke, *An Old Testament Theology*, 291–92.

The Noahic Covenants and the Kingdom of God

The Distinction between Clean and Unclean Animals

After God created man in his own image, he gave the original cultural mandate to man. He commanded that man has "dominion over" the creature of the earth as a vicegerent. In doing so, he was able to give all the glory and honor to his Lord and the Great King (Gen 1:26–30). After God finished recreating the new world through the means of the Flood judgment, he blessed Noah and his sons. And he ordered the new cultural mandate to have dominion over the newly created world (Gen 9:1–7). Strikingly, God ordered the new cultural mandate according to the principle of the covenant of common grace, which was absent in the original cultural mandate, given in Genesis 1:26–30. So, the proper interpretation and implication of the new cultural mandate within the context of the Noahic covenant of common grace is vitally important not only for a proper perspective on the subsequent redemptive history but also for a biblical worldview in the present world.

Meanwhile, Yahweh made a distinction between clean and unclean animals before Noah and his covenant family entered the Ark along with other animals and birds under the Prediulvian Noahic covenant. He made the distinction between clean and unclean animals that he did not make before because animal sacrifice on the altar had a redemptive typological meaning and significance.[14]

Most importantly, he made this distinction in the process of the formation of the theocratic kingdom in the Ark. Interestingly, Yahweh commanded Noah to take "seven pairs of all clean animals" (מִכֹּל ׀ הַבְּהֵמָה הַטְּהוֹרָה שִׁבְעָה שִׁבְעָה), both male and female, while he commanded Noah to take only one pair of each unclean animal into the Ark. In addition, he ordered Noah to take "seven pairs of the birds of the heavens" (מֵעוֹף הַשָּׁמַיִם שִׁבְעָה שִׁבְעָה), both male and female:

> 1 Then the Lord said to Noah, "Go into the ark, you and all your household, for I have seen that you are righteous before me in this generation. 2 *Take with you seven pairs of all clean animals* [מִכֹּל ׀ הַבְּהֵמָה הַטְּהוֹרָה תִּקַּח־לְךָ שִׁבְעָה שִׁבְעָה], the male and his mate, and *a pair of the animals that are not clean* [וּמִן־הַבְּהֵמָה אֲשֶׁר לֹא טְהֹרָה הִוא שְׁנָיִם], the male and his mate, 3 and *seven pairs of the birds of the heavens* [מֵעוֹף הַשָּׁמַיִם שִׁבְעָה שִׁבְעָה] also, male and female, to keep their offspring alive on the face of all the earth." (Gen 7:1–3)

Yahweh envisioned that world history and life on the earth would continue after the Flood judgment. And the Kingdom of God in the Ark, as a theocratic kingdom, was a typological kingdom. So, it would fade away after the Flood judgment. Afterwards, animal sacrifice on the altar would be renewed. But animal sacrifice had to be offered to God using only clean animals. That is the reason why Yahweh ordered Noah to take "seven pairs of all clean animals" along with "seven pairs of the birds of the heavens." But "a pair of the animals" was good enough as a means of reproduction

---

14. For the discussion of the distinction between clean and unclean animals, and its biblical theological significance in redemptive history, see Kline, *Kingdom Prologue*, 254–56.

among unclean animals because unclean animals were not permitted to be sacrificed on the altar when animal sacrifice was resumed after the Flood judgment.

In fact, when the Flood judgment was over and Noah and his covenant family, along with the animals and birds, came out from the Ark, Noah offered on the altar a burnt offering of "some of every clean animal and some of every clean bird." Here we find biblical theological reasoning as to why Yahweh commanded Noah to take seven pairs of clean animals and birds instead of one pair (Gen 8:20–22).

In the Postdiluvian Noahic covenant, God permitted the consumption of animals, without making a distinction between clean and unclean animals. This is the sign that the theocratic kingdom in the Ark was over, and the new world order began through the resumption of the covenant of common grace. It is interesting to note that God allowed the consumption of vegetables and fruits in the beginning with Adam and Eve. However, it is apparent that God was silent about whether human beings should consume animal meats in the beginning. In the Garden of Eden, God had given plants and fruits as food for Adam and Eve while green plants were given as food for every animal and birds as noted in the following:

> 28 And God blessed them. And God said to them, "Be fruitful and multiply and fill the earth and subdue it and have dominion over the fish of the sea and over the birds of the heavens and over every living thing that moves on the earth." 29 And God said, "Behold, I have given you every plant yielding seed that is on the face of all the earth, and every tree with seed in its fruit. You shall have them for food. 30 And to every beast of the earth and to every bird of the heavens and to everything that creeps on the earth, everything that has the breath of life, I have given every green plant for food." And it was so. (Gen 1:29–30)

Verse 28 is a classic verse about God's cultural mandate as the Great King to man who is a vicegerent. The language of eating is absent in verse 28. Rather, God used the language of ruling, saying to "have dominion over the fish of the sea and over the birds of the heavens and over every living thing" on the earth. The idea of dominion "over every living thing" on the earth embraces not only ruling as God's vicegerent, but also eating and consuming them.

It is true that God allowed for the first time outwardly the consumption of "every living thing" within the historical context of making the Postdiluvian Noahic covenant.[15] Nevertheless, that does not mean that God prohibited eating animal flesh before the Postdiluvian Noahic covenant.

---

15. Kline's analysis is helpful here. Kline argues that God permitted man to consume animals from the beginning of his creation, although there is no explicit mention of it in the original context of God's creation: "Moreover, there is a special literary purpose in the reference to the permission for the use of plants for food in Genesis 1:29, namely to prepare for the exceptional stipulation in Genesis 2:16, 17 prohibiting the use of the fruit of the tree of knowledge. These considerations show how unwarranted is the assumption that the silence of this passage concerning man's use of animal flesh as food must be intended as a prohibition of such . . . If Genesis 9:3 were interpreted as simply permitting the eating of meat as well as vegetables, it would, in any case, not be the first such authorization even

The Noahic Covenants and the Kingdom of God

Although God allowed the consumption of animal flesh without any distinction between clean and unclean animals, God specified that they were not to eat the blood of animals. In giving this commandment, God had a redemptive historical concern in mind: the blood from animal sacrifices on the altar was a precursor of the final Sacrifice, who shed his blood in the New Covenant. In that sense, the prohibition of eating the blood of animals was also related to the ceremonial law, which was centered on animal sacrifice, typifying the blood of Jesus, as the blood of the New Covenant, who fulfilled the ceremonial law in the Old Testament.

After Noah offered an animal sacrifice on the altar, God blessed Noah and his covenant family. And he ordered a cultural mandate to be fruitful and multiply, and to subdue the earth. God's cultural mandate was not intended to exploit but to exercise stewardship over his creation, God's servants and vicegerents. God's cultural mandate after the recreation process parallels the original cultural mandate given by God in Genesis 1:28. Moreover, God pronounced the fear and dread of mankind upon "every beast of the earth and upon every bird of the heavens," every creeping animal, and "all the fish of the sea." God, canceling a distinction between clean and unclean animals, permitted eating "every moving thing" (כָּל־רֶמֶשׂ), which includes animal, birds, and fish:

> 1 And God blessed Noah and his sons and said to them. "Be fruitful and multiply and fill the earth. 2 The fear of you and the dread of you shall be upon every beast of the earth and upon every bird of the heavens, upon everything that creeps on the ground and all the fish of the sea. Into your hand they are delivered. 3 *Every moving thing* [כָּל־רֶמֶשׂ] that lives shall be food for you. And as I gave you the green plants, I give you everything." (Gen 9:1–3)[16]

In the exposition of Genesis 9:3, Calvin notes that animal consumption was allowed by God from the beginning of the original creation. Calvin argues that animal sacrifices to God and permission "to kill wild beasts" to make "garments and tents" before the deluge are the biblical evidence that God permitted "the eating of flesh" from the beginning:

> The Lord proceeds further, and grants animals for food to men, that they may eat their flesh. And because Moses now first relates that this right was given to

---

in the postlapsarian period, judging from Genesis 4:4 (cf. 3:21). However, what Genesis 9:3 actually authorized was the eating of all kinds of meats, thus removing the prohibition against the eating of unclean animals that had been instituted for Noah's family within the special symbolic situation in the ark-kingdom. Instead of posing a problem for our thesis, Genesis 9:3 is another argument for it. For by its illusion to an earlier situation where the eating of meat had been temporarily restricted to the flesh of clean animals, this passage discloses the fact that the eating of meat had been permitted all along and was not a privilege first granted after the Deluge." Kline, *Kingdom Prologue*, 55.

16. Animal consumption was allowed by God from the beginning in the Garden of Eden. But some scholars argue that it began after the Flood judgment, based upon the description of Genesis 9:3. Representatively, Waltke explains it as follows: "Their rule is further assisted by God's placing the fear of humans in all other living creatures (9:2) and his holding the whole animal kingdom accountable for the death of any of those who are the image of God. Moreover, the custodians of the earth may now eat animals, but not wantonly—they must not eat their lifeblood." Waltke, *An Old Testament Theology*, 296–97.

men, nearly all commentators infer, that it was not lawful for man to eat flesh before the deluge, but that the natural fruits of the earth were his only food. But the argument is not sufficiently firm. For I hold to this principle; that God here does not bestow on men more than he had previously given, but only restores what had been taken away, that they might again enter on the possession of those good things from which they had been excluded. For since they had before offered sacrifices to God, and were also permitted to kill wild beasts, from the hides and skins of which, they might make for themselves garments and tents, I do not see what obligation should prevent them from the eating of flesh.[17]

Interpreting Genesis 9:3, Wenham is agnostic on whether God permitted the consumption of unclean animals as well:

"That is alive" precludes the consumption of animals that have died of natural causes (cf. Lev 11:40; Deut 14:21). Whether this permission to eat meat meant that Noah could eat unclean as well as clean creatures is uncertain. The silence of the text on this issue is usually taken to mean that he was not restricted just to clean creatures. However, the frequent mention of the difference between clean and unclean animals elsewhere in the story makes it problematic to assert that total freedom is being given here (7:2, 8; 8:20).[18]

Here, Wenham bypasses and undermines the importance of making the distinction between clean and unclean animals in Genesis 7:2, 8, and 8:20. It is important to remember that those distinctions were forming in the Noahic theocratic kingdom, which God did away with after the Flood judgment. So, when God permitted the consumption of animal flesh, he did not note the distinction between clean and unclean animals that he made earlier when the Noahic covenant community entered the Ark, forming the theocratic kingdom. And after the Flood judgment was over, the Noahic covenant community along with the animals, came out from the Ark. In doing so, the Kingdom of God in the Ark, as a theocratic kingdom, faded away. At the same time, the distinction between clean and unclean animals ceased. God did not make a distinction between clean and unclean animals when he permitted the consumption of animals, noting that "every moving thing that lives shall be food for you." In that sense, a distinction between clean and unclean animals is closely related with the formation of the theocratic kingdom, which was represented in the Noahic Ark and the covenant community of Israel in the Promised Land.

After God made the Sinaitic covenant with the covenant community of Israel, the theocratic kingdom of Israel was inaugurated. And the theocratic kingdom was eventually formed and settled in the Promised Land after forty years in the wilderness. At this time, God made a distinction between clean and unclean animals, alluding to the time right before the formation of the theocratic kingdom in the Ark under the

---

17. Calvin, *The Book of Genesis*, 9:3.
18. Wenham, *Genesis 1—15*, 192–93.

Prediluvian Noahic covenant. But under the Sinaitic covenant, God described clean and unclean animals with more detailed analysis, naming them. And he commanded the covenant community of Israel to consume only the clean animals (Lev 12:1–47; Deut 14:3–21). In the end of the analysis of the distinction between clean and unclean animals, the dietary law is summarized as follows: "This is the law about beast and bird and every living creature that moves through the waters and every creature that swarms on the ground, to make *a distinction between the unclean and the clean* [לְהַבְדִּיל בֵּין הַטָּמֵא וּבֵין הַטָּהֹר] and the living creature that may be eaten and the living creature that may not be eaten" (Lev 11:46–47).

Through Jesus' life, death, resurrection, and ascension, the New Covenant was inaugurated. The Pentecost event was a divine sign that the gospel of the good news should be preached and spread to all nations beyond the boundaries of the Promised Land. And the church of the New Covenant was formed and expanded through the evangelical endeavors of the disciples of Jesus and believers from Jerusalem to other regions. And the Sinaitic covenant dissolved through the inauguration of the New Covenant. And the decisive termination of the Sinaitic covenant was realized in the destruction of the temple and the fall of Jerusalem through God's covenant lawsuit against the unfaithful covenant community of Israel in A.D. 70. And the inauguration of the New Covenant and the termination of the Sinaitic covenant also revealed the end of the distinction between clean and unclean animals, as well as clean and unclean people, because the end of the Sinaitic covenant also signified the end of the theocratic kingdom in the Promised Land. This is the reason why God showed two different visions to Cornelius and Peter in relation to the abrogation of the distinction between clean and unclean people, as well as the distinction between clean and unclean animals (Acts 10:1–48).

As we already explored, God prohibited the consumption of unclean animals to the covenant community of Israel under the Sinaitic covenant. Peter followed the traditional observation of this food law, not consuming unclean animals, as defined and commanded in Leviticus 11:1–47. So, initially, Peter did not understand why God commanded him through a vision to consume unclean animals. God responded to Peter that the distinction between clean and unclean animals had ceased and was invalidated. And the implication is that the distinction between clean and unclean animals along with the distinction between clean and unclean people was here terminated by the inauguration of the New Covenant.

> 9 The next day, as they were on their journey and approaching the city, Peter went up on the housetop about the sixth hour to pray. 10 And he became hungry and wanted something to eat, but while they were preparing it, he fell into a trance 11 and saw the heavens opened and something like a great sheet descending, being let down by its four corners upon the earth. 12 In it were all kinds of animals and reptiles and birds of the air. 13 And there came a voice to him: "Rise, Peter; Kill and eat." 14 But Peter said, "By no means, Lord; *for I have never*

eaten anything that is common or unclean." 15 And the voice came to him again a second time, *"What God has made clean, do not call common."* 16 This happened three times, and the thing was taken up at once to heaven (Acts 10:9–16).[19]

Likewise, God originally made a distinction between clean and unclean animals with the formation of the theocratic kingdom in the Ark. After the Flood judgment, the theocratic kingdom in the Ark ceased, along with the distinction between clean and unclean animals. When God renewed the covenant of common grace with the Postdiluvian Noahic covenant, he allowed the consumption of animals, fish, and birds without any distinction between clean and unclean animals. With the formation of the theocratic kingdom of Israel under Moses, God resumed the distinction between clean and unclean animals, allowing the consumption of only clean animals. Later on, with the inauguration of the New Covenant and the termination of the theocratic kingdom in the Promised Land, God permanently obviated both the distinction between clean and unclean animals along with the distinction between clean and unclean people.

The Prohibition of Eating Animal Blood

After Adam and Eve were expelled from the holy Garden of Eden, mankind began their pilgrimage in the old world. In doing so, Yahweh directed them to have altar worship among the covenant community. We find the first explicit incident of altar worship in the story of Cain and Abel, who were the covenant children of Adam. Interestingly, Yahweh rejected Cain's offering of "the fruit of the ground" while he accepted Abel's offering of "the firstborn of his flock and of their fat portions" (Gen 4:1–7). This first explicit incident of altar worship in the old world suggests that Yahweh encouraged altar worship, sacrificing animals from the beginning of world history outside of the Garden of Eden. At the same time, it is not difficult to imagine that Yahweh informed the covenant community not to consume animal blood, which carried the meaning and significance of atonement and redemption.

In Genesis 9:4, God prohibited eating animal blood. The prohibition of eating animal blood is related to the earthly altar, as we already noted. It is interesting to note that the distinction between clean and unclean animals was abrogated in the Postdiluvian Noahic covenant in the consumption of all animals. Yet God informed the covenant community not to consume animal blood, because animal blood, sacrificed on the earthly altar as the sign of the blood of the New Covenant, should continue within the covenant community.[20]

---

19. The followers of Judaism and the Seventh-Day Adventist Church still maintain the distinction between clean and unclean animals, regulated as dietary laws under the Sinaitic covenant. In a word, it is because they fail to read the dietary laws in light of redemptive history.

20. For a comprehensive discussion of the relation between the prohibition of eating animal blood and the earthly altar, see Kline, *Kingdom Prologue*, 254–60.

Later on, Yahweh again commanded the covenant community of Israel not to consume animal blood, encapsulating it as a part of ceremonial law under the Sinaitic covenant (Lev 17:10–16). Yahweh said that those who violate the regulation of ceremonial law on the consumption of animal blood would be cut off. In a word, the violator would face capital punishment. The prohibition of consumption of animal blood not only applied to the covenant community of Israel, but also to "strangers who sojourn among them" under the Sinaitic covenant:

> 10 "If any one of the house of Israel or of the strangers who sojourn among them eats any blood, I will set my face against that person who eats blood and will cut him off from among his people. 11 For the life of the flesh is in the blood, and I have given it for you on the altar to make atonement for your souls, for it is the blood that makes atonement by the life. 12 Therefore I have said to the people of Israel, No person among you shall eat blood, neither shall any stranger who sojourns among you eat blood. 13 Any one also of the people of Israel, or of the strangers who sojourn among them, who takes in hunting any beast or bird that may be eaten shall pour out its blood and cover it with earth. 14 For the life of every creature is its blood: its blood is its life. Therefore I have said to the people of Israel, You shall not eat the blood of any creature, for the life of every creature is its blood. Whoever eats it shall be cut off." (Lev 17:10–14)

Yet the prohibition of eating animal blood was not permanent, but temporary. Its implication was applicable as long as the earthly altar worship continued. With the inauguration of the New Covenant, the mediator of the New Covenant offered himself as the final sacrifice, shedding the blood of the New Covenant as the symbol of covering the sins of all the elect. At the same time, animal sacrifice on the earthly altar dissolved, and the prohibition of eating animal blood was obviated within the covenant community of the New Covenant.

At the Jerusalem Council in A.D. 48 or 49, there were some theological and practical discussions among the participants (Acts 15:1–35). Some of the Pharisaic Christians insisted that the Gentile Christians were required to obey the whole Mosaic law, as the condition of justification and salvation, including circumcision (Acts 15:1–5). In the midst of the discussion, Peter argued that God obviated the barrier between the Jews and the Gentiles in Jesus Christ through the work of the Holy Spirit. And he insisted that salvation does not lie in the obedience of the whole Mosaic law, including circumcision, rather it is purely by grace in Jesus: "But we believe that we will be saved through the grace of the Lord Jesus just as they will" (Acts 15:11).

During the latter part of the Jerusalem Council, James proposed to draft a letter to the Antioch church, which included abstaining animal blood:

> 19 Therefore my judgment is that we should not trouble those of the Gentiles who turn to God, 20 but should write to them *to abstain from the things polluted by idols, and from sexual immorality, and from blood.* 21 For from ancient

generations Moses has had in every city those who proclaim him, for he is
read every Sabbath in the synagogues. (Acts 15:19–21)

James' proposal was accepted and the apostles and the elders chose Judas called Barsabbas and Silas along with Paul and Barnabas to send the Jerusalem Council's letter to the Gentile believers in the Antioch church. The Jerusalem Council's letter also included the commandment to abstain from animal blood.

> 27 We have therefore sent Judas and Silas, who themselves will tell you the same things by word of mouth. 28 For it has seemed good to the Holy Spirit and to us to lay on you no greater burden than these requirement: 29 that *you abstain from what has been sacrificed to idols, and from blood, and from what has been strangled, and from sexual immorality*. If you keep yourselves from these, you will do well. Farewell. (Acts 15:27–29)

It is important to remember that the Jerusalem Council's decision to abstain from animal blood within the church community was made within the historical context of the earthly altar in the temple of Jerusalem, which was effective until it was destroyed in A.D. 70, even though the New Covenant had been inaugurated earlier in Jesus Christ's life, death, resurrection, and ascension. When the earthly altar in the temple of Jerusalem was destroyed by the soldiers of the Roman Empire in A.D. 70, the divinely approved animal sacrifice became extinct. And the abstinence from eating animal blood within the covenant community was permanently obviated as well.

The Institution of Capital Punishment

It is important to note that God instituted capital punishment within the historical context of the recovery of the covenant of common grace. God prohibited the killing of man because man was created in "the image of God," distinguishing man and animals. The institution of capital punishment in the historical context of the recovery of the covenant of common grace is perfectly fitting because capital punishment for the crime of killing an innocent man is necessary to provide a stable environment in society as long as humans exist in the present world:

> 3 Every moving thing that lives shall be food for you. And as I gave you the green plants, I give you everything. 4 But you shall not eat flesh with its life, that is its blood. 5 And for your lifeblood I will require a reckoning: from every beast I will require it and from man. From his fellow man I will require a reckoning for the life of man. 6 'Whoever sheds the blood of man, by man shall his blood be shed, for God made man in his own image.' (Gen 9:3–6)[21]

---

21. For the affirmation of the institution and execution of capital punishment in the case of an active manslayer in the realm of the state until the Parousia in light of Genesis 9:3–6, see Kline, *Kingdom Prologue*, 250–53; Robertson, *The Christ of the Covenants*, 115–25; Waltke, *An Old Testament Theology*, 303–4.

As the mediator of the New Covenant, Jesus drew his disciples and the crowds, delivering his famous sermon, known as the Sermon on the Mount (Matt 5:1—7:29). It is interesting to note that Jesus' Sermon on the Mount was delivered during the early stage of his public life and ministry. Nevertheless, Jesus' Sermon on the Mount was the message of the eschatological mission to all nations under the New Covenant. It was a proclamation of the inauguration of the new era of eschatological mission in redemptive history.

God's command was to kill and destroy all seven tribes, including innocent children, women, and the elderly, when the Israelites entered and conquered the Promised Land under the leadership of Joshua. He commanded them to wage holy war, executing the war of *cherem*, which signifies total destruction without any mercy. But when Jesus came, the good news of the gospel spread from the holy land to all nations. Now, the order was reversed. Believers should persevere under persecution in the present world. As believers of the New Covenant community disperse from the Promised Land to all nations, they should not have the heart of total destruction, namely *cherem*, but a heart of love. That was the reason why Jesus proclaimed, "Love your enemies and pray for those who persecute you." And it is a perfectly suitable message to believers in the context of the eschatological mission and ministry of the church under the New Covenant in the last days.

> 43 You have heard that it was said, 'You shall love your neighbor and hate your enemy.' 44 But I say to you, Love your enemies and pray for those who persecute you, 45 so that you may be sons of your Father who is in heaven. For he makes his sun rise on the evil and on the good, and sends rain on the just and on the unjust. (Matt 5:43–45)

In Jesus' mind, when he delivered the Sermon on the Mount, he already envisioned the eschatological church mission, which would be inaugurated after his life, death, resurrection, and the Pentecost event. And that mission will be fulfilled progressively but surely through the works of the Holy Spirit, using the covenant community of the church under the New Covenant. But Jesus' message for the eschatological church mission should not be read and interpreted as a means to discard capital punishment by the state, warranted and instituted by the Postdiluvian Noahic covenant. His message should not be understood as the political ideal of pacifism. In a word, Jesus was not a pacifist. As such, the mission of the New Covenant church, as a realm of the spiritual kingdom, is to execute unconditional love as Jesus proclaimed to "love your enemies" through the process of evangelical and missionary endeavors and the gospel ministry.

However, the state, as a realm of the political kingdom, is not an institution of God's special grace, but of his common grace. So the primary task of the state is to execute divine justice and to protect civilians, preserving the well-being of society and religious freedom. The Roman Empire was a cruel regime in the first century to the Jews, as well as to the Christians. Yet the first-century Jews awaited the coming of the Messianic earthly kingdom under the rule of the Messiah in the Promised Land, overcoming the supreme power of the Roman Empire. Having the establishment of the earthly Messianic kingdom in mind, the exponents of Pharisaic Judaism and the Herodians asked the question whether they should pay "taxes to Caesar or not." Jesus' answer was to "render to Caesar the things that are Caesar's, and to God the things that are God's." This dialogue between Jesus, the Pharisees and the Herodians is important because it reflects that Jesus' ideal was not the establishment of the earthly Messianic kingdom that the first-century Jews yearned for and dreamt about:

> 15 Then the Pharisees went and plotted how to entangle him in his words. 16 And they sent their disciples to him, along with the Herodians, saying, "Teacher, we know that you are true and teach the way of God truthfully, and you do not care about anyone's opinion, for you are not swayed by appearances. 17 Tell us, then, what you think. Is it lawful to pay taxes to Caesar, or not?" 18 But Jesus, aware of their malice, said, "Why put me to the test, you hypocrites? 19 Show me the coin for the tax." And they brought him a denarius. 20 And Jesus said to them, "Whose likeness and inscription is this?" 21 They said, "Caesar's." Then he said to them, *"Therefore render to Caesar the things that are Caesar's, and to God the things that are God's."* 22 When they heard it, they marveled. And they left him and went away. (Matt 22:15–22)[22]

The dialogue indirectly reveals that Jesus made a proper distinction between church and state, which was already hinted at in the Postdiluvian Noahic covenant with the recovery of the covenant of common grace.

In the historical context of the recovery of the covenant of common grace, God allowed the government to be armed so that the government authorities may punish evildoers, even executing capital punishment when it is necessary to protect citizens and the well-being of the state. As Jesus made a proper distinction between the church and the state, the apostles adopted it after the pattern of Jesus. In this context, Paul explains the role of state as the institution of God's common grace to execute his justice in his epistle to the Romans, making a proper distinction between church and state:

> 1 Let every person be subject to the governing authorities. For there is no authority except from God, and those that exist have been instituted by God. 2 Therefore whoever resists the authorities resists what God has appointed, and those who resist will incur judgment. 3 For rulers are not a terror to good conduct, but to bad. Would you have no fear of the one who is in authority? Then do what is good, and you will receive his approval, 4 for he is God's servant for your good. But if you do wrong, be afraid, for he does not bear the sword in vain. *For he is the servant of God, and an avenger who carries out God's wrath*

---

22. Cf. Mark 12:13–17; Luke 20:20–26.

on the wrongdoer. 5 Therefore one must be in subjection, not only to avoid God's wrath but also for the sake of conscience. (Rom 13:1–5)[23]

In that sense, capital punishment, instituted in the Postdiluvian Noahic covenant in the realm of state, is warranted by God. As Paul explains it, capital punishment is a legitimate exercise under the New Covenant in the realm of the political kingdom, represented by the state. And it should not be ignored or abolished as long as world history and the institution of the state continues.

Summary

We explored the Noahic covenants, differentiating the Prediluvian Noahic covenant and the Postdiluvian Noahic covenant. In doing so, on the one hand, we endeavored to view the Prediluvian Noahic covenant in light of the covenant of grace, which is a redemptive covenant. On the other hand, we demonstrated that the Postdiluvian Noahic covenant is a renewal or recovery of the covenant of common grace, which was inaugurated in Genesis 3:16–19 and was temporarily abrogated during the Flood judgment. In this manner, we have argued that the Postdiluvian Noahic covenant provides the groundwork for the possibility of world history until the day of final judgment.

We identified the Prediluvian Noahic covenant as the covenant of royal grant because God bestowed and granted the Kingdom of God in the Ark after Noah fulfilled his mission, completing the architectural work of the Ark as God's warrior in a corrupt world. And the Kingdom of God in the Ark may be considered as a precursor to the eternal Kingdom of God in heaven.

While we identified the Postdiluvian Noahic covenant as the renewal of common grace, we visited a redemptive historical significance of the distinction between clean and unclean animals in the context of the formation of the theocratic kingdom in the Ark. In that sense, we interpreted God's command to eat "every living thing" in the historical context of the Postdiluvian Noahic covenant as not being the first time God allowed the consumption of animal meat. Rather, it is God's order that animal meat, without any distinction between clean and unclean animals, may be eaten. And this permit went out as he renewed the covenant of common grace through the Postdiluvian Noahic covenant. In addition, God ordained the institution of capital punishment in the case of an active man-slayer. And this is important for the well-being of society and state and reflects the institution of God's common grace in the present world.

---

23. Peter along with Paul basically offers the identical teaching that believers have obligation to obey civil authority under the Lordship of Jesus Christ: "Be subject for the Lord's sake to every human institution, whether it be to the emperor as supreme, or to governors as sent by him to punish those who do evil and to praise those who do good" (1 Pet 2:13–14).

3

The Abrahamic Covenant and the Kingdom of God

ABRAHAM'S LIFE IS EXTENSIVELY recounted, beginning with his calling by God, his pilgrimage, and his death (Gen 11:27—25:11). In the midst of his life, God made a covenant with Abraham that was a significant event and turning point in redemptive history.[1]

Jeffrey Niehaus argues that the recent archaeological findings and the discoveries of the ancient Near Eastern treaties should discard the classic covenant theology, formulated in the Reformed tradition of the seventeenth century:

> However, a rejection of the theologically constructed covenant established by covenant theology in its classic form (i.e. "the covenant of grace" construed out of the Noahic through the new covenants) does not make one *ipso facto* a classical dispensationalists either. Both classical covenant theology and classical dispensational theology are in fact archaic and ought to be discarded (or radically modified at least in terms of their understanding of covenants, as, to some extents, progressive dispensationalism has done with respect to classical dispensatinoalism) in favor of the realistic view of the Bible—that is, a view which understands Scripture in terms of its ancient Near Eastern context. It is *a priori* unlikely that systems developed in the seventeenth century (covenant theology) or in the nineteenth century (classical dispensational theology)—long before archaeological discoveries showed us what covenants actually were and how they worked in the ancient near East—could, lacking such evidence, have arrived at a proper understanding of covenantal matters in the Bible. That both systems failed to do so can now be seen to be the case.[2]

---

1. For interpretation of the Abrahamic covenant from different perspectives, see J. Collins, *Introduction to the Hebrew Bible*, 91–98; Dumbrell, *Covenant and Creation*, 47–79; Edwards, *A History of Redemption*, 54–68; Kline, *God, Heaven, and Har Magedon*, 93–110; *Kingdom Prologue*, 292–382; Lunn, "Patterns in the Old Testament Metanarrative," 237–49; Murray, *The Covenant of Grace*, 16–20; Robertson, *The Christ of the Covenants*, 127–66; Vangemeren, *The Progress of Redemption*, 100–30; Vos, *Biblical Theology*, 66–90; Wenham, *Genesis 1—15*, 255–335; Wenham, *Genesis 16—50*, 1–161; Williams, *Far as the Curse Is Found*, 100–30.

2. Niehaus, "Covenant and Narrative, God and Time," 535. Critiquing the classic covenant theology of the seventeenth century, Niehaus fails to read correctly its identity. The classic covenant theology did not construct the covenant theology, interpreting from "the Noahic through the new covenants" in

However, we will argue that the discoveries of the ancient Near East treaties do not discard but affirm the classic covenant theology. The Abrahamic covenant is a representative example. Classic covenant theology interpreted the Abrahamic covenant as the covenant of grace, inaugurated in Genesis 3:15. The Abrahamic covenant, in light of the ancient Near East treaties, may be considered a covenant of royal grant, granted by the Great King to the vassal king or faithful vassal who successfully accomplished a warrior's mission, defeating enemies in the name of the Great King. At this juncture, we will demonstrate that the Abrahamic covenant, as a covenant of royal grant, is harmonious and compatible with the idea of the covenant of grace.

We will see that God made promises to Abraham with his sworn oath, including a covenant people and land, both vital components of the theocratic kingdom as a type of the fully realized Kingdom of God in heaven. Historically, Bible interpreters and theologians overlooked the connection between the Abrahamic covenant and the judgment of Sodom and Gomorrah. It is my contention that God's judgment upon the cities of Sodom and Gomorrah was a redemptive judgment in the historical context of the Abrahamic covenant. In destroying these cities, God did not use a common grace war but a holy war against the wicked and corrupt cities. God demonstrated a pattern of redemptive judgment, which will be displayed once again, when he separates the elect from the non-elect with the Second Coming of the Son of Man.

In addition, we will demonstrate how the sacrifice of Isaac on the Mount of Moriah was a Messianic prophecy. It is important to note that God revealed in the Abrahamic covenant the coming of the Messiah as "the Son of Man," who will be sacrificed on the altar of Golgotha, to forgive all sins and to bestow all the promised redemptive blessings for the elect. Furthermore, God's promised blessings to Abraham, indicated by such expressions as "in your offspring," "in you," and "through you" were adopted and transformed later by the apostles to note the Christological designation as "in Christ Jesus," "in Christ," and "through Jesus Christ."

Finally, Bible interpreters and theologians, by and large, have ignored the relationship between Abraham's justification by faith and the Abrahamic covenant. It is my assessment that Abraham's justification by faith in Genesis 15:6, in the historical context of the Abrahamic covenant, provided a soteriological pattern that sinners are justified by faith apart from works of the law. Paul, as well as the other apostles, adopted this, and it became one of his key messages.

---

light of the covenant of grace. Rather, the classic covenant theology formulated and developed biblical hermeneutics and theology through the lens of the distinction between the covenant of works and covenant of grace, inaugurated in Genesis 3:15 after the first Adam's fall. In doing so, the redemptive historical order of creation, fall, redemption, and consummation as well as law and gospel is well safeguarded in the classic covenant theology.

Biblical Theology

The Calling of Abraham and the Promise of the Theocratic Kingdom in Canaan

God called Abraham[3] who was a descendent of Shem in the line of the Noahic covenant family. God inaugurated redemptive history after the fall of Adam and Eve, proclaiming the primitive gospel (Gen 3:15). Ever since then, he sovereignly directed the history of redemption, bestowing saving grace to the elect.

God revealed his plan of redemption, calling Abraham from Ur of the Chaldeans. Through his promise to Abraham, God revealed his plan for the establishment of the theocratic kingdom in Canaan.[4] God promised Abraham that he would form "a great nation" (לְגוֹי גָּדוֹל), a type of the heavenly theocratic kingdom, which will be consummated when Jesus returns:

> 1 Now the Lord said to Abram, "Go from your country and your kindred and your father's house *to the land* [אֶל־הָאָרֶץ] that I will show you. 2 And I will make of you *a great nation* [לְגוֹי גָּדוֹל], and I will bless you and make your name great, so that you will be a blessing. 3 I will bless those who bless you, and him who dishonors you I will curse, *and in you all the families of the earth shall be blessed* [וְנִבְרְכוּ בְךָ כֹּל מִשְׁפְּחֹת הָאֲדָמָה]. (Gen 12:1–3)

God's promise to Abraham to form "a great nation" was in fact significant because the nation would be different from pagan nations under God's common grace. "A great nation" would be composed of the covenant people of Abraham's descendants, who would dwell in the holy land that God promised to give them by oath. This nation would be ruled by God, the Great King, along with the kings as vicegerent rulers in his place. In that sense, "a great nation" is a holy theocratic kingdom, a type of the

---

3. We will use Abraham's name as Abraham consistently in this discussion, even though God did not change Abram's name into Abraham until he was ninety-nine years old: "No longer shall your name be called Abram, but your name shall be Abraham, for I have made you the father of a multitude of nations" (Gen 17:5).

4. The three components of the theocratic kingdom as holy land, covenant people, and king, as well as its specific characteristics, are insightfully summarized by Kline as follows: "Theocracy implies an external realm. It does not refer to a spiritual reign of God in the hearts of his people by itself, but included the geopolitical dimension. On the other hand, theocracy involves something more than a general providential rule of God over men and nations. It denotes a particular kingdom realm that God claims in a special way as his own . . . In a theocracy the people of the realm as well as the land itself are specially consecrated to God. This special religious relationship is defined through covenants, divinely determined and instituted, in which God identifies with the kingdom-people, bestowing on them his name to be borne and confessed by them. Because the name of God is identified with the theocratic people and is at stake in their history, the covenants that govern this relationship contain guarantees of dominion and power and glory for the loyal theocratic community . . . Theocracy is not a combination of church and state institutions. It is a simple unique institution, a structure sui generis. It is the kingdom realm whose great king is the Lord, where all activity is performed in the name of the Great-King enthroned, confessed, and worshipped in the cultic epicenter, whence theocratic holiness radiates outward, permeating all, so that the whole realm, land and people, is a sanctuary of the Creator-Lord." Kline, *Kingdom Prologue*, 49–51.

everlasting Kingdom of God in heaven, which will only be fully realized after the final redemptive judgment when Jesus returns.

The Promise of Blessings to All Nations through the Offspring of Abraham

God promised "a great nation" that will be established in Canaan as a type of the everlasting Kingdom of God in heaven. At the same time, God promised blessings to all nations in Abraham. Thus, God spoke his prophetic word to Abraham saying, "In you all the families of the earth shall be blessed" (Gen 12:3). This is an indication that God will continuously direct the grand drama of redemptive history through covenantal promises. And it will be fully realized with the coming of the Messiah, which is the central fulfillment of the promises of the Abrahamic covenant.

In fact, God confirmed his original promise to Abraham later, including the theocratic kingdom in the Promised Land and blessings to all nations *in him*:

> 17 The Lord said, "Shall I hide from Abraham what I am about to do, 18 seeing that Abraham shall surely become *a great and mighty nation*, and *all the nations of the earth shall be blessed in him*? 19 For I have chosen him, that he may command his children and his household after him to keep the way of the Lord by doing righteousness and justice, so that the Lord may bring to Abraham what he has promised him." (Gen 18:17–19)

During the earthly ministry of Jesus and the apostolic age, most Jews, committed to first-century Judaism as a whole, did not understand that Jesus Christ was the fulfillment of the Abrahamic covenant. The first-century Jews did not grasp this because they did not read the Hebrew scriptures from the perspective of redemptive history; instead, they denied Jesus as the coming Messiah despite the progressive revelation from various perspectives since Genesis 3:15.

Meanwhile, the apostles, after the crucifixion, resurrection, and ascension of Jesus and the Pentecost event, began to proclaim that Jesus is the fulfillment of the Abrahamic covenant. One of the central elements of the covenant is abundant soteriological blessings through faith in Jesus Christ. Accordingly, Matthew began his Gospel by stating that Jesus Christ is the descendent of Abraham who is the father of the Old Testament religion of Israel:

> 1 The book of the genealogy of Jesus Christ, the son of David, the son of Abraham . . . 16 and Jacob the father of Joseph the husband of Mary, of whom Jesus was born, who is called Christ. 17 So all the generations from Abraham to David were fourteen generations, and from David to the deportation to Babylon fourteen generations, and from the deportation to Babylon to the Christ fourteen generations. (Matt 1:1, 16–17)

After Peter experienced the Pentecost event, he began proclaiming the good news of the gospel to the Jews. He noticed that the promised seed of Abraham in the Abrahamic covenant is Jesus Christ. Peter alludes to the Pentecost event as a turning point in redemptive history that signifies the beginning of the spread of the gospel in Jesus to all nations. In that sense, Peter interprets the Abrahamic covenant in light of Jesus Christ, who is the fulfillment of the Messianic prophecy of the Old Testament, including the Abrahamic covenant:

> 13 The God of Abraham, the God of Isaac, and the God of Jacob, the God of our fathers, glorified his servant Jesus, whom you delivered over and denied in the presence of Pilate, when he decided to release him. 14 But you denied *the Holy and Righteous One* [τὸν ἅγιον καὶ δίκαιον], and asked for a murderer to be granted to you, 15 and you killed *the Author of life* [τὸν ἀρχηγὸν τῆς ζωῆς], whom God raised from the dead. To this we are witnesses . . . 22 Moses said, "The Lord God will raise up for you a prophet like me from your brothers. You shall listen to him in whatever he tells you. 23 And it shall be that every soul who does not listen to that prophet shall be destroyed from the people. 24 And all the prophets who have spoken, from Samuel and those who came after him, also proclaimed these days. 25 You are the sons of the prophets and of the covenant that God made with your fathers, saying to Abraham, and *in your offspring shall all the families of the earth be blessed* [ἐν τῷ σπέρματί σου [ἐν]ευλογηθήσονται πᾶσαι αἱ πατριαὶ τῆς γῆς]. (Acts 3:13–15, 22–25)

In these words, Peter sheds new light on his interpretation of the Abrahamic covenant. He interprets from the perspective of redemptive history, where the blessings of the covenant apply to "all the families of the earth" in Jesus Christ, who came as the singular figure, the offspring of Abraham. So the prophetic word in the Abrahamic covenant, "in your offspring," actually points to the covenantal blessings *in Jesus Christ* who is "the Holy and Righteous One" (τὸν ἅγιον καὶ δίκαιον) and "the Author of life" (τὸν ἀρχηγὸν τῆς ζωῆς).

First-century Jews appealed to the Abrahamic covenant for their religious and national roots. Paul, before his Damascus Road conversion experience, was at the center of Pharisaic Judaism, opposing Jesus and Christianity. He thought the rejection of Jesus Christ and the persecution of Christians were the right way of life for the glory of God. However, after his Damascus Road conversion experience, Paul realized that first-century Judaism misunderstood the heart of the Abrahamic covenant. So Paul testified to the Galatians that the centerpiece of the Abrahamic covenant is indeed Jesus Christ, who is its fulfillment. Paul realized that Abraham, as the father of faith, was justified and saved by the principle of the gospel in Jesus, just as believers are under the New Covenant.

Paul notes that believers in Jesus Christ are "the sons of Abraham" (υἱοί Ἀβραάμ), regardless of their ethnic background. Paul uses this method of representative expression for the children of God to embrace even Gentiles, including both males and females:

> 5 Does he who supplies the Spirit to you and works miracles among you do so by works of the law, or by hearing with faith—6 just as Abraham "believed God, and it was counted to him as righteousness"? 7 Know then that it is those of faith who are *the sons of Abraham* [υἱοί Ἀβραάμ]. 8 And the Scripture, foreseeing that *God would justify the Gentiles by faith* [ἐκ πίστεως δικαιοῖ τὰ ἔθνη ὁ θεός], preached the gospel beforehand to Abraham, saying, "*In you shall all the nations be blessed*" [ἐνευλογηθήσονται ἐν σοὶ πάντα τὰ ἔθνη] 9 So then, those who are of faith are blessed along with Abraham, the man of faith . . . 15 To give a human example, brothers: even with a man-made covenant, no one annuls it or adds to it once it has been ratified. 16 Now the promises were made to Abraham and to his offspring. It does not say, "*And to offsprings*," [καὶ τοῖς σπέρμασιν] referring to many, but referring to one, "*And to your offspring*," *who is Christ* [καὶ τῷ σπέρματί σου, ὅς ἐστιν Χριστός]. (Gal 3:5–9, 15–16)

Like Peter, Paul interprets the Abrahamic covenant from a Christocentric perspective as he endeavors to defend the good news of the gospel against the background of another gospel, spreading in different churches in the region of Galatia.

Calling out and making a covenant with Abraham was one of the most important turning points of redemptive history. God called out Abraham while he was living in the midst of a pagan culture and religion in Ur of the Chaldeans. Making a covenant with Abraham, God introduced the gospel of grace and bestowed saving grace unto Abraham. This historical episode suggests that Abraham's faith, as the father of the Old Testament Israelites, did not originate with man's religious tradition, teaching, and proclamation, but solely through God himself. In that sense, we may identify Yahweh as the original evangelist and missionary, as demonstrated through the calling of Abraham. This was also the case in the proclamation of the primitive gospel to Adam and Eve after they committed the original sin in the Garden of Eden (Gen 3:15).[5]

Similarly, calling Paul as the apostle for the Gentile mission was a very significant turning point in redemptive history. Before his conversion, Paul did not understand that one of the key elements of the Abrahamic covenant is salvation by God's grace through faith in the coming Son of Man. As one of his generation's representative spokesmen of Pharisaic Judaism, Paul fell into the legalistic understanding of salvation and religious tradition of Judaism which was fundamentally different from the religion of Old Testament Israel, which was in turn deeply rooted in the Abrahamic covenant. In the midst of confusion and struggle, Paul met Jesus at the heavenly throne and received the gospel "through a revelation of Jesus Christ" (δι' ἀποκαλύψεως Ἰησοῦ

---

5. Interpreting Genesis 12:1–3, Williams insightfully suggests that Yahweh in the Old Testament is "a missionary God": "Israel is elected to be God's channel of blessing to all nations. Again, the three promises given to Abraham in Genesis 12:1–3 (a seed, a land, and God's covenant blessing) are given for the sake of the fulfillment of Israel's missionary mandate. The goal of God's covenant with Abraham is that people from every nation, not just Israel, will be redeemed. The Old Testament is a missionary book because Yahweh is a missionary God." Williams, *Far As the Curse Is Found*, 118.

Χριστου) as he defended the authority of his apostleship and the authenticity of his proclamation of the gospel to the Galatians:

> 11 For I would have you know, brothers, that the gospel that was preached by me is not man's gospel. 12 For I did not receive it from any man, nor was I taught it, but I received it *through a revelation of Jesus Christ* [δι' ἀποκαλύψεως Ἰησοῦ Χριστοῦ]. 13 For you have heard of my former life in Judaism, how I persecuted the church of God violently and tried to destroy it . . . 15 But when he who had set me apart before I was born, and who called me by his grace, 16 was pleased to reveal his Son to me, in order that I might preach him among the Gentiles, I did not immediately consult with anyone, 17 nor did I go up to Jerusalem to those who were apostles before me, but I went away into Arabia, and returned again to Damascus. (Gal 1:11–13, 16–17)

As such, the apostolic apology for the defense of the gospel of Jesus Christ was deeply rooted in the Abrahamic covenant, which had been fundamentally misunderstood and misrepresented by first-century Judaism. And the apostles rightly offered this apology under the guidance and inspiration of the Holy Spirit.

Paul summarized the gospel he preached as "according to my gospel through Christ Jesus" (κατὰ τὸ εὐαγγέλιόν μού διὰ Χριστοῦ Ἰησοῦ, my own translation). In doing so, he emphasized that he received his gospel, not from men but "through a revelation of Jesus Christ" who was crucified, resurrected, and ascended into heaven where he was already inaugurated to rule as the exalted King in the heavenly Kingdom of God (Rom 2:16; 16:25–27; 2 Tim 2:8–10).

Knowing that the promised blessings of the Abrahamic covenant would be fulfilled and given in Jesus Christ, who is "the offspring of Abraham," Paul began to proclaim the good news of the gospel of Jesus Christ to the Gentiles, as well as to the Jews. For example, Paul used representative methods of expression such as "in Christ Jesus" (ἐν Χριστῷ Ἰησου), "in Christ" (ἐν Χριστῷ), and "through Jesus Christ" (διὰ Ἰησοῦ Χριστου). These expressions convey all the redemptive spiritual blessings given by God in Jesus to the elect, from election to the inheritance of the heavenly Kingdom of God. And this most definitely applied to the believers in Ephesus:

> 1 Paul, an apostle of Christ Jesus by the will of God, to the saints who are in Ephesus, and are faithful *in Christ Jesus* [ἐν Χριστῷ Ἰησοῦ]: 2 Grace to you and peace from God our Father and the Lord Jesus Christ. 3 Blessed be the God and Father of our Lord Jesus Christ, who has blessed us *in Christ* [ἐν Χριστῷ] with every spiritual blessing in the heavenly places, 4 even as he chose us in him before the foundation of the world, that we should be holy and blameless before him. In love 5 he predestined us for adoption as sons *through Jesus Christ* [διὰ Ἰησοῦ Χριστοῦ], according to the purpose of his will, 6 to the praise of his glorious grace, with which he has blessed us in the Beloved . . . 11 In him we have obtained all inheritance, having been predestined according to

the purpose of him who works all things according to the council of his will, 12 so that we who were the first to hope *in Christ* [ἐν τῷ Χριστῳ] might be to the praise of his glory. 13 In him you also, when you heard the word of truth, the gospel of your salvation, and believed in him, were sealed with the promised Holy Spirit, 14 who is the guarantee of our inheritance until we acquire possession of it, to the praise of his glory. (Eph 1:1–6, 11–14)

Accordingly, Paul, like other apostles, adopted the Christological designations such as "in Christ," "in Christ Jesus," and "through Jesus Christ," reflecting the Abrahamic covenant designation of "in your offspring" and "in you." The apostles' use of the Christological designations through the reflection of the Abrahamic covenant in light of Jesus' life, death, resurrection, ascension and the Pentecost event exemplifies how all the apostles read and interpreted the Hebrew scriptures from a redemptive historical perspective.

The Covenant of Royal Grant and Covenant Ratification Oath

God promised Abraham again and reassured him of the establishment of the theocratic kingdom in Canaan through the covenant community of Abraham's offspring. Throughout his pilgrimage, Abraham walked on the Promised Land where God would establish the holy theocratic kingdom. Although Abraham walked on the Promised Land, he still did not have his own covenant child that God promised. In the midst of Abraham's personal struggle with not having his own covenant child, God revealed to him "in a vision" (בַּמַּחֲזֶה) that his covenant offspring would be numerous as the stars in heaven:

> 1 After these things the word of the Lord came to Abram *in a vision* [בַּמַּחֲזֶה]: "Fear not, Abram, I am your shield; your reward shall be very great." 2 But Abram said, "O Lord God, what will you give me, for I continue childless, and the heir of my house is Eliezer of Damascus?" 3 And Abram said, "Behold, you have given me no offspring, and a member of my household will be my heir." 4 And behold, the word of the Lord came to him: "This man shall not be your heir; your very own son shall be your heir." 5 And he brought him outside and said, "Look toward heaven, and number the stars, if you are able to number them." Then he said to him, "So shall your offspring be." 6 *And he believed the Lord, and he counted it to him as righteousness* [וְהֶאֱמִן בַּיהוָה וַיַּחְשְׁבֶהָ לּוֹ צְדָקָה]. (Gen 15:1–6)

In his exegesis of Genesis 15:6, Collins fundamentally misinterprets justification by faith, which is one of the central components of the Abrahamic covenant. He argues that "there is no contrast between faith and law implied in Genesis."[6] However, this

---

6. Collins' interpretation of Genesis 15:6 by and large reflects contemporary biblical and theological scholarship, which denies the contrast between law and faith (or gospel) in the depiction of soteriology and redemptive history: "The statement in Gen 15:6, 'And he [Abraham] believed in the Lord, and the Lord reckoned it to him as righteousness,' has played an important and controversial role in Christian theology. It is cited by St. Paul in Gal 3:6. Paul argues that since Abraham is also told

is not so. God differentiated faith and law in the depiction of Abraham's covenantal pilgrimage. God forensically declared Abraham as righteous before his circumcision. In that sense, Genesis 15:6, "And he believed the Lord, and he counted it to him righteousness," is the primal example of soteriological blessing of justification by faith. Abraham's reception of circumcision, as the sign of the covenant, clearly suggests that Abraham was justified by faith apart from obedience or works of the law. In fact, many years after Abraham was justified by faith, Abraham, his son Ishmael, and "all the men of his house" were circumcised (Gen 17:22–27).[7]

It is important to note that Paul adopted this primal example of justification by faith, as represented in Genesis 15:6, in the historical context of the Abrahamic covenant. He quoted it in Galatians 3:6 to demonstrate that both Jews and Gentiles are justified by faith. So justification by faith for both Jews and Gentiles is one of the essential components of Paul's gospel.

After the Damascus Road conversion experience, Paul reflected on the Abrahamic covenant. He realized that Abraham as the father of faith was not justified by works, but by faith (Rom 4:1–25; Gal 3:6–14). So Paul revisited Abraham's story to note and confirm justification by faith. Paul's unpacking of sinners' justification by faith throughout his epistles was one of the central proclamations of his message. Again, it is important to note that Paul found the primary example of justification by faith in the historical context of the Abrahamic covenant, in which Yahweh declared Abraham as righteous when Abraham had faith in him even before he received circumcision, the sign of the covenant. In that sense, Genesis 15:6 is a classical biblical paradigm and reference from the Old Testament for Paul's proclamation of justification by faith in his Gentile mission and also for his epistles, as well as for the message of the other apostles.[8]

---

that all the peoples of the earth will be blessed in him (Gen 12:3), this shows that Gentiles can be justified by faith, not by the law. This argument later played a fundamental role in the theology of Martin Luther. Needless to say, there is no contrast between faith and law implied in Genesis (although it is true that there is no requirement of legal observance). Faith here is trust in the promise. In Jewish interpretation, the key element is that the promise relates to possession of the land. The promise to Abraham is seen as the original charter for possession of the land of Israel." Collins, *Introduction to the Hebrew Bible*, 92.

7. Bruce explains very concisely and clearly that Abraham's justification by faith before the reception of circumcision is a clear biblical indication that "Gentiles as well as Jews" are justified by faith apart from obedience "in the death and resurrection of Christ": "As for Abraham, it is important to observe that his faith was reckoned to him as righteousness long before he was circumcised: this shows that the way of righteousness by faith is in no way dependent on circumcision, but is open to Gentiles as well as Jews. Abraham is thus the spiritual father of all believers, irrespective of their racial origin. And the testimony that his faith was reckoned to him righteousness means that to all who believe in God, whose saving power has been manifested in the death and resurrection of Christ, their faith will similarly be reckoned as righteousness." Bruce, *Paul: Apostle of the Heart Set Free*, 329.

8. Vos as a redemptive historical theologian, who correctly emphasizes the progressive character of divine revelation in the Bible, recognizes that Genesis 15:6 is "the first explicit Biblical reference to faith." However, he is unable to read that justification by faith in Genesis 15:6 provides the primal pattern of justification by faith within the historical context of the Abrahamic covenant: "Gen. 15:6 is the

The Abrahamic Covenant and the Kingdom of God

Abraham's justification by faith apart from receiving circumcision, the sign of the covenant, signifies that believers in the Old Testament were saved by God's grace and justified not by the obedience of the law but by faith alone, as with the believers under the New Covenant. Reflecting on Genesis 15:6, Paul expresses the classical understanding of justification by faith "apart from works of the law" (χωρὶς ἔργων νόμου): "For we hold that *one is justified by faith apart from works of the law*" [δικαιουσθαι πίστει ἄνθρωπον χωρὶς ἔργων νόμου] (Rom 3:28).[9]

As discussed previously, in general, there were two different forms of treaties in the ancient Near East. One is the form of the treaty of royal grant. It was a treaty that the Great King promised to grant land or properties to the faithful vassal who fought the victorious war on behalf of the Great King and his kingdom. And one of the characteristics of it lies in that the sworn oath to the treaty was made not by the vassal king and his servants but by the Great King. Also, an animal was slain during the treaty ratification ceremony. One of the representative examples of the treaty of royal grant has been found in the treaty between Abban and Yarimlim. This treaty records the treaty ratification ceremony between the Great King, Abban, and the vassal, Yarimlim of Alalakh. It goes back to the time of Abraham, reflecting the ancient Near East culture, international relationship, and religion of that time.

> The city of Amame, the city of Aushun, the city of Zikir, the city of Murar, the city of Iriddi: Yarimlim [held them]. Zitraddu, the mayor of [Iriddi] turned against Yarimlim *and* led the [robber] MUSNADDU. He let *the robber band* enter Iriddi; his city and all its land he turned away from Abba-AN, king . . . With . . . and the mighty [weapon] . . . with silver, gold, lapis lazuli, *crystal* and the mighty [weapon] of Addu he captured and destroyed Iriddi, and he captured the MUSNADDU, his enemy. He returned safely to Aleppo *and said*: Can I give my brother a pile of ruins? In exchange for Iriddi [that] rebelled [against] him [and that I captured] and [destroyed, I shall give Yarimlim] the city of Alalakh, and the city of Murar over and above his portion I shall add to it. Abba-AN is under oath to Yarimlim, and also he cut the neck of a lamb. *He swore*: I shall never take back what I gave you. If in days to come Yarimlim sins against Abba-AN, [if] he repeats anything Abba-AN says to him and reveals *it* to another king, if he lets go of the hem of Abba-AN's robe and takes hold of another king's robe, he [shall forfeit] his cities and territories. Further, if a successor of Yarimlim sins against Abba-AN or a successor of Abba-AN, if he lets go of the hem of Abba-AN's robe or the hem of the robe of a successor of Abba-AN and takes hold of the hem of another king's robe, he shall forfeit his city and his territories. If successors of

---

first explicit Biblical reference to faith. Broadly speaking, faith bears a two-fold significance in Scriptural teaching and experience: it is, firstly, dependence on the supernatural power and grace of God; and secondly, the state or act of projection into a higher, spiritual world." Vos, *Biblical Theology*, 83.

9. For further readings on my thoughts of John Calvin's understanding of covenant and justification by faith, and other related theological and hermeneutical issues in light of contemporary discussions, see Jeon, *Calvin and the Federal Vision*, 1–42; Jeon, *Covenant Theology*, 1–29.

> Yarimlim wish to sell one of his cities, then their older brother shall buy *it*; he may sell it only to a successor of Abba-AN, *but* to another king he may not sell it. If [there is] no successor to Yarimlim, *but* [there is] a successor to Abba-AN, if... his cities... [Akhi-saduq] son of... [Irpadda]... [Niqmaddu]... (*gap*) ... made Yarimlim swear by the gods.[10]

The other form is the suzerainty treaty. This was a treaty in which the Great King stipulated regulations and laws upon the vassal and his kingdoms. The dual sanctions were announced and strictly applied by the principles of blessings and curses through the treaty lawsuit. When two kingdoms made the suzerainty treaty, the vassal king and his people made an oath as a means of ratifying the treaty. In the presence of the Great King and his servants, the vassal king and his people made an oath. The treaty ratification ceremony by an oath signified that the vassal king and his servants would comply with all the detailed components of the treaty. And the Great King may protect the vassal king and his kingdom from military threats and attacks from other kingdoms. However, if the vassal king and his kingdom violated the stipulations of the treaty with the Great King and his suzerain kingdom, the curses of the treaty would fall upon the former through the execution of the treaty lawsuit.[11]

The Hittite treaties around the fourteenth and thirteenth centuries B.C. were the representative paradigm of the suzerainty treaties in the ancient Near East. The treaty between Suppiluliuma, the Great King of the Hittites, and Mattiwaza of Mitanni is one of the representative examples of the suzerainty treaties in the second millennium B.C. The Hittite treaty as a suzerainty treaty makes a close parallel to the Sinaitic covenant (Ex 19–24), the covenant renewal in Moab (Deut 1:1—34:12), and another covenant renewal at Shechem (Josh 24:1–33). The common distinctive characteristics of the suzerainty treaty are that the treaty oath was sworn by the vassal and his people along with the announcement and execution of dual sanctions such as blessings and curses, following the written codes of stipulations:

> A duplicate of this tablet has been deposited before the sun-goddess of Arinna, because the sun-goddess of Arinna regulates kingship and queenship. In the Mitanni land *a duplicate* has been deposited before Teshub, the lord of the KURINNU of Kahat. At regular [intervals] shall they read it in the presence of the king of the Mitanni land and in the presence of the sons of the Hurri country. Whoever will remove this tablet from before Teshub, the lord of the KURINNU of Kahat, and put it in a hidden place, if he breaks it or causes anyone else to change the wording of the tablet—at the conclusion of this

---

10. Arnold and Beyer, *Readings from the Ancient Near East*, 96–97. For the different forms of the Ancient Near East treaties, similar to the covenants of the Old Testament, see ibid., 96–103; Pritchard, *The Ancient Near East*, 205–25.

11. Scholars have endeavored to formulate comparative studies from divergent theological perspectives between the ancient Near Eastern treaties and biblical covenants. See Hillers, *Covenant: The History of a Biblical Idea*; Kline, *The Structure of Biblical Authority*; McCarthy, *Old Testament Covenant*; Mendenhall, *Law and Covenant in Israel and the Ancient Near East*.

treaty we have called the gods to be assembled and the gods of the contracting parties to be present, to listen and to serve as witnesses . . . If you, Mattiwaza, the prince, and *you* the sons of the Hurri country do not fulfill the words of this treaty, may the gods, the lords of the oath, blot you out, *you* Mattiwaza and *you* the Hurri men together with your country, your wives and all that you have . . . May they overturn your throne, *yours*, of Mattiwaza. May the oaths sworn in the presence of these gods break you like reeds, you, Mattiwaza, together with your country. May they exterminate from the earth your name and your seed *born* from a second wife that you may take . . . If *on the other hand* you, Mattiwaza, the prince, and *you*, the Hurrians, fulfill this treaty and *this* oath, may these gods protect you, Mattiwaza, together with your wife, the daughter of Hatti land, her children and her children's children, and also *you*, the Hurrians, together with your wives, your children, and your children's children and together with your country.[12]

The Assyrian treaties from the first millennium B.C. have a similar pattern to that found in the suzerainty treaty in the Hittite treaties from the second millennium B.C. However, there was a distinctive visible ceremony during the Assyrian treaty ratification ceremony. The vassal and his servants made an oath before the Great King, while an animal was torn into two pieces. The torn animal signified that the curses of the treaty would befall the vassal, his servants, and their land if they do not obey the stipulations of the treaty.

This spring lamb has not been brought out its fold for sacrifice, nor for a banquet, nor for a purchase, nor for (divination concerning) a sick man, nor to be slaughtered for [. . .]: it has been brought to conclude the treaty of Assurnerari, king of Assyria with Mati'-ilu. If Mati'-ilu [sins] against th[is] sworn treaty, then, just as this spring lamb has been brought from its fold and will not return to its fold and [not behold] its fold again, (in like manner) may, alas, Mati'-ilu, together with his sons, daughters, [magnates] and the people of his land [be ousted] from his country, and not [behold] his country again . . .

If Mati'-ilu [should sin] against this treaty, so may, just as the head of this spring lamb is c[ut] off, and its knuckle placed in its mouth, [. . .] the head of Mati'-ilu be cut off, and his sons [and magnates] be th[rown] into . . .

If Mati'-ilu should sin against this [treaty], so may, just as the shou[lder of this spring lamb] is torn out and [placed in . . .], the shoulder of Mati'-ilu, of his sons, [his magnates] and the people of his land be torn out and [placed] in [. . .].[13]

---

12. Arnold and Beyer, *Readings from the Ancient Near East*, 97–98. A close parallel between the ancient Near Eastern treaties and covenants in the Old Testament remarkably discards the historical critical approach to the formulation of the Old Testament canon, affirming the antiquity of the Pentateuch.

13. Ibid., 101.

Strikingly, an Assyrian treaty-like pattern in the first millennium B.C. was evident in the covenant made by God with the covenant community of Judah in Jerusalem during the reign of King Zedekiah:

> 17 "Therefore, thus says the Lord: You have not obeyed me by proclaiming liberty, Every one to his brother and to his neighbor; behold, I proclaim to you liberty to the sword, to pestilence, and to famine, declares the Lord. I will make you a horror to all the kingdoms of the earth. 18 And the men who transgressed my covenant and did not keep the terms of the covenant that they made before me, I will make them *like the calf that they cut in two and passed between its parts*—19 the officials of Judah, the officials of Jerusalem, the eunuchs, the priests, and all the people of the land who passed between the parts of the calf. 20 And I will give them into the hand of their enemies and into the hand of those who seek their lives. Their dead bodies shall be food for the birds of the air and the beasts of the earth. 21 And Zedekiah king of Judah and his officials I will give into the hand of their enemies and into the hand of those who seek their lives, into the hand of the army of the king of Babylon which has withdrawn from you. 22 Behold, I will command, declares the Lord, and will bring them back to this city. And they will fight against it and take it and burn it with fire. I will make the cities of Judah a desolation without inhabitant." (Jer 34:17–21)

Yahweh revealed that curses can befall even the covenant community of Judah. He used the Babylonian kingdom to curse the covenant community because they violated the covenant before Yahweh, the Great King, even though they had passed "between the parts of the calf" like the vassal king and servants. Likewise, the Lord, as the Great King, cursed the covenant community when they violated the covenant by executing the covenant lawsuit.

Jeremiah's prophecy against Judah and her Babylonian exile, due to the execution of the covenant lawsuit, suggests that God's curses against the covenant community were not based upon the Abrahamic covenant but the Sinaitic covenant (Ex 19–24). In the process of making the Sinaitic covenant, the covenant community of Israel made a sworn oath to the covenant before Yahweh, the Great King (Ex 19:8; 24:3, 7).[14] That is

---

14. The sprinkling of the blood on the covenant people during the Sinaitic covenant ratification ceremony suggests that God's saving grace was applied to the elect not by the principle of the law but by the principle of the covenant of grace, even under the Sinaitic covenant. So, the sprinkling of the blood by Moses in Exodus 24:8 may not be considered as a sworn oath made by the covenant community of Israel as suggested by Robertson: "First the law was read. The people responded with a verbal commitment to obedience (Exod. 24:7). Then Moses sprinkled the blood on the people as he declared: 'Behold, the blood of the covenant, which the Lord has made with you' (Exod. 24:8). This blood of sprinkling symbolized not only the cleansing of the people. It also consecrated them to keep the covenant on pain of death. The same pledge-to-death which played such a prominent role in the inauguration of the Abrahamic covenant manifested itself in the inauguration of the Mosaic covenant. Sheer statistical considerations may have occasioned the substitution of the blood-sprinkling ritual for the ceremony of passing between the pieces. An entire nation hardly could be paraded between the

the reason God poured out his wrath against the covenant community of Israel when they disobeyed the law given to them through Moses, the mediator of the covenant on Mount Sinai. In this sense, we can identify the Sinaitic covenant as the covenant of law.

Having identified the Sinaitic covenant as the covenant of law, we need to explore the background of the Abrahamic covenant and why it fits to the pattern of a covenant of royal grant. Abraham fought the war to bring back his nephew "Lot with his possessions, and the women and the people" when they had been captive in Sodom. It is important to note that Abraham fought the war to bring back his nephew Lot, other people, and all the possessions in the name of Yahweh, the Great King (Gen 14:8–24). After Abraham returned from war as a victorious warrior, Yahweh, the Great King, recognized Abraham as the faithful warrior-servant. And he promised great reward to Abraham: "*After these things* the word of the Lord came to Abram in a vision: 'Fear not Abram, I am your shield; *your reward shall be* great'" (Gen 15:1).[15] As a reward, Yahweh promised to grant the land to Abraham's descendents through the covenant ratification ceremony in Genesis 15. In that sense, the Abrahamic covenant may be rightly identified and designated as a covenant of royal grant as demonstrated with the treaty of royal grant in the ancient Near East.[16] As a covenant of royal grant, the Abrahamic covenant is a comprehensive reflection of promissory character of the covenant, which has been designated as the covenant of grace in the Reformed tradition, including the classic covenant theology of the seventeenth century. In that sense, it is remarkable to discover how the idea of the Abrahamic covenant of grace, defined in the Reformed tradition, including the classic covenant theology in the seventeenth century, is harmonious with the concept of the covenant of royal grant.[17]

---

pieces of slain animals. But an equally significant ceremony of blood-sprinkling could be instituted." Robertson, *The Christ of the Covenants*, 135.

15. Italics are mine. Here, Kline's discussion is helpful and comprehensive: "Coming on the heels of this episode, the Lord's word to Abraham (Gen 15:1) has the character of a royal grant to an officer of the king for faithful military service. God identifies himself by the military figure of a shield (cf. Deut 33:29; Ps 18:2), otherwise read as suzerain, and promises: 'Your reward will be very great" (also read 'who will reward you very greatly'). The term *sakar*, 'reward,' is used for the compensation due to those who have conducted a military campaign. In Ezekiel 29:19 it refers to the spoil of Egypt which the Lord gives Nebuchadnezzar as wages for his army (cf. Isa 40:10; 62:11). The imagery of Genesis 15:1 is that of the Great King honoring Abraham's notable exhibition of compliance with covenant duty by the reward of a special grant that would more than make up for whatever enrichment he had foregone at the hand of the king of Sodom for the sake of faithfulness to Yahweh, his Lord. The broader record of the Lord's dealings with Abraham includes numerous key expressions paralleled in the ancient royal grants to loyal servants: such a servant is one who obeys, keeps the charge, serves perfectly, walks before his lord." Kline, *Kingdom Prologues*, 323–24.

16. For the discussion of the Abrahamic covenant as a covenant of royal grant in parallel to the treaty of royal grant in the ancient Near East, see Horton, *Introducing Covenant Theology*, 40–50; Kline, *God, Heaven and Har Magedon*, 102–3; Kline, *Kingdom Prologue*, 323–26; Niehaus, "Covenant and Narrative, God and Time," 544–46; Weinfeld, "The Covenant of Grant in the Old Testament and in the Ancient Near East," 184–203; Weinfeld, *Deuteronomy and the Deuteronomic School*, 78–79.

17. For a comprehensive and critical analysis of the development and adaptation of covenant theology in the Reformed tradition from Calvin to Murray and Kline, including the classic covenant

In the process of the covenant ratification ceremony of the Abrahamic covenant in Genesis 15, there was a distinctive phenomenon. Abraham as a vassal did not give a sworn oath before the Lord Almighty, the Great King, which was a general pattern of the suzerainty treaty in the ancient Near East:

> 17 When the sun had gone down and it was dark, behold, *a smoking fire pot and a flaming torch passed between these pieces.* 18 *On that day the Lord made a covenant with Abram, saying,* "*To your offspring I give this land,* from the river of Egypt to the great river, the river Euphrates, 19 the land of the Kenites, the Kenizzites, the Kadmonites, 20 the Hittites, the Perizzites, the Rephaim, 21 the Amorites, the Canaanites, the Girgashites and the Jebusites." (Gen 15:17–21)

In the process of the covenant ratification ceremony, the distinctive visible phenomena appeared and "a smoking fire pot and a flaming torch passed" between the torn pieces of the animals. In fact, "a flaming torch" between the carcasses was the visible sign of the theophanic glory.[18] It signified that Abraham as a vassal did not make an oath to the covenant. Rather, Yahweh as the Great King made an oath to the covenant. This visible presence of the theophanic glory indicates God's oath to Abraham that he would fulfill all the covenantal promises through the execution of his mighty power and sovereign grace in redemptive history. In addition, God made an oath that the theocratic kingdom in the Promised Land would surely be established. And God provided more detailed geographic boundaries of the Promised Land where Abraham's covenant descendents would dwell. The visible presence of the theophanic

---

theology of the seventeenth century, see Jeon, *Covenant Theology*, 1–334.

18. The appearances of the theophanic glory in Abraham's life, culminating in Genesis 15:17, are well articulated and summarized by Vos: "To Abraham at first revelation came after the earlier indefinite fashion. In Gen. 12.4 Jehovah 'speaks' to him, but no sooner has he entered the promised land than a change of expression is introduced. In Gen. 12.7 we read that Jehovah 'appeared' unto Abraham (literally, He 'let himself be seen by Abraham'). Here is something more than mere speech. The emergence of a new element is also recognized by the building of the altar, for the altar is a shrine or house of God. In Gen. 15:13 we have again the indefinite statement that Jehovah 'said to Abraham.' But in Gen. 15.17 a visible manifestation, a theophany takes place. In the form of the smoking furnace and the flaming torch God passes by. The theophany here assumes the character of something fearful. In chapter 17.1 we read again that Jehovah let Himself be seen by Abraham; and that this was a theophany follows from the statement of vs. 22, 'And he left off talking with him, and God went up from Abraham.'" Vos, *Biblical Theology*, 69. Furthermore, Vos insightfully observes that the theophanic glory as "the walking of God (alone)" between the torn animal pieces signifies God's sworn oath to keep his promises before Abraham: "At no point of the Old Testament, the life of Moses perhaps excluded, was there such a divine condescension as during the life of Abraham. If we except Gen. 15, there was a remarkable absence of the frightful in these theophanies. There is something here somewhat resembling God's ancient walk with men in the days of paradise or the life of Enoch. In recognition of all this he was by later generations called 'the friend of God', Jas. 2.23. And even in the midst of the terror of 15.12, there was a most impressive witness to the divine condescension in the remarkable setting of the theophany itself. There is probably no case surpassing this in anthropomorphic realism within the Old Testament. The dividing of the animals and the walking of God (alone) between the pieces literally signifies that God invokes upon Himself the fate of dismemberment in case He should not keep faith with Abraham [cp. Jer. 34.18–19]." Ibid., 86.

glory, passing between the pieces of torn animals, suggests that saving grace, bestowed on sinners, would be possible not through men's meritorious obedience but through God's sovereign grace alone. It was also a redemptive historical event which foreshadowed the Messiah's sacrificial death at Golgotha, which opened the way for the forgiveness of sins and salvation, including all the redemptive blessings.

Likewise, Genesis 15:17 can be considered the visible ceremony of the covenant ratification oath, made by Yahweh in the presence of Abraham. The visible phenomenon of a "flaming torch" was the presence of the theophanic glory, making an oath to the covenant in front of a mere creature, Abraham. Later, after Abraham passed the probation period, offering his promised son, Isaac, on Moriah, the Mount of the Lord, Yahweh confirmed his original oath to the covenant through the prophetic word:

> 15 And the angel of the Lord called to Abraham a second time from heaven 16 and said, "By myself I have sworn, declares the Lord, because you have done this and have not withheld your son, your only son, 17 I will surely bless you, and I will surely multiply your offspring as the stars of heaven and as the sand that is on the seashore. And your offspring shall possess the gate of his enemies, 18 *and in your offspring shall all the nations of the earth be blessed, because you have obeyed my voice.* (Gen 22:15–18)

Likewise, Yahweh's sworn oath to the covenant with Abraham through the prophetic word is the confirmation of his oath that he already made through the visible phenomenon in Genesis 15:17. The author of the book of Hebrews confirms that Yahweh made an oath before Abraham to demonstrate that all the promises of the covenant would be fulfilled without a mistake. Abraham experienced a glimpse of the fulfillment of the covenant promises during his own lifetime:

> 13 For when God made a promise to Abraham, since he had no one greater by whom to swear, *he swore by himself* [ὤμοσεν καθ' ἑαυτοῦ], 14 saying, "Surely I will bless you and multiply you." 15 And thus Abraham, having patiently waited, obtained the promise. 16 For people swear by something greater than themselves, and in all their disputes *an oath is final for confirmation* [πέρας εἰς βεβαίωσιν ὁ ὅρκος]. 17 So when God desired to show more convincingly to the heirs of the promise the unchangeable character of his purpose, *he guaranteed it with an oath* [ἐμεσίτευσεν ὅρκῳ], 18 so that by two unchangeable things, in which it is impossible for God to lie, we who have fled for refuge might have strong encouragement to hold fast to the hope set before us. (Heb 6:13–18)

In this passage, the author of Hebrews reflects upon and interprets the history of Yahweh making his promises to Abraham. And Yahweh guaranteed to fulfill his promises through the prophetic voice of his angel "with an oath" (ἐμεσίτευσεν ὅρκῳ). Yahweh's verbal sworn oath to Abraham after passing the probation period on Moriah, the Mount of the Lord, is another confirmation that the visible presence of theophanic glory in Genesis 15:17 is Yahweh's sworn oath to the covenant.

BIBLICAL THEOLOGY

Covenantal Obedience and the Sign of the Abrahamic Covenant

The covenant ratification oath, made by God to Abraham in Genesis 15:17, suggests that all the rich promises of the Abrahamic covenant would be completely fulfilled. One of the covenantal promises is that personal salvation, bestowed on the elect, may be applied by the mighty work of the Holy Spirit in Jesus Christ, who passed through the valley of death. Nevertheless, God commanded the covenant community members to live a life of obedience and holiness. This signifies that believers should be "the salt of the earth" (τὸ ἅλας τῆς γῆς) and "the light of the world" (τὸ φῶς τοῦ κόσμου) (Matt 5:13–16). Whatever they do, they must live for the glory of God. So God, through his oracle, revealed the unbreakable covenantal bond between him and Abraham, emphasizing the importance of covenantal obedience in believers' lives:

> 1 When Abram was ninety-nine years old the Lord appeared to Abram and said to him, "*I am God almighty; walk before me, and be blameless* [אֲנִי־אֵל שַׁדַּי הִתְהַלֵּךְ לְפָנַי וֶהְיֵה תָמִים] 2 that I may make my covenant between me and you, and may multiply you greatly." (Gen 17:1–2)

Yahweh revealed himself to Abraham as "I am God Almighty" (אֲנִי־אֵל שַׁדַּי). This signifies how "God Almighty" will fulfill all the promises made to Abraham through the gradual process of history, slowly but surely. In return, Yahweh demanded covenantal obedience from Abraham in response to his rich covenantal promises and blessings. So, he commanded Abraham to "walk before me, and be blameless" (הִתְהַלֵּךְ לְפָנַי וֶהְיֵה תָמִים:). This binding relationship between Yahweh and Abraham is the pattern of the covenantal relationship under the New Covenant: God saves his people in Jesus Christ through grace alone. In response, believers should be set apart and live their lives in the present world for the glory of God as the New Covenant community of Jesus Christ.

God commanded Abraham to perform the rite of circumcision as a sign of membership in the covenant community. Receiving the sign of circumcision did not mean that the recipient was saved by means of circumcision. Rather, it meant the recipient belonged to the covenant community, making a covenantal commitment to live a holy life which represents the Kingdom of God in the present sinful world:

> 9 And God said to Abraham, "As for you, you shall keep *my covenant*, you and your offspring after you throughout their generations. 10 *This is my covenant* [זֹאת בְּרִיתִי], which you shall keep, between me and you and your offspring after you: Every male among you shall be circumcised. 11 You shall be circumcised in the flesh of your foreskins, *And it shall be a sign of the covenant between me and you* [וְהָיָה לְאוֹת בְּרִית בֵּינִי וּבֵינֵיכֶם]. 12 He who is eight days old among you shall be circumcised. Every male throughout your generations, whether born in your house or bought with your money from any foreigner who is not of your offspring, 13 both he who is born in your house and he who is bought

with your money, shall surely be circumcised. So shall *my covenant* be in your flesh *an everlasting covenant* [לִבְרִית עוֹלָם]. 14 Any uncircumcised male who is not circumcised in the flesh of his foreskin shall be cut off from his people; *he has broken my covenant* [אֶת־בְּרִיתִי הֵפַר]." (Gen 17:9–14)

Commanding circumcision as a sign of the covenant, God assured Abraham that the covenant was "an everlasting covenant" (לִבְרִית עוֹלָם). The Abrahamic covenant as "an everlasting covenant" suggests that all the rich covenantal promises will certainly be fulfilled as the history of redemption progresses, according to the divine plan. Furthermore, it signifies that the Abrahamic covenant is an unbreakable covenant because God will fulfill all the promises of the covenant, even though God threatened his curse on any "uncircumcised male" in the covenant community, saying that "he has broken my covenant."

When God made a covenant with Noah and the world, including the earth after the Flood judgment, he used the rainbow as a sign of the covenant—located not around or in the human body, but in the sky. This suggests that the Postdiluvian Noahic covenant is not a covenant of grace but a covenant of common grace, which provides a stable world environment until the final redemptive judgment when Jesus Christ returns. That is why God placed the sign of the Postdiluvian Noahic covenant in the sky (Gen 9:8–17).[19]

In the Sinaitic covenant, God commanded the covenant community of Israel to keep the Sabbath holy, the fourth commandment (Ex 20:8–11). Moreover, God established the Sabbath day as holy, as a sign of the Sinaitic covenant (Ex 31:12–18). Keeping the Sabbath holy, as a sign of the Sinaitic covenant, indicates that the covenant is primarily the national covenant of Israel with Yahweh because he commanded the entire covenant community of Israel to keep the Sabbath holy. It was a breakable covenant although the principle of the covenant of grace, inaugurated in Genesis 3:15, confirmed and expanded through the Abrahamic covenant, was continuously applied even under the Sinaitic covenant (Gal 3:15–29). Later, through Jeremiah's prophecy, God identifies how the Sinaitic covenant as the Old Covenant was breakable while the New Covenant

---

19. For a comprehensive biblical theological analysis of the Post-diluvian Noahic Covenant in Genesis 8:20—9:17 as the renewal or recovery of the covenant of common grace, see Kline, *Kingdom Prologue*, 244–62; Vos, *Biblical Theology*, 51–55. The common grace character of the Post-diluvian Noahic Covenant is persuasively summarized by Vos as follows: "We now come to the Noachian Revelation which took place after the flood. In this positive constructive measures were taken for the further carrying out of the divine purpose. Here again the reminder is in place that the principles disclosed and the measures taken did not directly relate to the prosecution of redemption, although an indirect bearing upon that also must not be overlooked. That the development of natural life is proximately dealt with, follows from the following: what is ordained by God and the promise made have equal reference to the entire Noachian family. But we know that the work of redemption was carried on in the line of Shem only; the arrangement made is not even confined to the human race; it is made with every living creature, nay, with the earth herself; that the *berith* is a *berith* of nature appears from the *berith* sign; the rainbow is a phenomenon of nature, and absolutely universal in its reference. All the signs connected with redemption are bloody, sacramentally dividing signs." Ibid., 51.

is unbreakable because God will make it with his people through the Messiah, the mediator of the New Covenant as well as the fulfiller of the requirement of the covenant, bestowing all the redemptive blessings that God promised (Jer 31:31–34).

The Abrahamic Covenant and the Judgment upon Sodom and Gomorrah

God cursed the world through the Flood judgment due to the corruption of the people, exempting only Noah and his family. After the Flood, God promised Noah and the whole earth that there would never be "a flood to destroy the earth" again. This promise to Noah indicates that God would never curse the world by a flood again on a global scale. And it also explains how God will not use the Flood as a means of the final redemptive judgment at the Parousia:

> 11 I establish my covenant with you, that never again shall all flesh be cut off by the waters of the flood, and never again shall there be a flood to destroy the earth . . . 15 I will remember my covenant that is between me and you and every living creature of all flesh. And the waters shall never again become a flood to destroy all flesh. (Gen 9:11,15)

The post-Flood promise to Noah was fulfilled, surprisingly, within the historical context of the Abrahamic covenant. Certainly, God promised Noah that he would not destroy the world through the Flood judgment again. Nevertheless, God did not reveal to Noah the means or method of the final judgment. The judgment upon Sodom and Gomorrah was a type of the final eschatological judgment.[20]

The Bible identifies Sodom and Gomorrah as spiritually and morally corrupt cities where homosexuality was rampant. God sent two angels to save Lot's family, the covenant family, before the judgment of the cities. Knowing that there were male visitors in Lot's house, "the men of Sodom" surrounded the house and declared that they would like to engage in sexual activities. This episode indicates the homosexual nature of Sodom and Gomorrah:

> 4 But before they lay down, the men of the city, the men of Sodom, both young and old, all the people to the last man, surrounded the house. 5 And they

---

20. Edwards comprehensively captures and describes the fundamental nature of judgment upon Sodom and Gomorrah as a type of the eschatological judgment: "But this was now in a great measure forgotten; now therefore God was pleased again, in a most amazing manner, to show his wrath against sin, in the destruction of these cities; which was after such a manner as to be the liveliest image of hell of any thing that ever had been; and therefore the apostle Jude says, 'They suffer the vengeance of eternal fire,' Jude 7. God rained storms of fire and brimstone upon them. The way that they were destroyed probably was by thick flashes of lightning. The streams of brimstone were so thick as to burn up all these cities; so that they perished in the flames of divine wrath. By this might be seen the dreadful wrath of God against the ungodliness and unrighteousness of men; which tended to show men the necessity of redemption, and so to promote that great work." Edwards, *A History of the Work of Redemption*, 64.

called to Lot, "Where are the men who came to you tonight? *Bring them out to us, that we may know them* [הוֹצִיאֵם אֵלֵינוּ וְנֵדְעָה אֹתָם]. (Gen 19:4–5)

As such, the episode before the judgment of Sodom and Gomorrah suggests that homosexuality was common in the cities. In that sense, "bring them out to us, that we may know them" may be better translated as "bring them out to us so that we may have sexual relations with them."[21] In addition, this episode suggests that homosexuality is against God's creation ordinance, the regulation of life, and the institution of the family in the Garden of Eden.

Against such corruption and wickedness, God completely destroyed Sodom and Gomorrah, located on the east side of the edge of Canaan, with his fiery judgment. These two cities represented the sinful pattern of life near the holy land. Notably, God saved Abraham's nephew Lot and his family from the destruction of the cities through the intervention of his angels:

> 12 Then the men said to Lot, "Have you anyone else here? Sons-in-law, sons, daughters, or anyone you have in the city, bring them out of the place. 13 For we are about to destroy this place, because the outcry against its people has become great before the Lord, and the Lord has sent us to destroy it." 14 So Lot went out and said to his sons-in-law, who were to marry his daughters, "Up! Get out of this place, for the Lord is about to destroy the city." But he seemed to his sons-in-law to be jesting. 15 As morning dawned, the angels urged Lot, saying, "Up! Take your wife and your two daughters who are here, lest you be swept away in the punishment of the city." 16 But he lingered. So the men seized him and his wife and his two daughters by the hand, the Lord being merciful to him, and they brought him out and set him outside the city. 17 And as they brought them out, one said, "Escape for your life, Do not look back or stop anywhere in the valley. Escape to the hills, lest you be swept away." (Gen 19:12–17)

Lot and his family members, as a covenant community, escaped to Zoar, a safe area. We must pay special attention to Zoar, which was a part of Canaan, the Promised Land. Zoar is described as a beautiful land; it was "like the garden of the Lord" (כְּגַן־יְהוָה) which has the image of the Paradise Land represented in the Garden of Eden before the fall (Gen 13:10).[22] Zoar, as the garden of the Lord, actually reflects Canaan as the Promised Land to Abraham and alludes to the everlasting Kingdom of God, which will be consummated after the final redemptive judgment. After Lot's covenant community escaped the city, the judgment of fire came down from heaven. The judgment was a type of final judgment; it clearly separated the covenant community from the

---

21. The Septuagint adequately reflects the original Hebrew meaning and translates it as "ἐξάγαγε αὐτοὺς πρὸς ἡμᾶς ἵνα συγγενώμεθα αὐτοῖς" which may be translated in English as "bring them out to us so that we may have sexual relations with them."

22. The Septuagint translates כְּגַן־יְהוָה as "ὡς ὁ παράδεισος τοῦ θεοῦ" which carries the meaning of "like the paradise of the Lord."

non-covenant community. In that sense, the judgment was a redemptive judgment, which is related to redemption and salvation:

> 23 The sun had risen on the earth when Lot came to Zoar. 24 Then the Lord rained on Sodom and Gomorrah sulfur and fire from the Lord out of heaven. 25 And he overthrew those cities, and all the valley, and all the inhabitants of the cities, and what grew on the ground. 26 But Lot's wife, behind him, looked back, and she became a pillar of salt. (Gen 19:23–26)

Jesus prophesied that the world in the last days will be similar to the world in the days of Noah and Lot. Our present world will face the final redemptive judgment. Jesus' prophecy to his disciples reveals that the Flood judgment during the time of Noah and the fiery judgment upon Sodom and Gomorrah during the time of Lot were the Old Testament types of the final eschatological judgment:

> 26 Just as it was *in the days of Noah* [ἐν ταῖς ἡμέραις Νῶε], so will it be *in the days of the Son of Man* [ἐν ταῖς ἡμέραις τοῦ υἱοῦ τοῦ ἀνθρώπου]. 27 They were eating and drinking and marrying and being given in marriage, until the day when Noah entered the ark, and the flood came and destroyed them all. 28 Likewise, just as it was *in the days of Lot* [ἐν ταῖς ἡμέραις Λώτ]—they were eating and drinking, buying and selling, planting and building, 29 but on the day when Lot went out from Sodom, fire and sulfur rained from heaven and destroyed them all—30 so will it be *on the day when the Son of Man is revealed* [ᾗ ἡμέρᾳ ὁ υἱὸς τοῦ ἀνθρώπου ἀποκαλύπτεται]. (Luke 17:26–30)

Jesus noted that "the days of Noah" (ταῖς ἡμέραις Νῶε) were the last days of the original world before the corrupt world faced the universal flood judgment. Similarly, "the days of the Son of Man" (ταῖς ἡμέραις τοῦ υἱοῦ τοῦ ἀνθρώπου) are the last days of the present world which are the days between the first and Second Coming of the Son of Man. And "the days of the Son of Man" can also be identified as the last days or the semi-eschatological age.

God used the method of holy war when he executed redemptive judgment upon Sodom and Gomorrah. God revealed two different types of war in redemptive history. In fact, God allowed two different types of war when he commanded Israel to conquer the Promised Land. One was a common grace war, which is the common method of war among nations that we witness in the contemporary world; it respects international law along with peace treaties. God commanded the covenant community of Israel to wage a common grace war outside of the boundaries of the Promised Land when they marched into the Promised Land (Deut 20:10–15). The other was a holy war: the war of "total destruction" (חרם). God commanded the covenant community of Israel to wage a holy war within the boundaries of the Promised Land when they conquered the Promised Land (Deut 20:16–18). The holy war was the war of Yahweh, and Yahweh fought against the sinful world himself, although he commanded the

The Abrahamic Covenant and the Kingdom of God

covenant community of Israel to fight the holy war in his place when they conquered the Promised Land.[23]

Throughout the redemptive history of the Old Testament, Yahweh waged holy war several times, separating the covenant community from non-covenant communities. Yahweh fought the holy war, the war of total destruction, when he executed the redemptive judgment against the corrupt world while saving the Noahic covenant community in the Ark. Similarly, Yahweh fought against the corrupt cities of Sodom and Gomorrah through the means of a holy war, separating the covenant community of Abraham's nephew, Lot, and the non-covenant community within the cities. As such, the pattern of holy war in redemptive history demonstrates the coming of the final holy war. God will execute the final redemptive judgment, separating the elect and reprobates, at the Parousia. The demonstration of the holy war against Sodom and Gomorrah within the context of the Abrahamic covenant is the divine demonstration that the ultimate realization of the heavenly Kingdom of God, as the ultimate fulfillment of the Abrahamic covenant, will be granted to the covenant community of the elect in Jesus Christ after the final redemptive judgment.

Isaac on Mount Moriah and the Son of Man

In the inauguration of redemptive history, God prophesied that the Messiah will come as "the woman's offspring" (Gen 3:15). According to the four Gospels, Jesus, as the Messiah, revealed his own identity as "the Son of God" and "the Son of Man." Jesus, as the fulfillment of the Messianic prophecy of the Old Testament, emphasized his sinless humanity with his self-designation as "the Son of Man." Meanwhile, Jesus emphasized his divinity and the specific nature of the triune God against rejection by Judaism in the first century with his self-identification as "the Son of God."[24]

Isaac, as the promised son of Abraham, bound on the altar of Mount Moriah by his father, Abraham, can be considered and seen as a figure, alluding to the Son of Man

---

23. For the divergent patterns and practices of holy war in the history of Ancient Israel from different perspectives and understandings, see Jones, "'Holy War' or 'Yahweh War'?", 642–58; Jones, "The Concept of Holy War," 299–322; Kang, *Divine War in the Old Testament and in the Ancient Near East*; Longman and Reid, *God Is a Warrior*; von Rad, *Holy War in Ancient Israel*. Surprisingly, overall the scholars, exploring the patterns of holy war in the history of Ancient Israel, bypass and ignore the significance of Yahweh's holy war in the Flood judgment and judgment upon Sodom and Gomorrah, which are powerful historical demonstrations of the classical paradigm of Yahweh's holy war. In contemporary international wars and disputes, the radical Islamic fundamentalists have often claimed and raged holy war (*Jihad*) in the name of Allah. The radical Islamic claim on holy war, at best, is a pseudo-holy war when we examine it from the biblical concept of holy war, vividly patterned in redemptive history.

24. For Jesus as the Son of Man as well as the Son of God in light of Pauline theology in the milieu of the four Gospels, see Herman N. Ridderbos, *Paul and Jesus*, 21–130. The historical critical interpretation of Jesus as the Son of Man as well as the Son of God has been represented by Rudolf Bultmann, *Theology of the New Testament*, 26–133.

on the altar of Golgotha as the only begotten Son.[25] In that sense, Isaac on the altar of Mount Moriah was the first divine revelation in the Old Testament that the Messiah, "the woman's offspring," would actually come as "the Son of Man," although the specific words "the Son of Man" were not used in the context of the sacrifice (Gen 22:9–13).

Abraham was about to sacrifice his promised son, Isaac, on the altar of Mount Moriah. Then, suddenly, the voice of the angel of the Lord intruded from heaven and told Abraham to stop. Yahweh prepared a ram to sacrifice as a burnt offering "on the Mount of the Lord" (בְּהַר יְהוָה) (Gen 22:9–14). The dramatic transition of sacrifice from Isaac to a ram is a divine revelation about the mission of the coming of the Son of Man. Indeed, it is a Messianic prophecy that the Messiah as the Son of Man will come to sacrifice himself as "the Lamb of God" and be slaughtered as an innocent lamb at Golgotha, the Mount of the Lord. All the animal sacrifices on the altar of the Lord in the Old Testament prefigured Jesus as the final and "once for all" sacrifice (Heb 7:26–28). Hence, echoing the attempted sacrifice of Isaac on Mount of the Lord, John the Baptist shouted that the Messiah as "the Lamb of God" would be slaughtered to atone and forgive the sins of the elect. In the same vein, a ram, prepared by Yahweh on the Mount of the Lord, alluded to "the Lamb of God" (ὁ ἀμνὸς τοῦ θεοῦ) who is Jesus Christ:

> 29 The next day he saw Jesus coming toward him, and said, "*Behold, the Lamb of God, who takes away the sin of the world* [ἴδε ὁ ἀμνὸς τοῦ θεοῦ ὁ αἴρων τὴν ἁμαρτίαν τοῦ κόσμου]! 30 This is he of whom I said, 'After me comes a man who ranks before me, because he was before me.' 31 I myself did not know him, but for this purpose I am baptizing with water, that he might be revealed to Israel." (John 1:29–31; cf. Isa 53:7)

Abraham offered the ram as a burnt offering, which was related primarily to atonement for sins. In fact, Yahweh accepted the burnt offerings as "the pleasing aroma" which signifies the soothing or appeasing of Yahweh's anger due to human sin (Gen 8:20–22; Lev 1:3–17).

After Abraham offered the burnt offering on the altar, he shouted that "the Lord will provide," which echoes his prophetic answer to Isaac: "God will provide for himself the lamb for a burnt offering, my son" (Gen 22:8). Witnessing the burnt offering provided by Yahweh, Abraham shouted prophetically that "the Lord will provide" (יְהוָה יִרְאֶה). It signifies that Yahweh will provide the burnt offerings to be sacrificed on the altar. And from that time on, the oral tradition was transmitted by saying "on the mount of the Lord it shall be provided" (Gen 22:14). Later, Yahweh commanded

---

25. Kline interprets Isaac's sacrifice as the intrusion of eschatological judgment: "It was the ethics of the Cross, itself an intrusion of final judgment into mid-history, that was intruded into the Old Testament age in the divine command to sacrifice Isaac. The provision of the sacrificial substitute once Abraham had manifested the obedience of faith advises us of the inadequacy of sinful human life for making atonement. God had not defined Isaac's life as the life that was actually to be sacrificed as an atonement for sin. Meanwhile, Abraham's confrontation with the Intrusion's demand had served to try the father of believers whether he was prepared to live by every word that proceeded out of the mouth of God." Kline, *The Structure of Biblical Authority*, 169.

that the temple be built on Mount Zion. The Chronicler identifies Mount Zion as Mount Moriah, the place of the altar, offering the burnt offering by Abraham (2 Chr 3:1). Ultimately, Yahweh provided the Lamb of God as a once for all sacrifice, which is the ultimate fulfillment of the prophetic voice of "the Lord will provide." Fulfilling his earthly mission, Jesus as the Lamb of God offered himself to atone for the sins of the elect at Golgotha near the place of the Solomonic temple where Abraham's burnt offering was offered on Mount Moriah. After the death, resurrection, and ascension of the Lamb of God, the apostle John saw the exalted Lamb of God through a vision where he is ruling both visible and invisible realms; he is receiving honor, glory, and worship at the heavenly throne (Rev 5:6–14).

After Abraham passed his trial, being willing to sacrifice his only promised son on Mount Moriah, God confirmed how the Messiah as Abraham's offspring would indeed come. Abraham's obedience, displayed by his willingness to sacrifice his promised son on the altar of Mount Moriah, resembles Jesus' perfect obedience, sacrificing himself as the final sacrifice: "And *in your offspring* [בְזַרְעֲךָ] shall all the nations of the earth be blessed, because you have obeyed my voice"(Gen 22:18).

We need to pay attention to God's promise to Abraham after he successfully passed the trial to sacrifice his promised son, Isaac, on the altar of Mount Moriah. The promise was to bless "all the nations of the earth" in the offspring of Abraham. And God used the promised designation as "in your offspring" (בְזַרְעֲךָ).[26] The Abrahamic promise designation as "in your offspring" became an apostolic foundation, now using the language of "in Christ Jesus," "in Christ," and "through Christ Jesus" to indicate the promised blessings of the elect in Jesus Christ, who passed his trial through his sinless, obedient life and sacrificial death as the mediator of the New Covenant.

After Abraham died, God confirmed again to Isaac, the promised son of Abraham, that he would form the theocratic kingdom in the Promised Land. And "all the nations of the earth" shall be blessed in the offspring of the promised child of Abraham. Again, the redemptive blessings of "in your offspring" signify how God would give all the redemptive blessings to the elect *in Christ Jesus*, who would come as the seed of Abraham. Once again, God reminded Isaac that he would use Abraham's obedience as the ground to bless his descendents in the Promised Land because his obedience mirrored the perfect obedience of Jesus Christ, the Son of Man:

> 1 Now there was a famine in the land, besides the former famine that was in the days of Abraham. And Isaac went to Gerar to Abimelech king of the Philistines. 2 And the Lord appeared to him and said, "Do not go down to Egypt; dwell in the land of which I shall tell you. 3 Sojourn in this land, and I will be with you and will bless you, for to you and to your offspring I will give all these lands, and I will establish the oath that I swore to Abraham your father. 4 I will

---

26. The Septuagint translation of בְזַרְעֲךָ as ἐν τῷ σπέρματί σου is perfectly harmonious with the apostolic designation of the Abrahamic Covenant expression *in Christ, in Christ Jesus, and through Christ Jesus*.

multiply your offspring as the stars of heaven and will give to your offspring all these lands. And *in your offspring all the nations of the earth shall be blessed* [וְהִתְבָּרֲכוּ בְזַרְעֲךָ כֹּל גּוֹיֵי הָאָרֶץ], 5 because Abraham obeyed my voice and kept my charge, my commandments, my statutes, and my laws." (Gen 26:1–5)

Later, God revealed through Old Testament prophecy that the Son of Man would come. But he also revealed that the Son of Man will come as the eschatological King who will rule the heavenly Kingdom of God. God revealed the coming Son of Man as the eschatological figure who will rule the fully realized Kingdom of God through Daniel's prophetic night visions. To do so, the Messiah had to pass through a trial as the mediator of the New Covenant. Only then would the realized Kingdom of God be granted by the heavenly Father. At last, he fulfilled all the earthly missions given by God. And God would grant his realized kingdom to his Son where he will rule the kingdom as the Great King, as well as "the Son of Man" (בַּר אֱנָשׁ), who was already revealed through the sacrifice of the promised son, Isaac, on Mount of Moriah. The ruling of the Son of Man, as well as the Kingdom of God, will be everlasting after the Son of Man returns in eschatological glory "with the clouds of heaven":

> 13 "I saw in the night visions, and behold, with the clouds of heaven there came one *like a son of man* [כְּבַר אֱנָשׁ], and he came to the Ancient of Days and was presented before him. 14 And to him was given dominion and glory and a kingdom, that all people, nations, and languages should serve him; his dominion is an everlasting dominion, which shall not pass away, and his kingdom one that shall not be destroyed." (Dan 7:13–14)

During his earthly ministry, Jesus Christ had the self-consciousness that he came to the world as "the Son of Man" as prophesied through Daniel's night visions. For example, in the discourse with Zacchaeus in Jericho, Jesus revealed his own identity as "the Son of Man" (ὁ υἱὸς τοῦ ἀνθρώπου). And the earthly mission of the Son of Man was to save "the lost," adopting them as "a son of Abraham" (υἱὸς Ἀβραάμ), regardless of their ethnic identity and social status. Thus, Jesus interprets the recipient of the blessings of the Abrahamic covenant from the perspective of the New Covenant of which he is the mediator. He is the fulfillment of Isaac, who was sacrificed on Mount of Moriah as the promised son of Abraham:

> 8 And Zacchaeus stood and said to the Lord, "Behold, Lord, the half of my goods I give to the poor. And if I have defrauded anyone of anything, I restore it fourfold. 9 And Jesus said to him, "Today salvation has come to this house, since he also is *a son of Abraham* [υἱὸς Ἀβραάμ]. 10 For *the Son of Man* [ὁ υἱὸς τοῦ ἀνθρώπου] came to seek and to save the lost." (Luke 19:8–10)

As we observed, God rejoiced in seeing Abraham's obedience to sacrifice his promised child, Isaac, which established a foundation for God to grant all the promised blessings. Nevertheless, Abraham's obedience was not a meritorious obedience, although God used his obedience to make a ground to bless "all the nations of the earth" in his offspring. Abraham's obedience prophetically anticipated Jesus' perfect and meritorious obedience through his life and death, which is the foundation for the salvation of the elect in him, to whom he grants the full right to inherit the Kingdom of God in heaven.[27]

Summary

We endeavored to prove that God promised the holy theocratic kingdom, which includes the covenant people and the Promised Land in Canaan. Through the ceremony of covenant ratification by oath, God assured Abraham that all the promises would be realized and fulfilled. God's promise of the holy theocratic kingdom in Canaan was a type of the everlasting kingdom of heaven in Jesus Christ.

We found that the recent discoveries of the treaties in the ancient Near East do not contradict the classic covenant theology developed in the seventeenth century. Rather, they affirm it. We used the Abrahamic covenant as a test case. The designation of the Abrahamic covenant as a covenant of grace in the classic covenant theology is compatible with the concept of the covenant of royal grant, in parallel with the treaty of royal grant, which was one of the two different patterns on the treaties in the ancient Near East.

---

27. Kline notes that Abraham's obedience, intending to sacrifice Isaac as the son of promise on the altar of Mount Moriah, was *meritorious*, besides the affirmation of his saving faith through his obedient life. And Abraham's meritorious obedience had redemptive historical significance, providing grounds to grant the theocratic kingdom to his descendents. In promoting this view, Kline carefully avoids legalism, because Abraham's obedience served not to bestow personal salvation on the elect but the theocratic kingdom in the Promised Land, which is the type of the everlasting theocratic kingdom. However, I think *meritorious obedience should be limited to the first and last Adams*, although the first Adam failed to obey perfectly in the Garden of Eden. From the perspective of biblical theology, meritorious obedience should be applied only to sinless and perfect obedience, demonstrated by the obedience of Jesus Christ as the last Adam through his life and death as the mediator of the New Covenant, while the first Adam as the representative covenantal head failed to obey. Kline establishes his own biblical theological argument of how Abraham's obedience was meritorious, with which I disagree: "That Abraham's obedience had special historic significance as the basis for God's future favorable action towards his descendents is confirmed by the Lord's late repetition of the substance of this oracle, now to Isaac (Gen 26:2ff.). Having restated his commitment to fulfill the covenant promises to Isaac and his line, the Lord concluded: 'because Abraham obeyed my voice and kept my charge, my commandments, my statutes, and my laws' (Gen 26:5, cf. v. 24). Here the significance of Abraham's works cannot be limited to their role in validation of his own faith. His faithful performance of his covenantal duty is here clearly declared to sustain a causal relationship to the blessing of Isaac and Israel. It had a meritorious character that procured a reward enjoyed by others . . . Because of Abraham's obedience redemptive history would take the shape of an Abrahamite Kingdom of God from which salvation's blessings would rise up and flow out to the nations. God was pleased to constitute Abraham's exemplary works as the meritorious ground for granting to Israel after the flesh the distinctive role of being formed as the typological kingdom, the matrix from which Christ should come . . . Though not the ground of the inheritance of heaven, Abraham's obedience was the ground for Israel's inheritance of Canaan. Salvation would not come because of Abraham's obedience, but because of Abraham's obedience salvation would come of the Abrahamites, the Jews (John 4:22)." Kline, *Kingdom Prologue*, 324–25.

We explored how the judgment upon Sodom and Gomorrah was redemptive judgment through holy war and separated the covenant community from the non-covenant community and the corrupt world. It was a type of the final redemptive judgment at the Parousia. The redemptive judgment within the historical context of the Abrahamic covenant was the divine demonstration that the ultimate realization of the promises of the Abrahamic covenant would be fulfilled with the eschatological redemptive judgment.

Through the sacrifice of Isaac on the altar of Mount Moriah by Abraham, we endeavored to seek the image of the Son of Man sacrificed on the altar of Golgotha. In that sense, the sacrifice of Isaac on the altar was a Messianic prophecy of how "the woman's offspring" would come as "the Son of Man" to forgive the sins of the elect and bestow all the redemptive blessings that God promised to Abraham, including personal salvation.

We established the apostolic designation of "in Christ Jesus," "in Christ," and "through Christ Jesus" to note redemptive blessings, including personal salvation, adopted from the Abrahamic covenant wherein God promised redemptive blessings to Abraham and his descendents by the means of the phrases "in your offspring" and "in you."

We endeavored to support a thesis that Abraham's justification by faith within the historical context of the Abrahamic covenant provided for the first time in redemptive history a soteriological pattern that sinners are justified by faith apart from obedience or works of the law. Representatively, Paul used this soteriological motif after his Damascus Road conversion experience and proclaimed it for both Jews and Gentiles, as did the other apostles.

4

The Mosaic Covenant and the Kingdom of God

THE ABRAHAMIC COVENANT COMMUNITY in the line of Abraham, Isaac, and Jacob significantly increased in numbers, as God promised in his covenant with Abraham. The descendents of the Abrahamic covenant lived under Egyptian bondage for more than four centuries until God delivered them through his miraculous power, appointing Moses as their leader and prophet. When the Israelites arrived at Mount Sinai, God made a covenant with his people. Moses played the role of mediator between God and the Israelites in the covenant-making process (Ex 19—24).[1]

What is the true nature of the Mosaic covenant in redemptive history? Is it a covenant of law or a covenant of grace or a third covenant? Throughout church history, even the best minds have greatly struggled to identify and interpret the Mosaic covenant. After Robertson compares the external forms of the Pentateuchal material and Hittite treaties, he identifies the Mosaic covenant as "the covenant of law":

> In the case of the Mosaic covenant, the prominence of this external form of God's will provides ample justification for the characterization of the Mosaic covenant as the covenant of law. This characterization has the full support of the New Testament Scriptures. "The law was given through Moses," says the apostle John (John 1:17). In his letter to the Galatians, Paul clearly characterizes the Mosaic period as the epoch of "law" (Gal. 3:17).[2]

---

1. For divergent interpretations on the Mosaic covenant, see J. Collins, *Introduction to the Hebrew Bible*, 67–77; Dumbrell, *Covenant and Creation*, 80–126; Durham, *Exodus*, 255–348; Edwards, *A History of Redemption*, 68–92; Gentry and Wellum, *A Biblical Theological Understanding of the Covenants*, 301–88; Golding, *Covenant Theology*, 155–58, 164–75; Hahn, *Kinship by Covenant*, 49–92; Horton, *Introducing Covenant Theology*, 83–104; Kline, *God, Heaven, and Har Magedon*, 110–37; Kline, *Kingdom Prologue*, 8–117; LaRondelle, *Our Creator Redeemer*, 29–41; Murray, *The Covenant of Grace*, 20–22; Noth, *The History of Israel*, 127–38; Robertson, *The Christ of the Covenants*, 167–99; Turretin, *Institutes of Elenctic Theology*, 2:224–69; Vos, *Biblical Theology*, 100–82; Waltke, *An Old Testament Theology*, 405–44; Williams, *Far as the Curse Is Found*, 132–47.

2. Robertson, *The Christ of the Covenants*, 173. Robertson self-consciously identifies the Mosaic covenant as the covenant of law, making a clear distinction between the Mosaic covenant of law and the Edenic covenant of works, which was applied to Adam and Eve at the Garden of Eden before they committed the original sin: "This phrase 'covenant of law' must not be confused with the traditional

However, Robertson's identification of the Mosaic covenant as "the covenant of law" does not provide a comprehensive and complicated understanding of the Mosaic covenant. On the other hand, Turretin demonstrates a balanced understanding of the Mosaic covenant. He notes that the external form of the Mosaic covenant is clothed with "the form of a covenant of works" while the internal substance of the Mosaic covenant was nothing else but "the covenant of grace." In such a fashion, Turretin writes:

> However, we recognize only two covenants mutually distinct in species (to wit, the covenant of works, which promises life to the doer; and the covenant of grace, which promises salvation to believers). Although we confess that the Sinaitic covenant as to mode of dispensation was different from both, still as to substance and species we deny that it is constituted a third covenant and hold that it was nothing else than a new economy of the covenant of grace. It was really the same with the covenant made with Abraham, but different as to accidents and circumstances (to wit, clothed as to external dispensation with the form of a covenant of works through the harsh promulgation of the law; not indeed with that design, so that a covenant of works might again be demanded with the sinner [for this was impossible], but that a daily recollection and reproaching of the violated covenant of works might be made; thus the Israelites felt their sin and the curse of God besides hanging over them and acknowledged the impossibility of a legal righteousness; driven away from that hope, they so much the more ardently thirsted for the righteousness of redemption and were led along by the hand to Christ). Hence in it there was a mixture of the law and the gospel: the former to strike into sinners and press upon the neck of the stiff-necked (*schlerotragelou*) people; the latter to lift up and console the conscience contrite and overpowered by a sense of sin.[3]

In light of the modern discoveries of ancient Near Eastern treaties, Turretin's identification of the Mosaic covenant is simply brilliant, though a minor revision is required.[4] The thesis is that the Reformed interpretation in the seventeenth century, represented by Turretin's identification of the Mosaic covenant, has been remarkably

---

terminology which speaks of a 'covenant of works.' The phrase 'covenant of works' customarily refers to the situation at creation in which man was required to obey God perfectly in order to enter into a state of eternal blessedness. Contrary to this relation established with man in innocence, the Mosaic covenant of law clearly expresses itself to man in sin. This latter covenant never intended to suggest that man by perfect moral obedience could enter into a state of guaranteed covenantal blessedness. The integral role of a substitutionary sacrificial system within the legal provisions of the Mosaic covenant clearly indicates a sober awareness of the distinction between God's dealings with man in innocence and with man in sin." Ibid., 173–74.

3. Turretin, 2:262–63.

4. As a seventeenth century continental Reformed theologian, Turretin's identification of the Mosaic covenant is simply brilliant,because the external form of the Mosaic covenant in light of the ancient Near Eastern treaties in second millennium B.C. has the covenant of law while the internal substance of the Mosaic covenant was the covenant of grace, which was represented by the previous Abrahamic covenant. However, we identify the external form of the Mosaic covenant not as the covenant of works but the covenant of law to differentiate it from the Adamic covenant of works.

affirmed by the discoveries of treaties of the ancient Near East. So, the argument is that the external form of the Mosaic covenant was the covenant of law in light of the Hittite treaties in the mid-second millennium B.C. in the ancient Near East. However, the internal substance of the Mosaic covenant is the covenant of grace, which is represented by the previous covenant, the Abrahamic covenant. So, the elect under the Mosaic economy are saved by the principle of the covenant of grace exactly like believers under the New Covenant.

Thus, we will demonstrate that the Mosaic covenant has the form of the suzerainty covenant, which is similar to the form of the suzerainty treaty in the ancient Near East. In this respect, the Mosaic covenant is very different from the Abrahamic covenant in which God made a covenant with Abraham almost four centuries before the Mosaic covenant. In the process of the covenant ratification ceremony, the covenant community of Israel made a sworn oath to Yahweh to obey the Mosaic law. However, Yahweh made a sworn oath to Abraham when he ratified the covenant. Israel's sworn oath to the Mosaic covenant had very significant implications. Likewise, we will argue that the external form of the Mosaic covenant as the covenant of law had significant implications for Israel, because God applied Israel's obedience and disobedience to the Mosaic law for typological blessings and curses during the forty years of wilderness wandering and in the Promised Land.

However, it is important to know that the typological implications of the Mosaic covenant as the covenant of law did not nullify the continuity of the covenant of grace, inaugurated in Genesis 3:15. In light of that, we will seek to demonstrate that the individual salvation of those within the covenant community of ancient Israel and the possession of the land of Canaan under the Mosaic covenant were by the principle of the covenant of grace, promised in the previous Abrahamic covenant. So, in light of the internal substance of the covenant, the Mosaic covenant was an administration of the covenant of grace.

The covenant renewals at Moab after the forty years in the wilderness and at Shechem after the conquest of the land of Canaan affirm and demonstrate that the Mosaic covenant had the external form of the covenant of law while its internal substance was the covenant of grace.

Recently, scholars have discussed whether the Mosaic covenant was a republication of the covenant of works in a limited sense. In doing so, some have argued that the republication view fits neither the teaching of the Westminster Standards nor the teaching of the Bible. However, it is our assessment that the republication view is harmonious both to the teachings of the Bible and the Westminster Standards, although a minor revision is still required.

Biblical Theology

The External Form of the Sinaitic Covenant and Oath to the Covenant

The Sinaitic Covenant has the structure of a suzerainty treaty of the ancient Near East, represented by the Hittite treaties in the mid-second millennium B.C.

The preamble identifies the Great King as "I am the Lord your God" (Ex 20:2a). The historical prologue explains Yahweh's historical relationship to the vassal, the covenant community. Yahweh proclaims the historical relationship with the covenant people, naming himself as the One "who brought you out of the land of Egypt, out of the house of slavery" (Ex 20:2b). Then follow the covenant stipulations, which require faithful obedience and commitment to the Great King, Yahweh. The stipulations are well described in the revelation of the Ten Commandments (Ex 20:3–17). Interestingly, there is no separate section for blessings and curses. Rather, blessings and curses are seen throughout the stipulations in verses 5, 6, 7, 11, and 12. Later, before the covenant ratification ceremony, Yahweh states blessings and curses again in prophecy in respect to the conquest of Canaan (Ex 23:20–33). Through the covenant ratification ceremony (Ex 24), the Sinaitic covenant was officially inaugurated with a sworn oath to the covenant by the covenant community.[5]

When we compare the Abrahamic covenant (Gen 11:27—25:11) and the Sinaitic covenant (Ex 19—24), several distinct differences are found. Perhaps one of the most significant differences is the oath to the covenant. In the Abrahamic covenant, Yahweh, not Abraham, made a sworn oath to the covenant:

> 17 When the sun had gone down and it was dark, behold, *a smoking fire pot and a flaming torch passed between these pieces.* 18 *On that day the Lord made a covenant with Abram, saying, "To your offspring I give this land*, from the river of Egypt to the great river, the river Euphrates, 19 the land of the Kenites, the Kenizzites, the Kadmonites, 20 the Hittites, the Perizzites, the Rephaim, 21 the Amorites, the Canaanites, the Girgashites and the Jebusites." (Gen 15:17–21)

In the Abrahamic covenant ratification ceremony, Yahweh made a sworn oath to the covenant as a visible presence of the theophanic glory passed between the torn pieces of the animals. Yahweh's sworn oath before Abraham in the process of the covenant ratification ceremony signified that he would fulfill all the promises, executing his sovereign will and power throughout redemptive history that he made in his covenant with Abraham.

However, in the Mosaic covenant, Yahweh as the Great King did not make a sworn oath to the covenant. Rather, Abraham's descendents, the entire covenant community of Israel, made a sworn oath in the process of the covenant ratification

---

5. For discussions on the parallel structure or form between the Sinaitic covenant and the suzerainty treaty, found in the ancient Near East, see Gentry and Wellum, *Covenant through Kingdom*, 305–9; Kline, *The Structure of Biblical Authority*, 113–123; McCarthy, *Old Testament Covenant*, 10–21; Robertson, *The Christ of the Covenants*, 168–69; Waltke, *An Old Testament Theology*, 409–12.

ceremony. The initial sworn oath was made by the covenant community of Israel before Moses received the Book of the Covenant by Yahweh:

> 7 So Moses came and called the elders of the people and set before them all these words that the LORD had commanded him. 8 *All the people answered together and said, "All that the LORD has spoken we will do."* And Moses reported the words of the people to the LORD. 9 And the LORD said to Moses. "Behold, I am coming to you in a thick cloud, that the people may hear when I speak with you, and may also believe you forever." When Moses told the words of the people to the LORD, 10 the LORD said to Moses, "Go to the people and consecrate them today and tomorrow, and let them wash their garments." (Ex 19:7–10)

The covenant community of Israel, including children and elderly alike, made a sworn oath to keep all the laws and regulations that Yahweh gave them through the mediator of the covenant, Moses. Later, Moses climbed Mt. Sinai, enveloped in the theophanic glory, and received "the Book of the Covenant" from Yahweh. After returning from Mt. Sinai, Moses read "the Book of the Covenant" to the covenant community of Israel. The Israelites responded with a sworn oath in the presence of Yahweh:

> 4 And Moses wrote down all the words of the LORD. He rose early in the morning and built an altar at the foot of the mountain, and twelve pillars, according to the twelve tribes of Israel. 5 And he sent young men of the people of Israel, who offered burnt offerings and sacrificed peace offerings of oxen to the LORD. 6 And Moses took half of the blood and put it in basins, and half of the blood he threw against the altar. 7 *Then he took the Book of the Covenant and read it in the hearing of the people. And they said, "All that the LORD has spoken we will do, and we will be obedient."* (Ex 24:4–7)

The shout of the covenant community, "*All that the LORD has spoken we will do, and we will be obedient*" (v. 7b), had significant implications. It had identical meaning to the covenant ratification ceremony performed by God before Abraham as the entire covenant community as vassals passed through torn animals in the presence of the Great King, Yahweh. So, when the covenant community as vassals violated the regulations of the law, death or curses fell upon them. When the covenant community of Israel made a sworn oath to the covenant, the Mosaic covenant became effective, and they began to live their lives under the terms of the Mosaic covenant of law.

The Continuity of the Covenant of Grace

As already explored in the Mosaic covenant, Yahweh did not make a sworn oath to the covenant. Rather, the people of Israel as a whole made a sworn oath to the covenant during the covenant ratification ceremony. However, it is important to recognize that personal salvation under the Mosaic covenant did not depend upon obedience to the law. Rather, it was by faith through God's grace in Christ alone. It is crucial to remember this because the principle of the covenant of grace, inaugurated in Genesis 3:15, was not vitiated by the Mosaic covenant of law. The principle of the covenant of grace was at work even under the Mosaic covenant when the Israelites received the law from Yahweh. As such, Yahweh clearly demonstrated the continuation of the principle of the covenant of grace, sprinkling blood during the covenant ratification ceremony of the Mosaic covenant:

> 4 And Moses wrote down all the words of the LORD. He rose early in the morning and built an altar at the foot of the mountain, and twelve pillars, according to the twelve tribes of Israel. 5 And he sent young men of the people of Israel, who offered burnt offerings and sacrificed peace offerings of oxen to the LORD. 6 And Moses took half of the blood and put it in basins, and half of the blood he threw against the altar. 7 Then he took the Book of the Covenant and read it in the hearing of the people. And they said, "All that the LORD has spoken we will do, and we will be obedient." 8 *And Moses took the blood and threw it on the people and said, "Behold the blood of the covenant that the LORD has made with you in accordance with all these words."* (Ex 24:4–8)

Exodus 24:8 indicates that Yahweh washed away and forgave the sins of his people through "the blood of the covenant," which signified the blood of the Messiah, Jesus Christ as the mediator of the New Covenant. It is a profound mystery that the efficacy of the blood of the New Covenant was retrospective applied to the elect even under the Mosaic covenant, ultimately back to Genesis 3:15.[6] It is the only divine means to save and forgive sinners after the first Adam's fall. Moses' sprinkling of animal blood on the covenant community of Israel, the Book of the Covenant, and the altar was "the blood of the covenant," which typified the blood of the New Covenant shed by Jesus Christ. This is important to note because it signifies that the covenant community of Israel in the Old Testament was saved by faith through God's grace, and their sins were forgiven through the blood of Christ as people are under the New Covenant.[7]

---

6. Scott Hahn rejects the idea that there is a redemptive historical continuity between the Mosaic covenant and the New Covenant. He argues that "the Mosaic system as finalized in the Deuteronomic covenant can not be the economy of salvation." His rejection of redemptive historical continuity between the Old and New Covenants is a fundamental misreading of Pauline theology: "In contrast to the Abrahamic covenant, the Mosaic covenant—at least as renewed after the golden calf and other rebellions—is secondary and subordinate in Paul's eyes. For Paul, the Mosaic system as finalized in the Deuteronomic covenant can not be the economy of salvation, because under it Israel *did not receive*—and *is not receiving*—the blessings promised to Abraham. Instead, curses have come. Therefore, the Mosaic covenant is a temporary, penitential, and highly mediated arrangement which is valid only until the coming of the definitive 'seed' spoken of in the oath of the Aqedah (Gen 22:18). The Book of Deuteronomy—the final form of the Mosaic covenant—reflects its self-retiring nature, when it speaks of the inevitable failure of the people and the actualization of its severe curses, after which there will be a new exodus and a supernatural initiative on the part of God to 'circumcise the hearts' of the people." Hahn, *Kinship by Covenant*, 276.

7. Calvin rightly affirms that the sprinkling of blood on the people of Israel in the covenant-making process on Mt. Sinai was the sign of "a ratification of the Covenant." The Mosaic covenant was also "the covenant of gratuitous adoption," made with the people of Israel unto "eternal salvation"

Likewise, the author of the book of the Hebrews proclaims that the Mosaic covenant was inaugurated with "the blood of the covenant," even as the New Covenant was inaugurated with the blood of Christ:

> 15 Therefore he is the mediator of a new covenant, so that those who are called may receive the promised eternal inheritance, since a death has occurred that redeems them from the transgressions committed under the first covenant. 16 For where a will is involved, the death of the one who made it must be established. 17 For a will takes effect only at death, since it is not in force as long as the one who made it is alive. 18 Therefore not even the first covenant was inaugurated without blood. 19 For when every commandment of the law had been declared by Moses to all the people, he took the blood of calves and goats, with water and scarlet wool and hyssop, and sprinkled both the book itself and all the people, 20 saying, "This is the blood of the covenant that God commanded for you." 21 And in the same way he sprinkled with the blood both the tent and all the vessels used in worship. 22 Indeed, under the law almost everything is purified with blood, and without the shedding of blood there is no forgiveness of sins. (Heb 9:15–22)

The author of the book of Hebrews identifies the Mosaic covenant as "the first covenant," which was inaugurated with the sprinkling of animal blood. Similarly, God inaugurated the New Covenant with Jesus Christ as the mediator of the New Covenant by the shedding of his own blood on the cross. In doing so, the promised inheritance of the heavenly Kingdom of God along with the forgiveness of sins are guaranteed for the people of God who are in Jesus Christ.

The Mosaic law has three facets, namely the moral, ceremonial, and judicial laws. Yahweh revealed these laws through the Sinaitic covenant. The Ten Commandments can be categorized as moral law (Ex 20:3–17). Judical law to govern the nation of Israel

---

because it was "sealed with the blood of Christ in type and shadow" as Hebrews 9:19 proclaims: "This offering, however, comprised in it a ratification of the Covenant, as appears immediately afterwards; for, in order to increase the sanctity and security of covenants, they have in all ages, and even amongst heathen nations been accompanied with sacrifices. To this end Moses, the victims being slain, pours half the blood upon the altar, and keeps half in basins to sprinkle the people, that by this symbol the Covenant might be ratified, whereof he was the mediator and surety . . . But the case of this sacrifice was peculiar; for God desired the Jews to be reminded of the one solid confirmation of the Covenant, which He made with them; as if He had openly shewn that it would then only be ratified and effectual, when it should be sealed with blood. And this the Apostle (Heb. ix. 19) carefully takes into consideration, when he says, that after the Law had been declared, Moses 'sprinkled both the book and all the people' with blood; for, although there is no express mention here made of the book, the Apostle does not unreasonably comprise it under the word 'altar.' He also alludes to another kind of sacrifice, treated of in Numbers xix. 5, and therefore mentions 'the scarlet-wool and hyssop.' The sum is, that the blood was, as it were, the medium whereby the covenant was confirmed and established, since the altar, as the sacred seat of God, was bathed with half of it, and then the residue was sprinkled over the people. Hence we gather that the covenant of gratuitous adoption was made with the ancient people unto eternal salvation, since it was sealed with the blood of Christ in type and shadow." Calvin, *The Four Last Books of Moses*, 319–20.

was revealed as well (Ex 21:1—23:9). Ceremonial law was summarily mentioned (Ex 20:22–26; 14–19).[8] After the Sinaitic covenant was inaugurated, Yahweh commanded Moses to build the tabernacle. When the tabernacle was erected, Yahweh revealed the detailed regulations of ceremonial law in the book of Leviticus. The postscript of Leviticus, "These are the commandments that the Lord commanded Moses for the people of Israel on Mount Sinai" (Lev 27:34), suggests that the book of Leviticus provides detailed laws and regulation for the covenant community under the Sinaitic covenant, in order to reveal and explain the full account of ceremonial law and other related regulations. The ceremonial law pointed to the sacrificial and atoning death of the Messiah, and it was fulfilled by the suffering and sacrificial death of Jesus Christ as the mediator of the New Covenant. So, the revelation of the ceremonial law in the Sinaitic covenant serves as biblical evidence that the internal substance of the Sinaitic covenant was the covenant of grace.

Moreover, Yahweh reminded the covenant community about the conquest of the Promised Land in the covenant-making process of the Sinatic covenant (Ex 23:20–33). The possession of the Promised Land was one of the essential promises of the Abrahamic covenant with Yahweh's sworn oath.[9] So, Yahweh made sure that the conquest and possession of the Promised Land would be a *grant* to the covenant people:

> 23 "When my angel goes before you and brings you to the Amorites and the Hittites and the Perizzites and the Canaanites, the Hivites and the Jebusites, and I blot them out, 24 you shall not bow down to their gods nor serve them, nor do as they do, but you shall utterly overthrow them and break their pillars in pieces. 25 You shall serve the LORD your God, and he will bless your bread and your water, and I will take sickness away from among you. 26 None shall miscarry or be barren in your land; I will fulfill the number of your days. 27 I will send my terror before you and will throw into confusion all the people against whom you shall come, and I will make all your enemies turn their backs to you. 28 And I will send hornets before you, which shall drive out the Hivites, the Canaanites, and the Hittites from before you. 29 I will not drive them out from before you in

---

8. The Westminster Confession of Faith describes God's law, given to the covenant community of Israel on Mount Sinai as moral, ceremonial, and judicial laws, as follows: "3. Besides this law, commonly called moral, God was pleased to give to the people of Israel, as a church under age, ceremonial laws, containing several typical ordinances, partly of worship, prefiguring Christ, His graces, actions, sufferings, and benefits; and partly, holding forth divers instructions of moral duties. All which ceremonial laws are now abrogated, under the new testament.

4. To them also, as a body politic, He gave sundry judicial laws, which expired together with the state of that people; not obliging any other now, further than the general equity thereof may require." The Westminster Confession of Faith, 19.3–4.

9. The Promised Land *is* at the same time "Sworn Land" because God promised the land of Canaan to Abraham through his sworn oath. Nevertheless, Bruce Waltke does not identify "Sworn Land" as the "Promised Land" in his discussion of the divine oath in Genesis 22:1–19: "In truth, however, an oath is the most solemn attestation of the truth or inviolability of one's words. People don't go to jail for breaking a contract, but they do go to jail for lying under oath. We should speak of the 'Sworn Land,' not the 'Promised Land.'" Waltke, *An Old Testament Theology*, 321.

one year, lest the land become desolate and the wild beasts multiply against you. 30 Little by little I will drive them out from before you, until you have increased and possess the land. 31 *And I will set your border from the Red Sea to the Sea of the Philistines, and from the wilderness to the Euphrates, for I will give the inhabitants of the land into your hand, and you shall drive them out before you.* 32 You shall make no covenant with them and their gods. 33 They shall not dwell in your land, lest they make you sin against me; for if you serve their gods, it will surely be a snare to you." (Ex 23:23–33)

It is interesting to observe that Yahweh did not reveal the *way* he would grant the land of Canaan to the descendents of Abraham, Isaac, and Jacob when he made the covenant with them. Later on, Yahweh revealed to the covenant community *how* he would grant the Promised Land in the historical context of the Sinaitic covenant. It was by way of a holy war, executing redemptive judgment to separate the covenant community and the non-covenant community during the conquest of the Promised Land. Yahweh commanded the Israelites not to fight a common grace war but a holy war against the inhabitants of Canaan in the Promised Land. In particular, the statement of verse 23 that "When my angel goes before you and brings you to the Amorites and the Hittites and the Perizzites and the Canaanites, the Hivites and the Jebusites, and I blot them out" is the divine declaration of prophecy of holy war, which will be executed during the conquest of the Promised Land. Yahweh's proclamation, "I blot them out," is the revelation of his powerful will that he will execute redemptive judgment upon the inhabitants of Canaan through holy war. As such, Yahweh prophesied that the possession of the land of Canaan would be a grant to the covenant community through the execution of holy war. Verse 31b, *"for I will give the inhabitants of the land into your hand, and you shall drive them out before you,"* suggests that Yahweh will grant the Promised Land through his power and will. The inclusion of this prophecy of the possession of the land of Canaan within the historical context of the Sinaitic covenant suggests that its internal substance was the covenant of grace.

The Witnesses of the Covenant Ratification of the Mosaic Covenant

When Moses received the Book of the Covenant, the visible presence of theophanic glory was on Mt. Sinai. Moses as the prophet and mediator of the covenant was privileged to witness the Beauty of the theophanic glory.[10] This is not only the testimony

---

10. Martin Noth interprets the Sinaitic covenant from a historical critical perspective. In doing so, he denies Moses' role as the mediator of the Sinaitic covenant: "It is this view of Moses, however, as offered by the oldest surviving tradition, which raises the historical problem of his personality. Since the Pentateuch narrative was compiled step by step from a series of originally independent themes, the regular appearance of Moses in most of these themes cannot be original but must be the result of later assimilation; and the inevitable question is to which theme or tradition Moses was originally attached and where we must look for his position in history ... This suggests that Moses had no historical connection with the event which took place on Sinai. Historically, it is therefore hardly justifiable to

of Moses' reception of the Book of the Covenant from Yahweh; it is also a foretaste of the glory of the heavenly Kingdom of God on Mt. Sinai.[11] While Moses ascended to Mt. Sinai and was enveloped in the presence of theophanic glory, the covenant community of Israel observed the theophanic glory "at the foot of the mountain:"

> 16 On the morning of the third day there were thunders and lightnings and a thick cloud on the mountain and a very loud trumpet blast, so that all the people in the camp trembled. 17 Then Moses brought the people out of the camp to meet God, and they took their stand at the foot of the mountain. 18 Now Mount Sinai was wrapped in smoke because the LORD had descended on it in fire. The smoke of it went up like the smoke of a kiln, and the whole mountain trembled greatly. 19 And as the sound of the trumpet grew louder and louder, Moses spoke, and God answered him in thunder. (Ex 19:16–20)

> 15 Then Moses went up on the mountain, and the cloud covered the mountain. 16 The glory of the LORD dwelt on Mount Sinai, and the cloud covered it six days. And on the seventh day he called to Moses out of the midst of the cloud. 17 Now the appearance of the glory of the LORD was like a devouring fire on the top of the mountain in the sight of the people of Israel. 18 Moses entered the cloud and went up on the mountain. And Moses was on the mountain forty days and forty nights. (Ex 24:15–18)

The visible dwelling of the glory of the Lord on Mount Sinai was Yahweh's visible demonstration to the covenant community that God himself was a divine witness of the Sinaitic covenant. Likewise, the covenant community of Israel observed the extraordinary and terrifying scene of theophanic glory at Mt. Sinai, as testified in Exodus 19:18 and 24:17. It is a testimony that Yahweh was present as a witness of the Sinaitic covenant. Moreover, this is the visible testimony that Yahweh bestowed the covenant on the people of Israel. And the visible and thunderous presence of the theophanic glory in the process of establishing the covenant signified that Yahweh would pour out his blessings to the obedient and curses upon the disobedient, according to the terms of the Mosaic covenant of law.

---

describe him as the organizer and law-giver of Israel. The fact that it is impossible to name any specific human person who played an active or interpretative part on that occasion makes the Sinai event even more mysterious." Noth, *The History of Israel*, 136.

11. Reflecting on Exodus 24:12 in light of interpretation tradition by Philo and others, James Kugel insists that Moses experienced transformation and became divine. However, we need to remember that Moses as the mediator of the Sinaitic covenant never became divine. He was merely a human mediator of the Sinaitic covenant and ruler of the covenant community of Israel: "If the mountain actually ascended into heaven, and Moses with it, then surely Moses was transformed in the process; one cannot ascend into heaven and remain an ordinary human being. Indeed, Scripture seemed to imply as much when it had God say, 'Come up *to Me* on the mountain' (Exod. 24:12). Did not Moses' ascent into heaven mean that he himself became, as it were, divine?" Kugel, *The Bible As It Was*, 375.

The Mosaic Covenant and the Kingdom of God

After the Sinaitic covenant was ratified, Yahweh commanded Moses to make the ark of the testimony (Ex. 25:10–22). In doing so, he ordered placed in the ark the testimony, which would be the Ten Commandments, written on the two stone tablets:

> 16 And you shall put into the ark the testimony that I shall give you. 17 "You shall make a mercy seat of pure gold. Two cubits and a half shall be its length, and a cubit and a half its breadth. 18 And you shall make two cherubim of gold; of hammered work shall you make them, on the two ends of the mercy seat. 19 Make one cherub on the one end, and one cherub on the other end. Of one piece with the mercy seat shall you make the cherubim on its two ends. 20 The cherubim shall spread out their wings above, overshadowing the mercy seat with their wings, their faces one to another; toward the mercy seat shall the faces of the cherubim be. 21 And you shall put the mercy seat on the top of the ark, and in the ark you shall put the testimony that I shall give you. 22 There I will meet with you, and from above the mercy seat, from between the two cherubim that are on the ark of the testimony, I will speak with you about all that I will give you in commandment for the people of Israel. (Ex 25:16–22)

According to the masterful design of Yahweh, the tabernacle and its pieces were completed. And Yahweh commanded Moses to erect the tabernacle of the tent of meeting according to his specific guidelines (Ex 40:1–15). Moses erected the tabernacle as Yahweh commanded him (Ex 40:16–33). In the process of the erection of the tabernacle, Moses took the testimony and put it inside the ark:

> 16 This Moses did; according to all that the LORD commanded him, so he did. 17 In the first month in the second year, on the first day of the month, the tabernacle was erected. 18 Moses erected the tabernacle. He laid its bases, and set up its frames, and put in its poles, and raised up its pillars. 19 And he spread the tent over the tabernacle and put the covering of the tent over it, as the LORD had commanded Moses. 20 He took the testimony and put it into the ark, and put the poles on the ark and set the mercy seat above on the ark. 21 And he brought the ark into the tabernacle and set up the veil of the screen, and screened the ark of the testimony, as the LORD had commanded Moses. (Ex 40:16–21)

Taking the testimony and placing it in the ark had a very significant meaning as the Sinaitic covenant was inaugurated. Naming the Ten Commandments, written on the two stone tablets by Yahweh, as "the testimony" carries significant meaning for Yahweh's relationship with the covenant community. "The testimony" itself will be the future written witness to execute Yahweh's blessings and curses, according to the covenant community's obedience and disobedience to the Mosaic law. Furthermore, it is important to note that the erection of the tabernacle as the earthly dwelling place of Yahweh, along with the placing of the testimony into the ark, comes in the final chapter of Exodus (Ex 40:1–33). This suggests that the book of Exodus can be identified as the book of the Mosaic covenant. Moreover, in light of the good news of the gospel of Jesus Christ, the book of Exodus can be identified as the gospel of Moses, where the good news of the gospel was proclaimed and deeply embedded in the Mosaic law through the types and shadows of the sacrificial death of Jesus Christ.[12]

Republication of the Covenant of Works

Historically, the Mosaic covenant has been understood as a republication of the covenant of works in a limited sense by prominent orthodox scholars.[13] We would argue that John Calvin laid out the foundation of the idea of republication of the covenant of works in his interpretation of the Mosaic covenant during the Protestant Reformation. Calvin held that believers under the Old Covenant were saved by the principle of the covenant of grace, as we are saved under the New Covenant. The benefit of the covenant of grace, inaugurated in Genesis 3:15, persisted even under the Old Covenant. Receiving the Mosaic law on Mt. Sinai did not vitiate the continuation of redemptive history and benefits. Nevertheless, Calvin argued that "the covenant of the Law" operated under the Mosaic economy. Israel under the Old Covenant was under "the covenant of the Law" where God executed blessings and curses in the Promised Land according to their obedience or disobedience to the Mosaic law. Interpreting Jeremiah 31 and 32, Calvin carefully contrasts between the Old and New Covenants. In doing so, he identifies the Old Covenant as "a temporary covenant" while he sees the New Covenant as "a perpetual covenant:"

> We must notice *the contrast between the covenant of the Law, and the covenant of which the Prophet now speaks* [emphasis mine]. He called it in the thirty-first chapter a new covenant, and gave the reason for it, because their fathers

---

12. Comparing the Book of Exodus with the New Testament Gospels, Kline insightfully identifies the Book of Exodus as "the Gospel of Moses": "In this over-all pattern the Book of Exodus anticipates the form of the New Testament Gospels. The latter also have two main divisions. The first part, like Exodus 1–18, presents the covenant mediator, Jesus, the new and greater Moses, the Messiah-Son sent by the Father and certified for his mediatorial role by his unparalleled words and deeds. The second division of the Gospels is the passion narrative section, which, like Exodus 19—40, is the record of covenant ratification, the blood of the Cross being the blood of the New Covenant. We may, therefore, speak of the Book of Exodus in its over-all structure as the Gospel of Moses, a covenant witness document, which is what a gospel is." Kline, *God Heaven and Har Magedon*, 121.

13. For historical, theological, and biblical affirmation and defense of the concept of the republication of the covenant of works under the Mosaic covenant in the Reformed tradition, see Ferry, "Cross-Examining Moses' Defense: An Answer to Ramsey's Critique of Kline and Karlberg," 163–68 ; Ferry, "Works in the Mosaic Covenant: A Reformed Texamony," 76–103; Fesko, "Calvin and Witsius on the Mosaic Covenant," 25–43; Fesko, "The Republication of the Covenant of Works," 197–212; Hart, "Princeton and the Law: Enlightened and Reformed," 44–75; Jeon, *Covenant Theology*, 14–102.

For various writings which oppose to the concept of a republication of the covenant of works in a limited sense under the Mosaic covenant, see Elam, Van Kooten, and Bergquist, *Merit and Moses*; Dennison, "Merit or 'Entitlement' in Reformed Covenant Theology: A Review," 3–152; Letham, "'Not a Covenant of Works in Disguise' (Herman Bavinck)," 143–77; Ramsey, "In Defense of Moses," 373–400; Venema, "The Law of Moses: Not a Disguised Covenant of Works," 212–27 ; Venema, "The Mosaic Covenant: A Republication of the Covenant of Works?" 35–101.

had soon fallen away after the Law was proclaimed, and because its doctrine was that of the letter, and deadly, and also fatal. But he now calls it a *perpetual covenant*. That the covenant of the Law was not valid, this was accidental to it; for the Law would remain in force, were we only to keep it; but through men's fault it happened that the covenant of the Law became void and immediately vanished ... We must, at the same time, bear in mind that this covenant peculiarly belongs to the kingdom of Christ. For though it was a part of God's grace, which was manifested in delivering his people from captivity, yet the continued stream of his grace ought to be extended to the coming of Christ. The Prophet then, no doubt, brings Christ before us, together with the new covenant; for without him there is not the least hope that God would make another covenant, as it appears evident from the whole Law and the teaching of the Prophets. Then Christ is here opposed to Moses, and the Gospel to the Law. It hence follows, that the Law was a temporary covenant, for it had no stability, as it was that of the letter; but that the Gospel is a perpetual covenant, for it is inscribed on the heart.[14]

The brilliancy of Calvin's redemptive historical hermeneutics and theology lies in the fact that Calvin did not fall into legalism when he designated the Mosaic covenant as "the covenant of the Law." This is because the implication of "the covenant of the Law" only applied to the ministry of death. So, the Mosaic covenant as "the covenant of the Law" led sinners ultimately to Christ. Likewise, Calvin clearly articulated that believers under the Mosaic covenant were saved by the principle of the covenant of grace. In doing so, Calvin avoided legalism when he designated the Mosaic covenant as "the covenant of the Law."

The history of ancient Israel under the Mosaic covenant proves that the covenant community of Israel failed to obey the Mosaic laws and God poured out his covenant curses upon Israel during the forty years in the wilderness and in the Promised Land. Why did God administer temporary blessings and curses upon Israel? There was a pedagogical purpose, which was vividly manifested in the realization that sinners could not fulfill the requirements of God's holy law. So the curses of the Mosaic law in redemptive history ultimately point to Christ, the mediator of the New Covenant, who fulfilled the requirements of the Mosaic law through his life and sacrificial death on the cross.

It is our thesis that Calvin's designation of the Mosaic covenant as "the covenant of the Law" provided a hermeneutical and theological foundation for the Calvinists' designation of the Mosaic covenant as a republication of the covenant of works. The Westminster Standards (1643–1648)[15] reflects the mature thought of covenant theology, well developed among the English Puritans in the seventeenth century. In particular, the antithesis between the covenant of works and the covenant of grace is

---

14. Calvin, *Jeremiah*, 32:40.

15. The Westminster Standards includes the Westminster Confession of Faith, the Larger Catechism, and the Shorter Catechism.

beautifully reflected as a confessional form. In the analysis of the Mosaic covenant, the Westminster Standards do not identify the Mosaic covenant as a republication of the covenant of works explicitly. However, that does not mean that the concept of the republication of the covenant of works under the Mosaic covenant is not harmonious with the Confessional teaching. We argue that the comprehensive teaching of the Westminster Standards embraces the idea of the republication of the covenant of works. Therefore, the idea that the republication of the covenant of works in respect to the Mosaic covenant is not Confessional should be rejected.[16]

Charles Hodge is a representative of Reformed orthodox theologians at Princeton Theological Seminary in the nineteenth century along with Benjamin Warfield. Hodge clearly articulated the concept of the republication of the covenant of works under the Mosaic covenant.[17] Hodge rightly affirmed that the first Adam was under the covenant of works. After the first Adam's breach of the covenant of works, no one can accomplish the requirements of the covenant of works except Jesus Christ, the mediator of the New Covenant. According to Hodge, human beings are either in the first Adam or in the last Adam. Those who are under the first Adam are still under the covenant of works. However, those who are in Jesus Christ are under the full benefit of the covenant of grace because Jesus Christ as the mediator of the New Covenant fulfilled all the requirements of the covenant of works.

Interpreting 2 Corinthians 3:6, Hodge articulates that personal salvation under the Mosaic covenant was by the principle of the covenant of grace, inaugurated in Genesis 3:15 after the first Adam's fall. At the same time, "the law of Moses" was "a re-enactment of the covenant of works," where "the promise of life" was suspended "on the condition of perfect obedience." Moreover, Hodge argues that the Mosaic covenant was also "a national covenant" where "national promises" depended upon "the condition of national obedience." In that sense, it was a purely legal covenant:

> This view is presented repeatedly in Paul's epistles, and is argued out in due form in Rom. 3,21–31, Rom. 4, and Gal. 3. To reconcile these apparently conflicting representations it must be remembered that the Mosaic economy was designed to accomplish different objects, and is therefore presented in Scriptures under different aspects. What, therefore, is true of it under one aspect, is not true under another. 1. The law of Moses was, in the first place, a re-enactment of the covenant of works. A covenant is simply a promise suspended upon a condition. The covenant of works, therefore, is nothing more than the promise of life suspended on the condition of perfect obedience. The phrase is used as a concise and convenient expression of the eternal principles of justice on which

---

16. For a comprehensive explanation of the teaching of the Westminster Standards that the republication of the covenant of works under the Mosaic covenant is not absent or contradictory but harmonious, see Fesko, *The Theology of the Westminster Standards*, 125–67; Jeon, *Covenant Theology*, 40–45.

17. For Hodge's view on covenant theology, including the Mosaic covenant and other related issues, see Hart, "Princeton and the Law: Enlightened and Reformed," 44–65; Jeon, *Covenant Theology*, 69–79.

God deals with rational creatures, and which underlie all dispensations, the Adamic, Abrahamic, Mosaic and Christian. Our Lord said to the lawyer who asked what he should do to inherit eternal life, "What is written in the law? How readest thou? And he answering said, Thou shalt love the Lord thy God with all thy heart, and with all thy soul, and with all thy strength, and with all thy mind; and thy neighbor as thyself. And he said unto him, Thou hast answered right, this do and thou shalt live," Luke 10, 26–28. This is the covenant of works. It is an immutable principle that where there is no sin there is no condemnation, and where there is sin there is death. This is all that those who reject the gospel have to fall back upon. It is this principle which is rendered so prominent in the Mosaic economy as to give its character of law. Viewed under this aspect it is the ministration of condemnation and death. 2. The Mosaic economy was also a national covenant; that is, it presented national promises on the condition of national obedience. Under this aspect also it was purely legal. But 3, as the gospel contains a renewed revelation of the law, so the law of Moses contained the revelation of the gospel. It presented in its priesthood and sacrifices, as types of the office and work of Christ, the gratuitous method of salvation through a Redeemer. This necessarily supposes that faith and not works was the condition of salvation . . . The law, in every form, moral or Mosaic, natural or revealed, kills. In demanding works as the condition of salvation, it must condemn all sinners. But the gospel, whether as revealed in the promise to Adam after his fall, or in the promise to Abraham, or in the writings of Moses, or in its full clearness in the New Testament, gives life. As the old covenant revealed both the law and the gospel, it either killed or gave life, according to the light in which it was viewed. And therefore Paul sometimes says it does the one, and sometimes the other. *But the spirit giveth life.* The spirit or the gospel, gives life in a sense correlative to that in which *the letter* (i.e. the law) kills.[18]

This is the hermeneutical and theological background in which Hodge carefully articulated and laid out his understanding of the concept of the republication of the covenant of works under the Mosaic covenant. In that sense, the antithesis between the covenant of works and the covenant of grace was a hermeneutical principle to properly understand and interpret redemptive history, containing the grand drama of the creation, fall, redemption and consummation.

It is important to know that Hodge's thought on the republication of the covenant of works under the Mosaic covenant was well received during his time. It is because his teaching was not only biblical but also harmonious with the Westminster Standards which were the confessional standards at Old Princeton.

---

18. Hodge, *1&2 Corinthians*, 433–34.

Biblical Theology

The Mosaic Covenant as the Covenant of Law and Its Implication

As already explored, personal salvation under the Sinaitic covenant was based upon God's grace alone in Christ, deeply rooted in the eternal covenant of redemption compacted by the triune God. Nevertheless, the continuation and national security of the theocratic kingdom of Israel in the Promised Land depended upon the obedience of the covenant community of Israel (Lev 18:1–5). In that sense, we suggest that the Mosaic covenant as the covenant of law was applied in the history of the ancient Israel after the covenant was inaugurated on Mt. Sinai. In light of this, the Mosaic covenant as the covenant of law was a temporary covenant which applied to the covenant community of ancient Israel until the fall of Jerusalem in A.D. 70 by the military campaign of the Roman Empire. Furthermore, it was a breakable covenant, because the covenant community of Israel made a sworn oath to the Mosaic covenant. Yahweh used blessings and curses, based upon the terms of the covenant throughout the history of ancient Israel, after the inauguration of the Mosaic covenant.

Nevertheless, the Old Testament defines the Mosaic covenant as an everlasting covenant. For example, Yahweh regulated food offerings for the tabernacle after he made the covenant with the Israelites. In doing so, he guided the regulation of bread for the tabernacle which would be a part of an everlasting covenant:

> 5 "You shall take fine flour and bake twelve loaves from it; two tenths of an ephah shall be in each loaf. 6 And you shall set them in two piles, six in a pile, on the table of pure gold before the LORD. 7 And you shall put pure frankincense on each pile, that it may go with the bread as a memorial portion as a food offering to the LORD. 8 *Every Sabbath day Aaron shall arrange it before the LORD regularly; it is from the people of Israel as a covenant forever* [בְּיוֹם הַשַּׁבָּת בְּיוֹם הַשַּׁבָּת יַעַרְכֶנּוּ לִפְנֵי יְהוָה תָּמִיד מֵאֵת בְּנֵי־יִשְׂרָאֵל בְּרִית עוֹלָם:]. 9 And it shall be for Aaron and his sons, and they shall eat it in a holy place, since it is for him a most holy portion out of the LORD's food offerings, a perpetual due." (Lev 24:5–10)

This indicates that the original historical context of the Mosaic covenant identified the covenant as "an everlasting covenant."[19] Later, Isaiah prophesied that the earth would be cursed because people have "transgressed the laws, violated the statutes, broken the everlasting covenant." Isaiah's prophecy about a curse upon the earth due to the violation of the everlasting covenant is another confirmation that the Mosaic covenant was an everlasting covenant like the Abrahamic covenant, as well as the Davidic covenant.

> 1 Behold, the LORD will empty the earth and make it desolate, and he will twist its surface and scatter its inhabitants. 2 And it shall be, as with the people, so with the priest; as with the slave, so with his master; as with the maid, so

---

19. KJV translates Leviticus 24:8 as follows: "Every Sabbath he shall set it in order before the LORD continually, *being taken* from the children of Israel by an everlasting covenant." It properly translates "בְּרִית עוֹלָם" as "an everlasting covenant."

with her mistress; as with the buyer, so with the seller; as with the lender, so with the borrower; as with the creditor, so with the debtor. 3 The earth shall be utterly empty and utterly plundered; for the LORD has spoken this word. 4 The earth mourns and withers; the world languishes and withers; the highest people of the earth languish. 5 *The earth lies defiled under its inhabitants; for they have transgressed the laws, violated the statutes, broken the everlasting covenant* [הָאָרֶץ חָנְפָה תַּחַת יֹשְׁבֶיהָ כִּי־עָבְרוּ תוֹרֹת חָלְפוּ חֹק הֵפֵרוּ בְּרִית עוֹלָם]. 6 Therefore a curse devours the earth, and its inhabitants suffer for their guilt; therefore the inhabitants of the earth are scorched, and few men are left. (Isa 24:1–6)

As discussed, the Mosaic covenant was a temporary covenant because it was specifically applied to the covenant community of Israel during the forty years of pilgrimage in the wilderness, and in the Promised Land. However, the Old Testament identified it as an everlasting covenant. What is the major reason to call the Mosaic covenant an everlasting covenant when it was a temporary or breakable covenant? It is because all the requirements of the Mosaic covenant of law would be fulfilled in the coming Messiah, Jesus Christ, while the history of ancient Israel proved that the Israelites failed to accomplish the requirements of the Mosaic law even though they made a sworn oath to obey it in the presence of Yahweh.

Jesus Christ, the Messiah, was well aware that one of his earthly missions was to fulfill the requirements of the Mosaic law, which the covenant community of Israel failed to do. In the beginning of his public ministry, Jesus delivered the Sermon on the Mount (Matt 5:1—7:29). He spoke about the law, proclaiming that he did not come "to abolish the Law or the Prophets . . . but to fulfill them":

> 17 "Do not think that I have come to abolish the Law or the Prophets; I have not come to abolish them but to fulfill them. 18 For truly, I say to you, until heaven and earth pass away, not an iota, not a dot, will pass from the Law until all is accomplished [17 Μὴ νομίσητε ὅτι ἦλθον καταλῦσαι τὸν νόμον ἢ τοὺς προφήτας· οὐκ ἦλθον καταλῦσαι ἀλλὰ πληρῶσαι. 18 ἀμὴν γὰρ λέγω ὑμῖν· ἕως ἂν παρέλθῃ ὁ οὐρανὸς καὶ ἡ γῆ, ἰῶτα ἓν ἢ μία κεραία οὐ μὴ παρέλθῃ ἀπὸ τοῦ νόμου, ἕως ἂν πάντα γένηται.]. 19 Therefore whoever relaxes one of the least of these commandments and teaches others to do the same will be called least in the kingdom of heaven, but whoever does them and teaches them will be called great in the kingdom of heaven. 20 For I tell you, unless your righteousness exceeds that of the scribes and Pharisees, you will never enter the kingdom of heaven. (Matt 5:17–20)

In these words, Jesus showed that a part of the mission of his first coming was to fulfill the Old Testament prophecy. In addition, he anticipated that he would fulfill all the requirements of the Mosaic law through his life and death, whereas the covenant community of Israel failed to obey it, as the history of ancient Israel testified.

The Mosaic covenant as the covenant of law was immediately effective after Yahweh ratified it to the covenant community (Ex 19—24). After Yahweh made the covenant with Israel on Mt. Sinai, he commanded Moses to climb up Mount Sinai to receive "the tablets of stone, with the law and the commandment." So, Moses climbed up "into the mountain of God" with his assistant Joshua (Ex 24:12-14).

The people of Israel built the tabernacle according to Yahweh's masterful design, given to Moses (Ex 35:30—39:43). As the people of Israel obediently built the tabernacle according to Yahweh's masterful design and commandment to Moses, they brought the tabernacle parts to Moses. And Moses blessed the people of Israel (Ex 39:32-43). Moses erected the tabernacle according to all that Yahweh commanded him (Ex 40:1-33). As Moses erected the tabernacle, the glory of the Lord moved from Mount Sinai to the tabernacle. And the shining and beautiful glory filled the tabernacle:

> 34 Then the cloud covered the tent of meeting, and the glory of the LORD filled the tabernacle. 35 And Moses was not able to enter the tent of meeting because the cloud settled on it, and the glory of the LORD filled the tabernacle. 36 Throughout all their journeys, whenever the cloud was taken up from over the tabernacle, the people of Israel would set out. 37 But if the cloud was not taken up, then they did not set out till the day that it was taken up. 38 For the cloud of the LORD was on the tabernacle by day, and fire was in it by night, in the sight of all the house of Israel throughout all their journeys. (Ex 40:34-38)

After the erection of the tabernacle, the glory of the Lord was visibly present on it. The glory of the Lord had the visible form of the cloud "on the tabernacle by day." And it changed into the visible form of fire on the tabernacle by night. The entire house of Israel saw the visible form of the glory of the Lord throughout all their pilgrimage in the wilderness. Strikingly, the visible form of the glory of the Lord on the tabernacle became the means of Yahweh's blessings and curses in the wilderness, according to the terms of the Mosaic law.

After the tabernacle was erected, the covenant community began to take a journey toward the Promised Land, following the visible guidance of the glory of the Lord. The first journey from the wilderness of Mount Sinai to the wilderness of Paran took place as the cloud of the Lord lifted from "over the tabernacle of testimony":

> 11 In the second year, in the second month, on the twentieth day of the month, the cloud lifted from over the tabernacle of the testimony, 12 and the people of Israel set out by stages from the wilderness of Sinai. And the cloud settled down in the wilderness of Paran. 13 They set out for the first time at the command of the LORD by Moses. 14 The standard of the camp of the people of Judah set out first by their companies, and over their company was Nahshon the son of Amminadab. 15 And over the company of the tribe of the people of Issachar was Nethanel the son of Zuar. 16 And over the company of the tribe of the people of Zebulun was Eliab the son of Helon. (Num 10:11-16)

The Mosaic Covenant and the Kingdom of God

In the midst of the pilgrimage to the Promised Land, Yahweh told Moses to send the twelve representatives out from the twelve tribes of Israel to spy out the land of Canaan. Moses sent out twelve spies to the land of Canaan (Num 13:1–24). After forty days, twelve representatives returned from spying out of the land of Canaan. They came to Moses, Aaron, and the entire covenant community of Israel in the wilderness of Paran at Kadesh. Ten out of twelve representatives gave a negative report. However, Caleb gave a positive report of the Land of Canaan (Num 13:25–33). Paying attention to the bad report from the ten representatives, the entire covenant community of Israel wept and grumbled against Moses and Aaron. And they were against Yahweh, saying "Let us choose a leader and go back to Egypt" (Num 14:1–4).

Witnessing rebellion and disobedience to Yahweh, Moses and Aaron grieved. Joshua and Caleb, who spied the land of Canaan, tried to appease the entire covenant community of Israel, saying "The land, which we passed through to spy it out, is an exceedingly good land."[20] However, the covenant community did not trust Caleb's and Joshua's report. Instead, they tried to stone Caleb and Joshua:

> 5 Then Moses and Aaron fell on their faces before all the assembly of the congregation of the people of Israel. 6 And Joshua the son of Nun and Caleb the son of Jephunneh, who were among those who had spied out the land, tore

---

20. Canaan, as the Promised Land under the Mosaic Covenant, was the type of the everlasting Kingdom of Heaven. When the covenant people of Israel inherited the Promised Land, they didn't look back to the Garden of Eden, but meditated on the everlasting Kingdom of Heaven, which was typified by Canaan. In that sense, the Promised Land was not "Eden recaptured" or "paradise recovered" as Dumbrell argues: "The fertility of the land is the subject of comment in Deut. 26 (v.9) and thus the gift of the first fruits in that chapter is linked not only with Yahweh's ownership, but also with the fact of historical redemption. We note that the references to the land in chapter 26 in terms of its potential yield are similar in type to those reported by the scouts who had been sent out (cf. Num. 13:27) to evaluate the future homeland. In Deuteronomy the promised land is extravagantly idealized. It is the very quintessence of fertility and fruitfulness . . . From a covenant point of view, the implications of all this are as important as they are obvious. *One can hardly escape the impression that what is being depicted through such references is Eden recaptured, paradise recovered*. Since it had been anticipated that the promised land would be a sanctuary for Yahweh, such a picture is a consistent one. In keeping with its sanctuary status and equally consistent with such high expectation surrounding the use of the land, everything which was unclean or which threatened to pollute Israel was required to be removed." Dumbrell, *Covenant and Creation*, 119–20, emphasis added. Similarly, Goldsworthy insists that the entrance of the people of Israel into the Promised Land after their redemption from Egypt is "a picture of a return to Eden." The concept of "a return to Eden" in the Promised Land, however, undermines the important fact that God's redemptive history never looks back but always flows toward the future, which is final judgment and consummation. Moreover, he confuses 'regeneration,' which is a personal soteriological term, for a synonym of 'recreation': "If the covenant with Abraham stands behind the whole process of redemption in Israel, behind the covenant with Abraham stands God's original commitment to the creation. In the end-of-chapter summaries I have emphasized the theme of creation and re-creation. That which God *generated* through the fall of mankind. Redemption and salvation are seen as the process of *regeneration*, which affects the whole degenerated creation, including mankind. Thus the captivity in Egypt is a historical experience which underlines the reality of the fall into sin and the ejection from the Kingdom of God as it was experienced in the garden of Eden. Redemption from Egypt into the Promised Land, the land flowing with milk and honey, is a picture of a return to Eden. The kingship of David recalls the rule or dominion that God gave to Adam in Eden." Goldsworthy, *According to Plan*, 188.

their clothes 7 and said to all the congregation of the people of Israel, "The land, which we passed through to spy it out, is an exceedingly good land. 8 If the LORD delights in us, he will bring us into this land and give it to us, a land that flows with milk and honey. 9 Only do not rebel against the LORD. And do not fear the people of the land, for they are bread for us. Their protection is removed from them, and the LORD is with us; do not fear them." 10 Then all the congregation said to stone them with stones. But the glory of the LORD appeared at the tent of meeting to all the people of Israel. (Num 14:5–10)

As the covenant community tried to stone Caleb and Joshua, the visible glory of the Lord appeared at the tent of meeting to the entire covenant community of Israel. In the midst of this crisis, Moses interceded for them, asking Yahweh to pardon their sins and disobedience (Num 14:13–19). Listening to Moses' intercession, Yahweh told Moses that he pardoned the sins of the entire covenant community. Yahweh's forgiveness of the sins of Israel was profound, in that Israel was under the covenant of grace in terms of their personal salvation and redemptive blessings. This is another affirmation that the internal substance of the Mosaic covenant was the covenant of grace.

Nevertheless, Yahweh pronounced his execution of the covenant lawsuit against the men who observed God's glory and signs in Egypt and in the wilderness but chose not to obey his words. And he cursed the disobedient so that they would not see the land of Canaan, the Promised Land (Num 14:20–25). The prophetic pronouncement of curse and death upon the disobedient Israel was another profound historical evidence that Israel was also under the covenant of law in which Yahweh executed blessings and curses, life and death, according to the obedience and disobedience of Israel under the Mosaic covenant.

Yahweh instructed Moses and Aaron that, with the exception of Caleb and Joshua, all the people "from twenty years old and upward" would not come into the land of Canaan, which he had sworn by an oath to give to the covenant community of Israel. Yahweh pronounced curses against the disobedient covenant community that their children would suffer forty years in the wilderness and they would all die in the wilderness. And the ten representatives, who were sent to spy out the land of Canaan and returned and brought up "a bad report about the land," died by a plague before Yahweh immediately:

26 And the LORD spoke to Moses and to Aaron, saying, 27 "How long shall this wicked congregation grumble against me? I have heard the grumblings of the people of Israel, which they grumble against me. 28 Say to them, 'As I live, declares the LORD, what you have said in my hearing I will do to you: 29 your dead bodies shall fall in this wilderness, and of all your number, listed in the census from twenty years old and upward, who have grumbled against me, 30 not one shall come into the land where I swore that I would make you dwell, except Caleb the son of Jephunneh and Joshua the son of Nun. 31 But your little ones, who you said would become a prey, I will bring in, and they

shall know the land that you have rejected. 32 But as for you, your dead bodies shall fall in this wilderness. 33 And your children shall be shepherds in the wilderness forty years and shall suffer for your faithlessness, until the last of your dead bodies lies in the wilderness. 34 According to the number of the days in which you spied out the land, forty days, a year for each day, you shall bear your iniquity forty years, and you shall know my displeasure.' 35 I, the LORD, have spoken. Surely this will I do to all this wicked congregation who are gathered together against me: in this wilderness they shall come to a full end, and there they shall die." 36 And the men whom Moses sent to spy out the land, who returned and made all the congregation grumble against him by bringing up a bad report about the land—37 the men who brought up a bad report of the land died by plague before the LORD. 38 Of those men who went to spy out the land, only Joshua the son of Nun and Caleb the son of Jephunneh remained alive. (Num 14:26–38)

Yahweh's pronouncement of the suffering of forty years in the wilderness and the death of the disobedient people "from twenty years old and upward," except Caleb and Joshua, and the immediate death of the men who returned and brought a bad report of the Promised Land suggest that Yahweh executed blessings and curses of the Mosaic covenant of law after the covenant was ratified and inaugurated.[21]

As Yahweh renewed the Mosaic covenant with the covenant community, Moses reminded the people of Israel their history from Mount Sinai to the plain of Moab (Deut 1:6—3:29). Strikingly, Yahweh's pronouncement of curse against the men of "twenty years old and upward" was fulfilled during their sojourn in the wilderness for forty years. Moses reminded the covenant community about this in his description of the time in the wilderness:

14 And the time from our leaving Kadesh-barnea until we crossed the brook Zered was thirty-eight years, until the entire generation, that is, the men of war, had perished from the camp, as the LORD had sworn to them. 15 For indeed the hand of the LORD was against them, to destroy them from the camp,

---

21. Kline insightfully compares Israel's forty years wilderness with the Babylonian captivity. And he rightly considers the forty years wilderness and the Babylonian captivity, both enacted against disobedient Israel, as Yahweh's execution of the curse sanction of the Sinaitic covenant of law: "This period of roughly forty years was comparable to the late time of the nation's removal to Babylon. It was a virtual exile from the promised land even before they entered it, an executing of the curse sanction of the Sinaitic covenant of works. Here we must recall our earlier, introductory analysis of the relation of the Sinaitic covenant to the Abrahamic kingdom promise. The law did not abrogate God's promise covenant to Abraham. The Lord's sovereign grace relationship to the promised seed of Abraham, the true Israel, remained intact during the forty year hiatus from the typological kingdom program. Moreover, since (as we observed above) God's typological kingdom grant to Abraham assured the continuance of the Israelite covenant nation until the advent of the messianic seed of Abraham, the renewal of the broken Law covenant and the typological order after the forty years disruption was assured." Kline, *God, Heaven and Har magedon*, 132–33. Although Kline uses the phrase, "the Sinaitic covenant of works," we recommend changing it to "the Sinaitic covenant of law." In so doing, we can avoid confusion between the Adamic covenant of works and the Sinaitic covenant of law.

until they had perished. 16 "So as soon as all the men of war had perished and were dead from among the people, 17 the LORD said to me, 18 'Today you are to cross the border of Moab at Ar. 19 And when you approach the territory of the people of Ammon, do not harass them or contend with them, for I will not give you any of the land of the people of Ammon as a possession, because I have given it to the sons of Lot for a possession.' (Deut 2:14–19)

Almost nine centuries after the Sinaitic covenant was inaugurated, Jeremiah witnessed the basest time in ancient Israel's history. He was an eyewitness to the fall of the southern kingdom of Judah at the time of the reign of King Zedekiah. Before the fall of Jerusalem by the power of the Babylonian kingdom, Yahweh warned through the prophet Jeremiah that the southern kingdom of Judah would face catastrophic judgment because "the house of Judah have broken the covenant" made with their forefathers on Mt. Sinai:

1 The word that came to Jeremiah from the LORD: 2 "Hear the words of this covenant, and speak to the men of Judah and the inhabitants of Jerusalem. 3 You shall say to them, Thus says the LORD, the God of Israel: Cursed be the man who does not hear the words of this covenant 4 that I commanded your fathers when I brought them out of the land of Egypt, from the iron furnace, saying, Listen to my voice, and do all that I command you. So shall you be my people, and I will be your God, 5 that I may confirm the oath that I swore to your fathers, to give them a land flowing with milk and honey, as at this day." Then I answered, "So be it, LORD." 6 And the LORD said to me, "Proclaim all these words in the cities of Judah and in the streets of Jerusalem: Hear the words of this covenant and do them. 7 For I solemnly warned your fathers when I brought them up out of the land of Egypt, warning them persistently, even to this day, saying, Obey my voice. 8 Yet they did not obey or incline their ear, but everyone walked in the stubbornness of his evil heart. Therefore I brought upon them all the words of this covenant, which I commanded them to do, but they did not." 9 Again the LORD said to me, "A conspiracy exists among the men of Judah and the inhabitants of Jerusalem. 10 They have turned back to the iniquities of their forefathers, who refused to hear my words. They have gone after other gods to serve them. The house of Israel and the house of Judah have broken my covenant that I made with their fathers. 11 Therefore, thus says the LORD, behold, I am bringing disaster upon them that they cannot escape. Though they cry to me, I will not listen to them. 12 Then the cities of Judah and the inhabitants of Jerusalem will go and cry to the gods to whom they make offerings, but they cannot save them in the time of their trouble. 13 For your gods have become as many as your cities, O Judah, and as many as the streets of Jerusalem are the altars you have set up to shame, altars to make offerings to Baal. 14 "Therefore do not pray for this people, or lift up a cry or prayer on their behalf, for I will not listen when they call to me in the time of their trouble. 15 What right has my beloved in my house, when she has done many vile deeds? Can even sacrificial flesh avert your

doom? Can you then exult? 16 The LORD once called you 'a green olive tree, beautiful with good fruit.' But with the roar of a great tempest he will set fire to it, and its branches will be consumed. 17 The LORD of hosts, who planted you, has decreed disaster against you, because of the evil that the house of Israel and the house of Judah have done, provoking me to anger by making offerings to Baal." (Jer 11:1–17)

The history of ancient Israel after the inauguration of the Sinaitic covenant proves that this covenant was breakable and temporary. In the execution of blessings and curses according to the terms of the Mosaic covenant of law, Israel experienced blessings and curses in the wilderness for forty years and in the Promised Land. When Yahweh blessed Israel, the Israelites enjoyed the blessings and meditated on the future blessings in the heavenly Kingdom of God, the ultimate blessing of the covenant of grace. However, when Israel underwent Yahweh's curses in the wilderness and in the Promised Land due to their disobedience, they were given a foretaste of the final judgment of hell. So, the blessings and curses in the history of ancient Israel, according to the terms of the covenant of law, were shadows and types of the heavenly absolution and hellish blight. Through this historical reality, Yahweh envisioned the eschatological blessings of the heavenly Kingdom of God and the eschatological curses of hell. This can be identified as the Old Covenant eschatology, revealed and manifested in the history of ancient Israel after the inauguration of the Sinaitic covenant.

The Sign of the Mosaic Covenant and National Covenant of Israel

When Yahweh made the Abrahamic covenant, he assigned circumcision as the sign of the covenant. Thus, he commanded Abraham that every covenant son born into the covenant family should be circumcised when he was eight days old (Gen 17:1–14). Later, Yahweh commanded Moses that the covenant son should be circumcised so that "on the eighth day the flesh of his foreskin" should be circumcised even under the Mosaic covenant:

> 1 The LORD spoke to Moses, saying, 2 "Speak to the people of Israel, saying, 'If a woman conceives and bears a male child, then she shall be unclean seven days. As at the time of her menstruation, she shall be unclean. 3 And on the eighth day the flesh of his foreskin shall be circumcised. 4 Then she shall continue for thirty-three days in the blood of her purifying. She shall not touch anything holy, nor come into the sanctuary, until the days of her purifying are completed. 5 But if she bears a female child, then she shall be unclean two weeks, as in her menstruation. And she shall continue in the blood of her purifying for sixty-six days. (Lev 12:1–5)

Yahweh's command to circumcise the covenant son of the people of Israel was significant. It meant that the promised blessings of the covenant of grace, represented by the Abrahamic covenant were continued even after the inauguration of the Mosaic covenant at Mount Sinai (Ex 19—24).

After the people of Israel crossed the Jordan River, Yahweh commanded Joshua to circumcise the whole nation of Israel at Gilgal. The sons of Israel, who were born during the forty years in the wilderness, were not circumcised. So, according to Yahweh's command, Joshua circumcised all the sons before the people of Israel waged holy war against the city of Jericho:

> 2 At that time the LORD said to Joshua, "Make flint knives and circumcise the sons of Israel a second time." 3 So Joshua made flint knives and circumcised the sons of Israel at Gibeath-haaraloth. 4 And this is the reason why Joshua circumcised them: all the males of the people who came out of Egypt, all the men of war, had died in the wilderness on the way after they had come out of Egypt. 5 Though all the people who came out had been circumcised, yet all the people who were born on the way in the wilderness after they had come out of Egypt had not been circumcised. 6 For the people of Israel walked forty years in the wilderness, until all the nation, the men of war who came out of Egypt, perished, because they did not obey the voice of the LORD; the LORD swore to them that he would not let them see the land that the LORD had sworn to their fathers to give to us, a land flowing with milk and honey. 7 So it was their children, whom he raised up in their place, that Joshua circumcised. For they were uncircumcised, because they had not been circumcised on the way. 8 When the circumcising of the whole nation was finished, they remained in their places in the camp until they were healed. 9 And the LORD said to Joshua, "Today I have rolled away the reproach of Egypt from you." And so the name of that place is called Gilgal to this day. (Josh 5:2–9)

In light of redemptive history, the circumcision of the sons of the entire nation at Gilgal was significant. It signified that the blessings and promises of the covenant of grace after the inauguration of the Abrahamic covenant were continued even under the Mosaic covenant of law. Moreover, it was divine wisdom to command the circumcision of the entire nation before the people of Israel began to conquer the Promised Land under the leadership of Joshua. The sons of Israel were able to carry the visible sign of the covenant of grace in their own bodies as they waged holy war against the inhabitants of Canaan, who were not only uncircumcised pagans but also idol worshippers. According to the Mosaic law, idol worship resulted in capital punishment. So, the continuation of the circumcision of the sons of Israel under the Mosaic covenant was another good indication that the internal substance of the Mosaic covenant was the covenant of grace, even though its external form had the covenant of law.

However, Yahweh did not assign circumcision as the sign of the Mosaic covenant. Rather, he constituted keeping the Sabbath holy as the sign of the Mosaic covenant between Yahweh and the people of Israel.

> 12 And the LORD said to Moses, 13 "You are to speak to the people of Israel and say, 'Above all you shall keep my Sabbaths, for this is a sign between me and you throughout your generations, that you may know that I, the LORD, sanctify you. 14 You shall keep the Sabbath, because it is holy for you. Everyone who profanes it shall be put to death. Whoever does any work on it, that soul shall be cut off from among his people. 15 Six days shall work be done, but the seventh day is a Sabbath of solemn rest, holy to the LORD. Whoever does any work on the Sabbath day shall be put to death. 16 Therefore the people of Israel shall keep the Sabbath, observing the Sabbath throughout their generations, as a covenant forever. 17 It is a sign forever between me and the people of Israel that in six days the LORD made heaven and earth, and on the seventh day he rested and was refreshed.'" 18 And he gave to Moses, when he had finished speaking with him on Mount Sinai, the two tablets of the testimony, tablets of stone, written with the finger of God. (Ex 31:14–18)

Likewise, after the inauguration of the Mosaic covenant, Yahweh revealed to Moses that the sign of the covenant between him and the people of Israel would not be circumcision but keeping the Sabbath holy.

Why did Yahweh assign keeping the Sabbath holy as the sign of the Mosaic covenant? In fact, the inauguration of the Mosaic covenant was the official inauguration of the theocratic kingdom of Israel with the people of Israel, anticipating the possession of the Promised Land and the future king of Israel. After the Exodus, the people of Israel arrived and encamped at Mount Sinai. Moses went up Mount Sinai to Yahweh. And Yahweh revealed to Moses that the people of Israel would be "a kingdom of priests and a holy nation." As such, the people of Israel were set apart from pagan nations on the earth:

> 1 On the third new moon after the people of Israel had gone out of the land of Egypt, on that day they came into the wilderness of Sinai. 2 They set out from Rephidim and came into the wilderness of Sinai, and they encamped in the wilderness. There Israel encamped before the mountain, 3 while Moses went up to God. The LORD called to him out of the mountain, saying, "Thus you shall say to the house of Jacob, and tell the people of Israel: 4 You yourselves have seen what I did to the Egyptians, and how I bore you on eagles' wings and brought you to myself. 5 Now therefore, if you will indeed obey my voice and keep my covenant, you shall be my treasured possession among all peoples, for all the earth is mine; 6 and you shall be to me a kingdom of priests and a holy nation. These are the words that you shall speak to the people of Israel." (Ex 19:1–6)

Charles Hodge persuasively argues that personal salvation under the Mosaic covenant depended on the principle of the covenant of grace. Nevertheless, the people of Israel as a holy nation were under "a legal covenant" which has a principle of "Do this and live," represented in Leviticus 18:5:

> Besides this evangelical character which unquestionably belongs to the Mosaic covenant, it is presented in two other aspects in the Word of God. First, it was a national covenant with the Hebrew people. In this view the parties were God and the people of Israel; the promise was national security and prosperity; the condition was the obedience of the people as a nation to the Mosaic law; and the mediator was Moses. In this respect it was a *legal covenant*. It said, 'Do this and live.'[22]

Therefore, as Hodge argues, the Mosaic covenant as "a national covenant" was not a covenant of grace but "a legal covenant." That is one reason why Israel's keeping the Sabbath holy was the visible sign of a holy nation, which would be the theocratic kingdom of Israel in the Promised Land. After the inauguration of the Mosaic covenant on Mount Sinai, the people of Israel kept the Sabbath holy as a holy nation. During the forty years in the wilderness, the people of Israel anticipated the Sabbath rest in the Promised Land, which was the fulfillment of the Abrahamic covenant. As the people of Israel kept the Sabbath holy in the Promised Land after they entered it, they anticipated heavenly rest, which would be fully realized in the heavenly Kingdom of God, which was typified by the theocratic kingdom of Israel. So, the complete cessation of work and rest on the Sabbath day by the people of Israel as a holy nation was to symbolize rest in the heavenly Kingdom of God. This is the reason why Yahweh pronounced the death penalty against violators of the Sabbath among the people of Israel.

When the people of Israel were in the wilderness, they found a man who violated the Sabbath day by collecting sticks. People brought him to Moses, Aaron and to the entire assembly of Israel. According to Yahweh's command to Moses, the entire assembly of Israel took him outside of the camp and stoned him to death:

> 32 While the people of Israel were in the wilderness, they found a man gathering sticks on the Sabbath day. 33 And those who found him gathering sticks brought him to Moses and Aaron and to all the congregation. 34 They put him in custody, because it had not been made clear what should be done to him. 35 And the LORD said to Moses, "The man shall be put to death; all the congregation shall stone him with stones outside the camp." 36 And all the congregation brought him outside the camp and stoned him to death with stones, as the LORD commanded Moses. (Num 15:32–36)

It was Yahweh's wisdom to order the death penalty against the people of Israel, who violated the regulation of the Sabbath day. The people of Israel as a holy nation under the Mosaic covenant had to typify the eternal rest of the heavenly Kingdom of God, which would be consummated in the Second Coming of Jesus Christ. After the inauguration of the New Covenant, Jesus Christ began to rule the heavenly Kingdom of God with his exalted enthronement in heaven. So, the theocratic kingdom of Israel in the Promised Land fulfilled its purpose on earth and it was officially terminated by

---

22. Hodge, *Systematic Theology*, 2:375, emphasis mine.

the fall of Jerusalem in A.D. 70. At the same time, keeping the Sabbath holy as the *sign* of the Mosaic covenant between Yahweh and the people of Israel was terminated as well. In that sense, the violation of the Sabbath day by the covenant members under the New Covenant is no longer the subject of death penalty, but church discipline.

The Renewals of the Mosaic Covenant

The descendents of Abraham, Isaac, and Jacob became numerous like the stars in the sky, as God had promised in the process of making the Abrahamic covenant. The covenant community of Israel grew and reached several million. In his own sovereign time, God led the covenant community of Israel out of Egyptian bondage under the leadership of the prophet Moses.

When the Israelites came to Mt. Sinai, God made the covenant with them through the mediator Moses (Ex 19—24). At the end of forty years in the wilderness, Yahweh renewed the Mosaic covenant at the plain of Moab. The Book of Deuteronomy records the Mosaic covenant renewal at the end of the pilgrimage in the wilderness before the people of Israel crossed the Jordan River to enter the Promised Land. Under the leadership of Joshua, the covenant community of Israel conquered the Promised Land. After the end of Joshua's life, Yahweh again renewed the Mosaic covenant at Shechem (Josh 24). The covenant renewals also reveal and confirm that the Mosaic covenant had the external form of the covenant of law while its internal substance was the covenant of grace.

The Covenant Renewal at Moab

The first generation of the Exodus almost completely died due to Yahweh's curse during the period of forty years in the wilderness because of their disobedience to the Mosaic law. This historical episode suggests that the Israelites under the Sinaitic covenant were under the covenant of law, in which God applied blessings and curses according to the terms of the law.

Those who were born during the wilderness period escaped Yahweh's curse and were ready to enter the Promised Land. God renewed the Mosaic covenant at the plain of Moab through the prophet Moses before the covenant community of Israel crossed the Jordan River and entered the Promised Land. So the Book of Deuteronomy can be identified as the Book of the covenant renewal of the Mosaic covenant.[23]

---

23. Bruce Waltke denies Moses' authorship of the Pentateuch. Adopting Martin Noth's historical critical hypothesis that Deuteronomy was composed by "an exilic author," Waltke argues that Deuteronomy is the foundation of "the paradigmatic prologue of the Deuteronomic history," originally proclaimed "to the exiles around 550 BC." In this regard, he denies the antiquity of the Pentateuch, as well as its Mosaic authorship: "The book of Deuteronomy was probably written during the exile (ca. 550 BC), about eight centuries after Moses mediated the renewed covenant. By his at least fifty-six additional verses, the Deuteronomist transforms Moses' covenant renewal document into a historical

Remarkably, the structure of the Book of Deuteronomy is similar to the Hittite treaties of the second millennium B.C. The structure of the ancient agreements, represented in the Hittite treaties, include the preamble, historical prologue, stipulations, treaty ratification, and dynastic disposition. Similarly, the Book of Deuteronomy demonstrates the treaty structure, which includes the preamble (1:1–5), historical prologue (1:6—4:49), stipulations (5:1—26:19), dual sanctions (27:1—30:20), and dynastic disposition (31:1—34:12).[24]

Under the Mosaic covenant, blessings and curses or life and death were applied to the covenant people of Israel because it is, in a sense, the covenant of law. Therefore, when the Israelites obeyed God's laws and commandments, he blessed them. However, he cursed them when they disobeyed the Mosaic law. The death of the Exodus generation, including Moses, during the forty years in the wilderness, is historical proof that the Israelites were under the covenant of law. Nevertheless, the Israelites were under the blessings of the covenant of grace, when we consider their personal salvation and the possession of the Promised Land. In that sense, the internal or spiritual substance of the Sinaitic covenant was the covenant of grace.

The Book of Deuteronomy, as the renewal of the Sinaitic covenant, has the structure of the suzerainty covenant, which is the covenant of law. So Moses prophesied that blessings and curses would be applied to the covenant community of Israel when they entered the Promised Land. During the covenant ratification ceremony, Yahweh

---

narrative, probably originally addressed to the exiles but intended for the universal faith community. That community recognizes it as such, and it becomes part of their canon (*norma normanda*) for their faith and practice. The line between story (Moses) and plot (Deuteronomist) is attenuated, however, because the Deuteronomist adds so few verses of his own and many of them are only historical notices . . . By his additions the Deuteronomists shifts the addresses from 'that day' to 'this day,' even as Moses had made a similar shift from the audience of the original covenant at Horeb to its renewal at Moab. This historical form of the covenant renewal now constitutes the basis of the paradigmatic prologue of the Deuteronomic history (= 'Former Prophets'), originally addressed to the exiles around 550 BC but also intended for all Israel and recognized as such as shown by its incorporation into the canon." Waltke, *An Old Testament Theology*, 502.

For the classical defense of the Mosaic authorship of the Pentateuch and its antiquity, see Allis, *The Five Books of Moses*; Kline, *Treaty of the Great King*; Young, *Thy Word is Truth*.

24. The covenant structure of Deuteronomy in light of the ancient Near Eastern treaties has been found in Kline, *Treaty of the Great King*, 1–150. Kline summarizes the covenantal structure of Deuteronomy as follows: "It will be useful to have a simple outline of the matter before us : 1. Preamble (1:1–5). 2. Historical Prologue (1:6–P4:49). 3. Stipulations (5—26). 4. Curses and Blessings or Covenant Ratification (27—30). 5. Succession Arrangements or Covenant Continuity, in which are included the invocation of witnesses and directions for the disposition and public reading of the treaty (31—34)." Ibid., 28. Dillard and Longman properly recognize Kline's contribution that he defends "the antiquity of Deuteronomy" and Deuteronomy as a Mosaic covenant renewal book at the plain of Moab: "During this period researchers also began to notice that the literary structure found in ancient Near Eastern treaties between nations also resembled the structure of Deuteronomy. M. G. Kline argued that the book of Deuteronomy was specifically constructed along the lines of a second-millennium international treaty as distinct from the treaty pattern during the Assyrian period in the first millennium. As a consequence, Kline provided a strong argument for the antiquity of Deuteronomy. Although not all have followed Kline's argument, the relationship of Deuteronomy to ancient Near Eastern covenants and treaties has continued to play a large role in scholarship." Dillard and Longman, *An Introduction to the Old Testament*, 96.

did not make a sworn oath to the covenant. Rather, the covenant community made a sworn oath to the covenant, including children and future generations who were not yet born. After the historical prologue was addressed, Moses explained the stipulations of the law (Deut 5:1—26:49). Moses commanded that the covenant community would have the covenant ratification ceremony after they entered the Promised Land at Mount Gerizim and Mount Ebal (Deut 27:1-26). Strikingly, the twelve curses were announced by Moses. And the covenant people were required to shout "Amen." The act of shouting "Amen" by the covenant community was a self-maledictory oath to the covenant in the presence of Yahweh:

> 11 That day Moses charged the people, saying, 12 "When you have crossed over the Jordan, these shall stand on Mount Gerizim to bless the people: Simeon, Levi, Judah, Issachar, Joseph, and Benjamin. 13 And these shall stand on Mount Ebal for the curse: Reuben, Gad, Asher, Zebulun, Dan, and Naphtali. 14 And the Levites shall declare to all the men of Israel in a loud voice: 15 "'Cursed be the man who makes a carved or cast metal image, an abomination to the LORD, a thing made by the hands of a craftsman, and sets it up in secret.' And all the people shall answer and say, 'Amen.' 16 "'Cursed be anyone who dishonors his father or his mother.' And all the people shall say, 'Amen.' 17 "'Cursed be anyone who moves his neighbor's landmark.' And all the people shall say, 'Amen.' 18 "'Cursed be anyone who misleads a blind man on the road.' And all the people shall say, 'Amen.' 19 "'Cursed be anyone who perverts the justice due to the sojourner, the fatherless, and the widow.' And all the people shall say, 'Amen.' 20 "'Cursed be anyone who lies with his father's wife, because he has uncovered his father's nakedness.' And all the people shall say, 'Amen.' 21 "'Cursed be anyone who lies with any kind of animal.' And all the people shall say, 'Amen.' 22 "'Cursed be anyone who lies with his sister, whether the daughter of his father or the daughter of his mother.' And all the people shall say, 'Amen.' 23 "'Cursed be anyone who lies with his mother-in-law.' And all the people shall say, 'Amen.' 24 "'Cursed be anyone who strikes down his neighbor in secret.' And all the people shall say, 'Amen.' 25 "'Cursed be anyone who takes a bribe to shed innocent blood.' And all the people shall say, 'Amen.' 26 "'Cursed be anyone who does not confirm the words of this law by doing them.' And all the people shall say, 'Amen.' (Deut 27:11-26)

What makes the covenant renewal at Moab special was Yahweh did not make a sworn oath to the covenant. Instead, the entire covenant community made a sworn oath to the covenant, which signifies and confirms that the Mosaic covenant renewal at Moab was the covenant of law in respect to the external form of the covenant. After dual sanctions such as blessings and curses were announced, the covenant community entered the sworn covenant of Yahweh:

> 9 Therefore keep the words of this covenant and do them, that you may prosper in all that you do. 10 "You are standing today all of you before the LORD

> your God: the heads of your tribes, your elders, and your officers, all the men of Israel, 11 your little ones, your wives, and the sojourner who is in your camp, from the one who chops your wood to the one who draws your water, 12 so that you may enter into the sworn covenant of the LORD your God, which the LORD your God is making with you today, 13 that he may establish you today as his people, and that he may be your God, as he promised you, and as he swore to your fathers, to Abraham, to Isaac, and to Jacob. 14 It is not with you alone that I am making this sworn covenant, 15 but with whomever is standing here with us today before the LORD our God, and with whomever is not here with us today. (Deut 29:9–16)

We need to pay special attention to Deuteronomy 29:12, where Moses says "so that you may enter into the sworn covenant of the LORD your God, which the LORD your God is making with you today." Entering into "the sworn covenant of the LORD your God" is actually making a sworn oath to the covenant by the covenant community before Yahweh. In this historical context of the covenant ratification ceremony, Moses reminded the covenant community of the Abrahamic covenant, in which Yahweh made a sworn oath to the covenant before Abraham. It is the reason why Moses noted that Yahweh "swore to your fathers, to Abraham, to Isaac, and to Jacob" (v. 13b).

Moses also prophesied that the blessings of the Abrahamic covenant would be applied to the covenant community. Therefore, a future exile would be based upon Israelites' disobedience to the Mosaic covenant of law. And the restoration from the curse of the exile would be based upon the promissory nature of the Abrahamic covenant, in which Yahweh made a sworn oath before Abraham:

> 25 "When you father children and children's children, and have grown old in the land, if you act corruptly by making a carved image in the form of anything, and by doing what is evil in the sight of the LORD your God, so as to provoke him to anger, 26 I call heaven and earth to witness against you today, that you will soon utterly perish from the land that you are going over the Jordan to possess. You will not live long in it, but will be utterly destroyed. 27 And the LORD will scatter you among the peoples, and you will be left few in number among the nations where the LORD will drive you. 28 And there you will serve gods of wood and stone, the work of human hands, that neither see, nor hear, nor eat, nor smell. 29 But from there you will seek the LORD your God and you will find him, if you search after him with all your heart and with all your soul. 30 When you are in tribulation, and all these things come upon you in the latter days, you will return to the LORD your God and obey his voice. 31 For the LORD your God is a merciful God. He will not leave you or destroy you or forget the covenant with your fathers that he swore to them. (Deut 4:25–31)

In the process of the renewal of the Mosaic covenant at Moab, Moses reminded the people of the promises of the Abrahamic covenant, made to the covenant community of the Promised Land, Abraham, Isaac, and Jacob. In doing so, Moses proclaimed and remembered that God made a sworn oath to Abraham, Isaac, and Jacob for the Abrahamic covenant. Moses emphasized that the possession of the land of Canaan would not be because of the righteousness of Israel. Rather, Yahweh would drive out the Canaanites on account of their wickedness through holy war against them:

> 1 "Hear, O Israel: you are to cross over the Jordan today, to go in to dispossess nations greater and mightier than yourselves, cities great and fortified up to heaven, 2 a people great and tall, the sons of the Anakim, whom you know, and of whom you have heard it said, 'Who can stand before the sons of Anak?' 3 Know therefore today that he who goes over before you as a consuming fire is the LORD your God. He will destroy them and subdue them before you. So you shall drive them out and make them perish quickly, as the LORD has promised you. 4 "Do not say in your heart, after the LORD your God has thrust them out before you, 'It is because of my righteousness that the LORD has brought me in to possess this land,' whereas it is because of the wickedness of these nations that the LORD is driving them out before you. 5 Not because of your righteousness or the uprightness of your heart are you going in to possess their land, but because of the wickedness of these nations the LORD your God is driving them out from before you, and that he may confirm the word that the LORD swore to your fathers, to Abraham, to Isaac, and to Jacob. 6 "Know, therefore, that the LORD your God is not giving you this good land to possess because of your righteousness, for you are a stubborn people. (Deut 9:1–6)

In the wilderness, the covenant community destroyed the cities and people of Sihon and Og, which were located in the eastern side of the Jordan River. The defeat of Sihon, the King of the Amorites and Og, and the King of Bashan, were quite a remarkable event because the covenant community settled there before they crossed the Jordan River (Num 21:21–35). During the covenant renewal, Moses reflected on the defeat of King Sihon and King Og in his address of the historical prologue to the covenant community (Deut 2:28—3:22). Remarkably, Moses revealed the method of the defeat of King Sihon and King Og. It was a holy war which separated the covenant community and non-covenant community. In doing so, Yahweh commanded the covenant community to wage a holy war, the war of total destruction against the cities and people of King Sihon:

> 26 "So I sent messengers from the wilderness of Kedemoth to Sihon the king of Heshbon, with words of peace, saying, 27 'Let me pass through your land. I will go only by the road; I will turn aside neither to the right nor to the left. 28 You shall sell me food for money, that I may eat, and give me water for money, that I may drink. Only let me pass through on foot, 29 as the sons of Esau who live in Seir and the Moabites who live in Ar did for me, until I go over the Jordan into the land that the LORD our God is giving to us.' 30 But Sihon the king of Heshbon would not let us pass by him, for the LORD your

> God hardened his spirit and made his heart obstinate, that he might give him into your hand, as he is this day. 31 And the LORD said to me, 'Behold, I have begun to give Sihon and his land over to you. Begin to take possession, that you may occupy his land.' 32 Then Sihon came out against us, he and all his people, to battle at Jahaz. 33 And the LORD our God gave him over to us, and we defeated him and his sons and all his people. 34 *And we captured all his cities at that time and devoted to destruction every city, men, women, and children. We left no survivors.* 35 Only the livestock we took as spoil for ourselves, with the plunder of the cities that we captured. (Deut 2:26–35)

Verse 34 suggests that Yahweh commanded the covenant community to fight not a common grace war but a holy war against the cities and people of Sihon. And they executed this holy war with the total destruction of "every city, men, women, and children." Afterwards, the covenant community moved up to Bashan. There, they executed another holy war against Og the King of Bashan, all his people, and the kingdom of Og in Bashan:

> 1 "Then we turned and went up the way to Bashan. And Og the king of Bashan came out against us, he and all his people, to battle at Edrei. 2 But the LORD said to me, 'Do not fear him, for I have given him and all his people and his land into your hand. And you shall do to him as you did to Sihon the king of the Amorites, who lived at Heshbon.' 3 So the LORD our God gave into our hand Og also, the king of Bashan, and all his people, and we struck him down until he had no survivor left. 4 And we took all his cities at that time-there was not a city that we did not take from them-sixty cities, the whole region of Argob, the kingdom of Og in Bashan. 5 All these were cities fortified with high walls, gates, and bars, besides very many unwalled villages. 6 And we devoted them to destruction, as we did to Sihon the king of Heshbon, devoting to destruction every city, men, women, and children. 7 But all the livestock and the spoil of the cities we took as our plunder. (Deut 3:1–7)

In recounting this past history, Moses suggests that Yahweh *granted* the land of Bashan through the execution of holy war against the kingdom of Og. In particular, verse 6 says "and we devoted them to destruction, as we did to Sihon the king of Heshbon, devoting to destruction every city, men, women, and children." This shows that the defeat of the kingdom of Og was possible through Yahweh's execution of holy war, the war of total destruction.

The defeat of the kingdom of Sihon and the kingdom of Og has very significant redemptive historical meaning. It was the visible demonstration of Yahweh's will and mighty power that the conquest of the Promised Land would be possible through the execution of holy war. In other words, to grant Israel the Promised Land that was sworn to Abraham, Isaac, and Jacob, Yahweh would not use the method of ordinary or common grace war, but holy war, the war of total destruction (*cherem*). From the perspective of God's eschatological judgment, it would be the eschatological judgment, separating covenant community and non-covenant community. The eschatological judgment against the non-covenant community in the Promised Land was, in fact, a type of the final judgment at the Parousia.

At the end of the covenant ratification ceremony, Moses set before the covenant community life and death, and blessing and curse. Blessing and curse would be based upon obedience or disobedience in the Mosaic law. In doing so, Moses clearly explained that to take possession of the land of Canaan would be based upon the Abrahamic covenant where Yahweh made a sworn oath to the covenant. Meanwhile, the *continuation* of life and blessing in the Promised Land would be dependent upon the covenant community's faithful obedience to the Mosaic law:

> 15 "See, I have set before you today life and good, death and evil. 16 If you obey the commandments of the LORD your God that I command you today, by loving the LORD your God, by walking in his ways, and by keeping his commandments and his statutes and his rules, then you shall live and multiply, and the LORD your God will bless you in the land that you are entering to take possession of it. 17 But if your heart turns away, and you will not hear, but are drawn away to worship other gods and serve them, 18 I declare to you today, that you shall surely perish. You shall not live long in the land that you are going over the Jordan to enter and possess. 19 I call heaven and earth to witness against you today, that I have set before you life and death, blessing and curse. Therefore choose life, that you and your offspring may live, 20 loving the LORD your God, obeying his voice and holding fast to him, for he is your life and length of days, that you may dwell in the land that the LORD swore to your fathers, to Abraham, to Isaac, and to Jacob, to give them." (Deut 30:15–20)

Joshua succeeded the leadership of Moses before his death (Deut 31:1–8). Moses, as the mediator of the Sinaitic covenant, was not able to cross the Jordan River and enter the Promised Land, although he strongly desired it. However, the gracious God allowed Moses to see the Promised Land from Mount Nebo, right before his death. In doing so, Yahweh reminded Moses of the Promised Land, which was an essential part of the promises of the Abrahamic covenant, made also to Isaac and Jacob:

> 1 Then Moses went up from the plains of Moab to Mount Nebo, to the top of Pisgah, which is opposite Jericho. And the LORD showed him all the land, Gilead as far as Dan, 2 all Naphtali, the land of Ephraim and Manasseh, all the land of Judah as far as the western sea, 3 the Negeb, and the Plain, that is, the Valley of Jericho the city of palm trees, as far as Zoar. 4 And the LORD said to him, "This is the land of which I swore to Abraham, to Isaac, and to Jacob, 'I will give it to your offspring.' I have let you see it with your eyes, but you shall not go over there." 5 So Moses the servant of the LORD died there in the land of Moab, according to the word of the LORD, 6 and he buried him in the valley in the land of Moab opposite Beth-peor; but no one knows the place of his burial to this day. 7 Moses was 120 years old when he died. His eye was

undimmed, and his vigor unabated. 8 And the people of Israel wept for Moses in the plains of Moab thirty days. Then the days of weeping and mourning for Moses were ended. (Deut 34:1–8)

Likewise, Moses was not able to walk into the west side of the Jordan River of the Promised Land, even though he was the prophet that led the covenant community of Israel during the Exodus and for forty years in the wilderness, after God made the Sinaitic covenant with the covenant community of Israel. In the process of the Exodus, making the Sinaitic covenant, and forty years in the wilderness, Yahweh endowed Moses not only with the office of prophet but also with a dynastic leadership. In fact, Moses led the Israelites as the kingly leader. So, Moses as the vassal king led the covenant people of the Great King, Yahweh. Nevertheless, the task of conquering the west side of the Jordan River of the Promised Land was not given to Moses, but to Joshua.[25]

The Covenant Renewal at Shechem

As Joshua was appointed to be the leader of Israel after Moses, Yahweh endowed him with "the spirit of wisdom" as Moses laid his hands on Joshua before he passed away and gave his torch of leadership to Joshua:

> 9 And Joshua the son of Nun was full of the spirit of wisdom, for Moses had laid his hands on him. So the people of Israel obeyed him and did as the LORD had commanded Moses. 10 And there has not arisen a prophet since in Israel like Moses, whom the LORD knew face to face, 11 none like him for all the signs and the wonders that the LORD sent him to do in the land of Egypt, to Pharaoh and to all his servants and to all his land, 12 and for all the mighty power and all the great deeds of terror that Moses did in the sight of all Israel. (Deut 34:9–12)

We need to pay attention to the concluding remarks of the Book of Deuteronomy. Verse 9 suggests and anticipates the successful campaign of conquering the land of Canaan. As Joshua became the new political leader of the Israelites, Yahweh endowed him with "the spirit of wisdom." And the covenant community of Israel obeyed Joshua.

25. The Book of Deuteronomy as the renewal document of the Sinaitic covenant is "a dynastic covenant," as Kline suggests. In fact, Moses' role was as a vassal king who represented the covenant community of Israel on behalf of Yahweh, the Great King. And Joshua succeeded Moses' role as a vassal king: "There, east of the Jordan in the plains of Moab, the mission of Moses came to a close with his mediating a renewal of the Sinaitic covenant. The documentation of this covenant is found in the Book of Deuteronomy, whose over-all structure, like the Sinaitic treaty tablets, conformed to that of the international suzerain-vassal treaties of the second millennium BC . . . This summons to Israel to swear anew their covenantal commitment to Yahweh was more specifically a call to affirm their acceptance of his new representative, Joshua, the appointed successor of Moses (Num 27:15–23; Deut 3:28; 31:3, 7; 34:9). The Deuteronomic Covenant was a dynastic covenant. Such covenants became of force at the death of the current king—in the case of Deuteronomy, the death of the heavenly Sovereign's earthly representative. Accordingly, the Book of Deuteronomy closes with a notice of the death of Moses, attesting that the Deuteronomic Covenant was now in effect." Kline, *God, Heaven and Har Magedon*, 134.

The Mosaic Covenant and the Kingdom of God

Under the wise and strong leadership of Joshua, Israel crossed the Jordan River (Josh 3:1–17). Just as Yahweh divided the water when Israel crossed the Red Sea, he divided the water of the Jordan River so that the people of Israel began to walk into the land of Canaan. Afterwards, the people of Israel began to conquer the land of Canaan from Jericho to Southern and Northern Canaan (Josh 6:1—12:24). As Joshua aged, Yahweh commanded him to divide and allocate the Promised Land, even though there remained a lot of land to possess (Josh 13:1–7). Joshua divided and allotted the conquered land of Canaan to the tribes of Israel (Josh 13:8—21:45). In fact, the conquest of Canaan under the leadership of Joshua was successful because the people of Israel obeyed Joshua's command. However, it is important to remember that Yahweh *granted* "to Israel all the land that he swore to give" to Abraham, Isaac, and Jacob:

> 43 Thus the LORD gave to Israel all the land that he swore to give to their fathers. And they took possession of it, and they settled there. 44 And the LORD gave them rest on every side just as he had sworn to their fathers. Not one of all their enemies had withstood them, for the LORD had given all their enemies into their hands. 45 Not one word of all the good promises that the LORD had made to the house of Israel had failed; all came to pass. (Josh 21:43–45)

In that sense, the conquest and allotment of the Promised Land under the leadership of Joshua was the visible fulfillment of the land promised in the Abrahamic covenant which can be identified as the covenant of royal grant.[26]

The covenant renewal of the Mosaic covenant at Shechem is written in Joshua 24:1–33. The form of the covenant renewal at Shechem has the form of the covenant of law, in light of the suzerain treaties in the ancient Near East. It includes the preamble (v.1), historical prologue (vv. 2–13), stipulations (vv. 14–24), blessings and curses (vv. 14–20), and covenant ratification (vv. 16–19, 21, 24–25).[27]

---

26. Martin Noth, as a major exponent of the Deuteronomistic history, denies that the conquest of Canaan was *historical* because he interprets it in light of the historical critical perspective. His explanation of the Deuteronomistic history is well summarized as follows: "If we begin by enquiring about the source of the information which enables us to establish the outward course of the history of Israel as a whole and in many of its details, we must refer, in the first place, to the Old Testament with its wealth of historical material, but also to a great mass of sources outside the Old Testament. In the Old Testament one must mention first of all the great historical work which comprises the books of Deuteronomy, Joshua, Judges, Samuel, Kings, which we call 'deuteronomistic' by reason of its language and spirit, and which offers the very first exposition of the 'history of Israel' up to the events of the year 587 B.C. The author of this compilation passed on numerous sources from different periods, of different extent and different origin and nature, partly *in extenso*, partly in extracts, and developed the whole work from these sources. He thereby conveyed to posterity a mass of valuable traditional material and without his work we should know very little about the earlier phases of the history of Israel." Noth, *The History of Israel*, 42.

27. While the renewal of the Sinaitic covenant at Shechem took place, there was no appointment of Joshua's successor. In that sense, the Shechem covenant was "not a dynastic covenant," as Kline indicates: "Mention of the Sabbath rest (Josh 23:1; cf. 21:44) is followed by the record of an assembly (or two assemblies if Joshua 23 and 24 describe separate occasions) called by Joshua to set the kingdom in order. Like his master Moses, Joshua at the close of his life summoned the nation to renew their

One of the distinctive external characteristics of the Mosaic covenant as the covenant of law is that not Yahweh but the covenant community made a sworn oath to keep the covenant. Meanwhile, Yahweh made a sworn oath to the covenant when he made the covenant with Abraham (Gen 15:17–20). In that sense, the Abrahamic covenant set a classical paradigm of the covenant of grace, which can be identified as the covenant of royal grant in light of the ancient Near Eastern treaties. The Mosaic covenant renewal at Shechem has a very compact external form. However, it reveals that the people of Israel clearly made a sworn oath to the covenant to keep the Mosaic law:

> 14 "Now therefore fear the LORD and serve him in sincerity and in faithfulness. Put away the gods that your fathers served beyond the River and in Egypt, and serve the LORD. 15 And if it is evil in your eyes to serve the LORD, choose this day whom you will serve, whether the gods your fathers served in the region beyond the River, or the gods of the Amorites in whose land you dwell. But as for me and my house, we will serve the LORD." 16 Then the people answered, "Far be it from us that we should forsake the LORD to serve other gods, 17 for it is the LORD our God who brought us and our fathers up from the land of Egypt, out of the house of slavery, and who did those great signs in our sight and preserved us in all the way that we went, and among all the peoples through whom we passed. 18 And the LORD drove out before us all the peoples, the Amorites who lived in the land. Therefore we also will serve the LORD, for he is our God." 19 But Joshua said to the people, "You are not able to serve the LORD, for he is a holy God. He is a jealous God; he will not forgive your transgressions or your sins. 20 If you forsake the LORD and serve foreign gods, then he will turn and do you harm and consume you, after having done you good." 21 And the people said to Joshua, "No, but we will serve the LORD." 22 Then Joshua said to the people, "You are witnesses against yourselves that you have chosen the LORD, to serve him." And they said, "We are witnesses." 23 He said, "Then put away the foreign gods that are among you, and incline your heart to the LORD, the God of Israel." 24 And the people said to Joshua, "The LORD our God we will serve, and his voice we will obey." 25 So Joshua made a covenant with the people that day, and put in place statutes and rules for them at Shechem. (Josh 24:14–25)

In the process of the covenant renewal, Joshua as the covenant mediator on behalf of Yahweh pronounced stipulations, including dual sanctions such as blessings and curses. In doing so, the covenant community of Israel made a sworn oath to the

---

covenantal vows to the Lord. The elements of the treaty pattern that informed the Sinaitic and the Deuteronomic Covenant documentation are found again in Joshua 24. Thus, preamble (v. 20); historical prologue (vv. 2b–13; cf. vv. 17, 18); stipulations (vv. 14, 23, 25); document clause –incorporation of this treaty in the Torah documentation (v. 26); sanctions (vv. 19, 20). Note also the common ceremonial features of ratificatory oath (vv. 15–24) and witnesses (vv. 22, 26, 27). Unlike the concluding covenant mediated by Moses, this was not a dynastic covenant. It did not appoint a successor to Joshua but rather marked the end of the Moses-Joshua phase of the establishing of the typological kingdom in Canaan." Kline, *God, Heaven and Har Magedon*, 136–37.

covenant. The people of Israel made a sworn oath, saying "Therefore we also will serve the LORD, for he is our God" (v. 18b), "No, but we will serve the LORD" (v. 21b), and "The LORD our God we will serve, and his voice we will obey" (v. 24b). As the covenant community of Israel made a sworn oath to the covenant, the Mosaic covenant was publically and officially renewed.

Meanwhile, Joshua gave to the people of Israel the summary account of the ancient history of Israel from Terah, the father of Abraham to the Conquest of Canaan through a historical prologue (Josh 24:2–13). The section of historical prologue is a brief summary of the historical fulfillment of the promises of the Abrahamic covenant. The two essential components of the promises of the Abrahamic covenant were covenant community and the Promised Land to form the holy Kingdom of God as the theocratic kingdom. The partial fulfillment of the promises of the Abrahamic covenant is beautifully manifested at the end of the historical prologue:

> 11 And you went over the Jordan and came to Jericho, and the leaders of Jericho fought against you, and also the Amorites, the Perizzites, the Canaanites, the Hittites, the Girgashites, the Hivites, and the Jebusites. And I gave them into your hand. 12 And I sent the hornet before you, which drove them out before you, the two kings of the Amorites; it was not by your sword or by your bow. 13 I gave you a land on which you had not labored and cities that you had not built, and you dwell in them. You eat the fruit of vineyards and olive orchards that you did not plant.' (Josh 24:11–13)

Yahweh, through Joshua, pronounced the summary account of the conquest of Canaan after the people of Israel crossed the Jordan River. Verse 11a summarizes that Israel crossed the Jordan River and came to the city of Jericho: "And you went over the Jordan and came to Jericho." However, crossing the Jordan River was not a natural but a supernatural process, made possible through Yahweh's power, as when he divided the Red Sea in the Exodus. In fact, Yahweh executed redemptive judgment against the Egyptian warriors through holy war when Israel crossed the Red Sea as they came out of Egyptian bondage. So, when Israel crossed the Jordan River through Yahweh's power, dividing the water before the ark of the covenant of Yahweh, he commanded Joshua to erect twelve memorial stones. The twelve stones, representing the twelve tribes, became a memorial to the people of Israel of when Yahweh dried up the Jordan River until Israel passed over, just as he had done for them at the Red Sea (Josh 4:1–24).

After Israel crossed over the Jordan River through the power of Yahweh, he commanded Joshua to circumcise all the sons of Israel who were born during the forty years in the wilderness. Until then, all the males of Israel who came out of Egypt, "all the men of war, had died in the wilderness on the way after they came out of Egypt" (Josh 5:2–9). It is important to remember that circumcision was the sign or seal of the Abrahamic covenant. Yahweh's command to Joshua to circumcise all the males of Israel who were born in the wilderness after they crossed the Jordan River, suggests that Israel as a chosen people was under the spiritual benefits of the internal substance of the Abrahamic covenant, even though they were also under the Mosaic covenant of law as previously discussed.

At the same time, Yahweh prepared Israel's military campaign against the Canaanites through circumcision. Joshua circumcised all "the sons of Israel" who were born in the wilderness according to Yahweh's command:

> 3 So Joshua made flint knives and circumcised the sons of Israel at Gibeath-haaraloth. 4 *And this is the reason why Joshua circumcised them: all the males of the people who came out of Egypt, all the men of war, had died in the wilderness on the way after they had come out of Egypt. 5 Though all the people who came out had been circumcised, yet all the people who were born on the way in the wilderness after they had come out of Egypt had not been circumcised.* 6 For the people of Israel walked forty years in the wilderness, until all the nation, the men of war who came out of Egypt, perished, because they did not obey the voice of the LORD; the LORD swore to them that he would not let them see the land that the LORD had sworn to their fathers to give to us, a land flowing with milk and honey. 7 So it was their children, whom he raised up in their place, that Joshua circumcised. For they were uncircumcised, because they had not been circumcised on the way. 8 When the circumcising of the whole nation was finished, they remained in their places in the camp until they were healed. 9 And the LORD said to Joshua, "Today I have rolled away the reproach of Egypt from you." And so the name of that place is called Gilgal to this day. (Josh 5:3–9)

Verses 4 and 5 testify that "all the men of war" of the Exodus generation were circumcised. Nevertheless, they all died in the wilderness through Yahweh's covenant lawsuit against their disobedience. Circumcision of "the whole nation" before the military campaign in the Promised Land signifies that one of the reasons for circumcision under the Mosaic covenant was closely related to military warfare against the inhabitants of the land of Canaan. That is why Yahweh ordered the circumcision of "the whole nation" before the people of Israel waged holy war against the city of Jericho.

The famous military battle between David and Goliath at the valley of Elah more clearly demonstrates that the circumcision of the people of Israel under the Mosaic covenant was closely integrated and related to Yahweh's holy war against the inhabitants in the Promised Land (1 Sam 17:1–58). Saul and all the men of Israel were waging war against Goliath and the Philistines. When the armies of Israel saw Goliath, they ran away from him and were terrified. At this critical moment, David under the inspiration of the Spirit of the Lord came out and shouted that the war would be between the circumcised men of Israel as "the armies of the living God" and uncircumcised Philistines, led by Goliath:

> 24 All the men of Israel, when they saw the man, fled from him and were much afraid. 25 And the men of Israel said, "Have you seen this man who has come up? Surely he has come up to defy Israel. And the king will enrich the man who kills him with great riches and will give him his daughter and make his father's house free in Israel." 26 *And David said to the men who stood by him, "What shall be done for the man who kills this Philistine and takes away the reproach from Israel? For who is this uncircumcised Philistine, that he should defy the armies of the living God?"* 27 And the people answered him in the same way, "So shall it be done to the man who kills him." 28 Now Eliab his eldest brother heard when he spoke to the men. And Eliab's anger was kindled against David, and he said, "Why have you come down? And with whom have you left those few sheep in the wilderness? I know your presumption and the evil of your heart, for you have come down to see the battle." 29 And David said, "What have I done now? Was it not but a word?" 30 And he turned away from him toward another, and spoke in the same way, and the people answered him again as before. 31 When the words that David spoke were heard, they repeated them before Saul, and he sent for him. 32 And David said to Saul, "Let no man's heart fail because of him. Your servant will go and fight with this Philistine." 33 And Saul said to David, "You are not able to go against this Philistine to fight with him, for you are but a youth, and he has been a man of war from his youth." 34 But David said to Saul, "Your servant used to keep sheep for his father. And when there came a lion, or a bear, and took a lamb from the flock, 35 I went after him and struck him and delivered it out of his mouth. And if he arose against me, I caught him by his beard and struck him and killed him. 36 *Your servant has struck down both lions and bears, and this uncircumcised Philistine shall be like one of them, for he has defied the armies of the living God."* 37 And David said, "The LORD who delivered me from the paw of the lion and from the paw of the bear will deliver me from the hand of this Philistine." And Saul said to David, "Go, and the LORD be with you!" (1 Sam 17:24–37)

In the end, David won the battle against Goliath "with a sling and with a stone" without a sword in his hand. And the circumcised armies of Israel defeated and killed the uncircumcised armies of the Philistines (1 Sam 17:48–54). The famous battle between David and Goliath at the valley of Elah was Yahweh's holy war against the Philistines. All the Philistines, along with their champion, Goliath, were totally destroyed by David and the armies of Israel. Moreover, the battle was depicted by David as a battle between the armies of the living God and uncircumcised Philistines. In that regard, we can consider that Yahweh used circumcision as a visible and bodily sign for his armies while he was waging holy war against the inhabitants of Canaan under the Mosaic covenant.

We need to pay attention to Joshua 24:13 which states, "I gave you a land on which you had not labored and cities that you had not built, and you dwell in them. You eat the fruit of vineyards and olive orchards that you did not plant." The statement "I gave you a land" is the language of a royal grant, signifying Yahweh's free gift based upon the promise of the Abrahamic covenant. Although Yahweh gave the land of Canaan as a gift of the covenant of royal grant, based upon the Abrahamic covenant, he gave it through war. Therefore, Yahweh commanded the covenant community to fight against the kings and inhabitants of the seven tribes who lived in the land of Canaan. Interestingly, the war was not a common grace war, but a holy war, which was the war of total destruction, already commanded to the prophet Moses and the covenant community when Yahweh renewed the Mosaic covenant at the plain of Moab (Deut 7:1–5; 20:16–18).[28]

After crossing the Jordan River, Yahweh commanded the people of Israel to attack the city of Jericho, giving specific guidelines. As the covenant community followed and obeyed the guidelines of Joshua, the wall of Jericho collapsed and all the people and livestocks were totally destroyed. Only Rahab the prostitute and people with her in her house were saved (Josh 6:1–27). The war against the city of Jericho was a holy war instigated by Yahweh, separating the covenant and non-covenant community:

> 15 On the seventh day they rose early, at the dawn of day, and marched around the city in the same manner seven times. It was only on that day that they marched around the city seven times. 16 And at the seventh time, when the priests had blown the trumpets, Joshua said to the people, "Shout, for the LORD has given you the city. 17 And the city and all that is within it shall be devoted to the LORD for destruction. Only Rahab the prostitute and all who are with her in her house shall live, because she hid the messengers whom we sent. 18 But you, keep yourselves from the things devoted to destruction, lest when you have devoted them you take any of the devoted things and make the camp of Israel a thing for destruction and bring trouble upon it. 19 But all silver and gold, and every vessel of bronze and iron, are holy to the LORD; they shall go into the treasury of the LORD." 20 So the people shouted, and the trumpets were blown. As soon as the people heard the sound of the trumpet, the people shouted a great shout, and the wall fell down flat, so that the people went up into the city, every man straight before him, and they captured the city. 21 Then they devoted all in the city to destruction, both men and women, young and old, oxen, sheep, and donkeys, with the edge of the sword. (Josh 6:15–21)

---

28. Walther Eichrodt insightfully summarizes a close relationship between the day of the Lord and holy war in the history of the ancient Israel, executing his judgment against the enemies of Israel: "The same tendency is reflected in the increasing consistency with which *the hope of the overthrow and punishment of all Israel's enemies* envisages a final reckoning of Yahweh with the nations on 'his Day'. From the earliest times Yahweh's mighty presence as Lord and Helper had never been experienced more intensely than in the day of battle, which was thus rightly termed 'his day'. It was then that men rejoiced in the consciousness of his unlimited power, putting to flight all those that hated him, and confounding every assault on his sovereignty. The sacred object of the Ark provided empirical support for this sense of having Yahweh in their midst; and the rites by which the war was sanctified also helped to concentrate men's thoughts on the presence of the God of Battles. Hence the holy war belongs pre-eminently to the ages in which men were aware of being in an especially close relationship with the exalted God, and of experiencing his saving presence." Eichrodt, *Theology of the Old Testament*, 459.

The Mosaic Covenant and the Kingdom of God

Verse 21 summarizes that the specific character of Israel's war against the city of Jericho was not a common grace war but holy war.[29] In fact, the holy war against Jericho set the classical paradigm, which suggests that conquering the land of Canaan would also be considered as a holy war.[30]

29. Walter Kaiser, Jr. recognizes that wars in the process of the conquest of the Promised Land were holy wars. However, his understanding of holy war lacks a redemptive historical understanding, according to which holy war during the conquest of the Promised Land was the type of final holy war, which will take place at the Second Coming of the Messiah: "Such wars have been named 'holy wars' by Gerhard von Rad. They were in actuality 'Yahweh's wars' (1 Sa 18:18; 25:28); therefore, such battles were not to be initiated by any leader or group without consulting the Lord first (1 Sa 28:5–6; 30:7–8; 2 Sa 5:19, 22, 23). After Israel had been assured by Yahweh that the anticipated battle was his own, then the trumpets were sounded and the cry went up: 'Yahweh has given [the enemy] into your hands' (Jdg 3:28; 6:3; 7:15; 1 Sa 13:3). The war began with Yahweh's promise of success and an exhortation to fight valiantly. Israel must only trust and not be afraid (Jos 1:6, 9; 6:2; 8:1; 10:8; 11:6). The men were then 'consecrated' to the Lord, for their mission set them apart from all mundane activity (1 Sa 21:6; 2 Sa 11:11). Yahweh went before the army and dwelt in the camp (Dt 23:14; Jdg 4:14) and 'fought' on behalf of Israel (Dt 1:30). The military leader of the army, though often specially endowed with powers, was ultimately dependent on the Lord, for the Lord could save by few or by many (Jdg 7:2ff.; 1 Sa 13:15ff.). This is vividly brought out by Joshua's vision of the 'commander of the Lord' who stood with sword in hand ready for action (Jos 5:13–15)." Kaiser, Jr., *The Promise-Plan of God*, 101.

30. Scholars, influenced by the historical critical school deny the historicity of the fall of Jericho. Denying the historicity of the fall of Jericho is at the same time the denial of the Final judgment, which will follow the Second Coming of Jesus Christ, because the two judgments are redemptive historically integrated and connected together. For example, Collins denies the historicity of the fall of Jericho along with the holy war, arguing that it is *fictitious*: "The story of Jericho has been something of an embarrassment for conservative Biblicists because of the negative findings of archaeological research. A more fundamental problem is posed, however, by the morality exemplified in the story. Joshua instructs the Israelites that 'the city and all that is in it shall be devoted to the Lord for destruction' (6:17), with the exception of the prostitute Rahab, who helped the Israelite spies. When the Israelites enter the city, we are told that 'they devoted to destruction by the edge of the sword all in the city, both men and women, young and old, oxen, sheep, and donkeys' (6:21). This dedication and destruction is known as *herem*, or the ban. The custom was known outside Israel. King Mesha of Moab, in the ninth century B.C.E., boasted that he took Nebo from Israel, 'slaying all, seven thousand men, boys, women, girls and maid-servants, for I had devoted them to destruction for (the god) Ashtar-Chemosh' (*ANET*, 320). The story of the capture of Jericho is almost certainly fictitious, but this does not lessen the savagery of the story. We are not dealing in Joshua with a factual report of the ways of ancient warfare. Rather, the slaughter of the Canaanites, here and elsewhere, is presented as a theologically correct ideal." Collins, *Introduction to the Hebrew Bible*, 193.

Similarly, von Rad understands the conquest of Canaan in light of the Deuteronomistic history. In doing so, he denies the authentic historicity of the conquest of Canaan, waging the holy war with total destruction, and he sees it as not actual history but a history, reflected and colored by faith: "But our final comment on it should not be that it is obviously an 'unhistorical' picture, because what is in question here is a picture fashioned throughout by faith. Unlike any ordinary historical document, it does not have its centre in itself; it is intended to tell the beholder about Jahweh, that is, how Jahweh led his people and got himself glory. In Jahweh's eyes Israel is always a unity: his control of history was no improvisation made up of disconnected events: in the saving history he always deals with all Israel. This picture makes a formidable claim, and actually in the subsequent period it proved to have incalculable power to stamp affairs. How this came about is quite interesting. Israel made a picture of Jahweh's control of history on his people's behalf whose magnificence far surpasses anything that older and more realistic accounts offered. Faith had so mastered the material that the history could be seen from within, from the angle of faith. What supports and shapes this late picture of Israel's taking possession of the land is a mighty zeal for and glorification of the acts of Jahweh." Von Rad, *Old*

However, Achan the son of Carmi of the tribe of Judah violated Yahweh's regulation in respect to "the devoted things" when he took some for himself. And Yahweh's anger burned against the covenant community. As a result, the soldiers of Israel were defeated by the soldiers of Ai because Yahweh was not with them (Josh. 7:1–9). Surprisingly, Yahweh considered Achan's personal violation in respect to the devoted things as a sin of Israel which was a violation of the Mosaic covenant of law:

> 10 The LORD said to Joshua, "Get up! Why have you fallen on your face? 11 Israel has sinned; they have transgressed my covenant that I commanded them; they have taken some of the devoted things; they have stolen and lied and put them among their own belongings. 12 Therefore the people of Israel cannot stand before their enemies. They turn their backs before their enemies, because they have become devoted for destruction. I will be with you no more, unless you destroy the devoted things from among you. 13 Get up! Consecrate the people and say, 'Consecrate yourselves for tomorrow; for thus says the LORD, God of Israel, "There are devoted things in your midst, O Israel. You cannot stand before your enemies until you take away the devoted things from among you." 14 In the morning therefore you shall be brought near by your tribes. And the tribe that the LORD takes by lot shall come near by clans. And the clan that the LORD takes shall come near by households. And the household that the LORD takes shall come near man by man. 15 And he who is taken with the devoted things shall be burned with fire, he and all that he has, because he has transgressed the covenant of the LORD, and because he has done an outrageous thing in Israel.'" (Josh 7:10–15)

So Joshua's messengers found Achan and his family. They brought Achan and his family along with their belongings and livestocks to the Valley of Achor. And the covenant community of Israel stoned and burned Achan and his family as Yahweh commanded them to do so. Then, Yahweh's anger against Israel died down (Josh 7:22–26).

Afterwards, the covenant community of Israel could conquer the city of Ai with the proper execution of holy war, which was prescribed and commanded by Yahweh (Josh 8:1–29). As Joshua and Israel obeyed Yahweh's command to fight a holy war against the King and soldiers of Ai, they were able to destroy "all the inhabitants of Ai," including woman and children:

> 24 When Israel had finished killing all the inhabitants of Ai in the open wilderness where they pursued them, and all of them to the very last had fallen by the edge of the sword, all Israel returned to Ai and struck it down with the edge of the sword. 25 And all who fell that day, both men and women, were 12,000, all the people of Ai. 26 But Joshua did not draw back his hand with which he stretched out the javelin until he had devoted all the inhabitants of Ai to destruction. 27 Only the livestock and the spoil of that city Israel took as

---

Testament Theology, 302.

their plunder, according to the word of the LORD that he commanded Joshua. 28 So Joshua burned Ai and made it forever a heap of ruins, as it is to this day. 29 And he hanged the king of Ai on a tree until evening. And at sunset Joshua commanded, and they took his body down from the tree and threw it at the entrance of the gate of the city and raised over it a great heap of stones, which stands there to this day. (Josh 8:24–29)

Likewise, the paradigm of holy war against the inhabitants of the Promised Land during the conquest of the city of Jericho was also applied to the conquest of the city of Ai. The fearful pattern of the total destruction of holy war was also applied after the conquest of Ai when Israel conquered Southern Canaan (Josh 10:29–43). The conquest of Southern Canaan under Joshua's leadership is summarized as follows:

40 So Joshua struck the whole land, the hill country and the Negeb and the lowland and the slopes, and all their kings. He left none remaining, but devoted to destruction all that breathed, just as the LORD God of Israel commanded. 41 And Joshua struck them from Kadesh-barnea as far as Gaza, and all the country of Goshen, as far as Gibeon. 42 And Joshua captured all these kings and their land at one time, *because the LORD God of Israel fought for Israel*. 43 Then Joshua returned, and all Israel with him, to the camp at Gilgal. (Josh 10:40–43)

The words of verse 40b, "He left none remaining, but devoted to destruction all that breathed, just as the LORD God of Israel commanded," sums up the fact that the conquest of southern Canaan was not accomplished through a natural process but through the supernatural intervention of Yahweh's power, executing his holy war against the inhabitants of that land. Joshua and Israel were simply human agents fighting a holy war on behalf of Yahweh. In fact, the conquest of Canaan was Yahweh's holy war, "because the LORD God of Israel fought for Israel" (v. 42b).

After the conquest of southern Canaan, Joshua and Israel headed toward northern Canaan, which was part of the Promised Land. And they conquered northern Canaan, reaching to Mount Hermon (Josh 11:1–23). During the process of the Mosaic covenant renewal at the plain of Moab, Yahweh commanded Israel through the mouth of Moses to fight a holy war in the conquest of the Promised Land (Deut 7:1–5; 20:16–18). So, Israel followed the exact guidelines of holy war when they conquered northern Canaan under the leadership of Joshua:

16 So Joshua took all that land, the hill country and all the Negeb and all the land of Goshen and the lowland and the Arabah and the hill country of Israel and its lowland 17 from Mount Halak, which rises toward Seir, as far as Baal-gad in the Valley of Lebanon below Mount Hermon. And he captured all their kings and struck them and put them to death. 18 Joshua made war a long time with all those kings. 19 There was not a city that made peace with the people of Israel except the Hivites, the inhabitants of Gibeon. They took them all in battle. 20 For it was the LORD's doing to harden their hearts that they

should come against Israel in battle, in order that they should be devoted to destruction and should receive no mercy but be destroyed, just as the LORD commanded Moses. (Josh 11:16–20)

After the successful initial campaign against the inhabitants of the land of Canaan, Yahweh commanded Joshua to divide and allot the land of Canaan. The East of the Jordan River was already divided and allotted to the tribe of Reuben, the tribe of Gad, and the half-tribe of Manasseh at the time of Moses (Josh. 13:8–33). Joshua divided and allotted the land West of the Jordan River to the nine and a half tribes of Israel, with the exception of the tribe of Levi (Josh 14:1—19:51). Afterwards, Yahweh commanded them to set apart six different cities as cities of refuge. So the unintentional manslayer was able to flee (Josh 20:1–9). Forty-eight cities with their pasturelands were given and allotted to the tribe of Levi, as Yahweh had commanded through Moses (Josh 21:1–45). The covenant community of Israel conquered and allotted the Promised Land which was sworn by Yahweh to be given to the descendents of Abraham, Isaac, and Jacob. And then, Yahweh renewed the Mosaic covenant with Israel through the mediator, Joshua (Josh 24:1–33). Thus, the external form of the Mosaic covenant, renewed at Shechem, was the covenant of law. However, the internal substance of the covenant was the covenant of grace.

Summary

We have seen that the Mosaic covenant reflects the suzerainty covenant, which is similar to the suzerainty treaties in the ancient Near East, manifested by the Hittite treaties in the second millennium B.C. In the Abrahamic covenant, Yahweh made a sworn oath to the covenant. It signified that he would fulfill all the covenantal promises by his sovereign will and power throughout redemptive history. However, in the Mosaic covenant, the covenant community of Israel as the covenantal descendents of Abraham made a sworn oath in the process of the covenant ratification ceremony. Israel, as the covenant community who had a sworn oath to the Mosaic covenant, started to live under the terms of the Mosaic covenant of law.

We have affirmed that personal salvation under the Mosaic covenant was by faith through God's grace in Christ alone. The principle of the covenant of grace inaugurated in Genesis 3:15 was constantly applied even under the Mosaic covenant, although the covenant community of Israel also received the Mosaic law. Yahweh did not reveal the method by which he promised to grant the land of Canaan in the historical context of the Abrahamic covenant; however, Yahweh did reveal to the covenant community how he granted the Promised Land in the historical context of the Mosaic covenant. It was by holy war, executing God's redemptive judgment to separate the covenant community and the non-covenant community during the conquest of the Promised Land. The inclusion of prophecy on the possession of the land of Canaan as God's grant within the historical context of the Mosaic covenant suggests that its internal substance was the covenant of grace.

We have endeavored to demonstrate that the visible glory of the Lord on Mount Sinai in the process of making the Mosaic covenant was Yahweh's visible demonstration to the covenant community of Israel that he was the divine witness of the Mosaic covenant. Moreover, the visible and thunderous presence of the theophanic glory in the process of making the Mosaic covenant signified that Yahweh would pour out blessings to the obedient and curses upon the disobedient according to the terms of the Mosaic covenant of law.

We have argued that considering the Mosaic covenant as a republication of the covenant of works in a limited sense is warranted biblically and confessionally. Calvin understood that believers under the Old Covenant were saved by the principle of the covenant of grace. Nevertheless, Calvin insisted that "the covenant of Law" was operative under the Mosaic covenant. Calvin's identification of the Mosaic law as "the covenant of Law" is significant because he interpreted that God executed blessings and curses in the Promised Land according to obedience and disobedience to the Mosaic law. Calvin's designation of the Mosaic covenant as "the covenant of the Law" provided a hermeneutical and theological foundation for the Calvinists' designation of the Mosaic covenant as a republication of the covenant of works. The Westminster Standards (1643–1648) do not explicitly identify the Mosaic covenant as a republication of the covenant of works. Nevertheless, the comprehensive teaching of the Westminster Standards is harmonious with the concept of the republication of the covenant of works. Charles Hodge was a representative theologian who articulated the idea of the republication of the covenant of works under the Mosaic covenant.

We have identified the Mosaic covenant as the covenant of law. It was applied in the history of ancient Israel after the covenant was inaugurated on Mount Sinai. The Mosaic covenant as the covenant of law was a temporary and breakable covenant which applied to the covenant community of the ancient Israel until the fall of Jerusalem in A.D. 70. Nevertheless, the Old Testament defines the Mosaic covenant as an "everlasting covenant." A major reason to define the Mosaic covenant as an everlasting covenant is the fact that all the requirements and promises of the Mosaic covenant of law would be fulfilled in the coming Messiah, Jesus Christ. The blessings and curses in the history of ancient Israel, according to the terms of the Mosaic covenant of law, were the type of the heavenly blessings and hellish curses. Through this historical experience, Yahweh revealed the blessings of the heavenly Kingdom of God and the curses of hell. We identified it as the Old Covenant eschatology, demonstrated in the history of ancient Israel after the inauguration of the Mosaic covenant.

We have argued that the continuation of the circumcision of the sons of Israel under the Mosaic covenant was an indication that the internal substance of the Mosaic covenant was the covenant of grace, although its external form had the covenant of law. Nevertheless, Yahweh did not assign circumcision as the sign of the Mosaic covenant. Rather, he instituted keeping the Sabbath holy as the sign of the Mosaic covenant between himself and the covenant community of Israel. For the people of Israel, keeping the Sabbath holy was the visible sign of a holy nation, which would be the theocratic kingdom of Israel in the Promised Land. The complete cessation from work and rest on the Sabbath day by the covenant community of Israel was to typify the everlasting rest in the heavenly Kingdom of God. The people of Israel as a holy nation under the Mosaic covenant had to typify the everlasting rest in the heavenly Kingdom of God, which would be fully realized in the Second Coming of Jesus Christ. So, Yahweh demonstrated the eschatological vision assigned by the mandate of keeping the Sabbath holy as the sign of the Mosaic covenant.

We have traced the renewals of the Mosaic covenant at Moab and Shechem. Yahweh renewed the Mosaic covenant at the plain of Moab through the prophet Moses before the covenant community of Israel crossed the Jordan River and entered the Promised Land. In that sense, the Book of Deuteronomy can be identified as the book of the covenant renewal of the Mosaic covenant.

We have identified Joshua 24:1–33 as the Mosaic covenant renewal at Shechem after the conquest of the western part of the lands near the Jordan River of the Promised Land. The conquest and allotment of the Promised Land under the leadership of Joshua was the visible fulfillment of the promise of land in the Abrahamic covenant, which can be identified as the covenant of royal grant. The form of the Mosaic covenant renewal at Shechem has the form of the covenant of law in light of the suzerainty treaties in the ancient Near East. As the covenant community of Israel made a sworn oath to the covenant, the Mosaic covenant was publically and officially renewed. Yahweh's command to Joshua to circumcise all the sons of Israel, who were born in the wilderness after they crossed the Jordan River, indicates that Israel as a chosen nation was under the redemptive benefits of the internal substance of the covenant of grace in the Abrahamic covenant even though they were also under the Mosaic covenant of law. The Mosaic covenant renewal at Schechem affirms that the external form of the Mosaic covenant was the covenant of law, while the internal substance of the covenant was the covenant of grace.

5

The Davidic Covenant and the Kingdom of God

THE ABRAHAMIC COVENANT WAS beautifully accomplished when Abraham's descendents, as the covenant community of Israel, entered, conquered, and settled in the Promised Land sworn to them by Yahweh. Before the covenant community of Israel entered the land of Canaan, Moses prophesied on the plain of Moab that the Israelites would install kings to govern the theocratic kingdom of Israel:

> 14 "When you come to the land that the LORD your God is giving you, and you possess it and dwell in it and then say, 'I will set a king over me, like all the nations that are around me,' 15 you may indeed set a king over you whom the LORD your God will choose. One from among your brothers you shall set as king over you. You may not put a foreigner over you, who is not your brother. 16 Only he must not acquire many horses for himself or cause the people to return to Egypt in order to acquire many horses, since the LORD has said to you, 'You shall never return that way again.' 17 And he shall not acquire many wives for himself, lest his heart turn away, nor shall he acquire for himself excessive silver and gold. 18 "And when he sits on the throne of his kingdom, he shall write for himself in a book a copy of this law, approved by the Levitical priests. 19 And it shall be with him, and he shall read in it all the days of his life, that he may learn to fear the LORD his God by keeping all the words of this law and these statutes, and doing them, 20 that his heart may not be lifted up above his brothers, and that he may not turn aside from the commandment, either to the right hand or to the left, so that he may continue long in his kingdom, he and his children, in Israel. (Deut 17:14–20)

Nevertheless, until the kingdom of Israel was inaugurated and built, the covenant community of Israel had to struggle through the period of the conquest of Canaan, under the leadership of Joshua, and disobedience and chaos during the period of Judges.

We will endeavor to explore and prove that the Davidic covenant was the covenant of the kingdom.[1] And the Davidic kingdom was the type of the everlasting

---

1. For divergent interpretation on the Davidic covenant, see J. Collins, *Introduction to the Hebrew Bible*, 233–39; Dumbrell, *Covenant and Creation*, 127–63; Edwards, *A History of Redemption*, 93–124;

Kingdom of God where Jesus Christ eternally reigns as the Great King. Saul was the first king of Israel. Nevertheless, he failed to win the holy war after he was inaugurated as the first king of Israel. We will note that this was the main reason why Yahweh did not make a covenant with Saul. After Saul failed to be the covenantal grantee of the kingdom of Israel, David was anointed as the king of Israel. He made it through the probation period, waging the holy war against the Philistines, and successfully completed the holy war, becoming the victorious warrior as the vassal on behalf of the Great King, Yahweh. Afterward, Yahweh made a covenant with David, granting the kingdom of Israel. In that sense, we will demonstrate that the Davidic covenant was the covenant of royal grant, in the same category as the Prediluvian Noahic covenant, the Abrahamic covenant, and the New Covenant.

Ryrie, as a dispensationalist, argues that "the Davidic millennial kingdom," promised in the Davidic covenant in 2 Samuel 7:12–16, will be fulfilled in the Second Coming of Christ, who will be the Ruler of the earthly millennial kingdom:

> Both Judaism and premillennial Christian theology give a major place to this concept of kingdom. It is Davidic in that the promises concerning the kingdom were made in the great covenant with David (2 Sam. 7:12–16). It is messianic since Messiah will be the Ruler. It will be realized at the second advent of Christ when he will establish His kingdom and fulfill those promises made to David . . . In summary, in the Davidic messianic kingdom Christ is the Ruler; He will rule over the earth and its inhabitants during the one thousand years that follow His second coming.[2]

However, it is our assessment that the idea that "the Davidic messianic kingdom" and "the millennial kingdom" are one is a fundamental misreading and misrepresentation of the prophecy of the Davidic covenant and its kingdom. The Davidic covenant does not anticipate the Messianic millennial kingdom. Rather, it anticipates that the first coming of the Messiah as the Son of David will take over the reigning of the Davidic kingdom as the eschatological Kingdom of God, which will be inaugurated

---

Peter Golding, *Covenant Theology*, 158–61; Hahn, *Kinship by Covenant*, 176–213; Horton, *Introducing Covenant Theology*, 56–57; Kline, *God, Heaven, and Har Magedon*, 138–40; Kline, *Kingdom Prologue*, 340–55; LaRondelle, *Our Creator Redeemer*, 43–55; McCarthy, *Old Testament Covenant*, 46–52; Murray, *The Covenant of Grace*, 22–24; Robertson, *The Christ of the Covenants*, 229–69; Ryrie, *Basic Theology*, 532–35; Turretin, *Institutes of Elenctic Theology*, 2:224–69; von Rad, *Old Testament Theology*, 1:308–18; Waltke, *An Old Testament Theology*, 405–44; Williams, *Far as the Curse Is Found*, 132–47.

2. Ryrie, *Basic Theology*, 461. Ryrie, making a sharp distinction between church and Israel, categorizes four different forms of kingdom in the present world: "1. *To the universal kingdom*. In the sense that the church is in the world it is part of God's universal kingdom. He designed it, brought it into being, and rules over it, as He does all aspects of His universe. 2. *To the Davidic/messianic kingdom*. The church is not a part of this kingdom at all. When this kingdom is established the church will have been resurrected and will reign with Christ over the millennial kingdom. 3. *To the mystery form of the kingdom*. Since the church is part of Christendom, she is part of this concept of the kingdom. 4. *To the spiritual kingdom*. The true church, the body of Christ, is equivalent to this concept of the kingdom." Ibid., 462.

in the Messiah's life, death, resurrection, and ascension. This is because the Davidic kingdom in the Promised Land was the type of the eschatological Kingdom of God, which will be fulfilled in Jesus Christ. In fact, the Messianic kingdom will be coming not as the earthly millennial kingdom but as the eschatological Kingdom of God. And it will be inaugurated through the first coming of the Messiah, and will be consummated at the Second Coming of Christ. In that sense, it is our assessment that the idea that the earthly millennial kingdom is the fulfillment of the Davidic covenant and its kingdom, as taught by dispensationalists, results from a lack of proper understanding of the Davidic kingdom in light of redemptive historical continuity and typology.

The Covenant of Royal Grant and the Divine Oath

The Abrahamic covenant was a classical paradigm of the covenant of royal grant. The Davidic covenant demonstrated that it was also a covenant of royal grant. The history of the covenant-making process of the Davidic covenant reflects the reason why it was the covenant of royal grant. God did not make a covenant with Saul, although he was the first king of Israel, because he failed to obey Yahweh during the probation period after his anointing as the king of Israel. So Yahweh forfeited Saul's kingship. Afterwards, David was anointed as the king of Israel, and he successfully completed his holy war against the Philistines, and began to rule Israel in Jerusalem. After David passed the probation period, God made a covenant with David (2 Sam 7:1–17). With this in mind, it is necessary to briefly explore the historical background to the Davidic covenant to identify it as a covenant of royal grant.[3]

The covenant community of Israel entered and conquered the land of Canaan, sworn by God to be granted to the descendents of Abraham, Isaac, and Jacob. It was the historical fulfillment of the Abrahamic covenant. Before the covenant community entered the Promised Land after wandering in the wilderness for forty years, Moses prophesied that kings to rule the kingdom of Israel would arise, as we briefly examined (Deut 17:14–20). Nevertheless, the Israelites had to live through a period of chaos and confusion, as seen in Judges, before the kingdom of Israel was visibly inaugurated and realized.

Yahweh anointed David as the king of Israel (1010–970 BC), a man who used to be a shepherd and warrior (2 Sam 5:1–5). At that point, the kingdom of Israel in Canaan, promised in the Abrahamic covenant, was inaugurated and visibly realized approximately after ten centuries passed. Through this redemptive historical realization, we can affirm that God is faithful to his covenant.

---

3. The comprehensive discussion about the Davidic covenant as a covenant of royal grant or a covenant of grant has been found in Collins, *Introduction to the Hebrew Bible*, 235; Hahn, *Kinship by Covenant*, 176–79; Weinfeld, "The Covenant of Grant in the Old Testament and in the Ancient Near East," 184–203.

However, before David was anointed as the king of Israel, Samuel anointed Saul as the first king of Israel under the blessings of Yahweh (1 Sam 10:1–27). After Saul was anointed as the king of Israel, the Ammonites under the leadership of Nahash attempted to attack the city of Jabesh. But Saul, leading the Israelites, fought against the Ammonites and slaughtered them, rescuing the city of Jabesh (1 Sam 11:1–11). After Saul's glorious victory against the Ammonites, the Israelites confirmed that Saul was, indeed, the king of Israel. So, the prophet Samuel led the covenant community of Israel into Gilgal and confirmed Saul as the king of Israel in the presence of Yahweh:

> 12 Then the people said to Samuel, "Who is it that said, 'Shall Saul reign over us?' Bring the men, that we may put them to death." 13 But Saul said, "Not a man shall be put to death this day, for today the LORD has worked salvation in Israel." 14 Then Samuel said to the people, "Come, let us go to Gilgal and there renew the kingdom." 15 So all the people went to Gilgal, and there they made Saul king before the LORD in Gilgal. There they sacrificed peace offerings before the LORD, and there Saul and all the men of Israel rejoiced greatly. (1 Sam 11:12–15)

However, Saul's kingship over Israel was under probation. He should have obeyed Yahweh and his command for a certain period of time, but he failed to do so. For example, Saul was about to lead the Israelites to fight against the Philistines at Gilgal. While he was waiting for Samuel to arrive, he became impatient and offered the burnt offering, which was not the king's but the priest's duty. In doing so, he violated a ceremonial law as defined in the Mosaic law. After Samuel arrived, he rebuked Saul and announced the end of Saul's kingship over Israel because of his disobedience to Yahweh's command:

> 5 And the Philistines mustered to fight with Israel, thirty thousand chariots and six thousand horsemen and troops like the sand on the seashore in multitude. They came up and encamped in Michmash, to the east of Beth-aven. 6 When the men of Israel saw that they were in trouble (for the people were hard pressed), the people hid themselves in caves and in holes and in rocks and in tombs and in cisterns, 7 and some Hebrews crossed the fords of the Jordan to the land of Gad and Gilead. Saul was still at Gilgal, and all the people followed him trembling. 8 He waited seven days, the time appointed by Samuel. But Samuel did not come to Gilgal, and the people were scattering from him. 9 So Saul said, "Bring the burnt offering here to me, and the peace offerings." And he offered the burnt offering. 10 As soon as he had finished offering the burnt offering, behold, Samuel came. And Saul went out to meet him and greet him. 11 Samuel said, "What have you done?" And Saul said, "When I saw that the people were scattering from me, and that you did not come within the days appointed, and that the Philistines had mustered at Michmash, 12 I said, 'Now the Philistines will come down against me at Gilgal, and I have not sought the favor of the LORD.' So I forced myself, and offered the burnt offering." 13 *And*

The Davidic Covenant and the Kingdom of God

> Samuel said to Saul, "You have done foolishly. You have not kept the command of the LORD your God, with which he commanded you. For then the LORD would have established your kingdom over Israel forever. 14 But now your kingdom shall not continue. The LORD has sought out a man after his own heart, and the LORD has commanded him to be prince over his people, because you have not kept what the LORD commanded you." 15 And Samuel arose and went up from Gilgal. The rest of the people went up after Saul to meet the army; they went up from Gilgal to Gibeah of Benjamin. And Saul numbered the people who were present with him, about six hundred men. (1 Sam 13:5–15)

Another one of Saul's failures came when Yahweh commanded Saul to fight a holy war against the Amalekites. Yahweh commanded Saul to totally destroy the Amalekites and to devote to "destruction all that they have." However, Saul and the Israelites spared Agag, the king of the Amalekites, and the best of the animals that they captured. In doing so, Saul as the king of Israel failed to fight a holy war as the vassal king on behalf of the Great King, Yahweh:

> 1 And Samuel said to Saul, "The LORD sent me to anoint you king over his people Israel; now therefore listen to the words of the LORD. 2 Thus says the LORD of hosts, 'I have noted what Amalek did to Israel in opposing them on the way when they came up out of Egypt. 3 *Now go and strike Amalek and devote to destruction all that they have. Do not spare them, but kill both man and woman, child and infant, ox and sheep, camel and donkey.'* 4 So Saul summoned the people and numbered them in Telaim, two hundred thousand men on foot, and ten thousand men of Judah. 5 And Saul came to the city of Amalek and lay in wait in the valley. 6 Then Saul said to the Kenites, "Go, depart; go down from among the Amalekites, lest I destroy you with them. For you showed kindness to all the people of Israel when they came up out of Egypt." So the Kenites departed from among the Amalekites. 7 And Saul defeated the Amalekites from Havilah as far as Shur, which is east of Egypt. 8 And he took Agag the king of the Amalekites alive and devoted to destruction all the people with the edge of the sword. 9 *But Saul and the people spared Agag and the best of the sheep and of the oxen and of the fattened calves and the lambs, and all that was good, and would not utterly destroy them. All that was despised and worthless they devoted to destruction.* 10 The word of the LORD came to Samuel: 11 "I regret that I have made Saul king, for he has turned back from following me and has not performed my commandments." And Samuel was angry, and he cried to the LORD all night. (1 Sam 15:1–11)[4]

---

4. God is not only the God of mercy but also the God of justice. God's command for Saul to fight a holy war against the enemies of the Kingdom of God is the divine revelation and prophecy that there will be final judgment against the Kingdom of Satan when the Parousia comes. So, God's command to fight a holy war against the enemies of the Kingdom of God should be interpreted in light of eschatology. However, Kugel along with other historical critical scholars discredits God's commandment for Saul to fight a holy war, arguing that that did not happen. Rather, it was the result of the Deuteronomistic historian's legendary historical imagination: "God's commandment to kill

Saul's duty was to fight a holy war as the vassal king in the presence of Yahweh, the Great King. However, he failed to fight the holy war correctly. In this sense, Saul as the first king of Israel failed to pass a probation period. So, he was disqualified from being the grantee of the covenant of kingdom. This is the historical background of David's anointing as the king of Israel after Saul. The entire covenant community of Israel, the twelve tribes of Israel, gathered together at Hebron when David was anointed as the king of Israel after Saul was disqualified as the grantee of the covenant of the kingdom:

> 1 Then all the tribes of Israel came to David at Hebron and said, "Behold, we are your bone and flesh. 2 In times past, when Saul was king over us, it was you who led out and brought in Israel. And the LORD said to you, 'You shall be shepherd of my people Israel, and you shall be prince over Israel.'" 3 So all the elders of Israel came to the king at Hebron, and King David made a covenant with them at Hebron before the LORD, and they anointed David king over Israel. 4 David was thirty years old when he began to reign, and he reigned forty years. 5 At Hebron he reigned over Judah seven years and six months, and at Jerusalem he reigned over all Israel and Judah thirty-three years. (2 Sam 5:1–5)

After David was anointed as the king of Israel, Yahweh did not make a covenant with him immediately. This is very important to remember, because it shows that he had to pass through a probationary period as Saul did. When David was anointed as the king of Israel, Jerusalem was under the control of the Jebusites. David and the Israelites attacked the Jebusites and conquered Jerusalem, known as "the stronghold of Zion" and "the city of David." Likewise, David, as a vassal king, fought a holy war on behalf of the Great King, Yahweh, and conquered Jerusalem. Thus, David moved the capital city from Hebron to Jerusalem (2 Sam 5:6–7). After David conquered Jerusalem, he fought against the Philistines according to the command of Yahweh and defeated them. In fact, Yahweh fought the holy war on behalf of David, the king of Israel, and his warriors when David obeyed Yahweh's guideline of a holy war:

> 17 When the Philistines heard that David had been anointed king over Israel, all the Philistines went up to search for David. But David heard of it and went down to the stronghold. 18 Now the Philistines had come and spread out in the Valley of Rephaim. 19 And David inquired of the LORD, "Shall I go up against the Philistines? Will you give them into my hand?" And the LORD

---

everything in sight—men, women, and little babies, as well as dumb beasts—has, for centuries, stuck in the throats of Bible readers. How could a God who is supposedly 'merciful and compassionate' even allow such a thing to happen—never mind actually *order* it to happen. Indeed, this passage and similar ones have been disowned by many modern theologians ('This is no God that I know,' declared Martin Buber), and more than one modern commentator has sought to explain away such passages as an 'anachronistic literary formulation' that could not actually have taken place." Kugel, *How to Read the Bible*, 448–49.

The Davidic Covenant and the Kingdom of God

> said to David, "Go up, for I will certainly give the Philistines into your hand." 20 And David came to Baal-perazim, and David defeated them there. And he said, "The LORD has burst through my enemies before me like a bursting flood." Therefore the name of that place is called Baal-perazim. 21 And the Philistines left their idols there, and David and his men carried them away. 22 And the Philistines came up yet again and spread out in the Valley of Rephaim. 23 And when David inquired of the LORD, he said, "You shall not go up; go around to their rear, and come against them opposite the balsam trees. 24 And when you hear the sound of marching in the tops of the balsam trees, then rouse yourself, for then the LORD has gone out before you to strike down the army of the Philistines." 25 And David did as the LORD commanded him, and struck down the Philistines from Geba to Gezer. (2 Sam 5:17–25)

Under the leadership of King David, Jerusalem became the political capital of Israel. Jerusalem also became the religious center of Israel because Israel was a theocratic kingdom in which kingdom and religion were fused together under the rule of Yahweh, the Great King. So, David brought the ark of Yahweh from Baale-Judah to Jerusalem. David and all the Israelites rejoiced before Yahweh when the ark of Yahweh was brought to Jerusalem:

> 1 David again gathered all the chosen men of Israel, thirty thousand. 2 And David arose and went with all the people who were with him from Baale-judah to bring up from there the ark of God, which is called by the name of the LORD of hosts who sits enthroned on the cherubim. 3 And they carried the ark of God on a new cart and brought it out of the house of Abinadab, which was on the hill. And Uzzah and Ahio, the sons of Abinadab, were driving the new cart, 4 with the ark of God, and Ahio went before the ark. 5 And David and all the house of Israel were making merry before the LORD, with songs and lyres and harps and tambourines and castanets and cymbals. 6 And when they came to the threshing floor of Nacon, Uzzah put out his hand to the ark of God and took hold of it, for the oxen stumbled. 7 And the anger of the LORD was kindled against Uzzah, and God struck him down there because of his error, and he died there beside the ark of God. 8 And David was angry because the LORD had burst forth against Uzzah. And that place is called Perez-uzzah, to this day. 9 And David was afraid of the LORD that day, and he said, "How can the ark of the LORD come to me?" 10 So David was not willing to take the ark of the LORD into the city of David. But David took it aside to the house of Obed-edom the Gittite. 11 And the ark of the LORD remained in the house of Obed-edom the Gittite three months, and the LORD blessed Obed-edom and all his household. 12 And it was told King David, "The LORD has blessed the household of Obed-edom and all that belongs to him, because of the ark of God." So David went and brought up the ark of God from the house of Obed-edom to the city of David with rejoicing. 13 And when those who bore the ark of the LORD had gone six steps, he sacrificed an ox and a fattened animal. 14

> And David danced before the LORD with all his might. And David was wearing a linen ephod. 15 So David and all the house of Israel brought up the ark of the LORD with shouting and with the sound of the horn. (2 Sam 6:1–15)[5]

King David's conquering of Jerusalem and bringing back the ark of Yahweh from Baale-Judah to Jerusalem were visible signs that he successfully passed through the probation period after he was anointed as the king of Israel. He executed and fought the holy war against the Philistines as the vassal king on behalf of the Great King, Yahweh. In the end, David as the vassal king was qualified to receive his kingdom by the Great King through the covenant of royal grant because he fought the victorious war. This is the historical background before the formal inauguration of the Davidic covenant.[6] Kline comprehensively summarizes the historical and theological background of the Davidic covenant as the covenant of royal grant as follows:

> The dynastic guarantees were a grant to David as the faithful servant (1 Kgs 3:6), who had waged the Lord's battle, secured the mountain city for his enthronement, and brought the ark-throne to Zion, the city of David, so identifying his kingdom as God's kingdom (1 Chr 13:1–13; 15:23–28). Significantly, the record of the Davidic Covenant comes immediately (2 Samuel 7) after the account of David's service (2 Samuel 5 and 6). In this respect David was a type of Christ, who earns the eternal kingship by fulfilling the intratrinitarian covenant of works, triumphing in the Har Magedon conflict over Satan.[7]

In this respect, we may identify the Davidic covenant as the covenant of royal grant which was already exemplified in the Prediluvian Noahic covenant and the Abrahamic covenant.

After David as the king of Israel passed the probation period, God made a covenant with David (2 Sam 7:1–17).[8] Interestingly, we do not find the language of the

---

5. Yahweh executed his covenant curse when Uzzah violated the Mosaic law in respect to the ark of God. Numbers 4:15 clearly warns that when anyone touches the ark of God, he will surely die. Thus Uzzah immediately died when he touched the ark of God.

6. For historical background for "the formal inauguration of the Davidic covenant," see Robertson, *The Christ of the Covenants*, 230–31.

7. Kline, *God Heaven and Har Magedon*, 139–40. Gentry and Wellum are not sure whether they can identify the Davidic covenant as "either a royal grant or a suzerain-vassal covenant." It is because they do not see the *continuation* of the Mosaic covenant of law under the Davidic covenant while it is the covenant of royal grant: "However, as 2 Samuel 7:14–15 makes clear: God demands faithfulness and obedience on the king's part—a faithfulness and obedience which, David understands, will effect nothing less than the divine rule in the entire world as God intended it for humanity in the covenant of creation (vv. 18–19). As noted in chapter 11, in effect, what verses 14–15 are saying is that the covenant will be fulfilled not by a faithful father alone (i.e., Yahweh keeping his promises), but also by a faithful son (i.e., the obedience of the king to Yahweh's Torah). This is one of the reasons why it is difficult to classify the Davidic covenant as either a royal grant or a suzerain-vassal covenant: it includes elements of both." Gentry and Wellum, *Kingdom through Covenant*, 642–43.

8. John Collins denies the historical validity of the Davidic covenant in 2 Samuel 7. He reads the historical context of the Davidic covenant in light of "the Deuteronomistic view of Israel's history."

divine oath to David in the original historical context of the Davidic covenant.[9] However, the Psalmist affirms that Yahweh made a sworn oath to David when he made a covenant with David:

> 1 I will sing of the steadfast love of the LORD, forever; with my mouth I will make known your faithfulness to all generations. 2 For I said, "Steadfast love will be built up forever; in the heavens you will establish your faithfulness." 3 *You have said, "I have made a covenant with my chosen one; I have sworn to David my servant: 4 'I will establish your offspring forever, and build your throne for all generations.'"Selah.* (Ps 89:1–4)

Yahweh's sworn oath to a covenant with David suggests that he will keep and fulfill all the promises that he made to David. Verse 4, "*I will establish your offspring forever, and build your throne for all generations,*" is the main highlight and summary of the promises of the Davidic covenant. It will surely be fulfilled, because Yahweh made a sworn oath to David.

The Psalmist again affirms that Yahweh made a sworn oath to David when he made the Davidic covenant:

> 33 [B]ut I will not remove from him my steadfast love or be false to my faithfulness. 34 I will not violate my covenant or alter the word that went forth from my lips. 35 *Once for all I have sworn by my holiness; I will not lie to David.* 36 His offspring shall endure forever, his throne as long as the sun before me. 37 Like the moon it shall be established forever, a faithful witness in the skies." Selah. (Ps 89:33–37)

The Psalmist highlights that the Davidic dynasty will be an everlasting one, based on Yahweh's sworn oath.

The Psalmist again confirms that Yahweh made "a sure oath" to David when he made a covenant with David:

In that regard, he argues that the Davidic covenant by the oracle of Nathan is the literary and edited product of the several Deuteronomists: "The role of the Deuteronomists in the composition of 2 Samuel 7 is controversial. On the one hand, the promise to David is certainly important in the Deuteronomistic view of Israel's history. Despite the tension with 1 Kings 5, the notion of 'rest' is typically Deuteronomic—cf. Deut 12:10. So is the statement that God 'brought Israel up out of the land of Egypt' (7:6) and the construction of a period of Judges between the exodus and the monarchy. The oracle assumes the story of David's origin as a shepherd and says that he was designated *nagid*, or prince, rather than king (7:8). Accordingly, some scholars argue that 2 Samuel 7 is simply a Deuteronomistic composition, although it may comprise more than one stage . . . On the other hand, it is unlikely that the Deuteronomists would have invented an unconditional promise that the kingdom would last forever. In Deuteronomic theology, covenants are conditional. The fortunes of the king depend on his observance of the law. The idea that God had promised David an everlasting dynasty by the oracle of Nathan was probably an established tradition in Jerusalem. The present formulation of the promise has been edited by the Deuteronomists, probably in more than one stage." Collins, *Introduction to the Hebrew Bible*, 234–35.

9. For discussion of the divine oath to David in respect to the Davidic covenant, see Hahn, *Kinship by Covenant*, 184–94.

> 10 For the sake of your servant David, do not turn away the face of your anointed one. 11 The LORD swore to David a sure oath from which he will not turn back: "One of the sons of your body I will set on your throne. 12 If your sons keep my covenant and my testimonies that I shall teach them, their sons also forever shall sit on your throne." (Ps 132:10–12)

Several Psalmists' affirmation of Yahweh's sworn oath to David with respect to the Davidic covenant suggests a very important truth. Yahweh will fulfill all the promises that he made to David when he made the covenant with David. In this respect, the Davidic covenant is a covenant of royal grant similar the Abrahamic covenant.

In many regards, we may consider David as a type of Christ who would come as the descendent of Abraham and David. Christ through his entire earthly life and the atoning death on the cross overcame the constant challenge of the power of the Kingdom of Satan and fulfilled the righteousness of the Adamic covenant of works, which the first Adam failed to accomplish.[10] Through this, God grants eternal life and the everlasting Kingdom of God as a gift for his people who are in Christ, who fought the victorious spiritual war against the challenge of the Kingdom of Satan. Similarly, God granted the kingdom of Israel to David after he fought and won a holy war in the Promised Land. He also promised to bestow the blessings of the Davidic kingdom on his descendents. The Davidic kingdom in the Promised Land was the type of the everlasting Kingdom of God, which would be consummated in Christ. In this sense, the Davidic covenant may rightly be identified as the covenant of royal grant.

The Davidic Kingdom and the Continuity of the Mosaic Covenant of Law

When Yahweh made a covenant with David, he emphasized that the kingdom of Israel in Canaan was under the Mosaic covenant. For example, Yahweh informed that Solomon would build a temple and warned that he would chastise him if Solomon disobeyed the law:

---

10. Jonathan Edwards considers David as "the greatest personal type of Christ of all under the Old Testament" when he explores the redemptive historical epoch from David to the Babylonian captivity: "This was a great dispensation of God, and a great step taken towards a further advancing of the work of redemption, according as the time drew near wherein Christ was to come. David, as he was ancestor of Christ, so he was the greatest personal type of Christ all under the Old Testament. The types of Christ were of three sorts; types of institution, or instituted types, and providential and personal types. The ordinance of sacrificing was the greatest of the instituted types; and the redemption out of Egypt was the greatest of the providential types; and David the greatest of the personal types. Hence Christ is often called David in the prophecies of scripture; as Ezek. xxxiv. 23, 24. 'And I will set up one shepherd over them, and he shall feed them, even my servant David: my servant David a prince among them;' and so in many other places: and he is very often spoken of as the seed of David, and the son of David." Edwards, *A History of the Work of Redemption*, 94.

> 12 When your days are fulfilled and you lie down with your fathers, I will raise up your offspring after you, who shall come from your body, and I will establish his kingdom. 13 He shall build a house for my name, and I will establish the throne of his kingdom forever. 14 *I will be to him a father, and he shall be to me a son. When he commits iniquity, I will discipline him with the rod of men, with the stripes of the sons of men,* 15 but my steadfast love will not depart from him, as I took it from Saul, whom I put away from before you. 16 And your house and your kingdom shall be made sure forever before me. Your throne shall be established forever." 17 In accordance with all these words, and in accordance with all this vision, Nathan spoke to David. (2 Sam 7:12–17)

In the historical context of Yahweh's covenant-making with David, he informed David that although the Davidic covenant was a covenant of royal grant, the Mosaic covenant of law was not void under the Davidic covenant.[11] Therefore, the dual sanctions of blessings and curses of the Mosaic covenant of law would be continuously applied in the kingdom of Israel in the Promised Land.[12]

We need to highlight that the dual sanctions of the blessings and curses of the Mosaic covenant of law would be applied under the Davidic covenant. Verse 14, "*I will be to him a father, and he shall be to me a son. When he commits iniquity, I will discipline him with the rod of men, with the stripes of the sons of men,*" is the prophecy in relation to David's son, Solomon. Furthermore, it is, in fact, the summary account that

---

11. Scott Hahn properly recognizes that the Davidic covenant retains "the conditional elements of the Mosaic covenant": "At the same time, the Davidic covenant appears to retain at least a note of the conditional elements of the Mosaic covenant. This is evident from several texts, especially from 2 Samuel 7:14 and Psalm 89:26–36. A question arises: How can conditionality be reconciled with the unconditional aspect of the Davidic grant? The texts themselves suggest a principle that integrates the conditional and unconditional aspects." Hahn, *Kinship by Covenant*, 197.

12. Kugel, adopting the viewpoint of several historical critical scholars, falsely argues that Nathan's oracle about "the Davidic dynasty forever" is "a pseudo-oracle" which was the work of editors of "the Deuteronomistic history": "What Nathan's oracle essentially promised was that a single dynasty, the house of David, would rule Israel forever. Forever is a long time, of course, and things did not turn out that way; but as we shall see, the house of David did rule in Judah for some four centuries, certainly an impressive record.

"In view of modern scholarship's overall skepticism about early dates—as well as everything we have seen specifically about the Deuteronomistic history and its sources—it would appear unlikely that such an oracle was ever delivered in David's own time. Instead, it seems to scholars to be a typical prediction after the fact, a pseudo-oracle composed sometime after (perhaps *long* after) the Davidic dynasty was an established reality. When exactly it might have been written is hard for them to say. The sentence about Solomon's building a temple ('He shall build a house for My name, and I will establish the throne of his kingdom forever') seems to interrupt the flow of the paragraph; take it out and you have one continuous theme, that God is establishing the Davidic dynasty forever. Since this interpretive sentence is very much in the style of Deuteronomy—Deuteronomy is the book where the temple is consistently described as a place for God's 'name' to dwell—scholars feel that this insertion must be the work of the compilers or subsequent editors of the Deuteronomistic history; they stuck this sentence into an already-existing text. Thus, this original oracle might arguably go back sometime before the mid-seventh century—but how far back is anyone's guess." Kugel, *How to Read the Bible*, 488.

Yahweh will execute his covenant lawsuit against the people of God and the Davidic kingdom when they disobey the Mosaic law.[13]

Before his death, David reminded his son Solomon about the covenant between Yahweh and himself. In particular, he reminded Solomon of 2 Samuel 7:11–17. In doing so, David emphasized the importance of obeying "the Law of Moses" for the prosperity and continuation of the Davidic kingdom:

> 1 When David's time to die drew near, he commanded Solomon his son, saying, 2 "I am about to go the way of all the earth. Be strong, and show yourself a man, 3 and keep the charge of the LORD your God, walking in his ways and keeping his statutes, his commandments, his rules, and his testimonies, as it is written in the Law of Moses, that you may prosper in all that you do and wherever you turn, 4 that the LORD may establish his word that he spoke concerning me, saying, 'If your sons pay close attention to their way, to walk before me in faithfulness with all their heart and with all their soul, you shall not lack a man on the throne of Israel.' (1 Kings 2:1–4)

The conditional clause in verse 4b, "If your sons pay close attention to their way, to walk before me in faithfulness with all their heart and with all their soul, you shall not lack a man on the throne of Israel," reveals that the Mosaic covenant of law was applied for the well-being and continuation of the Davidic earthly kingdom.

Later, the Psalmist reflects on the historical context of the Davidic covenant, and reaffirms that it is an everlasting covenant in which Yahweh assures that the Davidic kingdom will be forever. Nevertheless, Yahweh warns that if David's descendents, as the covenant community, violate the Mosaic covenant of law, he will execute the covenant curses upon "their transgression with the rod and their iniquity with stripes." This is a clear indication that the Mosaic covenant of law was continued after the Davidic covenant was inaugurated:

> 28 My steadfast love I will keep for him forever, and my covenant will stand firm for him. 29 I will establish his offspring forever and his throne as the days of the heavens. 30 *If his children forsake my law and do not walk according to my rules, 31 if they violate my statutes and do not keep my commandments, 32 then I will punish their transgression with the rod and their iniquity with stripes,* 33 but I will not remove from him my steadfast love or be false to my faithfulness. 34 I will not violate my covenant or alter the word that went forth from my lips. 35 Once for all I have sworn by my holiness; I will not lie to David.

---

13. John Collins insists that "the punishment of a rebellious king" is a reflection of "Deuteronomic theology." However, his historical critical presupposition of "Deuteronomic theology" undermines the important concept of the dual sanctions of blessings and curses that already existed from the inauguration of the Mosaic covenant on Mt. Sinai: "Nathan's oracle does provide for the punishment of a rebellious king: 'When he commits iniquity, I will punish him with a rod such as mortals use, with blows inflicted by human beings. But I will not take my steadfast love away from him as I took it from Saul' (7:14–15). Punishment for transgression is certainly in line with Deuteronomic theology." Collins, *Introduction to the Hebrew Bible*, 235.

> 36 His offspring shall endure forever, his throne as long as the sun before me.
> 37 Like the moon it shall be established forever, a faithful witness in the skies. Selah. (Ps 89:28–37)[14]

Psalm 132 as a royal psalm reflects why the Mosaic covenant of law continues under the Davidic covenant. The Psalmist beautifully portrays the continuation of the Mosaic covenant of law under the Davidic covenant as follows:

> 11 The LORD swore to David a sure oath from which he will not turn back: "One of the sons of your body I will set on your throne. 12 *If your sons keep my covenant and my testimonies that I shall teach them, their sons also forever shall sit on your throne.*" 13 For the LORD has chosen Zion; he has desired it for his dwelling place: 14 "This is my resting place forever; here I will dwell, for I have desired it. 15 I will abundantly bless her provisions; I will satisfy her poor with bread. 16 Her priests I will clothe with salvation, and her saints will shout for joy. 17 There I will make a horn to sprout for David; I have prepared a lamp for my anointed. 18 His enemies I will clothe with shame, but on him his crown will shine." (Ps 132:11–18)

Verse 12, "*If your sons keep my covenant and my testimonies that I shall teach them, their sons also forever shall sit on your throne,*" clearly suggests that the *continuation* of the Davidic dynasty will depend upon whether the covenant community of Israel are faithful to the Mosaic covenant of law.

Meanwhile, God did not allow David to build a temple, known as the house of God, because David was a holy warrior and fought bloody wars. Instead, God let David's son, Solomon, build the temple (2 Sam 7:11–13).

After Solomon was inaugurated as the king of Israel, Solomon built the temple, the house of Yahweh, according to God's command and design. The temple was the symbolic and visible place of Yahweh's dwelling among the covenant people of Israel. After seven years of labor, the temple was completed (1 Kings 6:1–37). Afterward, Solomon assembled "the elders of Israel and all the heads of the tribes, the leaders of the fathers' houses of the people of Israel" before him in Jerusalem. Until then, the ark of the covenant of Yahweh remained in the movable tabernacle in the city of David, Zion. When Solomon had built the permanent temple, it was time to move the ark of the covenant of Yahweh into the Most Holy Place of the temple. The priests brought the ark of the covenant of Yahweh "in the inner sanctuary of the house, in the Most

---

14. Kline insists that the typological and earthly administration of the Davidic kingdom was "an administration of the Sinaitic covenant of works." However, we would not use the term, "the Sinaitic covenant of works." I think that "an administration of the Sinaitic or Mosaic covenant of law" is a better way to make a proper distinction between the Adamic covenant of works and the Mosaic covenant of law: "In so far as the dynastic grant to David referred to the typological level of the kingdom it was *an administration of the Sinaitic covenant of works*, and accordingly it included a warning that for failure to obey the law of the theocratic king, occupants of David's throne would incur the curse of the covenant (2 Sam 7:14; Ps 89:30–32)." Kline, *God Heaven and Har Magedon*, 140, emphasis added.

Holy Place, underneath the wings of cherubim." Inside of the ark, there were "the two tablets of stone that Moses put there at Horeb" where Yahweh made the Mosaic covenant of law with the covenant community of Israel after they were released from Egyptian bondage. When the priest left the Holy Place, the glory cloud filled the house of Yahweh. In fact, the glory cloud was the visible glory of Yahweh. In doing so, the spectacular and shining glory of the heavenly Kingdom of God intruded into the earthly temple, which was designated as the dwelling place of Yahweh:

> 1 Then Solomon assembled the elders of Israel and all the heads of the tribes, the leaders of the fathers' houses of the people of Israel, before King Solomon in Jerusalem, to bring up the ark of the covenant of the LORD out of the city of David, which is Zion. 2 And all the men of Israel assembled to King Solomon at the feast in the month Ethanim, which is the seventh month. 3 And all the elders of Israel came, and the priests took up the ark. 4 And they brought up the ark of the LORD, the tent of meeting, and all the holy vessels that were in the tent; the priests and the Levites brought them up. 5 And King Solomon and all the congregation of Israel, who had assembled before him, were with him before the ark, sacrificing so many sheep and oxen that they could not be counted or numbered. 6 Then the priests brought the ark of the covenant of the LORD to its place in the inner sanctuary of the house, in the Most Holy Place, underneath the wings of the cherubim. 7 For the cherubim spread out their wings over the place of the ark, so that the cherubim overshadowed the ark and its poles. 8 And the poles were so long that the ends of the poles were seen from the Holy Place before the inner sanctuary; but they could not be seen from outside. And they are there to this day. 9 There was nothing in the ark except the two tablets of stone that Moses put there at Horeb, where the LORD made a covenant with the people of Israel, when they came out of the land of Egypt. 10 And when the priests came out of the Holy Place, a cloud filled the house of the LORD, 11 so that the priests could not stand to minister because of the cloud, for the glory of the LORD filled the house of the LORD. (1 Kings 8:1–11)

In Solomon's prayer of dedication for the temple, he affirmed that the continuation of the kingdom of Israel would depend upon whether or not David's sons and the covenant community of Israel would be obedient to the Mosaic law:

> 22 Then Solomon stood before the altar of the LORD in the presence of all the assembly of Israel and spread out his hands toward heaven, 23 and said, "O LORD, God of Israel, there is no God like you, in heaven above or on earth beneath, keeping covenant and showing steadfast love to your servants who walk before you with all their heart, 24 who have kept with your servant David my father what you declared to him. You spoke with your mouth, and with your hand have fulfilled it this day. 25 *Now therefore, O LORD, God of Israel, keep for your servant David my father what you have promised him, saying, 'You*

> shall not lack a man to sit before me on the throne of Israel, if only your sons pay close attention to their way, to walk before me as you have walked before me.' 26 Now therefore, O God of Israel, let your word be confirmed, which you have spoken to your servant David my father. (1 Kings 8:22–26)

Solomon's prayer of dedication confirms that the kingdom of Israel was promised by the Davidic covenant. Nevertheless, the *continuation* of the earthly kingdom of Israel would be conditional and would depend upon the attitude of the covenant community of Israel toward the Mosaic covenant of law. Solomon recalled Yahweh's *conditional promise* to his father David, saying "You shall not lack a man to sit before me on the throne of Israel, if only your sons pay close attention to their way, to walk before me as you have walked before me."

After Solomon's prayer of dedication, Solomon and the covenant community of Israel dedicated the temple of Yahweh (1 Kings 8:62–66; 2 Chr 7:4–10). Afterward Yahweh appeared to Solomon, and he reaffirmed that the continuation of the kingdom of Israel would be conditional because it would depend upon whether Solomon's sons and the covenant community of Israel were faithful to the Mosaic covenant of law:

> 1 As soon as Solomon had finished building the house of the LORD and the king's house and all that Solomon desired to build, 2 the LORD appeared to Solomon a second time, as he had appeared to him at Gibeon. 3 And the LORD said to him, "I have heard your prayer and your plea, which you have made before me. I have consecrated this house that you have built, by putting my name there forever. My eyes and my heart will be there for all time. 4 *And as for you, if you will walk before me, as David your father walked, with integrity of heart and uprightness, doing according to all that I have commanded you, and keeping my statutes and my rules, 5 then I will establish your royal throne over Israel forever, as I promised David your father, saying, 'You shall not lack a man on the throne of Israel.' 6 But if you turn aside from following me, you or your children, and do not keep my commandments and my statutes that I have set before you, but go and serve other gods and worship them, 7 then I will cut off Israel from the land that I have given them, and the house that I have consecrated for my name I will cast out of my sight, and Israel will become a proverb and a byword among all peoples. 8 And this house will become a heap of ruins. Everyone passing by it will be astonished and will hiss, and they will say, 'Why has the LORD done thus to this land and to this house?' 9 Then they will say, 'Because they abandoned the LORD their God who brought their fathers out of the land of Egypt and laid hold on other gods and worshiped them and served them. Therefore the LORD has brought all this disaster on them.'"* (1 Kings 9:1–9)

Solomon became very famous for his wisdom and wealth in the kingdom of Israel and among the neighboring kingdoms. King Solomon exceeded "all the kings of the earth in riches and in wisdom" and many people visited Solomon to hear his outstanding wisdom, which God had engraved into his mind. Visiting Solomon, they brought "articles of silver and gold, garments, myrrh, spices, horses, and mules, so much year by year" (1 Kings 10:23–25). Although Solomon was so blessed by Yahweh in his wisdom and wealth, he did not use them for the glory of Yahweh. Instead, he turned from Yahweh morally and religiously, failing to set an example for the covenant community of Israel. So Yahweh prophesied through the mouth of the prophet Ahijah that the kingdom of Israel would be divided into two because Solomon and the covenant community of Israel failed to keep the Mosaic covenant of law:

> 29 And at that time, when Jeroboam went out of Jerusalem, the prophet Ahijah the Shilonite found him on the road. Now Ahijah had dressed himself in a new garment, and the two of them were alone in the open country. 30 Then Ahijah laid hold of the new garment that was on him, and tore it into twelve pieces. 31 And he said to Jeroboam, "Take for yourself ten pieces, for thus says the LORD, the God of Israel, 'Behold, I am about to tear the kingdom from the hand of Solomon and will give you ten tribes 32 (but he shall have one tribe, for the sake of my servant David and for the sake of Jerusalem, the city that I have chosen out of all the tribes of Israel), 33 because they have forsaken me and worshiped Ashtoreth the goddess of the Sidonians, Chemosh the god of Moab, and Milcom the god of the Ammonites, and they have not walked in my ways, doing what is right in my sight and keeping my statutes and my rules, as David his father did. 34 Nevertheless, I will not take the whole kingdom out of his hand, but I will make him ruler all the days of his life, for the sake of David my servant whom I chose, who kept my commandments and my statutes. 35 But I will take the kingdom out of his son's hand and will give it to you, ten tribes. 36 Yet to his son I will give one tribe, that David my servant may always have a lamp before me in Jerusalem, the city where I have chosen to put my name. 37 And I will take you, and you shall reign over all that your soul desires, and you shall be king over Israel. 38 And if you will listen to all that I command you, and will walk in my ways, and do what is right in my eyes by keeping my statutes and my commandments, as David my servant did, I will be with you and will build you a sure house, as I built for David, and I will give Israel to you. 39 And I will afflict the offspring of David because of this, but not forever.'" 40 Solomon sought therefore to kill Jeroboam. But Jeroboam arose and fled into Egypt, to Shishak king of Egypt, and was in Egypt until the death of Solomon. (1 Kings 11:29–40)

As the prophet Ahijah prophesied, the kingdom of Israel was divided into the northern kingdom of Israel and the southern kingdom of Judah. Solomon's son, Rehoboam, became the king of the southern kingdom of Judah while Jeroboam became the king of the northern kingdom of Israel, just as the prophet Ahijah had foretold:

> 16 And when all Israel saw that the king did not listen to them, the people answered the king, "What portion do we have in David? We have no inheritance

in the son of Jesse. To your tents, O Israel! Look now to your own house, David." So Israel went to their tents. 17 But Rehoboam reigned over the people of Israel who lived in the cities of Judah. 18 Then King Rehoboam sent Adoram, who was taskmaster over the forced labor, and all Israel stoned him to death with stones. And King Rehoboam hurried to mount his chariot to flee to Jerusalem. 19 So Israel has been in rebellion against the house of David to this day. 20 And when all Israel heard that Jeroboam had returned, they sent and called him to the assembly and made him king over all Israel. There was none that followed the house of David but the tribe of Judah only. 21 When Rehoboam came to Jerusalem, he assembled all the house of Judah and the tribe of Benjamin, 180,000 chosen warriors, to fight against the house of Israel, to restore the kingdom to Rehoboam the son of Solomon. 22 But the word of God came to Shemaiah the man of God: 23 "Say to Rehoboam the son of Solomon, king of Judah, and to all the house of Judah and Benjamin, and to the rest of the people, 24 'Thus says the LORD, You shall not go up or fight against your relatives the people of Israel. Every man return to his home, for this thing is from me.'"So they listened to the word of the LORD and went home again, according to the word of the LORD. (1 Kings 12:16–24)

In fact, the division of the kingdom was the result of Solomon's disobedience to the Mosaic covenant of law. So, Yahweh executed his covenant lawsuit against Solomon and his kingdom because Solomon and the people of Israel disobeyed the Mosaic law and worshipped idols. Yet Yahweh spared the Davidic kingdom through the southern kingdom of Judah for the sake of David.

The author of Kings recounts the history of ancient Israel from Solomon's dynastic succession of the Davidic dynasty to the fall of the southern kingdom of Judah and the Babylonian exile. In doing so, he summarizes that the fall of the northern kingdom of Israel was due to the violation and disobedience of the Mosaic covenant of law:

6 In the ninth year of Hoshea, the king of Assyria captured Samaria, and he carried the Israelites away to Assyria and placed them in Halah, and on the Habor, the river of Gozan, and in the cities of the Medes. 7 And this occurred because the people of Israel had sinned against the LORD their God, who had brought them up out of the land of Egypt from under the hand of Pharaoh king of Egypt, and had feared other gods 8 and walked in the customs of the nations whom the LORD drove out before the people of Israel, and in the customs that the kings of Israel had practiced. 9 And the people of Israel did secretly against the LORD their God things that were not right. They built for themselves high places in all their towns, from watchtower to fortified city. 10 They set up for themselves pillars and Asherim on every high hill and under every green tree, 11 and there they made offerings on all the high places, as the nations did whom the LORD carried away before them. And they did wicked things, provoking the LORD to anger, 12 and they served idols, of which the LORD had said to them, "You shall not do this." 13 Yet the LORD warned

Israel and Judah by every prophet and every seer, saying, "Turn from your evil ways and keep my commandments and my statutes, in accordance with all the Law that I commanded your fathers, and that I sent to you by my servants the prophets." 14 But they would not listen, but were stubborn, as their fathers had been, who did not believe in the LORD their God. 15 They despised his statutes and his covenant that he made with their fathers and the warnings that he gave them. They went after false idols and became false, and they followed the nations that were around them, concerning whom the LORD had commanded them that they should not do like them. 16 And they abandoned all the commandments of the LORD their God, and made for themselves metal images of two calves; and they made an Asherah and worshiped all the host of heaven and served Baal. 17 And they burned their sons and their daughters as offerings and used divination and omens and sold themselves to do evil in the sight of the LORD, provoking him to anger. 18 Therefore the LORD was very angry with Israel and removed them out of his sight. None was left but the tribe of Judah only. 19 Judah also did not keep the commandments of the LORD their God, but walked in the customs that Israel had introduced. 20 And the LORD rejected all the descendants of Israel and afflicted them and gave them into the hand of plunderers, until he had cast them out of his sight. 21 When he had torn Israel from the house of David, they made Jeroboam the son of Nebat king. And Jeroboam drove Israel from following the LORD and made them commit great sin. 22 The people of Israel walked in all the sins that Jeroboam did. They did not depart from them, 23 until the LORD removed Israel out of his sight, as he had spoken by all his servants the prophets. So Israel was exiled from their own land to Assyria until this day. (2 Kings 17:6–23)

We may give special attention to the summary description of Israel's violation of the covenant in verse 16: "They despised his statutes and his covenant that he made with their fathers and the warnings that he gave them. They went after false idols and became false, and they followed the nations that were around them, concerning whom the LORD had commanded them that they should not do like them." In fact, the statement of verse 15a that "They despised his statutes and his covenant that he made with their fathers" clearly indicates that the covenant community of the northern kingdom of Israel broke the covenant that Yahweh made with their ancestors. And that covenant was the Mosaic covenant, made on Mount Sinai. So, the fall of the northern kingdom of Israel and the covenant community's exile and dispersion to Assyria was the result of Yahweh's covenantal curse because they broke the Mosaic covenant of law. Verse 23b, "So Israel was exiled from their own land to Assyria until this day," suggests that the survival remnant of the northern kingdom of Israel became the covenant diaspora community outside of the Promised Land in the midst of the powerful pagan Assyrian Empire. The dispersion of the covenant diaspora community in the pagan Assyrian Empire was due to the breaking and violation of the Mosaic covenant of law. In a word, it was the result of Yahweh's covenant curse against the

The Davidic Covenant and the Kingdom of God

covenant community of the northern kingdom of Israel. However, Yahweh used the covenant diaspora community in the midst of the Assyrian Empire to demonstrate the existence and works of the living God in light of the mission to Gentiles.

During the reign of Asa in the southern kingdom of Judah, there was religious reformation after the king heard "the prophecy of Azariah the son of Obed." The people of Judah gathered at Jerusalem, sacrificing to Yahweh. And there was a renewal ceremony of the Sinaitic covenant:

> 8 As soon as Asa heard these words, the prophecy of Azariah the son of Oded, he took courage and put away the detestable idols from all the land of Judah and Benjamin and from the cities that he had taken in the hill country of Ephraim, and he repaired the altar of the LORD that was in front of the vestibule of the house of the LORD. 9 And he gathered all Judah and Benjamin, and those from Ephraim, Manasseh, and Simeon who were residing with them, for great numbers had deserted to him from Israel when they saw that the LORD his God was with him. 10 They were gathered at Jerusalem in the third month of the fifteenth year of the reign of Asa. 11 They sacrificed to the LORD on that day from the spoil that they had brought 700 oxen and 7,000 sheep. 12 And they entered into a covenant to seek the LORD, the God of their fathers, with all their heart and with all their soul, 13 but that whoever would not seek the LORD, the God of Israel, should be put to death, whether young or old, man or woman. 14 *They swore an oath to the LORD with a loud voice and with shouting and with trumpets and with horns. 15 And all Judah rejoiced over the oath, for they had sworn with all their heart and had sought him with their whole desire, and he was found by them, and the LORD gave them rest all around.* (2 Chr 15:8–15)

During the covenant renewal ceremony, the covenant community made a sworn oath to Yahweh. Here we find the very important truth that Yahweh did not make a sworn oath to the covenant, but rather the covenant community did so in the renewal of the Sinaitic covenant. This is the historical and covenantal background that led to God's execution of blessings and curses according to Israel's obedience and disobedience to the Mosaic law. When Asa and the people of Judah obeyed the Mosaic law with all their heart, Yahweh blessed the southern kingdom of Judah, which preserved the Davidic dynasty. Verse 15, "*And all Judah rejoiced over the oath, for they had sworn with all their heart and had sought him with their whole desire, and he was found by them, and the LORD gave them rest all around,*" comprehensively reflects that the people of Judah rejoiced in the sworn oath that they made when there was a renewal of the Sinaitic covenant. And Yahweh blessed them with "rest all around" because they obeyed the Mosaic law with all their heart and desire.

During the reign of Zedekiah, Yahweh made the covenant with the people of Judah. Surprisingly, the people of Judah passed between the torn parts of the calf. In fact, it was the covenant community's sworn oath to the covenant. And the prophecy of the desolation of the cities of Judah was based upon breaking the covenant:

> 17 "Therefore, thus says the LORD: You have not obeyed me by proclaiming liberty, every one to his brother and to his neighbor; behold, I proclaim to you liberty to the sword, to pestilence, and to famine, declares the LORD. I will make you a horror to all the kingdoms of the earth. 18 *And the men who transgressed my covenant and did not keep the terms of the covenant that they made before me, I will make them like the calf that they cut in two and passed between its parts* 19 *the officials of Judah, the officials of Jerusalem, the eunuchs, the priests, and all the people of the land who passed between the parts of the calf.* 20 And I will give them into the hand of their enemies and into the hand of those who seek their lives. Their dead bodies shall be food for the birds of the air and the beasts of the earth. 21 And Zedekiah king of Judah and his officials I will give into the hand of their enemies and into the hand of those who seek their lives, into the hand of the army of the king of Babylon which has withdrawn from you. 22 Behold, I will command, declares the LORD, and will bring them back to this city. And they will fight against it and take it and burn it with fire. I will make the cities of Judah a desolation without inhabitant." (Jer 34:17–22)

By the way, the covenant that the people of Judah broke was not the Abrahamic covenant but the Sinaitic covenant. As the people of Israel made a sworn oath to the original ratification of the Sinaitic covenant (Ex 19:8; 24:3,7), so the people of Judah made a sworn oath while Yahweh was renewing the Sinaitic covenant (Jer 34:19–20). Verse 19, *"the officials of Judah, the officials of Jerusalem, the eunuchs, the priests, and all the people of the land who passed between the parts of the calf,"* provides a comprehensive and vivid picture that the people of Judah's passing between the torn parts of the calf was the covenant community's sworn oath to the covenant in the presence of the Great King, Yahweh. Likewise, in light of the Sinaitic covenant, the covenant, made with the people of Judah during the reign of Zedekiah, was the renewal of the Sinaitic covenant. Breaking the covenant after the people of Judah's sworn oath during the renewal of the Sinaitic covenant became the covenantal background of Yahweh's curse and wrath against the southern kingdom of Judah. Yahweh used the Babylonian kingdom when he executed the covenant lawsuit and the southern kingdom of Judah fell. The survivors were removed from the Promised Land, and went into Babylonian exile in 586 B.C.

Likewise, the theocratic kingdom which was promised to Abraham was fulfilled as the Davidic kingdom was inaugurated and visibly realized. Nevertheless, the people of Israel under the Davidic kingdom had to undergo dual sanctions, such as blessings and curses, described in the Mosaic covenant of law as recorded in the ancient history of Israel.

The Davidic Kingdom and the Continuity of the Abrahamic Covenant

The Abrahamic covenant is foundational for the formation of the Davidic covenant.[15] Through the psalm of thanks, David recognized that the inheritance of the land of Canaan and the covenant community was the fulfillment of the Abrahamic covenant, which is everlasting (1 Chr 16:7–43). David summarizes the foundational aspect of the Abrahamic covenant under the Davidic kingdom as follows:

> 14 He is the LORD our God; his judgments are in all the earth. 15 *Remember his covenant forever, the word that he commanded, for a thousand generations,* 16 *the covenant that he made with Abraham, his sworn promise to Isaac,* 17 *which he confirmed as a statute to Jacob, as an everlasting covenant to Israel,* 18 saying, "To you I will give the land of Canaan, as your portion for an inheritance." 19 When you were few in number, and of little account, and sojourners in it, 20 wandering from nation to nation, from one kingdom to another people, 21 he allowed no one to oppress them; he rebuked kings on their account, 22 saying, "Touch not my anointed ones, do my prophets no harm!" 23 Sing to the LORD, all the earth! Tell of his salvation from day to day. 24 Declare his glory among the nations, his marvelous works among all the peoples! (1 Chr 16:14–24)

David's psalm of thanks to Yahweh recognizes that the Abrahamic covenant is "an everlasting covenant to Israel." David's inauguration as the king of Israel and the inheritance of Canaan by the people of Israel, building the Davidic kingdom, were the earthly fulfillment of the Abrahamic covenant. In addition, it is important to note that David's recognition of the Abrahamic covenant as "an everlasting covenant to Israel" signifies that the ultimate fulfillment of the Abrahamic covenant will be fully realized in the heavenly Kingdom of God in Jesus Christ. Kline comprehensively summarizes the Davidic covenant as "an administration of the Abrahamic Covenant" as follows:

> At the same time, in so far as there was a reference to the New Covenant level of the kingdom, the Davidic Covenant was an administration of the Abrahamic Covenant as a covenant of sovereign grace and the promised dynasty of David culminated in the Messiah, the king in whom the dynasty was confirmed for ever (2 Sam 7:15, 16; Ps 89:3, 4, 28f., 33ff.).[16]

---

15. Scott Hahn comprehensively summarizes the close relationship and continuity between the Abrahamic and Davidic covenants: "First and foremost, both are grant-type covenants involving a divine oath that is directed at blessing nations through the promised seed. Second, the Abrahamic covenant involves three promissory elements (i.e., land, kingship, and world blessing). All three of these are fulfilled in the Davidic covenant, at least provisionally. Third, Abraham and David are both archetypal father figures whose faithful obedience caused their sons to receive a covenant grant of blessing by divine oath in connection with Jerusalem. Fourth, from a canonical reading of the Old Testament, Abraham and David are the sole witnesses to the royal priesthood of Melchizedek." Hahn, *Kinship by Covenant*, 196.

16. Kline, *God, Heaven and Har Magedon*, 140.

Psalm 105 recounts the ancient history of Israel from the Abrahamic covenant, through the Exodus and forty years in the wilderness, to the inheritance of the land of Canaan (Ps 105:1–45). In this historical psalm, the Abrahamic covenant is reaffirmed as "an everlasting covenant" as follows:

> 1 Oh give thanks to the LORD; call upon his name; make known his deeds among the peoples! 2 Sing to him, sing praises to him; tell of all his wondrous works! 3 Glory in his holy name; let the hearts of those who seek the LORD rejoice! 4 Seek the LORD and his strength; seek his presence continually! 5 Remember the wondrous works that he has done, his miracles, and the judgments he uttered, 6 O offspring of Abraham, his servant, children of Jacob, his chosen ones! 7 He is the LORD our God; his judgments are in all the earth. 8 *He remembers his covenant forever, the word that he commanded, for a thousand generations, 9 the covenant that he made with Abraham, his sworn promise to Isaac, 10 which he confirmed to Jacob as a statute, to Israel as an everlasting covenant,* 11 saying, "To you I will give the land of Canaan as your portion for an inheritance." 12 When they were few in number, of little account, and sojourners in it, 13 wandering from nation to nation, from one kingdom to another people, 14 he allowed no one to oppress them; he rebuked kings on their account, 15 saying, "Touch not my anointed ones, do my prophets no harm!" (Ps 105:1–15)

During the reign of Jehoahaz, the son of Jehu in the northern kingdom of Israel, Jehoahaz was "evil in the sight of the Lord and followed the sins of Jeroboam the son of Nebot, which he made Israel to sin." Yahweh's anger was poured out against the covenant community of Israel. Yahweh disciplined and cursed them through the hands of "Hazael king of Syria" and "Ben-hadad the son of Hazael." Yahweh used the kingdom of Syria to discipline the northern kingdom of Israel when Jehoahaz and the people of Israel became idol worshippers by erecting the Asherah and fell into sin:

> 1 In the twenty-third year of Joash the son of Ahaziah, king of Judah, Jehoahaz the son of Jehu began to reign over Israel in Samaria, and he reigned seventeen years. 2 He did what was evil in the sight of the LORD and followed the sins of Jeroboam the son of Nebat, which he made Israel to sin; he did not depart from them. 3 And the anger of the LORD was kindled against Israel, and he gave them continually into the hand of Hazael king of Syria and into the hand of Ben-hadad the son of Hazael. 4 Then Jehoahaz sought the favor of the LORD, and the LORD listened to him, for he saw the oppression of Israel, how the king of Syria oppressed them. 5 (Therefore the LORD gave Israel a savior, so that they escaped from the hand of the Syrians, and the people of Israel lived in their homes as formerly. 6 Nevertheless, they did not depart from the sins of the house of Jeroboam, which he made Israel to sin, but walked in them; and the Asherah also remained in Samaria.) 7 For there was not left to Jehoahaz an army of more than fifty horsemen and ten chariots and ten

thousand footmen, for the king of Syria had destroyed them and made them like the dust at threshing. (2 Kings 13:1–7)

Based on the Mosaic covenant of law, Yahweh could have cursed and destroyed the northern kingdom of Israel, executing the covenant lawsuit against them when the people of Israel fell into sin. Yet Yahweh spared them, although he disciplined the northern kingdom of Israel "all the days of Jehoahaz" during the reign of "Hazael king of Syria" due to the sins of Israel. Remarkably, Yahweh's grace and compassion on sinful Israel was based upon the Abrahamic covenant, in which he made a sworn oath to Abraham, Isaac, and Jacob:

> 22 Now Hazael king of Syria oppressed Israel all the days of Jehoahaz. 23 *But the LORD was gracious to them and had compassion on them, and he turned toward them, because of his covenant with Abraham, Isaac, and Jacob, and would not destroy them, nor has he cast them from his presence until now.* 24 When Hazael king of Syria died, Ben-hadad his son became king in his place. 25 Then Jehoash the son of Jehoahaz took again from Ben-hadad the son of Hazael the cities that he had taken from Jehoahaz his father in war. Three times Joash defeated him and recovered the cities of Israel. (2 Kings 13:22–25)

We need to pay special attention to a brief historical analysis of verse 23, "But the LORD was gracious to them and had compassion on them, and he turned toward them, because of his covenant with Abraham, Isaac, and Jacob, and would not destroy them, nor has he cast them from his presence until now." Here, the author of Kings certainly emphasizes that Yahweh's grace and compassion to the sinful community of the northern kingdom of Israel was "because of his covenant with Abraham, Isaac, and Jacob." The author of Kings as a member of the post-exilic covenant community reflected on the past history of the northern kingdom of Israel and was reminded that Yahweh's grace upon sinful Israel was based upon the Abrahamic covenant, which was efficacious even under the Mosaic covenant of law and the Davidic covenant of kingdom.

The Son of David and Jesus as the Davidic Messiah

The relationship between the Davidic kingdom and the messianic kingdom is so pertinent for a proper understanding of the Kingdom of God in redemptive history. Robertson properly relates "David's throne" to "Jesus Christ's session at God's right hand" in the present time, over against the modern dispensationalist's denial of it, as follows:

> The two features central to the Davidic covenant as noted earlier relate Israel's kingship immediately with God's throne. Both the line of David and the location of Jerusalem interrelate with the lordship of God himself. It is in this context of the Old Testament identification of the throne of David with the throne of God that the position of the modern dispensationalist must be assessed. The dispensationalist asserts that Jesus Christ's session at God's right hand had nothing to

do with his occupancy of David's throne. John F. Walvoord asserts: "A search of the New Testament reveals that there is not one reference connecting the present session of Christ with the Davidic throne." However, if it be understood that from the perspective of the Old Testament itself, David's throne was considered as coordinate with God's throne, this position hardly could be maintained. The fact that "the Christ," the anointed one of Israel, is seated at God's right hand, has everything to do with David's throne. Christ's present reign represents the fulfillment of the Old Testament anticipation in this regard.[17]

Unlike modern dispensationalists' *breach and disconnection* between David's throne and the Messiah's present reign at God's right hand in heaven, there is close connection between the two. In the history of ancient Israel, the kingdom of Israel was succeeded by the Son of David, which was one of the promises of the Davidic covenant. The New Testament writers' identification of Jesus Christ as the Son of David suggests that he came to the world as the Davidic Messiah, who is a redemptive historical fulfillment of the Old Testament prophecy that the Messiah would come as the Son of David.

Identifying Jesus as the Son of David also shows that the Davidic throne has been captured and succeeded by the Davidic Messiah's throne. In that sense, the Davidic throne is the type of the Messiah's throne in the kingdom of heaven. Likewise, there is a beautiful redemptive historical connection and succession between David's throne in the earthly Jerusalem and the Davidic Messiah's throne at the right hand of God in the heavenly Jerusalem.

During the reign of David and Solomon, the kingdom of Israel prospered under the blessings of Yahweh. However, after Solomon's day, the kingdom of Israel was divided into the northern kingdom of Israel and the southern kingdom of Judah. Ever since then, the kingdom of Israel never recovered to the pinnacle period of David and Solomon. Instead, the northern kingdom of Israel fell in 722 B.C. through the military campaign of Assyria. And the southern kingdom of Judah fell as well in 586 B.C. to the military attack of the Babylonian kingdom. So the Israelites questioned whether Yahweh's covenantal promise to David was everlasting. In fact, in the original covenant-making context Yahweh promised David that the kingdom of Israel, as the Davidic kingdom, would indeed be everlasting (2 Sam 7:12–16).

Psalm 89 is the psalm of the community's lament. It mourns curses that fell upon the covenant community of Israel due to disobedience to the Mosaic law. Nevertheless, it reminds them of Yahweh's covenantal promise to David. Moreover, it notes that the Davidic kingdom, promised in the covenant, would last forever "as the days of the heavens":

> 3 You have said, "I have made a covenant with my chosen one; I have sworn to David my servant: 4 'I will establish your offspring forever, and build your

---

17. Robertson, *The Christ of the Covenants*, 251.

The Davidic Covenant and the Kingdom of God

throne for all generations.'"Selah. . . . 27 And I will make him the firstborn, the highest of the kings of the earth. 28 *My steadfast love I will keep for him forever, and my covenant will stand firm for him. 29 I will establish his offspring forever and his throne as the days of the heavens.* 30 If his children forsake my law and do not walk according to my rules, 31 if they violate my statutes and do not keep my commandments, 32 then I will punish their transgression with the rod and their iniquity with stripes, 33 but I will not remove from him my steadfast love or be false to my faithfulness. 34 *I will not violate my covenant or alter the word that went forth from my lips. 35 Once for all I have sworn by my holiness; I will not lie to David. 36 His offspring shall endure forever, his throne as long as the sun before me. 37 Like the moon it shall be established forever, a faithful witness in the skies."* Selah. (Ps 89:3–4, 27–37)

Isaiah as a prophet of the southern kingdom of Judah witnessed the fall of the northern kingdom of Israel. In addition, Yahweh showed him through a vision that the southern kingdom of Judah would fall through the military power of the Babylonian kingdom. In this critical historical juncture, Isaiah prophesied that the Messiah would come as a "Wonderful Counselor, Mighty God, Everlasting Father, Prince of Peace." Moreover, he would come as the king "on the throne of David and over his kingdom." Isaiah's prophecy signifies that the Messiah would arrive as a divine figure:

2 The people who walked in darkness have seen a great light; those who dwelt in a land of deep darkness, on them has light shined. 3 You have multiplied the nation; you have increased its joy; they rejoice before you as with joy at the harvest, as they are glad when they divide the spoil. 4 For the yoke of his burden, and the staff for his shoulder, the rod of his oppressor, you have broken as on the day of Midian. 5 For every boot of the tramping warrior in battle tumult and every garment rolled in blood will be burned as fuel for the fire. 6 *For to us a child is born, to us a son is given; and the government shall be upon his shoulder, and his name shall be called Wonderful Counselor, Mighty God, Everlasting Father, Prince of Peace. 7 Of the increase of his government and of peace there will be no end, on the throne of David and over his kingdom, to establish it and to uphold it with justice and with righteousness from this time forth and forevermore. The zeal of the LORD of hosts will do this.* (Isa 9:2–8)

Isaiah's Messianic prophecy suggests that he would come as the king of the Davidic kingdom. This signifies that the Messianic kingdom will be not only everlasting but also a redemptive historical succession of the Davidic kingdom. In that sense, the kingdom of Israel as the Davidic kingdom is a type of the everlasting Kingdom of God in Jesus Christ.[18]

---

18. Ryrie as a dispensational theologian fails to see the Davidic kingdom in light of redemptive historical continuity. In doing so, he falsely argues that "the visible, earthly kingdom promised in the Davidic covenant" will be fulfilled in "the future, earthly kingdom" in the Second Coming of Jesus Christ: "A number of passages in Isaiah also predict and describe the visible, earthly kingdom

Isaiah's Messianic prophecy was fulfilled when Jesus Christ came to this world as *the Son of David*. The birth of Jesus was foretold by the angel Gabriel to the virgin Mary. And the angel announced that God would grant to Jesus "the throne of his father David," and he would rule over his kingdom forever:

> 26 In the sixth month the angel Gabriel was sent from God to a city of Galilee named Nazareth, 27 to a virgin betrothed to a man whose name was Joseph, of the house of David. And the virgin's name was Mary. 28 And he came to her and said, "Greetings, O favored one, the Lord is with you!" 29 But she was greatly troubled at the saying, and tried to discern what sort of greeting this might be. 30 And the angel said to her, "Do not be afraid, Mary, for you have found favor with God. 31 And behold, you will conceive in your womb and bear a son, and you shall call his name Jesus. 32 *He will be great and will be called the Son of the Most High. And the Lord God will give to him the throne of his father David, 33 and he will reign over the house of Jacob forever, and of his kingdom there will be no end* [32 οὗτος ἔσται μέγας καὶ υἱὸς ὑψίστου κληθήσεται καὶ δώσει αὐτῷ κύριος ὁ θεὸς τὸν θρόνον Δαυὶδ τοῦ πατρὸς αὐτοῦ, 33 καὶ βασιλεύσει ἐπὶ τὸν οἶκον Ἰακὼβ εἰς τοὺς αἰῶνας καὶ τῆς βασιλείας αὐτοῦ οὐκ ἔσται τέλος.]." (Luke 1:26–33)

Before Jesus Christ's conception through the power of the Holy Spirit and birth through the virgin Mary, God confirmed that Jesus Christ would come as the fulfillment of the Messianic prophecy of the Old Testament. And he would come as the king of the Davidic kingdom. His kingdom would be an everlasting one. Here, we need to pay close attention to the angel Gabriel's announcement to Mary. The angel's announcement in verses 32–33, "He will be great and will be called the Son of the Most High. And the Lord God will give to him the throne of his father David, and he will reign over the house of Jacob forever, and of his kingdom there will be no end," is God's affirmation that Jesus will come as the fulfillment of the Davidic Messianic prophecy in the Old Testament. And it signifies that God will give to Jesus Christ "the throne of his father David," and his Kingdom will be the everlasting Kingdom.[19]

---

promised in the Davidic covenant. Isaiah predicted the reign of Messiah 'on the throne of David and over his kingdom' (9:7). In other places he described some of the characteristics of that kingdom (chaps. 11; 24—25; 54; 60—61) . . . In other words, whatever form the kingdom would take in the present age (i.e., the mysteries of the kingdom) would not change or abrogate the promises of the Davidic Covenant concerning the future, earthly kingdom." Ryrie, *Basic Theology*, 533–34.

19. Ryrie, making a sharp distinction between Israel and the church as a dispensationalist, argues that Jesus will rule over "the house of Jacob" in the future millennial kingdom. So, he insists that the promise of Luke 1:33 is "not now being fulfilled" because the church is different from "the house of Jacob." Furthermore, he argues that although Christ is now "at the right hand of the Father," this cannot be identified with "the throne of David." Likewise, Ryrie fails to see that there is a redemptive historical continuity and succession between "the throne of David" and Jesus' inauguration of reigning over the Kingdom of God at the right hand of Father after his death, resurrection, and ascension: "1:33 As the Davidic Messiah, Jesus will reign over the *house of Jacob*, which will happen in the millennial kingdom. This promise is not now being fulfilled simply because the church is not the house of Jacob, and Christ is presently at the right hand of the Father, which is never equated with the throne of

The Davidic Covenant and the Kingdom of God

As Jesus began his public earthly ministry, the followers of Judaism paid attention to his message. However, they were deeply disappointed by Jesus' message about the Kingdom of God, or the kingdom of heaven. In fact, Jesus used the two terms interchangeably. At the time of Jesus' earthly ministry, Israel as the covenant community was under the control and subject of the Roman Empire. So the first-century Jews were eagerly waiting for the Messiah to come so that the Messianic earthly kingdom would be established and the Jews would be freed from the political oppression of the Roman Empire. They believed that the Messianic earthly kingdom in the Promised Land would be the fulfillment of the kingdom of the Davidic covenant.

Psalm 110:1–7 are, in fact, "A Psalm of David" which is a royal psalm. David as the king of Israel prophesied that the Davidic Messiah is a divine figure as we read Psalm 110 as follows:

> 1 The LORD says to my Lord: "Sit at my right hand, until I make your enemies your footstool." 2 The LORD sends forth from Zion your mighty scepter. Rule in the midst of your enemies! 3 Your people will offer themselves freely on the day of your power, in holy garments; from the womb of the morning, the dew of your youth will be yours. 4 The LORD has sworn and will not change his mind, "You are a priest forever after the order of Melchizedek." 5 The Lord is at your right hand; he will shatter kings on the day of his wrath. 6 He will execute judgment among the nations, filling them with corpses; he will shatter chiefs over the wide earth. 7 He will drink from the brook by the way; therefore he will lift up his head. (Ps 110:1–7)

David's prophetic psalm, "The LORD says to my Lord: 'Sit at my right hand, until I make your enemies your footstool'" (v.1), suggests that the Davidic Messiah as the Son of David will be coming as a divine Messiah:

> 35 And as Jesus taught in the temple, he said, "How can the scribes say that the Christ is the son of David? 36 David himself, in the Holy Spirit, declared, "' The Lord said to my Lord, Sit at my right hand, until I put your enemies under your feet.' 37 David himself calls him Lord. So how is he his son?" And the great throng heard him gladly. 38 And in his teaching he said, "Beware of the scribes, who like to walk around in long robes and like greetings in the marketplaces 39 and have the best seats in the synagogues and the places of honor at feasts, 40 who devour widows' houses and for a pretense make long prayers. They will receive the greater condemnation." (Mark 12:35–40; cf. Matt 22:41–46; Luke 20:41–44)

After the triumphant entry into Jerusalem, Jesus was teaching in the temple. And he asked how the scribes can say that "the Christ is the son of David," quoting Psalm 110:1. Jesus' question, however, is not a denial that the Messiah is the Son of David.

David." Ryrie, *The Ryrie Study Bible: ESV*, 1238.

Rather, it is his emphatic statement that the Davidic Messiah is not only the Son of David but also the Lord of David, the divine figure.[20]

From the beginning of Jesus' earthly ministry, he proclaimed the essence and nature of the Kingdom of God, or the kingdom of heaven. Calling twelve disciples, he taught and trained them, correcting their wrong conception of the Messianic earthly kingdom that they used to have as the followers of Judaism. Jesus taught and proclaimed that he is not only the Son of God, but also the King of the kingdom of heaven. This message provoked the followers of first-century Judaism because they thought Jesus was not only a false Messiah but also blasphemous, in light of their own interpretation of the Messianic prophecy in the Hebrew scriptures. For these reasons, the band of soldiers and the officers from the chief priests and the Pharisees, who represented the Jews, arrested and bound Jesus and handed him over to Pilate, the Roman governor. In the governor's headquarters, there was a remarkable dialogue between Pilate, the chief judge, and Jesus, the accused:

> 33 So Pilate entered his headquarters again and called Jesus and said to him, "Are you the King of the Jews?" 34 Jesus answered, "Do you say this of your own accord, or did others say it to you about me?" 35 Pilate answered, "Am I a Jew? Your own nation and the chief priests have delivered you over to me. What have you done?" 36 Jesus answered, "My kingdom is not of this world. If my kingdom were of this world, my servants would have been fighting, that I might not be delivered over to the Jews. But my kingdom is not from the world." 37 Then Pilate said to him, "So you are a king?" Jesus answered, "You say that I am a king. For this purpose I was born and for this purpose I have come into the world-to bear witness to the truth. Everyone who is of the truth listens to my voice." 38 Pilate said to him, "What is truth?" After he had said this, he went back outside to the Jews and told them, "I find no guilt in him. 39 But you have a custom that I should release one man for you at the Passover. So do you want me to release to you the King of the Jews?" 40 They cried out again, "Not this man, but Barabbas!" Now Barabbas was a robber. (John 18:33–40)

Pilate asked Jesus whether he was "the King of the Jews." This question he refused to answer directly. Instead, he answered (in verse 36), "My kingdom is not of this world. If my kingdom were of this world, my servants would have been fighting, that I might not be delivered over to the Jews. But my kingdom is not from the world." In

---

20. Schweitzer, commenting on Mark 12:35–37, incorrectly states that Jesus dissociated "the Davidic Sonship and the Messiahship." Jesus' dissociation between "the Davidic Sonship and the Messiahship" is the result of Schweitzer's historical critical reading of the life of Jesus: "Similarly He is playing with His secret *in* that crucial question regarding the Messiahship in Mark xii 35–37. There is no question of dissociating the Davidic Sonship from the Messiahship. He asks only how can the Christ in virtue of His descent from David be, as his son, inferior to David, and yet be addressed by David in the Psalm as his Lord? The answer is; by reason of the metamorphosis and Parousia in which natural relationships are abolished and the scion of David's line who is the predestined Son of Man shall take possession of His unique glory." Schweitzer, *The Quest of the Historical Jesus*, 393.

The Davidic Covenant and the Kingdom of God

doing so, Jesus indirectly denied that he came to the world to be the king of the earthly kingdom of Israel, which was a type of the heavenly Kingdom of God, and in which he would reign forever through his death, resurrection, ascension, and session at the right hand of God. In that sense, Jesus indirectly corrected the wrong conception of the Messianic earthly kingdom, which was a false expectation of the first-century followers of Judaism.

Peter was a staunch follower of Judaism before he witnessed Jesus' life, death, resurrection, and ascension as a disciple. However, after the Pentecost event, Peter began his official apostolic ministry with the anointing of the Holy Spirit, sent by the exalted Messiah from God the Father on the heavenly throne. And he delivered a remarkable and powerful message to the audience of the followers of Judaism and other residents in Jerusalem. In doing so, Peter proclaimed that David was not only a king but also a prophet of ancient Israel. As a prophet, David foresaw the resurrection of the crucified Messiah, and his session at the right hand of God:

> 29 "Brothers, I may say to you with confidence about the patriarch David that he both died and was buried, and his tomb is with us to this day. 30 Being therefore a prophet, and knowing that God had sworn with an oath to him that he would set one of his descendants on his throne, 31 he foresaw and spoke about the resurrection of the Christ, that he was not abandoned to Hades, nor did his flesh see corruption. 32 This Jesus God raised up, and of that we all are witnesses. 33 Being therefore exalted at the right hand of God, and having received from the Father the promise of the Holy Spirit, he has poured out this that you yourselves are seeing and hearing. 34 For David did not ascend into the heavens, but he himself says, "'The Lord said to my Lord, Sit at my right hand, 35 until I make your enemies your footstool.' 36 Let all the house of Israel therefore know for certain that God has made him both Lord and Christ, this Jesus whom you crucified." (Acts 2:29–36)[21]

Peter in his message affirmed that the Messiah had begun to reign over the Kingdom of God through his exaltation, involving his resurrection, ascension, and session at the right hand of God. Peter's proclamation that "God has made him both Lord and Christ, this Jesus whom you crucified" (v. 36 b) suggests that Jesus as the exalted "Lord and Christ" began to rule the Kingdom of God at the right hand of God, which is the redemptive historical succession and continuation of the Davidic throne.

---

21. Interpreting Acts 2:34, Ryrie makes no connection between the Messiah's present reign "at the right hand of the Father" and reign "on the throne of David" because as a dispensationalist he does not see a redemptive historical continuity and connection between the two: "2:34 Peter quotes Ps. 110:1. Messiah is now at the right hand of the Father awaiting the subjugation of His enemies, at which time He will reign on the throne of David. In the meantime, He has sent the Spirit." Ryrie, *The Ryrie Study Bible*, 1322.

BIBLICAL THEOLOGY

The Davidic Covenant and the Eschatological Kingdom of God

In light of redemptive historical continuity, the Davidic kingdom was beautifully succeeded by the reign of Jesus Christ, who began to reign over the eschatological Kingdom of God as the Son of David through his life, death, resurrection, and ascension.

However, dispensationalists fail to see this redemptive historical continuity between the reigning of the Davidic kingdom and the exalted Messiah's reign at the right hand of Father. For example, Ryrie fails to see that the Messianic kingdom, as the eschatological Kingdom of God, was already inaugurated when Jesus Christ was enthroned at the right hand of God after his resurrection and ascension. Instead, he falsely argues that "the messianic kingdom will be inaugurated at the Second Coming of Christ." Ryrie's failure to see the continuity between the Davidic kingdom and the Messianic kingdom at the right hand of the Father clearly reminds us that the idea of redemptive historical continuity and integration is vitally important for the proper understanding of the eschatological Kingdom of God:

> To build the kingdom on the first coming of Christ produces a theological error with many serious ramifications. By kingdom, I mean the rule of Messiah on earth as promised to David (2 Sam. 7:12–16). To claim that Christ established this Davidic kingdom at His first advent requires deliteralizing of the promises made to David and results in confusion between the church and the kingdom. Among other things, church ethics and kingdom ethics are intermixed, usually with the result that kingdom ethics are promoted more than church ethics. That mistake was made by some during the earthly life of Christ (Luke 19:11). The truth is that the messianic kingdom will be inaugurated at the second coming of Christ. At that time the land promise made to Abraham and his descendents will be fulfilled (Gen. 15:18–21). Then the promise made to David that his descendent (Messiah) will sit on the throne of the kingdom forever will be fulfilled. Without a Millennium in which all these promises can be fulfilled, the promises have to be canceled for some reason or be fulfilled in Israel's past or in the present nonliterally.[22]

---

22. Ryrie, *Basic Theology*, 592. Jonathan Edwards sees "Christ's ascension into heaven" and "his sitting at the right hand of God" as a unity. "Christ's ascension into heaven" was "his solemn enthronization, whereby the Father did set him upon the throne," to reign over visible and invisible kingdoms after his life, death, and resurrection: "Christ's ascension into heaven. In this I would include his sitting at the right hand of God. For Christ's ascension, and sitting at the right hand of God, can scarcely be looked upon as two distinct things: for Christ's ascension was nothing else, but ascending to God's right hand; it was his coming to sit down at his Father's hand in glory. This was another thing whereby Christ was put into a capacity for the accomplishing the effect of his purchase; as one that comes to be a deliverer of a people as their king, in order to it, and that he may be under the best capacity for it, is first installed on his throne . . . Christ's ascension into heaven was, as it were, his solemn enthronization, whereby the Father did set him upon the throne, and invest him with the glory of his kingdom which he had purchased for himself, that he might thereby obtain the success of his redemption in conquering all his enemies: Psa. cx. 1. 'Sit thou at my right hand, until I make thine enemies thy footstool.' . . . And as he ascended into heaven, God the Father did in a visible manner set him on the throne as king of the universe. He then put the angels all under him, and subjected heaven and earth

The Davidic Covenant and the Kingdom of God

After Jesus Christ's ascension, the exalted Messiah began to reign over the visible and invisible kingdoms on the throne of heaven at the right hand of the Father. Yet 120 believers, including Jesus' disciples, gathered in the upper room in Jerusalem and prayed together, waiting for the coming of the Holy Spirit. When the day of Pentecost came, the promised Holy Spirit visibly and audibly descended from heaven. And the visible and audible glory of the Holy Spirit filled the upper room, and the people who witnessed this remarkable scene were amazed and puzzled (Acts 2:1–13).

After Pentecost, Peter and John preached the good news of the gospel, and many people came to the Lord in Jerusalem. However, *a great persecution* took place as Stephen was martyred and believers in Jerusalem began to scatter to the regions of Judea, Samaria, and beyond. Paradoxically, God used the great persecution against the church in Jerusalem as a means of evangelism and mission to Judea and Samaria:

> 1 *And Saul approved of his execution. And there arose on that day a great persecution against the church in Jerusalem, and they were all scattered throughout the regions of Judea and Samaria, except the apostles.* 2 Devout men buried Stephen and made great lamentation over him. 3 But Saul was ravaging the church, and entering house after house, he dragged off men and women and committed them to prison. 4 *Now those who were scattered went about preaching the word.* 5 *Philip went down to the city of Samaria and proclaimed to them the Christ.* 6 And the crowds with one accord paid attention to what was being said by Philip when they heard him and saw the signs that he did. 7 For unclean spirits came out of many who were possessed, crying with a loud voice, and many who were paralyzed or lame were healed. 8 So there was much joy in that city. (Acts 8:1–8)

The remarkable story of Stephen's martyrdom powerfully demonstrates the exalted Jesus' standing "at the right hand of God" through revelation. In fact, the risen Jesus had ascended into heaven, promising his Second Coming (Acts 1:9–11). Nevertheless, heaven was enveloped so that the ascended Jesus was hidden from human eyes. Stephen's *seeing* "the glory of God, and Jesus standing at the right hand of God" via revelation right before his historic martyrdom is the affirmation that the exalted Davidic Messiah had already begun to rule the eschatological Kingdom of God in heaven:

> 54 Now when they heard these things they were enraged, and they ground their teeth at him. 55 But he, full of the Holy Spirit, gazed into heaven and saw the glory of God, and Jesus standing at the right hand of God. 56 And he said, "Behold, I see the heavens opened, and the Son of Man standing at the right hand of God." 57 But they cried out with a loud voice and stopped their ears and rushed together at him. 58 Then they cast him out of the city and stoned him. And the witnesses laid down their garments at the feet of a young man

---

under him, that he might govern them for the good of the people for whom he had died, Eph. i. 20, 21, 22." Edwards, *A History of the Work of Redemption*, 227.

> named Saul. 59 And as they were stoning Stephen, he called out, "Lord Jesus, receive my spirit." 60 And falling to his knees he cried out with a loud voice, "Lord, do not hold this sin against them." And when he had said this, he fell asleep. (Acts 7:54–60)

Under the Old Covenant, God used the covenant curse to disperse and scatter the covenant community outside of the Promised Land when they disobeyed the Mosaic covenant of law. By doing so, God created the Old Covenant diaspora community in the midst of pagan societies and nations. However, God used "a great persecution" against "the church in Jerusalem" after Pentecost to disperse the New Covenant community into Judea, Samaria, and beyond. In his providence, God began to use great persecution against the church to proclaim and spread the good news of the gospel, and to expand his spiritual kingdom from Jerusalem to Judea, Samaria, and the ends of the earth after Pentecost. Likewise, God created the New Covenant diaspora community to accomplish the Great Commission, given to the original disciples by the crucified and resurrected Jesus Christ (Matt 28:16–20). In fact, the New Covenant diaspora community became *pilgrims* in the present world after Pentecost, as they still are in the Global Mission Age of the twenty-first century.

The author of Hebrews wrote a letter to Jewish Christians who were experiencing hardship and great persecution. In his epistle, he emphasizes that Jesus came to the world as the Davidic Messiah. The Davidic Messiah came to the world not only as the Son of David but also as the Son of God. Furthermore, the exalted Davidic Messiah had already begun to rule the inaugurated eschatological Kingdom of God, sitting down "at the right hand of the majesty on high" (Heb 1:1–14). The reality of the inauguration of the eschatological Kingdom of God, and the reign over it by the Davidic Messiah, became a great source of courage and joy in the midst of Jewish Christians' pilgrimage and persecution in Greco-Roman pagan society.

The author of Hebrews assures his Jewish Christian readers that because Jesus sacrificed himself as the Davidic Messiah to redeem the elect from their sins, God awarded his kingdom to his Son, the Mediator of the New Covenant. So Jesus began to rule the eschatological Kingdom of God not at the earthly throne in Jerusalem but "seated at the right hand of the throne of God." The passive verb emphasizes that Jesus' inauguration as the king of the eschatological Kingdom of God is God's royal grant to his Son, who faithfully obeyed unto his crucifixion and death:

> 1 Therefore, since we are surrounded by so great a cloud of witnesses, let us also lay aside every weight, and sin which clings so closely, and let us run with endurance the race that is set before us, 2 *looking to Jesus, the founder and perfecter of our faith, who for the joy that was set before him endured the cross, despising the shame, and is seated at the right hand of the throne of God.* (Heb 12:1–2)

The author of Hebrews boldly proclaims that the Jewish Christians have come to "Mount Zion and to the city of the living God, the heavenly Jerusalem, and to innumerable angels in festal gatherings." Why did the author mention "the heavenly Jerusalem" to his audience, who were Jewish Christian pilgrims? At the time of his writing, Jerusalem as the heart of the Davidic Kingdom of Israel had become desolate and powerless under the oppressive regime of the Roman Empire. In other words, it was a hopeless situation. In that historical context, the author of Hebrews confirms for his audience that Jesus as the mediator of the New Covenant sprinkled his own blood of the covenant. God rewarded and granted his kingdom to his Son. So, the exalted Jesus as the Davidic Messiah began to rule the eschatological Kingdom of God, not in the earthly Jerusalem but in the heavenly Jerusalem:

> 18 For you have not come to what may be touched, a blazing fire and darkness and gloom and a tempest 19 and the sound of a trumpet and a voice whose words made the hearers beg that no further messages be spoken to them. 20 For they could not endure the order that was given, "If even a beast touches the mountain, it shall be stoned." 21 Indeed, so terrifying was the sight that Moses said, "I tremble with fear." 22 *But you have come to Mount Zion and to the city of the living God, the heavenly Jerusalem, and to innumerable angels in festal gathering, 23 and to the assembly of the firstborn who are enrolled in heaven, and to God, the judge of all, and to the spirits of the righteous made perfect, 24 and to Jesus, the mediator of a new covenant, and to the sprinkled blood that speaks a better word than the blood of Abel.* 25 See that you do not refuse him who is speaking. For if they did not escape when they refused him who warned them on earth, much less will we escape if we reject him who warns from heaven. 26 At that time his voice shook the earth, but now he has promised, "Yet once more I will shake not only the earth but also the heavens." 27 This phrase, "Yet once more," indicates the removal of things that are shaken-that is, things that have been made-in order that the things that cannot be shaken may remain. 28 *Therefore let us be grateful for receiving a kingdom that cannot be shaken, and thus let us offer to God acceptable worship, with reverence and awe,* 29 *for our God is a consuming fire.* (Heb 12:18–29)

The author of Hebrews sees the present reality of Jewish Christians in light of redemptive history and eschatology. Jewish Christians became the Jewish Christian diaspora in the midst of pagan Greco-Roman society. Due to great persecution, they were dispersed outside of Jerusalem and the Promised Land after Stephen's death. So they are yearning to return and see the earthly city of Jerusalem, where the sons of David had ruled the kingdom of Israel, and where the Old Covenant community still worshiped in the temple. In this historical context, the author of Hebrews comforts the Jewish Christian diaspora, who had already undergone great hardship and suffering because they believed in Jesus as the Messiah and the Son of God. He informs them that believers are united with Jesus Christ in his death and resurrection through faith. Through the mystical and spiritual union with a crucified and resurrected Christ, believers have come not to the earthly Jerusalem but to "the heavenly Jerusalem," where the exalted Christ is already ruling and reigning over visible and invisible kingdoms. In fact, "a kingdom" as the eschatological Kingdom of God has already been inaugurated with the Davidic Messiah's exaltation. The eschatological Kingdom of God will be fully consummated with the Second Coming of Jesus Christ. This is the redemptive historical background to the writer's exclamation, "*Therefore let us be grateful for receiving a kingdom that cannot be shaken, and thus let us offer to God acceptable worship, with reverence and awe*" (v. 29).

As Herman Bavinck properly understands, "the heavenly Jerusalem" should not be identified "with the believing community," but it is rather "a city built by God himself" and "the city of the living God," which is the heavenly city where the exalted Jesus Christ currently reigns as the King of kings and the Lord of lords:

> But this inheritance is destined to be revealed. Someday Christ will return visibly and then cause the whole believing community—indeed, the whole world—to participate in his glory. Not only are believers changed after his likeness (John 17:24; Rom. 8:17–18, 28; Phil. 3:21; Col. 3:4; 1 John 3:2), but also "the whole creation itself will be set free from its bondage to decay and obtain the freedom of the glory of the children of God" (Rom. 8:21). Earth and heaven will be renewed so that justice will be at home in them (2 Pet. 3:13; Rev. 21:1). The heavenly Jerusalem, which is now above and was the model for the earthly Jerusalem, then comes down to earth (Gal. 4:26; Heb. 11:10, 13–16; 12:22; 13:14; Rev. 3:12; 21:2ff.). This new Jerusalem is not identical with the believing community, even though it is figuratively called the bride of the Lamb (21:2,9) for Hebrews 12:22–23 clearly distinguishes among the heavenly Jerusalem, the assembly of the firstborn (the Old Testament faithful), and the spirits of the righteous made perfect (deceased Christians). The heavenly Jerusalem is a city built by God himself (Heb. 11:10). It is the city of the living God, inasmuch as God is not just its architect but also makes it his home (Rev. 21:3). In it the angels are the servants and constitute the royal entourage of the great king (Heb. 12:22), while the blessed are its citizens (Rev. 21:27; 22:3–4).[23]

Meanwhile, the apostle John witnessed the great persecution of the church under the reign of the Roman emperor Nero (54–68 A.D.), as well as the fall of Jerusalem and the destruction of the Jerusalem temple in 70 A.D. During Domitian's reign (81–96 A.D.), persecution intensified in the Roman Empire and many believers were tortured and martyred. Around the end of Domitian's reign, the apostle John was exiled to the island of Patmos and wrote the book of Revelation in response to the revelation of the exalted Jesus Christ. The apostle John received "the revelation of Jesus Christ" (Rev 1:1–3). And the heart of Revelation is the message that the eschatological Kingdom of God was already inaugurated with the Davidic Messiah's death, resurrection, and ascension. And the eschatological Kingdom of God will be fully realized and consummated with the Second Coming of the Davidic Messiah.

---

23. Bavinck, *Reformed Dogmatics*, 4:719.

The Davidic Covenant and the Kingdom of God

In the book of Revelation, 20:1–6 is closely related to the Davidic covenant, which is the covenant of kingdom. Nevertheless, among biblical scholars and theologians it is one of the most contested and debated passages not only in the book of Revelation but also in the Bible.[24] Anthony Hoekema properly interprets and summarizes Revelation 20:1–6 from the perspective of the eschatological Kingdom of God being "already and not yet," as follows:

> This then, is the amillennial interpretation of Revelation 20:1–6. So understood, the passage says nothing about an earthly reign of Christ over a primarily Jewish kingdom. Rather, it describes the reigning with Christ in heaven, between their death and Christ's Second Coming, of the souls of deceased believers. It also describes the binding of Satan during the present age in such a way that he cannot prevent the spread of the gospel.[25]

According to Revelation 20:1–6, John saw that Satan was bound "for a thousand years." So, the "ancient serpent" might not deceive "any longer, until the thousand years were ended." And John saw the martyred spirits, which were glorified and reigned with the exalted Jesus Christ "for a thousand years" in heavenly thrones:

> 1 Then I saw an angel coming down from heaven, holding in his hand the key to the bottomless pit and a great chain. 2 And he seized the dragon, that ancient serpent, who is the devil and Satan, and bound him for a thousand years, 3 and threw him into the pit, and shut it and sealed it over him, so that he might not deceive the nations any longer, until the thousand years were ended. After that he must be released for a little while. 4 *Then I saw thrones, and seated on them were those to whom the authority to judge was committed. Also I saw the souls of those who had been beheaded for the testimony of Jesus and for the word of God, and who had not worshiped the beast or its image and had not received its mark on their foreheads or their hands. They came to life and reigned with Christ for a thousand years. 5 The rest of the dead did not come to life until the thousand years were ended. This is the first resurrection.* 6 Blessed and holy is the one who shares in the first resurrection! Over such the second death has no power, but they will be priests of God and of Christ, and they will reign with him for a thousand years. (Rev 20:1–6)

---

24. Dennis Johnson comprehensively reflects that Revelation 20:1–6 is "probably the most controversial six verses in Revelation" and "interpreters of Scripture have debated for not quite two millennia:" "We have reached what are probably the most controversial six verses in Revelation. For this reason this chapter needs to be longer than others, and its discussion more detailed. John sees an angel descending from heaven, seizing, chaining, and locking the dragon into the abyss for a thousand years—in Latin, a millennium—to keep the dragon from continuing to deceive the nations for that extended period (Rev. 20:1–3). Then he sees thrones, and the souls of martyrs beheaded for their testimony, who come to life in 'the first resurrection' and reign with Christ for the same period of time, one thousand years (20:4–6). Over these two visions—what they mean, and where they fall in God's agenda for history—interpreters of Scripture have debated for not quite two millennia." Johnson, *Triumph of the Lamb*, 278–79.

25. Hoekema, *The Bible and the Future*, 238.

The apostle John saw a comprehensive historical vision through revelation. Revelation 20:1–6 is the representative and comprehensive picture of the exalted Jesus Christ already beginning to reign over the eschatological Kingdom of God as the King of kings and Lord of lords on the heavenly throne. Remarkably, the glorified martyred spirits, *"the souls of those who had been beheaded for the testimony of Jesus and for the word of God, and who had not worshiped the beast or its image and had not received its mark on their foreheads or their hands"* (v. 4b), participate in the reign of the exalted Jesus Christ in heaven "for a thousand years." They receive the blessings of "the first resurrection,"[26] so that they will not experience "the second death," which will be the curse of everlasting hell with bodily resurrection when the final judgment comes.

"A thousand years" summarizes the epoch which covers the period of the semi-eschatological Kingdom of God. It is an extensive period stretching from Jesus' enthronement, as seen in his resurrection, ascension, and session at the right hand of God, until the time of his Second Coming. Indeed, the eschatological Kingdom of God or Heaven is already inaugurated through Jesus' death, resurrection, ascension, and enthronement in heaven.[27] Jesus' redemptive ministry continues through the works of the Holy Spirit, although his glorified body has been enveloped in the heavenly realm. Jesus, as the Son of Abraham and the Son of David, has begun to reign as the king of the eschatological Kingdom of God, which is the fulfillment and succession of the Davidic earthly kingdom. The deceased believers as glorified spirits participate in the reign of the eschatological Kingdom of God in Jesus Christ. Yet the eschatological Kingdom of God will be fully realized only after the Second Coming of Jesus Christ. The Davidic covenant as the covenant of kingdom will be *fully and visibly* realized

---

26. As Hoekema suggests, "the first resurrection" is "not a bodily resurrection but rather the transition from physical death to life in heaven with Christ." Likewise, the deceased souls will participate in the blessings of "the first resurrection" in the heavenly Kingdom of God until the Second Coming of Christ: "Now John goes on to say, 'This is the first resurrection' (v.5b.). These words depict what happened to the believing dead whom John was describing at the end of verse 4, previous to the parenthetical statement just discussed. In the light of what was said above, we must understand these words as describing not a bodily resurrection but rather the transition from physical death to life in heaven with Christ. This transition is here called a 'resurrection'—an unusual use of the word, to be sure, but perfectly understandable against the background of the preceding context. This is indeed a kind of resurrection, since people who are thought to be dead are now seen to be, in a very real sense of the word, alive. The expression 'the first resurrection' implies that there will indeed be a 'second resurrection' (though this expression is not used) for these believing dead—the resurrection of the body which will take place when Christ returns at the end of the thousand-year period." Ibid., 237.

27. "A thousand years" should be understood as not literal but symbolical. As Hoekema correctly suggests, "the thousand-year period" covers "from the first coming of Christ to the Second Coming." And the reign of the millennium by the exalted Christ is present, "not an earthly but a heavenly one:" "We therefore understand the word *ezesan* (lived, or came to life) in verse 4 as describing the fact that the souls of believers who have died are now living with Christ in heaven and sharing in his reign during the intermediate state between death and the resurrection. The thousand-year period during which these souls live and reign with Christ is, as we saw, the entire gospel era, from the first coming of Christ to the Second Coming. In other words, the millennium is now, and the reign of Christ with believers during this millennium is not an earthly but a heavenly one." Ibid., 233.

The Davidic Covenant and the Kingdom of God

after the final judgment as well. Then, Jesus Christ, as *the Son of David*, will rule the fully realized Kingdom of God in a new heaven and a new earth, with the heavenly hosts and glorified believers.

Believers have always wanted to see the realized Kingdom of God. God showed the comprehensive picture of the glorious Kingdom of God through revelation to the apostle John. Certainly, the eschatological Kingdom of God will be visibly realized after the Second Coming of Christ, and it will be gloriously consummated in the new heaven and new earth:

> 1 *Then I saw a new heaven and a new earth, for the first heaven and the first earth had passed away, and the sea was no more. 2 And I saw the holy city, new Jerusalem, coming down out of heaven from God, prepared as a bride adorned for her husband.* 3 And I heard a loud voice from the throne saying, "Behold, the dwelling place of God is with man. He will dwell with them, and they will be his people, and God himself will be with them as their God. 4 He will wipe away every tear from their eyes, and death shall be no more, neither shall there be mourning nor crying nor pain anymore, for the former things have passed away." 5 And he who was seated on the throne said, "Behold, I am making all things new." Also he said, "Write this down, for these words are trustworthy and true." 6 And he said to me, "It is done! I am the Alpha and the Omega, the beginning and the end. To the thirsty I will give from the spring of the water of life without payment. 7 The one who conquers will have this heritage, and I will be his God and he will be my son. 8 But as for the cowardly, the faithless, the detestable, as for murderers, the sexually immoral, sorcerers, idolaters, and all liars, their portion will be in the lake that burns with fire and sulfur, which is the second death." (Rev 21:1–8)

What is John's visionary picture in verse 1? Most evangelical scholars' perspective is that the new heaven and new earth is a renewed cosmos, and the renewed earth will be the fulfillment of redemptive history. In that sense, the renewed earth will be heaven.[28] However, I think that it is a visionary picture of *a glorious union with the new*

---

28. Denying the existence and reality of heaven and hell, Richard Middleton argues that believers do not go to heaven after their death in the present age. He argues that "John's vision in Revelation 21 of the new Jerusalem" indicates that "the goal of heavenly preparation is an earthly future." His denial of heaven and hell is a popular reflection among contemporary evangelical scholars: "John's vision in Revelation 21 of the new Jerusalem is important because it makes the apocalyptic pattern that we have discerned in many other New Testament texts more explicit than most . . . Thus, when Jesus tells the disciples in John 14:3 that after preparing a place for them he will come and take them to be with him forever, many contemporary readers supply the place as (obviously) heaven. But that is based on an unbiblical set of assumptions, derived more from the history of theology than from the Bible itself. The fact that the city that God has prepared in heaven comes down to earth in Revelation 21 makes clear that the goal of heavenly preparation is an earthly future. We do not go to heaven; rather, what is prepared or stored in heaven is brought to us at Christ's return." Middleton, *A New Heaven and a New Earth*, 220. Similarly, George Ladd argues that "the new earth of Revelation 21" is the final goal of redemptive history: "The new earth of Revelation 21 is the final term in the revelation of how this redemption is to take place. Just as we can speak of the resurrection of the body even though the resurrection body will be very different

heaven and new earth. In that regard, as the new heaven and new earth will be gloriously united together, the eschatological Kingdom of God which has been anticipated in the Davidic covenant with the inauguration of the Davidic Kingdom of Israel, will be consummated gloriously.[29]

By the way, the glorious union between the new heaven and new earth, when the final judgment comes, was manifested typologically during the Flood judgment at the time of Noah. The Noahic covenant community entered the Ark before the Flood judgment began on the original earth (Gen 7:1–24). After the Flood judgment was over, God abated the flood waters from the earth. The Ark arrived to rest "on the mountains of Ararat" (Gen 8:1–12). As the flood waters dried from the earth, God completed his creative work for the renewed earth through the Flood judgment. And Noah removed "the covering of the ark" and the Noahic covenant community came out from the Ark according to God's command:

> 13 In the six hundred and first year, in the first month, the first day of the month, the waters were dried from off the earth. And Noah removed the covering of the ark and looked, and behold, the face of the ground was dry. 14 In the second month, on the twenty-seventh day of the month, the earth had dried out. 15 Then God said to Noah, 16 "Go out from the ark, you and your wife, and your sons and your sons' wives with you. 17 Bring out with you every living thing that is with you of all flesh-birds and animals and every creeping thing that creeps on the earth-that they may swarm on the earth, and be fruitful and multiply on the

---

from the physical bodies of this order, so we can speak of the redemption of the creation even though the new order is indeed a new earth. The new earth is the scene of the final goal of redemption: 'Behold, the dwelling of God is with men. He will dwell with them, and they shall be his people, and God himself will be with them' (Rev. 21:3). This feature—the fact that God will be God to his people—is the central element of God's covenant with his people throughout the entire course of redemptive history . . . Now, at last, this covenant promise finds the perfect fulfillment in the new earth of the Age to come . . . And so the Bible ends, with a redeemed society dwelling on a new earth that has been purged of all evil, with God dwelling in the midst of his people. This is the goal of the long course of redemptive history." George Ladd, *A Theology of the New Testament*, 682–83.

29. Wayne Grudem insightfully argues that John's vision of "a new heaven and a new earth" in Revelation 21:1–3 is a revelatory picture of "a new kind of unification of heaven and earth" in the new creation: "The Lord promises through Isaiah, 'For behold, I created *new heavens and a new earth*; and the former things shall not be remembered' (Isa. 66:22), and speaks of 'the new heavens and the new earth which I will make' (Isa. 66:22). Peter says, 'according to his promise we wait for *new heavens and a new earth* in which righteousness dwells' (2 Peter 3:13). In John's vision of events to follow the final judgment, he says, 'Then I saw *a new heaven and a new earth*; for the first heaven and the first earth passed away' (Rev. 21:1). He goes on to tell us that there will also be a new kind of unification of heavens and earth, for he sees the holy city, the 'new Jerusalem,' coming 'down out of heaven from God' (Rev. 21:2), and hears a voice proclaiming that 'the dwelling of God is with men. He will dwell with them, and they shall be his people, and God himself will be with them' (v. 3). So there will be a joining of heaven and earth in this new creation, and there we will live in the presence of God . . . These texts lead us to conclude that heaven is even now a place—though one whose location is now unknown to us and whose existence is now unable to be perceived by our natural senses. It is this place of God's dwelling that will be somehow made new at the time of the final judgment and will be joined to a renewed earth." Grudem, *Systematic Theology*, 1158–60.

earth." 18 So Noah went out, and his sons and his wife and his sons' wives with him. 19 Every beast, every creeping thing, and every bird, everything that moves on the earth, went out by families from the ark. (Gen 8:13–19)

In light of redemptive history, the Noahic Ark's arrival to rest "on the mountains of Ararat" was a union between the Noahic Ark and the renewed earth through the Flood judgment. This union is a type of the glorious union of the new heaven and new earth after the final judgment through fire when Jesus Christ comes back again as Judge and Consummator.

Having briefly explored the Noahic Flood judgment in the original world, we see that Revelation 21:1–8 is a comprehensive and pictorial revelation about the visible realization of the eschatological Kingdom of God (vv. 1–7) and the completion of the Kingdom of Satan (v. 8). This comprehensive and pictorial revelation suggests that after the Second Coming of Christ, the eschatological Kingdom of God in the new heaven and new earth (vv. 1–7) will be completely separated from the Kingdom of Satan in hell (v. 8). Likewise, Revelation 21:1–7 is a pictorial vision of *a glorious union between the perfected heaven and glorified earth*, including "the holy city," a glorious new Jerusalem "coming down out of heaven from God." The glorious picture of the new heaven and new earth along with the new Jerusalem signifies that the triune God is a supernatural designer and architect. Nevertheless, God will execute his final judgment, separating the everlasting Kingdom of God and the Kingdom of Satan. Verse 8 is a vivid picture of the completed Kingdom of Satan, where the resurrected unbelievers will be punished forever along with Satan and his demons. Richard Middleton, however, plainly endorses "annihilation of the person rather than the classical notion of eternal torment" as he denies the existence of heaven and hell:

> While much is still mysterious about final judgment, perhaps we can find a clue in Jesus's teaching that the meek will inherit the earth (Matt. 5:5). Could this mean that final judgment is akin to cosmic disinheritance, permanent exile from God's good creation? This might mean that final judgment should be construed as annihilation of the person rather than the classical notion of eternal torment. However, the extreme imagery that Jesus uses should warn us that this is not something anyone would want to experience; we dare not tame his vivid warning implicit in this imagery.[30]

30. Middleton, *A New Heaven and a New Earth*, 207. Reflecting on Revelation 21:1—22:21, Beale rightly observes that there will be ultimate separation between the dwelling place of the righteous in the new creation and "unrighteous false Christians and the non-Christian world" when God's final judgment comes: "It is noteworthy that the new creation is what the righteous inherit (v 7), so that unrighteous false Christians and the non-Christian world in general do not reside within the borders of the new cosmos. 21:1—22:5 shows that the blessing of God's presence permeates the entire new creation, whereas 21:8 and 27 indicate that God's judgment is revealed outside the confines of the new world (see also 22:15). Even though 'the second death' is a perfected punishment, those who suffer it do so outside the geography of the new universe, since, as we have already been told, 'there will be no more death . . . nor pain' in the new order of things (21:4). In similar fashion we have been told that there will be 'no more sea' in the new order; this figurative sea likely overlaps to some degree

Likewise, the theocratic kingdom in Canaan, promised in the Abrahamic covenant, will ultimately be consummated in the eschatological Kingdom of God in Christ. Similarly, the Davidic kingdom, inaugurated with King David, has been succeeded by Jesus Christ, the Son of David in the eschatological Kingdom of God. It will be consummated in the new heaven and new earth.

Summary

Saul became the first king of ancient Israel. Nevertheless, he violated God's law, offering the burnt offering, which was not the duty of a king but a priest. Furthermore, Saul failed to fight a holy war against the Amalekites, even though Yahweh commanded him to do so (1 Sam 15:1–11). In doing so, Saul as the first king of Israel failed to pass the probation period. After Saul's disqualification as the first king of Israel, David was anointed as the king of Israel (2 Sam 5:1–5). Like Saul, David was under probation, and he had to pass the probation period. David fought the holy war, conquering Jerusalem and the Philistines on behalf of Yahweh, the Great King (2 Sam 5:6–7; 5:17–25). In the end, David was qualified to be granted his kingdom by the Great King, Yahweh. In that sense, the Davidic covenant is the covenant of royal grant, which was exemplified in the Prediluvian Noahic covenant and the Abrahamic covenant.

In the historical context of Yahweh's making a covenant with David, he assured David that although the Davidic covenant was the covenant of royal grant, granting the kingdom eternally, the Mosaic covenant of law was continuously effective under the Davidic covenant. In that sense, the dual sanctions of blessings and curses of the Mosaic covenant should be continuously applied under the kingdom of Israel in the Promised Land (2 Sam 7:12–17).

David's psalm of thanks to Yahweh affirms that the Abrahamic covenant is "an everlasting covenant to Israel" (1 Chr 16:14–24). David's inauguration as the king of Israel and the inheritance of Canaan by the covenant community of Israel, building the Davidic kingdom was the earthly fulfillment of the Abrahamic covenant. Especially, David's recognition of the Abrahamic covenant as "an everlasting covenant to Israel" in 1 Chronicles 16:17b signifies that the ultimate fulfillment of the Abrahamic covenant will be fully realized in the heavenly Kingdom of God in Jesus Christ. Moreover, the author of 2 Kings as a member of the post-exilic covenant community reflected on the past history of the northern kingdom of Israel. And he noted that Yahweh's grace upon sinful Israel was based upon the Abrahamic covenant which was constantly efficacious even under the Mosaic covenant of law and the Davidic covenant of kingdom.

---

conceptually with 'the lake . . . which is the second death,' so that the reality underlying the figurative lake of the second death must exist somewhere else, perhaps in a different dimension from that of the new creation." Beale, *The Book of Revelation*, 1061.

The Davidic Covenant and the Kingdom of God

As the Davidic kingdom was inaugurated, Yahweh allowed the people of Israel to enjoy the blessings of the theocratic kingdom in the Promised Land, promised through the Abrahamic covenant. Through this, Yahweh visualized typologically the blessings of the everlasting Kingdom of God, ultimately realized in Jesus Christ who would come as the descendent of both Abraham and David.

In the history of ancient Israel, both the Abrahamic and Davidic covenants were described as everlasting. Furthermore, categorizing the Davidic covenant as everlasting has specific redemptive historical significance. It is important to recognize that the everlasting nature of the Davidic kingdom will not be fulfilled in the earthly millennial kingdom, as dispensationalists falsely argue. Rather, it will be inaugurated with the first coming of the Messiah, and then consummated in the heavenly Kingdom of God where Jesus Christ reins eternally as the great heavenly king.

In light of the Davidic covenant of kingdom, Revelation 20:1–6 is the representative and comprehensive picture that the exalted Jesus Christ as the Son of David is already inaugurated as the King of kings and Lord of lords on the heavenly throne. "A thousand years" summarizes the epoch which covers the semi-eschatological Kingdom of God from Jesus' enthronement at the right hand of God to his Second Coming. In fact, the Davidic kingdom was succeeded by Jesus Christ's reign in the eschatological Kingdom of God, inaugurated by his death, resurrection, ascension, and enthronement in heaven. Yet the eschatological Kingdom of God will be fully realized only after the Second Coming of Jesus Christ. And the Davidic covenant will be fully realized after the final judgment as well, with the consummation of the eschatological Kingdom of God.

6

The New Covenant and the Kingdom of God

THE HISTORY OF JESUS' birth, life, public ministry, death, and resurrection provoked Jewish society, as well as the Roman Empire. In particular, it disturbed the followers of Judaism in the first century. However, the four Gospels testify that Jesus as the Son of God came to this world as the Messiah, as the fulfillment of prophecy in the Old Testament. Moreover, he was the mediator of the New Covenant. Jesus encountered spiritual battles, fighting against Satan, especially after his baptism. During these spiritual battles, he defeated Satan and demons on behalf of the Kingdom of God. After Jesus won the spiritual battles on earth, he victoriously entered Jerusalem. Strikingly, God ratified the New Covenant through his crucifixion and death. In that sense, our thesis is that the New Covenant can be properly identified as a covenant of royal grant similar to the Prediluvian Noahic Covenant, the Abrahamic Covenant, and the Davidic Covenant.[1]

The grand drama of redemptive history, inaugurated in Genesis 3:15, anticipates that it will be ultimately fulfilled in Jesus Christ, the mediator of the New Covenant. Indeed, the Old Covenant, made with the covenant community of Israel through their mediator, Moses, would be ultimately fulfilled in Jesus Christ. However, the followers of Judaism do not find the good news of the gospel of Jesus Christ enveloped in shadows and types, although they read through the Hebrew scriptures. This is because they fail to read the Old Testament from a redemptive historical perspective. God revealed only one way to salvation for sinners throughout the Bible. Sinners can only be saved

---

1. For a divergent interpretation of the New Covenant, see Bavinck, *Reformed Dogmatics*, 223–24; J. Collins, *Introduction to the Hebrew Bible*, 344–46; Dumbrell, *Covenant and Creation*, 33–39; Edwards, *A History of Redemption*, 2–46; Golding, *Covenant Theology*, 162–63; Hahn, *Kinship by Covenant*, 217–331; Horton, *Introducing Covenant Theology*, 83–104; Kline, *God, Heaven, and Har Magedon*, 145–222; Kline, *Kingdom Prologue: Genesis*, 8–117; LaRondelle, *Our Creator Redeemer*, 57–115; Murray, *The Covenant of Grace*, 25–32; Ridderbos, *The Coming of the Kingdom*, 192–202; Robertson, *The Christ of the Covenants*, 271–300; Turretin, *Institutes of Elenctic Theology*, 2:232–61; Vos, *Biblical Theology*, 299–402; Waltke, *An Old Testament Theology*, 435–44; Williams, *Far as the Curse Is Found*, 132–47.

by God's grace, through faith in Jesus Christ alone. Therefore, we should read the Old Testament with a Christocentric perspective.[2]

The covenant community of Israel made an oath in the presence of Yahweh to uphold the Mosaic covenant. Nevertheless, they failed to keep the covenant and disobeyed the Mosaic law. At last, God executed the judgment of curses through the covenant lawsuit against Israel. The disobedience of the covenant community of Israel and God's judgment pointed them to the mediator of the New Covenant who would fulfill all the requirements of the Mosaic law, which they had failed to uphold. In that sense, we will suggest that the fall of Jerusalem in A.D. 70 at the hands of the Roman Empire occured because the covenant community of Israel broke the Mosaic covenant of law. The disobedience of Israel culminated in their rejection and crucifixion of Jesus Christ. In the end, God executed his covenant lawsuit against the covenant community of Israel, and poured his wrath on them by using the pagan Roman Empire, thereby marking the end of the theocratic kingdom of Israel in the Promised Land.

After the covenant of grace was inaugurated in Genesis 3:15, God never intended the covenant community in redemptive history to be an infallibly regenerate community. The covenant community under the New Covenant is no exception. However, Gentry and Wellum falsely argue that the covenant community under the New Covenant is "a regenerate community" while Israel under the Old Covenant is "a mixed community," including both "believers and unbelievers":

> Probably the most distinguishing difference between the two communities is that Israel is a *mixed* community (i.e., comprised of believers and unbelievers) while the church is a *regenerate* community (i.e., comprised of believers who have been born of the Spirit and have professed faith in Christ). It is important to stress that, not only is this difference taught in the New Testament, it is also anticipated in the Old Testament, particularly in Jeremiah 31.[3]

In contrast, we argue that the covenant community under the New Covenant embraces and includes both the elect and non-elect, similar to the covenant community under the Old Covenant.

---

2. The New Covenant is the culmination of the covenant of grace, inaugurated in Genesis 3:15. As Christ fulfilled his redemptive work on earth through his incarnation, life, death and resurrection, the benefits and application of the covenant of grace are fully revealed and manifested: "So when the fullness of time had come and Christ had completed his work on earth, the covenant of grace moved into a higher dispensation. Believers in Israel indeed knew that the Sinaitic dispensation was merely temporary and therefore anticipated the day of the new covenant with longing. And Jesus with the apostles who read the Old Testament in that way saw in it the same covenant of grace with the same benefits that now became fully manifest." Bavinck, *Reformed Dogmatics*, 3:223.

3. Gentry and Wellum, *Kingdom through Covenant*, 646.

BIBLICAL THEOLOGY

The Prophecy of the New Covenant

The New Covenant was prophesied and anticipated in the Old Testament, so it is necessary to briefly explore the prophecy of the New Covenant. The prophet Jeremiah (626–586 B.C.) witnessed the sad episode of the fall of the southern Kingdom of Judah by God's judgment, as the Lord executed his covenant lawsuit. Within this historical context, God gave a message of hope to Jeremiah. This message of hope is the New Covenant, made with his people through the mediator, the Messiah. The Old Covenant was *breakable* because the covenant community of Israel had made a sworn oath to the covenant, and the history of ancient Israel was not characterized by obedience but disobedience and failure. So God executed his judgment of curses against the northern Kingdom of Israel (722 B.C.) and the southern Kingdom of Judah (586 B.C.), using his covenant lawsuit.

As the prophet Jeremiah witnessed judgment upon the southern Kingdom of Judah and the Promised Land, God revealed the New Covenant, which is unbreakable:

> 31 "Behold, the days are coming, declares the LORD, when I will make a new covenant with the house of Israel and the house of Judah, 32 not like the covenant that I made with their fathers on the day when I took them by the hand to bring them out of the land of Egypt, my covenant that they broke, though I was their husband, declares the LORD. 33 But this is the covenant that I will make with the house of Israel after those days, declares the LORD: I will put my law within them, and I will write it on their hearts. And I will be their God, and they shall be my people. 34 And no longer shall each one teach his neighbor and each his brother, saying, 'Know the LORD,' for they shall all know me, from the least of them to the greatest, declares the LORD. For I will forgive their iniquity, and I will remember their sin no more." (Jer 31:31–34)[4]

The historical context of the revelation of the New Covenant should be interpreted in light of how the the New Covenant is wholly revealed in the New Testament. Yahweh promised to "make a New Covenant with the house of Israel and the house of Judah." It is important to recognize that the phrase, "the house of Israel and the house of Judah," embraces the twelve tribes of Israel, the promised descendents of the

---

4. James Kugel fundamentally misreads the prophecy of the New Covenant in Jeremiah 31:31–34, in stating that the passage presents "one of the most characteristic features of the religion of Judaism." However, we need to recognize that the prophecy of the New Covenant will be fulfilled in the Coming Messiah, the mediator of the New Covenant. So, to say that it reveals "the religion of Judaism" is not appropriate considering that it is incompatible to the true biblical religion of the ancient Israel: "This passage bespeaks one of the most characteristic features of the religion of Judaism. The idea that it is incumbent on the whole society to learn and obey Torah's ordinances—that indeed, the renewal of God's covenant and His future protection of Israel would depend on the people scrupulously obeying God's laws—meant that attention would henceforth be focused as never before on the proper interpretation and inculcation of those laws within the general population." Kugel, *How to Read the Bible*, 592.

The New Covenant and the Kingdom of God

Abrahamic covenant. Moreover, it is the *representative expression* of the elect, which includes both Jews and Gentiles.[5]

Just as God revealed the New Covenant to the prophet Jeremiah, so he also revealed the New Covenant to the prophet Ezekiel after the southern Kingdom of Judah fell under the siege of Babylon in 586 B.C. In fact, God waged holy war against the covenant community of Israel that had broken the Mosaic covenant of law. He poured out his wrath against his covenant people, executing his covenant lawsuit. In the darkest moment of the history of ancient Israel, God revealed the New Covenant to the prophet Ezekiel as "a covenant of peace." In fact, God's revelation of the New Covenant as "a covenant of peace" is significant, because under it God no longer prosecutes the covenant lawsuit against the covenant community as he did under the Mosaic covenant of law:

> 20 "Therefore, thus says the Lord GOD to them: Behold, I, I myself will judge between the fat sheep and the lean sheep. 21 Because you push with side and shoulder, and thrust at all the weak with your horns, till you have scattered them abroad, 22 I will rescue my flock; they shall no longer be a prey. And I will judge between sheep and sheep. 23 And I will set up over them one shepherd, my servant David, and he shall feed them: he shall feed them and be their shepherd. 24 *And I, the LORD, will be their God, and my servant David shall be prince among them. I am the LORD; I have spoken.* 25 *"I will make with them a covenant of peace and banish wild beasts from the land, so that they may dwell securely in the wilderness and sleep in the woods.* 26 *And I will make them and the places all around my hill a blessing, and I will send down the showers in their season; they shall be showers of blessing.* 27 And the trees of the field shall yield their fruit, and the earth shall yield its increase, and they shall be secure in their land. And they shall know that I am the LORD, when I break the bars of their yoke, and deliver them from the hand of those who enslaved them. 28 They shall no more be a prey to the nations, nor shall the beasts of the land devour them. They shall dwell securely, and none shall make them afraid. 29 And I will provide for them renowned plantations so that they shall no more be consumed with hunger in the land, and no longer suffer the reproach of the nations. 30 And they shall know that I am the LORD their God with them, and that they, the house of Israel, are my people, declares the Lord GOD. 31 And you are my sheep, human sheep of my pasture, and I am your God, declares the Lord GOD." (Ezek 34:20–31)

---

5. Ryrie, as a dispensationalist, interprets "the house of Israel and the house of Judah" literally. He insists that God will make the New Covenant "in the future with the whole nation of Israel." Thereby, he ignores the important fact that God will make his New Covenant with the elect, which includes both the Jews and Gentiles: "31:31–34 The principal Old Testament passage on the new covenant (cf. Isa. 59:20–21; Jer. 32:37–40; Ezek. 16:60–63; 37:21–28). See note on Heb. 8:6. It will be made in the future with the whole nation of Israel (v. 31); it will be unlike the Mosaic covenant in that it will be unconditional (v. 32); its provisions will include (1) a change of heart, (2) fellowship with God, (3) knowledge of the Lord, and (4) forgiveness of sins. All of this will be fulfilled for Israel when the Lord returns (Rom. 11:26–27)." Ryrie, *The Ryrie Study Bible*, 915.

Later, God revealed to Ezekiel that the New Covenant as "a covenant of peace" (בְּרִית שָׁלוֹם) will be an "everlasting covenant" (בְּרִית עוֹלָם), making it different from the Old Covenant which was a temporary and breakable because of Israel's sworn oath:

> 20 When the sticks on which you write are in your hand before their eyes, 21 then say to them, Thus says the Lord GOD: Behold, I will take the people of Israel from the nations among which they have gone, and will gather them from all around, and bring them to their own land. 22 And I will make them one nation in the land, on the mountains of Israel. And one king shall be king over them all, and they shall be no longer two nations, and no longer divided into two kingdoms. 23 They shall not defile themselves anymore with their idols and their detestable things, or with any of their transgressions. But I will save them from all the backslidings in which they have sinned, and will cleanse them; and they shall be my people, and I will be their God. 24 "My servant David shall be king over them, and they shall all have one shepherd. They shall walk in my rules and be careful to obey my statutes. 25 *They shall dwell in the land that I gave to my servant Jacob, where your fathers lived. They and their children and their children's children shall dwell there forever, and David my servant shall be their prince forever. 26 I will make a covenant of peace with them. It shall be an everlasting covenant with them. And I will set them in their land and multiply them, and will set my sanctuary in their midst forevermore.* 27 My dwelling place shall be with them, and I will be their God, and they shall be my people. 28 Then the nations will know that I am the LORD who sanctifies Israel, when my sanctuary is in their midst forevermore." (Ezek 37:20–28)[6]

In fact, the New Covenant is the climax and consummation of *all* the divine covenants with God's people. God will no longer execute the covenant lawsuit against his covenant people, because the mediator of the New Covenant has been cursed and slaughtered as the Lamb on the cross on behalf of God's elect. Under the New Covenant, God will never again pour out his wrath against his people as he did under the Old Covenant. The everlasting peace, joy, and love are consummated in the New Covenant for those who receive the blessings of election, calling, faith and repentance, justification, sanctification, and glorification. Thus it is proper for the New Covenant to be called "the covenant of peace" and an "everlasting covenant."

Meanwhile, Daniel went into Babylonian captivity along with other young Jews when King Nebuchadnezzar of Babylon and his soldiers attacked Jerusalem "in the

---

6. Ryrie interprets Ezekiel 37:21–28 in light of dispensational premillennialism. Thereby, he argues that "promises for Israel" will be visibly realized "at the second coming of Christ." They include restoration of the Promised Land, "unifications of the two kingdoms," and "Messiah's ruling over them," and others: "37:21–28 Promises for Israel that will be fulfilled at the second coming of Christ include restoration to the land of Palestine (v. 21), unification of the two kingdoms (v. 22), purification from all idolatry (v.23), Messiah's ruling over them (v.24; see note on 34:23), possession of the land forever (v. 25; cf. Gen. 15:18–21), and the presence of God and His sanctuary in their midst (vv. 26–28)." Ibid., 1002.

third year of the reign of Jehoiakim king of Judah," in 605 B.C. The Jews in Babylonian captivity included some "of the royal family and of the nobility, youths without blemish" (Dan 1:1–4). Later, the Babylonian Empire was destroyed by the Medes and the Persians in 539 B.C. When Daniel read the scroll of Jeremiah, he realized that the Babylonian exile would last seventy years "in the first year of Darius the son of Ahasuerus, by descent a Mede" around the fall of Babylon (Dan 9:1–2).

In fact, Jeremiah prophesied seventy years of the Babylonian captivity "in the fourth year of Jehoiakim the son of Josiah, king of Judah (that was the first year of Nebuchadnezzar king of Babylon)" (Jer 25:1). Yahweh spoke clearly through Jeremiah to the covenant community, who were "all the people of Judah." God revealed through Jeremiah that he would execute the covenant lawsuit against the covenant community which violated the Mosaic covenant of law. He used "Nebuchadnezzar the king of Babylon" to destroy the Promised Land and covenant community. However, the covenant community, after seventy years of Babylonian captivity, returned to the Promised Land, after Yahweh punished the Babylonian kingdom:

> 8 "Therefore thus says the LORD of hosts: Because you have not obeyed my words, 9 behold, I will send for all the tribes of the north, declares the LORD, and for Nebuchadnezzar the king of Babylon, my servant, and I will bring them against this land and its inhabitants, and against all these surrounding nations. I will devote them to destruction, and make them a horror, a hissing, and an everlasting desolation. 10 Moreover, I will banish from them the voice of mirth and the voice of gladness, the voice of the bridegroom and the voice of the bride, the grinding of the millstones and the light of the lamp. 11 *This whole land shall become a ruin and a waste, and these nations shall serve the king of Babylon seventy years. 12 Then after seventy years are completed, I will punish the king of Babylon and that nation, the land of the Chaldeans, for their iniquity, declares the LORD, making the land an everlasting waste.* 13 I will bring upon that land all the words that I have uttered against it, everything written in this book, which Jeremiah prophesied against all the nations. 14 For many nations and great kings shall make slaves even of them, and I will recompense them according to their deeds and the work of their hands." (Jer 25:8–14)

Yahweh had warned that he would fight a war of total destruction (*cherem*) against the covenant community that had violated the Mosaic covenant of law. In fact, he used the Babylonian kingdom to wage a holy war against the southern kingdom of Judah.

Realizing through his reading of Jeremiah that the cause of the desolation of Jerusalem and seventy years of Babylonian captivity of the Jews was sin against God, Daniel confessed his sin, as well as the sins of Israel, in a heartfelt prayer:

> 11 All Israel has transgressed your law and turned aside, refusing to obey your voice. And the curse and oath that are written in the Law of Moses the servant of God have been poured out upon us, because we have sinned against him. 12 He

> *has confirmed his words, which he spoke against us and against our rulers who ruled us, by bringing upon us a great calamity. For under the whole heaven there has not been done anything like what has been done against Jerusalem.* 13 As it is written in the Law of Moses, all this calamity has come upon us; yet we have not entreated the favor of the LORD our God, turning from our iniquities and gaining insight by your truth. 14 *Therefore the LORD has kept ready the calamity and has brought it upon us, for the LORD our God is righteous in all the works that he has done, and we have not obeyed his voice.* 15 And now, O Lord our God, who brought your people out of the land of Egypt with a mighty hand, and have made a name for yourself, as at this day, we have sinned, we have done wickedly. (Dan 9:11–15)

Daniel's prayer is historical proof that the Babylonian captivity and the desolation of Jerusalem were the result of transgression of the Mosaic covenant of law by the covenant community of Israel. Yahweh poured out the curses found "in the Law of Moses." Thus a great calamity fell upon not only all Israel but also on Jerusalem, the heart of the Promised Land. Listening to Daniel's sincere confession of sins and plea for mercy, Yahweh revealed a prophecy that the seventy years of the Babylonian captivity would end. The new era began in redemptive history as:

> 24 "Seventy weeks are decreed about your people and your holy city, to finish the transgression, to put an end to sin, and to atone for iniquity, to bring in everlasting righteousness, to seal both vision and prophet, and to anoint a most holy place. 25 Know therefore and understand that from the going out of the word to restore and build Jerusalem to the coming of an anointed one, a prince, there shall be seven weeks. Then for sixty-two weeks it shall be built again with squares and moat, but in a troubled time. 26 And after the sixty-two weeks, an anointed one shall be cut off and shall have nothing. And the people of the prince who is to come shall destroy the city and the sanctuary. Its end shall come with a flood, and to the end there shall be war. Desolations are decreed. 27 And he shall make a strong covenant with many for one week, and for half of the week he shall put an end to sacrifice and offering. And on the wing of abominations shall come one who makes desolate, until the decreed end is poured out on the desolator." (Dan 9:24–27)[7]

---

7. Historical critical scholars deny the validity of the prophets' future prophecy, because they deny any supernatural events and works performed by God. So, their understanding of history is purely naturalistic, getting rid of any supernatural elements in the Bible. Likewise, Collins as a historical critical scholar denies all the supernatural elements in the book of Daniel, even denying the historical existence of the prophet Daniel: "Conservative Christian scholars have expended enormous energy in efforts to salvage the historicity of Darius the Mede and other problematic data in Daniel. These efforts are misdirected. These stories are not exercises in history writing. They are legends, full of miraculous elements (the fiery furnace, the lions' den). They are meant to inspire awe and wonder, and are not to be taken as factual accounts. In fact, it is unlikely that Daniel ever existed. The name Daniel (Danel) was attached to a legendary figure from antiquity, who is known from the Ugaritic Epic of Aqhat, and who is mentioned in Ezek 14:14, 20, in conjunction with Noah and Job, as a paradigmatic righteous person. He is also mentioned in Ezek 28:3 as a paradigmatic wise man ("are you wiser

The New Covenant and the Kingdom of God

The decree of seventy weeks disclosed the Lord's plan "to bring in everlasting righteousness" through the Messiah's life, death, and resurrection. Yahweh designated a redemptive historical timeline as seven weeks and sixty-two weeks to restore and build Jerusalem along with the first coming of the Messiah. Verse 27 is a prophecy about the seventieth week, which covered the time period from the crucifixion of "an anointed one" to the final judgment, which will happen at the Second Coming of Jesus Christ. We need to pay special attention to the first part of verse 27: "And he shall make a strong covenant with many for one week, and for half of the week he shall put an end to sacrifice and offering." "He shall make a strong covenant with many for one week" suggests that God will ratify the New Covenant with the death of the Messiah. The elect as "many" will be saved by God's grace in Jesus Christ "for one week," which spans from the death of Jesus Christ to his Second Coming. The latter part of verse 27 signifies that the end of the seventieth week will be culminated with the pouring out of God's final wrath, as we read, "And on the wing of abominations shall come one who makes desolate, until the decreed end is poured out on the desolator." In that sense, "the decreed end" is the end of the seventieth week.[8]

---

than Daniel?"). The Daniel of the book of Daniel, however, would have been a younger contemporary of Ezekiel. It is likely that the biblical author borrowed the name of the legendary hero and assigned it to a fictional Judean in the Babylonian exile. The story of Daniel, then, is not historical. It is, however, meant to be exemplary." Collins, *Introduction to the Hebrew Bible*, 554–55.

Rejecting the historical existence of the prophet Daniel, Collins interprets Daniel 9:24–27 in light of a purely naturalistic history: "After Daniel has finished his prayer, an angel appears to him and explains the prophecy. The seventy years are really seventy weeks of years, or 490 years. After seven weeks, the initial restoration of Jerusalem takes place. Then sixty-two weeks pass uneventually. At the end of this period, an anointed one is cut off. The reference is not to the messiah in the usual sense of the term, but to the anointed high priest Onias III, who was murdered in 171 B.C.E. (see 2 Macc 4:23–28). Then, in the last week, troops come to destroy the city and the sanctuary. They disrupt the sacrificial cult for half of the week. The implication is that from the time that the cult is disrupted, and the 'desolating abomination' is installed in the temple, the time remaining is half a week or three and a half years (a time, times, and half a time).

"The interpretation of Daniel's prophecy is an important text for the history of apocalyptic speculation about the time of the end. It serves as the basis for such calculations already in the Dead Sea Scrolls. By modern calculations, the 490 years from the destruction of the temple should have ended in 196 B.C.E., but Daniel was written some thirty years after that. We do not know how the author calculated the length of time between the Babylonian exile and the Maccabean revolt. The Jewish historian Josephus, writing in the late first century C.E., said that Daniel was the greatest of the prophets, because he not only said what would happen, but when it would happen. We might wonder how Josephus could believe in the accuracy of Daniel's calculations, so long after the 490 years had elapsed, by any reckoning." Ibid., 568.

8. In fact, the prophecy of the seventieth week is the summary from the ratification of the New Covenant through the Messiah's death and resurrection, termination of the Old Covenant order in 70 A.D. through the fall of Jerusalem to the Roman army to the consummation of redemptive history through the Second Coming of the Messiah. Kline summarizes the seventieth week in light of redemptive history as follows: "As a priest who offers the true once-for-all sacrifice, Christ made obsolete in principle the typical sacrifices of the Old Covenant. But the point of v. 27b, in correspondence to v. 26b, is rather that Christ as Ruler and Judge effected the outward cessation of the old sacrificial system by destroying the old temple. A significant new feature added in v. 27b is that Christ's judgment on apostate Jerusalem takes place 'in the middle of the week'—the 'one week' (the seventieth week) just mentioned in v.27a.

In fact, the decree of seventy weeks was the summary of a future redemptive history, after the completion of seventy years of the Babylonian captivity. Remarkably, Yahweh disclosed a future redemptive history, focusing on the Messiah's Coming, his death, the fall of Jerusalem in 70 A.D., and the Second Coming of Jesus, which would be the consummation of redemptive history. As such, the prophecy of seventy weeks is a comprehensive summary of a future redemptive history from 539 B.C. to the consummation of redemptive history with the Second Coming of the Messiah. In that sense, we should interpret seventy weeks figuratively, as Kline properly suggests:

> This evidence that the seventy weeks were already under way, together with the necessity for immediate action on the Lord's part in order to fulfill the promissory prophecy of Jer 29:10, puts it beyond question that the seventy weeks of Dan 9:24 began in that very year, 539 BC. Since the Messiah and the fall of Jerusalem in 70 AD are features of the seventy weeks, that period is longer than a literal 490 years. The seventy weeks of this vision must then be figurative.[9]

Jesus Christ as the mediator of the New Covenant fulfilled all the requirements of the righteousness of the Mosaic covenant of law through his sinless life and atoning death on the cross. At the same time, Jesus Christ as the last Adam fulfilled the requirements of the Edenic covenant of works, which the first Adam failed to accomplish as the representative covenant head.

While the seventieth week as a whole is devoted to fulfilling for those in Christ the blessing sanctions of the New Covenant as the final administration of the Covenant of Grace, the terminating curse sanction of the Old Covenant is executed within the epoch. There is thus an overlapping of the Old and New Covenants, the old temple order retaining a qualified legitimacy for a while after the inauguration of the New Covenant, even though the latter meant the obsolescence in principle of the old order (cf. Heb 8:13). The overlap is the period from the Cross to 70 AD and the practice of the apostles and early church, especially in Jerusalem, as recorded in the Book of Acts was in accord with this overlap situation.

"The division of the seventieth week in the middle produces two symbolic periods of three and a half years each. The first is the overlap period extending to the fall of Jerusalem in 70 AD. The second covers the history of the church from its disengagement from the collapsed typal order in 70 AD to the consummation. The second symbolic three and a half year era reappears in the New Testament Apocalypse as a symbolic period which we will be identifying with the interim leading up to the antichrist crisis and the second advent of Christ." Kline, *God, Heaven and Har Magedon*, 153.

Interestingly, putting together John the Baptist's ministry and Christ's public ministry, Jonathan Edwards calculates that their public ministries made seven years, which was the seventieth week of Daniel's seventy weeks: "The forerunner of Christ's coming in his public ministry was John the Baptist: he came preaching repentance for the remission of sins, to make way for Christ's coming, agreeable to the prophecies of him, Isa. xl. 3, 4, 5. And Matt. iv. 5, 6. It is supposed that John the Baptist began his ministry about three years and an half before Christ; so that John's ministry and Christ's put together, made seven years, which was the last of Daniel's weeks; and this time is intended in Dan. ix. 27. 'He will confirm the covenant with many for one week.' Christ came in the midst of this week, viz. in the beginning of the last half of it, or the last three years and an half. As Daniel foretold, as in the verse just now quoted: 'and in the midst of the week he shall cause the sacrifice and the oblation to cease.' John Baptist's ministry consisted principally in preaching the law, to awaken men and convince them of sin, to prepare men for the coming of Christ, to comfort them, as the law is to prepare the heart for the entertainment of the gospel." Edwards, *A History of the Work of Redemption*, 187.

9. Kline, *God, Heaven and Har Magedon*, 147.

The New Covenant and the Kingdom of God

The Spiritual Battle Against the Kingdom of Satan and the Covenant of Royal Grant

The four Gospels can be rightly identified as the books of the New Covenant because they comprehensively explore the incarnation, life, earthly ministry, death, and resurrection of Jesus Christ, the mediator of the New Covenant. The authors of the Gospels testify to Jesus Christ's birth, life, death, and resurrection from different perspectives but with wonderful harmony.[10] They not only testify of Jesus' life, death, and resurrection, but also God's covenant-making process with his elect through the mediator of the New Covenant.[11] The analysis is that the New Covenant is the covenant of royal

---

10. Just as historical critical scholars deny the Mosaic authorship of the Pentateuch, so they also deny the authorship of the four Gospels by Matthew, Mark, Luke, and John. For example, James Robinson insists that the authors of the four Gospels are anonymous in light of the historical critical reading of these books: "To gain admission to the canon, Gospels were attributed to apostles (Matthew and John) or to those dependent on apostles for their information (Mark and Luke). But today, these persons are not thought to have been the actual authors. None of the text themselves give the author's name—all four are anonymous. They were composed in the last thirty years of the first century, half a century after the facts. Their actual authors are unknown, but all four Gospels are of course cited here by their traditional names, Matthew, Mark, Luke, and John." Robinson, *The Gospel of Jesus*, 4.

11. The Nag Hammadi religious documents were found in 1945 in the village of Nag Hammadi near the Nile River while two Egyptian farmers were digging the soil of a cave. The twelve leather bound documents were inside a sealed jar. Ever since then, scholars have paid deep interest in the contents and interpretation of the religious documents. Scholars have general consensus that the documents were translated from Greek to Coptic around the third or fourth century. The documents reflect so well the religious belief and practice of the Gnostic Christians in the early church. Most importantly, the documents contain several gospels such as "the Gospel of Thomas," "the Gospel of Mary," "the Gospel of Judas," and others. As we read the Nag Hammadi religious documents, including the gospels, it is not difficult to determine that the so-called gospels contained among the documents should not be identified as authentic Gospels of the New Testament. Rather, they are pseudo-gospels, because they do not contain Jesus Christ's incarnation, public life, death, and resurrection, which are the essential components of the stories of the four Gospels of the New Testament. The different gospels in the Nag Hammadi religious documents are the religious reflection of Gnostic Christianity in light of the Platonic dualism in the early church. The pseudo-gospels at Nag Hammadi are proof that Gnostic Christianity in the early church reinterpreted the stories and truth of Jesus Christ of the four Gospels in the New Testament in light of Platonic dualism. For the Nag Hammadi religious documents and critical analysis about these documents, see Meyer ed., *The Nag Hammadi Scriptures*.

Robert Funk, a founder of the Jesus Seminar and a historical critical scholar, recognizes that the hypothetical document of "Sayings Gospel Q" and "the Gospel of Thomas" do not contain the narrative stories about Jesus' incarnation, life, death, and resurrection, which are the backbone and foundation of the good news of the gospel. This is precisely the reason why we argue that the Gospel of Thomas is at best a pseudo-gospel, which was the religious reflection of Gnostic Christianity in the early church: "Saying Gospel Q antedates Matthew and Luke, since they both make use of it. Q specialists are inclined to date Q to about 50 C.E., thus making it the earliest written record of the words of Jesus. What about Thomas? On the theory that Thomas went through several editions, some Thomas specialists have proposed dating a hypothetical first edition of Thomas also to the decade 50–60 C.E. The startling insight this hypothetical scenario brings with it is that collections of Jesus' sayings, without narrative setting, preceded the creation of narrative gospels. Q and Thomas lack any reference to Jesus' death; they lack resurrection stories; they do not have any birth or childhood stories; and, even more significantly, they do not provide narrative settings that might place Jesus' utterances in some historical context. It suddenly becomes possible to speculate that the Christian overlay found in the New

grant after the pattern of the Prediluvian Noahic, Abrahamic and Davidic covenants. In fact, the New Covenant is not only the culmination of the redemptive covenants, inaugurated in Genesis 3:15, but is also the climax of the covenant of royal grant.[12]

Interestingly, God did not ratify the New Covenant in the beginning of Jesus' public life and ministry. Rather, he ratified the New Covenant at the end of Jesus' life and ministry through his crucifixion. However, before the crucifixion of Jesus Christ, he fought against the challenges of Satan and his servants, the demons. The first Adam failed to fight against the challenge of Satan as the representative covenantal head in the holy Garden of Eden. So he committed the original sin with his wife, Eve, nullifying the Edenic covenant of works (Gen 3:1–7). Meanwhile, Jesus Christ humbly accepted his role as the last Adam, and underwent a probationary period in his birth, life, and ministry. One of his earthly missions from the Father was to accomplish the requirement of the covenant of works wherein the first Adam failed.

Before Jesus began his public ministry, he went from Galilee to the Jordan River. At the Jordan River, he was baptized by John the Baptist. Of note, the baptism of Jesus was Trinitarian. At the scene of the baptism of the Son of God, there was an audible and visible sign of the triune God:

> 16 And when Jesus was baptized, immediately he went up from the water, and behold, the heavens were opened to him, and he saw the Spirit of God descending like a dove and coming to rest on him; 17 and behold, a voice from heaven said, "This is my beloved Son, with whom I am well pleased."(Matt 3:16–17; cf. Mark 1:19–21; Luke 3:21–22)[13]

Testament gospels may be just that—an overlay. The original, or at least an original, gospel probably consisted only of a collection of pronouncements attributed to Jesus, in which his birth, death, and resurrection played no role at all. In retrospect, it is intriguing to discover that this possibility had been opened up by Hermann Samuel Reimarus (1694–1768), the first critical scholar of the gospels, when he observed that who Jesus was and what he said may have differed from what the New Testament evangelists report he said and did." Funk, *Honest to Jesus*, 135.

12. The New Covenant is the covenant of royal grant, as Horton comprehensively explains: "The New Testament does not end up without a doctrine of covenant, but it does end up with a *royal grant* that is absolutely consistent with a 'last will and testament.' This royal grant is one-sided in terms of its basis yet calls for genuine partnership and future obedience as the reasonable response. Further, if we are to read about the kingship canonically, we find that this royal grant is made (as usually in the ancient world) on the basis of David's own performance. Yet does this square with Paul's appeal in Romans 4 to David as an example of one who, like Abraham, is justified by faith alone apart from works? A contradiction only emerges if we fail to distinguish between the typological and conditional aspects of the old covenant (based on the law) and the reality to which they point (based on promise). Like Abraham, David is the recipient of a covenant of grant because of past performance, but this royal grant concerns the perpetuity of his seed on the throne (as it did Abraham's in the land), not individual salvation ... Even more clearly than Abraham's, David's military campaigns presage the greater victory of his greater Son, receiving a greater prize for his conquest. With respect to individual salvation, therefore, Abraham, David, and the rest of us receive the eternal inheritance not by personal performance (past, present, and future), but on the basis of Christ's performance. This bounty is then inherited by us as a last will and testament." Horton, *Introducing Covenant Theology*, 56–57.

13. Interpreting Jesus' baptism at the Jordan River, Bultmann, from the perspective of a historical

The New Covenant and the Kingdom of God

The baptism of Jesus was the first explicit revelation of the triune God. Until then, the revelation of the triune God was implicit throughout the history of the Old Testament. Jesus' baptism was an official affirmation that he came to this world as the Son of God. The baptism was a pivotal moment because it officially marked the beginning of his public ministry to fulfill his earthly mission, which was commissioned by God the Father and empowered through the Holy Spirit. In his baptism, Jesus beheld "the Spirit of God descending like a dove and coming to rest on him." This remarkable scene was a Trinitarian affirmation that Jesus indeed *is* the Son of God. Moreover, the visible descent of "the Spirit of God" on Jesus was the visible glory of the Holy Spirit, intruded from the heavenly Kingdom of God. This visible phenomenon can be identified as Spiritophanic glory.[14]

When God made the Mosaic covenant with the covenant community of Israel on Mt. Sinai, there was visible glory. That glory was the glory of Yahweh, intruded from the heavenly Kingdom of God. The covenant community of Israel trembled as they saw the glory of Yahweh, which enveloped the prophet Moses, the mediator of the Old Covenant. Likewise, the visible glory before the covenant community of Israel was the glory of Yahweh as the theophanic glory which witnessed the covenant ratification ceremony:

> 15 Then Moses went up on the mountain, and the cloud covered the mountain. 16 *The glory of the LORD dwelt on Mount Sinai, and the cloud covered it six days. And on the seventh day he called to Moses out of the midst of the cloud.* 17 *Now the appearance of the glory of the LORD was like a devouring fire on the top of the mountain in the sight of the people of Israel.* 18 Moses entered the

---

critical and existential understanding of the life of Jesus, claims that Jesus *becomes* "the Son of God by the Spirit conferred upon him at the baptism." However, it is important to understand that the audible and visible scene of Jesus' baptism is the Trinitarian God's affirmation that Jesus *is* the Son of God: "The Gentile-Christian conception of Christ as Son of God varies according to which tradition influences it more. The synoptic gospels essentially represent the first type, inasmuch as they picture Jesus as the Son of God who reveals his divine power and authority through miracles. This is a way of thinking which was also capable of being appropriated even by such Christian thought as was determined by Jewish tradition; this was done when it attributed the 'power' in the life of the 'divine man' to the divine Spirit by analogy with David and the prophets. This is the vein in which the Gospel of Mark tells its story. According to it, Jesus becomes the Son of God by the Spirit conferred upon him at the baptism." Bultmann, *Theology of the New Testament*, 1:130–31.

14. Schweitzer, investigating the history of Jesus in the light of the historical critical understanding, falsely argues that Jesus *awoke to* his Messianic consciousness at his baptism in the Jordan River. Unlike Schweitzer's false claim, Jesus had the Messianic consciousness throughout his earthly life as the Son of God as well as the Son of Man: "The ministry of Jesus is therefore not in principle different from that of John the Baptist: there can be no question of a founding and development of the Kingdom within the hearts of men. What distinguishes the work of Jesus from that of the Baptist is only His consciousness of being the Messiah. He awoke to this consciousness at His baptism. But the Messiahship which he claims is not a present office; its exercise belongs to the future. On earth He is only a man, a prophet, as in the view implied in the speeches in the Acts of the Apostles. 'Son of Man' is therefore, in the passages where it is authentic, a purely eschatological designation of the Messiah, though we cannot tell whether His hearers understood Him as speaking of Himself in His future rank and dignity, or whether they thought of the Son of Man as a being quite distinct from Himself, whose coming He was only proclaiming in advance." Schweitzer, *The Quest of the Historical Jesus*, 239.

cloud and went up on the mountain. And Moses was on the mountain forty days and forty nights (Ex 24:15–18).

During Jesus' baptism, the heavenly Father audibly affirmed that Jesus is his beloved Son. The visible presence of the glory of the Holy Spirit was the prelude of the visible coming of the Holy Spirit at Pentecost, which was a turning point in redemptive history, proclaiming the good news of the gospel to all nations. Furthermore, the scene of Jesus' baptism was the ceremony of the Holy Spirit's anointing of Jesus as the king of the Kingdom of God. When David was anointed as the king of Israel, he was anointed by "all the elders of Israel" at Hebron (2 Sam 5:1–5; cf. 1 Chr 11:1–3).[15] However, Jesus as the Son of David was not anointed by human hands but by the Holy Spirit. It is significant that while David was anointed as the king of Israel, Jesus as the Davidic Messiah was anointed as the king of the eschatological Kingdom of God.[16]

After the Pentecost event, Peter went to Caesarea to preach the good news of the gospel to the Gentiles. In doing so, he reflected on John the Baptist who was the forerunner of Jesus:

> 34 So Peter opened his mouth and said: "Truly I understand that God shows no partiality, 35 but in every nation anyone who fears him and does what is right is acceptable to him. 36 As for the word that he sent to Israel, preaching good news of peace through Jesus Christ (he is Lord of all), 37 *you yourselves know what happened throughout all Judea, beginning from Galilee after the baptism that John proclaimed:* 38 *how God anointed Jesus of Nazareth with the Holy Spirit and with power. He went about doing good and healing all who were oppressed by the devil, for God was with him.* 39 And we are witnesses of all that he did both in the country of the Jews and in Jerusalem. They put him to death by hanging him on a tree, 40 but God raised him on the third day and made him to appear, 41 not to all the people but to us who had been chosen by God as witnesses, who ate and drank with him after he rose from the dead. 42 And he commanded us to preach to the people and to testify that he is the

---

15. Bruce Waltke properly indicates that John the Baptist as "the greatest of the prophets" identifies Jesus Christ as "the greatest of the kings" when he baptizes Jesus: "The prophet, armed with God's voice, has the authority to anoint, to rebuke, and finally to depose kings. Samuel, the first court prophet anoints Saul, rejects Saul, and anoints David. In the scramble for succession after David, the prophet Nathan awards the crown to Solomon, and faithful David obeys... This proper relationship between king and prophet is affirmed by Jesus, who is baptized by John the Baptist, the greatest of the prophets. As John the Baptist gives his prophetic anointing, he identifies Jesus as the greatest of the kings." Waltke, *An Old Testament Theology*, 399.

16. Jonathan Edwards explains anointing David by the oil was "a type of the Spirit of God." In the original scene of anointing David, "the type and the antitype were given both together." In that sense, it makes a perfect sense that the scene of Jesus' baptism was the visible ceremony of the Holy Spirit's anointing of Jesus as the king of the Kingdom of God without using the oil: "The oil that was used in anointing David was a type of the Spirit of God; and the type and the antitype were given both together; as we are told, 1 Sam. xvi. 13. 'Then Solomon took the horn of oil, and anointed him in the midst of his brethren; and the Spirit of the Lord came upon David from that day forward:' and it is probable, that it now came upon him in its prophetical influences." Edwards, *A History of the Work of Redemption*, 99.

one appointed by God to be judge of the living and the dead. 43 To him all the prophets bear witness that everyone who believes in him receives forgiveness of sins through his name." (Acts 10:34–43)

In verse 38, by stating "how God anointed Jesus of Nazareth with the Holy Spirit and with power. He went about doing good and healing all who were oppressed by the devil, for God was with him," Peter summarizes Jesus' public life and ministry with Jesus' water baptism by John the Baptist in the Jordan River. We need to pay particular attention to "how God anointed Jesus of Nazareth with the Holy Spirit and with power" (v. 38a). This signifies that "God anointed Jesus of Nazareth with the Holy Spirit and with power" in the Jordan River at his water baptism. In fact, God's anointing of "Jesus of Nazareth with the Holy Spirit and with power" is an official ceremony of anointing Jesus as the king of the Kingdom of God. Although Jesus as the Son of David was anointed as the king of the Kingdom of God, God's official grant of the kingdom to his Son was postponed until he passed the probation period which culminated in his death on the cross.

After Jesus' baptism, he was led by the Holy Spirit to the desert and was tempted by Satan. He fasted for forty days and nights, and he became hungry. Satan came to Jesus and the famous spiritual battle took place between Jesus and Satan. In the process of the spiritual battle, Jesus did not use physical force or military means. Rather, he used the Word of God. He faithfully cited and proclaimed Deuteronomy 8:3; 6:16, and 6:13 with his commanding voice against Satan. Satan was defeated and escaped from the presence of Jesus, where angels surrounded and served him (Matt 4:1–11; cf. Mark 1:12–13; Luke 4:1–13).

Jesus went throughout Galilee and preached the good news of the Kingdom of Heaven and also called the first disciples beside the Sea of Galilee. He cast out demons from the people who were possessed by them. And many people followed him from Galilee and different regions:

> 23 And he went throughout all Galilee, teaching in their synagogues and proclaiming the gospel of the kingdom and healing every disease and every affliction among the people. 24 So his fame spread throughout all Syria, and they brought him all the sick, those afflicted with various diseases and pains, those oppressed by demons, epileptics, and paralytics, and he healed them. 25 And great crowds followed him from Galilee and the Decapolis, and from Jerusalem and Judea, and from beyond the Jordan. (Matt 4:23–25)

When Jesus went to the region of the Gadarenes, he encountered two men who were possessed by demons. The men were so violent because many demons were working in them. At the request of the demons, Jesus drove the demons out of the men and into a large herd of pigs. The pigs, possessed by the demons, ran down the steep bank into the sea and drowned in the water:

> 28 And when he came to the other side, to the country of the Gadarenes, two demon-possessed men met him, coming out of the tombs, so fierce that no one could pass that way. 29 And behold, they cried out, "What have you to do with us, O Son of God? Have you come here to torment us before the time?" 30 Now a herd of many pigs was feeding at some distance from them. 31 And the demons begged him, saying, "If you cast us out, send us away into the herd of pigs." 32 And he said to them, "Go." So they came out and went into the pigs, and behold, the whole herd rushed down the steep bank into the sea and drowned in the waters. 33 The herdsmen fled, and going into the city they told everything, especially what had happened to the demon-possessed men. 34 And behold, all the city came out to meet Jesus, and when they saw him, they begged him to leave their region. (Matt 8:28–34; cf. Mark 5:1–20; Luke 8:26–39)

Jesus as the Son of God encountered the demons and fought a spiritual battle, healing the demon-possessed. It is interesting to note that Jesus cast out the demons from people using his own words. Meanwhile, he quoted the Word of God from Deuteronomy when he fought the spiritual battle against Satan in the desert after fasting for forty days and nights.

By casting out demons from people, Jesus demonstrated that he *is* the Messiah and the Son of God. Yet, the majority of the Jews did not accept Jesus as the Messiah and the Son of God. For example, people brought to Jesus a demon-possessed man who was blind and mute. When Jesus cast out the demon from the man, he was immediately healed and became able to see and speak. But the Pharisees did not believe Jesus' healing of the demon-possessed man. They said that Jesus drove out the demons by Beelzebub, the prince of demons. In response to the Pharisees' unbelief, Jesus said that he drove out demons not by Beelzebub but "by the Spirit of God."

> 22 Then a demon-oppressed man who was blind and mute was brought to him, and he healed him, so that the man spoke and saw. 23 And all the people were amazed, and said, "Can this be the Son of David?" 24 But when the Pharisees heard it, they said, "It is only by Beelzebul, the prince of demons, that this man casts out demons." 25 Knowing their thoughts, he said to them, "Every kingdom divided against itself is laid waste, and no city or house divided against itself will stand. 26 And if Satan casts out Satan, he is divided against himself. How then will his kingdom stand? 27 And if I cast out demons by Beelzebul, by whom do your sons cast them out? Therefore they will be your judges. 28 *But if it is by the Spirit of God that I cast out demons, then the Kingdom of God has come upon you.* (Matt 12:22–28)

In battling Satan and demons, Jesus never used military means, whereas Abraham and David used military means to fight battles in the name of Yahweh, the Great King. After Jesus won the series of spiritual battles against Satan and his demons, he entered Jerusalem as a victorious Davidic Messiah. But Jesus' triumphal entry into

Jerusalem was a humble one. He did not ride on chariot, led by powerful horses. Rather, he rode on a powerless donkey, and entered Jerusalem, the holy city of God:

> 1 Now when they drew near to Jerusalem and came to Bethphage, to the Mount of Olives, then Jesus sent two disciples, 2 saying to them, "Go into the village in front of you, and immediately you will find a donkey tied, and a colt with her. Untie them and bring them to me, 3 If anyone says anything to you, you shall say, 'The Lord needs them,' and he will send them at once." 4 This took place to fulfill what was spoken by the prophet, saying, 5 "Say to the daughter of Zion, 'Behold, your king is coming to you, humble, and mounted on a donkey, and on a colt, the foal of a beast of burden.'" 6 The disciples went and did as Jesus had directed them. 7 They brought the donkey and the colt and put on them their cloaks, and he sat on them. 8 Most of the crowd spread their cloaks on the road, and others cut branches from the trees and spread them on the road. 9 *And the crowds that went before him and that followed him were shouting, "Hosanna to the Son of David! Blessed is he who comes in the name of the Lord! Hosanna in the highest!"* 10 And when he entered Jerusalem, the whole city was stirred up, saying, "Who is this?" 11 And the crowds said, "This is the prophet Jesus, from Nazareth of Galilee." (Matt 21:1–11)

A victorious and humble Davidic Messiah, Jesus, entered Jerusalem. The crowds' shout to Jesus, "*Hosanna to the Son of David! Blessed is he who comes in the name of the Lord! Hosanna in the highest!*" (v. 9b), signifies that they recognized and revered Jesus as a prophet and the Davidic Messiah.[17] Not only as the mediator of the New Covenant but also as the Son of David, Jesus fought and won the spiritual battle against a series of challenges by Satan and his demons. Only after Jesus' victory over Satan and his demons did God ratify the New Covenant. In this respect, the New Covenant is a covenant of royal grant. Strikingly, the ceremony of the ratification of the New Covenant was visibly realized and manifested through the crucifixion and death of Jesus.

---

17. Schweitzer, exploring Jesus' triumphal entry to Jerusalem in the light of a historical critical reading of the life of Jesus, falsely concludes that Jesus' entry to Jerusalem was "Messianic for Jesus, but not Messianic for the people." However, Schweitzer's false claim undermines the importance of the crowd's shout to Jesus as "the Son of David," which inherently embraces the understanding and welcoming of Jesus as the Davidic Messiah: "The entry is therefore a Messianic act on the part of Jesus, an action in which His consciousness of His office breaks through, as it did at the sending forth of the disciples, in the explanation that the Baptist was Elias, and in the feeding of the multitude. But others can have had no suspicion of the Messianic significance of that which was going on before their eyes. The entry into Jerusalem was therefore Messianic for Jesus, but not Messianic for the people . . . Jesus therefore made His entry into Jerusalem as the Prophet, as Elias. That is confirmed by Matthew (xxi. II), although Matthew gives a Messianic colouring to the entry itself by bringing in the acclamation in which He was designated the Son of David, just as, conversely, he reports the Baptist's question rightly, and introduces it wrongly, by making the Baptist hear of the 'works of the Christ.'" Schweitzer, *The Quest of the Historical Jesus*, 391–92.

BIBLICAL THEOLOGY

The Ratification of the New Covenant and the Divine Oath

When God revealed the covenant of grace in Genesis 3:15, he prophesied that the blood of the covenant would be shed by the mediator of the covenant. This signifies that the only way for sinners to be forgiven is through the blood of the covenant. Therefore, God foreshadowed the blood of the covenant in animal blood, ceremonially shed in the Old Testament. It is noteworthy that all the animal blood which was dedicated on the altar of God throughout redemptive history in the Old Testament was decisively fulfilled through the blood of the Messiah. It is important to remember that the blood of the New Covenant, shed by the Messiah, was the promised blood of the covenant to the covenant people of Israel in the Old Testament.

Before his crucifixion, Jesus administered the Last Supper for his disciples and testified that his blood would be the blood of the covenant, shed for the forgiveness of sins for the elect:

> 26 Now as they were eating, Jesus took bread, and after blessing it broke it and gave it to the disciples, and said, "Take, eat; this is my body." 27 And he took a cup, and when he had given thanks he gave it to them, saying, "Drink of it, all of you, 28 *for this is my blood of the covenant, which is poured out for many for the forgiveness of sins.* 29 I tell you I will not drink again of this fruit of the vine until that day when I drink it new with you in my Father's kingdom." (Matt 26:26–28)

Jesus' phrase, "my blood of the covenant" indicates that the mediator of the New Covenant shed his blood as the means of *ratification* of the covenant. In this manner, the author of Hebrews identifies Christ as the mediator of the New Covenant. The blood of the New Covenant washes away sins, committed under the principle of the Mosaic covenant of law. This suggests that the blood of the New Covenant is intended not only for the elect under the New Covenant but also for the elect under the Mosaic covenant, as well as the elect in the period of the patriarchal age, including Adam and Eve:

> 11 But when Christ appeared as a high priest of the good things that have come, then through the greater and more perfect tent (not made with hands, that is, not of this creation) 12 he entered once for all into the holy places, not by means of the blood of goats and calves but by means of his own blood, thus securing an eternal redemption. 13 For if the sprinkling of defiled persons with the blood of goats and bulls and with the ashes of a heifer sanctifies for the purification of the flesh, 14 how much more will the blood of Christ, who through the eternal Spirit offered himself without blemish to God, purify our conscience from dead works to serve the living God. 15 *Therefore he is the mediator of a new covenant, so that those who are called may receive the promised eternal inheritance, since a death has occurred that redeems them from the transgressions committed under the first covenant.* (Heb 9:11–15)

The New Covenant and the Kingdom of God

The author of the book of Hebrews reflects on Jesus' life, death, resurrection, and ascension. With the inspiration of the Holy Spirit in mind, he affirms that Jesus is "the mediator of a new covenant."[18] Jesus entered the most holy place of the heavenly Kingdom of God after he was sacrificed on God's altar. Afterwards, God granted him the heavenly Kingdom of God and Jesus entered it through his life, death, resurrection, and ascension. The blood of the New Covenant of Christ redeems the people of God and grants "the promised eternal inheritance," the heavenly Kingdom of God for the elect, because of Christ's perfect and meritorious obedience through his life and death.[19]

Meanwhile, the sacrificial death of Jesus Christ on the cross was not only the ceremony of the ratification of the New Covenant but also God's oath to the covenant.

---

18. D. A. Carson properly notes that the prophet Jeremiah in the prophecy of Jeremiah 31:31–34 foresees "a time of no mediators" within the covenant community under the New Covenant. This is because Jesus Christ is clearly and unambiguously "the mediator of a new covenant," as the author of the book of Hebrews proclaims: "But the time is coming, Jeremiah says, when this proverb will be abandoned. 'Instead,' God promises, 'everyone will die for his own sin; whoever eats sour grapes—his own teeth will be set on edge' (Jer. 31:30). This could be true only if the entire covenantal structure associated with Moses' name is replaced by another. That is precisely what the Lord promises: he will make 'a new covenant with the house of Israel and with the house of Judah' that 'will not be like the covenant' he made with their forefathers at the time of the Exodus. The nature of the promised new covenant is carefully recorded: God will put his law in the hearts and on the minds of his people. Instead of having a mediated knowledge of God, 'they will all know me, from the least of them to the greatest,' and therefore 'no longer will a man teach his neighbor, or a man his brother, saying, 'Know the Lord'" (31:31 ff.). This does not foresee a time of no teachers; *in the context, it foresees a time of no mediators, because the entire covenant community under this new covenant will have a personal knowledge of God*, a knowledge characterized by the forgiveness of sin (31:34) and by the law of God written on the heart (31:33)." Carson, "Evangelicals, Ecumenism, and the Church," 359–60, emphasis added.

19. A close relationship between Jesus' message about the Kingdom of God, or the Kingdom of Heaven, and the New Covenant is well summarized by Ridderbos: "The whole structure of the gospel preached by Jesus is determined by the idea of the covenant. The clearest evidence of this fact, finally, is found in the only statement that has been preserved as spoken by Jesus himself and which explicitly mentions the covenant. It is his statement spoken on the occasion of the last Supper. In it Jesus refers to his forthcoming death and says: 'For this is my blood of the new testament (covenant) which is shed for many for the remission of sins' (Matt. 26:28, cf. Mark 14:24; Luke 22:20). These words are important because they place the whole of Jesus' messianic action in the light of the covenant. His death is its seal and provisional conclusion. But they are above all important because they reveal in an incomparable manner the foundation, the character and the scope of this relation in the covenant . . . This reference to Jeremiah 31 is so important because according to these words prophecy the Lord God himself will accomplish the fulfillment of the condition for the maintenance of the new covenant. For he will write his law in the hearts of his people. To this end he will forgive their former iniquity and will no longer remember their sins (Jer. 32:31, 34). According to these words at the last Supper, this fellowship of grace between God and his people is guaranteed by God himself and is consequently unbreakable and finds its foundation and strength in Christ's substitutive suffering and death. For it is his blood which, as the blood of the covenant, is shed for many for the remission of sins and thus makes the new and eternal covenant possible. He is the Mediator of this covenant and of the mercy for the renewal of the heart promised in it. It is clear that in this statement the whole of the salvation given in Christ and preached by him is concentrated in the idea of the covenant . . . Here is revealed the mystery of all the summarizing pronouncements giving expression to the salvation of the kingdom as the *gospel of the poor*, the *saving of those who were lost*, etc. The entire gospel of the kingdom can be explained in the categories of the covenant promised by God." Ridderbos, *The Coming of the Kingdom of God*, 200–1.

In redemptive history, God made a sworn oath when he made his covenants with Abraham and David. In other words, God made a sworn oath in the Abrahamic covenant and the Davidic covenant while he guaranteed his rich promises to Abraham and David.[20] However, the people of Israel made a sworn oath to the covenant in the Sinaitic covenant, not God (Ex 19—24). In that sense, the Abrahamic covenant and Davidic covenant were the representative examples of the covenant of royal grant in the Old Testament. The Sinaitic covenant was a form of the covenant of law while it was the covenant of grace in substance, saving the elect by the principle of the covenant of grace under the Mosaic economy.

The New Covenant is both the climax of the divine covenants and the covenant of royal grant. The divine oath in the ratification ceremony of the New Covenant suggests that in fact the New Covenant is the culmination and climax of the divine covenants revealed in the Old Testament. The author of Hebrews affirms that God made a sworn oath, sacrificing his only begotten Son on the cross

> 20 *And it was not without an oath. For those who formerly became priests were made such without an oath,* 21 but this one was made a priest with an oath by the one who said to him: "The Lord has sworn and will not change his mind, 'You are a priest forever.'" 22 This makes Jesus the guarantor of a better covenant. 23 The former priests were many in number, because they were prevented by death from continuing in office, 24 but he holds his priesthood permanently, because he continues forever. 25 Consequently, he is able to save to the uttermost those who draw near to God through him, since he always lives to make intercession for them. 26 For it was indeed fitting that we should have such a high priest, holy, innocent, unstained, separated from sinners, and exalted above the heavens. 27 He has no need, like those high priests, to offer sacrifices daily, first for his own sins and then for those of the people, since he did this once for all when he offered up himself. 28 *For the law appoints men in their weakness as high priests, but the word of the oath, which came later than the law, appoints a Son who has been made perfect forever.* (Heb 7:20-28)

The author of Hebrews explains that the Levitical high priests became high priests without an oath under the Old Covenant. However, Jesus became the eternal high priest with God's oath. David in his royal psalm prophesied that the Messiah

---

20. The crucifixion of Jesus Christ was not only the visible sign of the divine oath, but it was also the visible sign of the ratification of the New Covenant. In other words, God the Father made a sworn oath and ratified the New Covenant through the crucifixion of his only begotten Son. However, Scott Hahn misinterprets this, stating that "Christ ratified the New Covenant by fulfilling in himself," offering himself upon the cross: "By voluntarily offering himself 'upon the tree,' Christ ratified the New Covenant by fulfilling in himself—as the divine son—the curses that were deserved by those who were called to divine sonship as the seed of Abraham. The Aqedah not only secured but signified the divine oath and its attendant curse. In other words, the Adeqah served as a ritual preenactment of the curse entailed by God's covenant oath to bless the nations through Abraham's seed (Gen 22:16-18). This covenant oath meant that God himself assumed ultimate responsibility to bless the nations, even if that required that he bear the immense burden of the curse for their sin." Hahn, *Kinship by Covenant*, 256.

would be "a priest forever after the order of the Melchizedek." And the Messiah's eternal priesthood is effective with God's oath (Ps 110:4).[21] Verse 21, "but this one was made a priest with an oath by the one who said to him: 'The Lord has sworn and will not change his mind, You are a priest forever,'" is a redemptive historical interpretation of Psalm 110:4 in light of Jesus Christ's crucifixion and death as the eternal high priest. In this regard, the New Covenant is the culmination of the covenant of royal grant accompanied with God's oath, which visibly took place with the sacrificial death of Jesus Christ on the cross.

Jesus' Resurrection and the Reward of the Covenant of Royal Grant

Jesus' death on the cross was the defining moment in redemptive history. Judas Iscariot hanged himself after he sold Jesus to be crucified. The other disciples ran away out of fear before Jesus faced the crucifixion. Yet Jesus anticipated and prophesied his crucifixion and resurrection throughout his public ministry.[22]

One day, Jesus went to Jerusalem to observe the feast of the Jewish Passover. He cleared the temple courts when he found people exchanging money and others selling cattle, sheep, and doves. The Jews challenged Jesus when they witnessed him clearing the temple, questioning his authority. In response, Jesus showed indirectly that he anticipated his death and resurrection, speaking about his body figuratively as the temple:

---

21. Interpreting Psalm 110:4, Calvin notes that "the priesthood of Christ" is ratified "by the oath of God." In light of that, it makes perfect sense that "our salvation" absolutely depends upon Christ, the mediator of the New Covenant: "Admitting, then, that God had sworn that the Messiah would be the prince and governor of his people, according as Melchizedek was, this would have been nothing else than an unbecoming profanation of his name. When, however, it is quite apparent that something unusual and peculiar was denoted in this place, we may therefore conclude that the priesthood of Christ is invested with great importance, seeing that it is ratified by the oath of God. And, in fact, it is the very turning point upon which our salvation depends; because, but for our reliance on Christ our Mediator, we would be all debarred from entering into God's presence. In prayer, too, nothing is more needful for us than sure confidence in God, and therefore he not only invites us to come to him, but also by an oath hath appointed an advocate for the purpose of obtaining acceptance for us in his sight." Calvin, *Commentary on the Book of Psalms*, 110:4.

22. Jesus' cross and resurrection are the twin climactic moments of his redemptive works in his earthly life. Without them, there is neither the forgiveness of sins nor hope of an everlasting life in the Kingdom of God. Nevertheless, Bultmann as an existential liberal New Testament scholar argues that Jesus' resurrection is not "a historical event" but a mythical event. In doing so, he mythologizes Jesus' cross and resurrection in light of historical critical and existential understandings, thus stripping off the historical foundation of the good news of the gospel: "But what about the resurrection of Christ? Is it not an utterly mythical event? In any case, it is not a historical event that is to be understood in its significance. Can talking about Christ's resurrection be anything other than an expression of the significance of the cross? Does it say anything else than that Jesus' death on the cross is not to be seen as a human death but rather as God's liberating judgment of the world, the judgment that as such robs death of its power? Is it not precisely this truth that is expressed by the statement that the crucified one is not dead but risen?" Bultmann, *New Testament & Mythology*, 36.

> 19 Jesus answered them, "Destroy this temple, and in three days I will raise it up." 20 The Jews then said, "It has taken forty-six years to build this temple, and will you raise it up in three days?" 21 But he was speaking about the temple of his body. 22 When therefore he was raised from the dead, his disciples remembered that he had said this, and they believed the Scripture and the word that Jesus had spoken. (John 2:19–22)

Neither the Jews nor Jesus' disciples understood that Jesus anticipated his death and resurrection when he said, "Destroy this temple, and three days I will raise it up" at that moment.[23]

When Jesus visited the district of Caesarea Philippi, Jesus asked about the people's conception of the identity of the Son of Man. Peter made his famous confession about Jesus when the disciples were asked by Jesus, "Who do you say that I am?" Peter answered, "You are the Christ, the Son of the living God." Peter's confession was a turning point of Jesus' public ministry, because from that time Jesus began to predict his death and resurrection in the presence of his disciples:

> 13 Now when Jesus came into the district of Caesarea Philippi, he asked his disciples, "Who do people say that the Son of Man is?" 14 And they said, "Some say John the Baptist, others say Elijah, and others Jeremiah or one of the prophets." 15 He said to them, "But who do you say that I am?" 16 Simon Peter replied, "You are the Christ, the Son of the living God." 17 And Jesus answered him, "Blessed are you, Simon Bar-Jonah! For flesh and blood has not revealed this to you, but my Father who is in heaven. 18 And I tell you, you are Peter, and on this rock I will build my church, and the gates of hell shall not prevail against it. 19 I will give you the keys of the kingdom of heaven, and whatever you bind on earth shall be bound in heaven, and whatever you loose on earth shall be loosed in heaven." 20 Then he strictly charged the disciples to tell no one that he was the Christ. (Matt 16:13–20)

Peter's famous confession about the Son of Man in the district of Caesarea Philippi marked the end of Jesus' ministry in the area of Galilee. After this, he headed south towards Jerusalem, anticipating his death and resurrection. Jesus predicted his death and resurrection in Jerusalem to his disciples as he prepared for a final journey to Jerusalem with his disciples:

> 21 *From that time Jesus began to show his disciples that he must go to Jerusalem and suffer many things from the elders and chief priests and scribes, and be killed, and on the third day be raised.* ['Ἀπὸ τότε ἤρξατο ὁ Ἰησοῦς δεικνύειν τοῖς μαθηταῖς αὐτοῦ ὅτι δεῖ αὐτὸν εἰς Ἱεροσόλυμα ἀπελθεῖν καὶ πολλὰ παθεῖν ἀπὸ τῶν πρεσβυτέρων καὶ ἀρχιερέων καὶ γραμματέων καὶ ἀποκτανθῆ

---

23. Jesus' interpretation of the temple is a good example of how he interpreted the Old Testament in light of redemptive history, which will be fulfilled in him, the mediator of the New Covenant. In that sense, we may call Jesus a redemptive historical theologian.

ναι καὶ τῇ τρίτῃ ἡμέρᾳ ἐγερθῆναι.] 22 And Peter took him aside and began to rebuke him, saying, "Far be it from you, Lord! This shall never happen to you." 23 But he turned and said to Peter, "Get behind me, Satan! You are a hindrance to me. For you are not setting your mind on the things of God, but on the things of man." (Matt 16:21–23)

It is very important to note that Matthew's testimony about Jesus' death and resurrection here uses passive verbs (i.e., Jesus must "be killed" and "be raised"). It signifies that Jesus' resurrection was God's grant to his Son, who obeyed unto his death to accomplish his redemptive work through his life and earthly ministry.

Jesus again predicted his death and resurrection to his disciples as they gathered in Galilee. In doing so, Jesus used a future passive tense about his resurrection:

22 As they were gathering in Galilee, Jesus said to them, "The Son of Man is about to be delivered into the hands of men, 23 *and they will kill him, and he will be raised on the third day." And they were greatly distressed* [καὶ ἀποκτενοῦσιν αὐτόν, καὶ τῇ τρίτῃ ἡμέρᾳ ἐγερθήσεται. καὶ ἐλυπήθησαν σφόδρα. (Matt 17:22–23)

Here, Jesus' prediction about his resurrection, "he will be raised on the third day" (τῇ τρίτῃ ἡμέρᾳ ἐγερθήσεται), reveals that his resurrection will be God's grant as he prepares a triumphal entry into Jerusalem. On the way to Jerusalem, Jesus predicted his suffering, death, and resurrection in Jerusalem to his disciples:

17 And as Jesus was going up to Jerusalem, he took the twelve disciples aside, and on the way he said to them, 18 "See, we are going up to Jerusalem. And the Son of Man will be delivered over to the chief priests and scribes, and they will condemn him to death 19 and deliver him over to the Gentiles to be mocked and flogged and crucified, and he will be raised on the third day." (Matt 20:17–19)

The Gospel writers commonly testify about the bodily resurrection of Jesus Christ. When we pay close attention to the story of Jesus' bodily resurrection three days after his crucifixion and death, we realize that Jesus' resurrection was God the Father's grant to his Son, who was obedient unto his death, fighting against Satan and his kingdom:

1 Now after the Sabbath, toward the dawn of the first day of the week, Mary Magdalene and the other Mary went to see the tomb. 2 And behold, there was a great earthquake, for an angel of the Lord descended from heaven and came and rolled back the stone and sat on it. 3 His appearance was like lightning, and his clothing white as snow. 4 And for fear of him the guards trembled and became like dead men. 5 But the angel said to the women, "Do not be afraid, for I know that you seek Jesus who was crucified. 6 *He is not here, for he has risen, as he said. Come, see the place where he lay. 7 Then go quickly and tell his*

disciples that he has risen from the dead, and behold, he is going before you to Galilee; there you will see him. See, I have told you." [6 οὐκ ἔστιν ὧδε, ἠγέρθη γὰρ καθὼς εἶπεν· δεῦτε ἴδετε τὸν τόπον ὅπου ἔκειτο. 7 καὶ ταχὺ πορευθεῖσαι εἴπατε τοῖς μαθηταῖς αὐτοῦ ὅτι ἠγέρθη ἀπὸ τῶν νεκρῶν, καὶ ἰδοὺ προάγει ὑμᾶς εἰς τὴν Γαλιλαίαν, ἐκεῖ αὐτὸν ὄψεσθε· ἰδοὺ εἶπον ὑμῖν.] 8 So they departed quickly from the tomb with fear and great joy, and ran to tell his disciples. 9 And behold, Jesus met them and said, "Greetings!" And they came up and took hold of his feet and worshiped him. 10 Then Jesus said to them, "Do not be afraid; go and tell my brothers to go to Galilee, and there they will see me." (Matt 28:1–10; cf. Mark 16:1–8; Luke 24:1–12; John 20:1–10)

The announcement of an angel of the Lord to the women signifies a very important truth about Jesus' bodily resurrection. Verse 6a, "He is not here, for *he has risen,*" should be translated as "He is not here, for *he was raised,*" because the verb (ἠγέρθη) is an aorist passive third person singular, which carries the significant meaning that God the Father raised the Son from the grave after three days, as it was anticipated and prophesied. Furthermore, verse 7a, "Then go quickly and tell his disciples that *he has risen from the dead,*" should be also translated as "Then go quickly and tell his disciples that *he was raised from the dead,*" because "he was raised from the dead" (ἠγέρθη ἀπὸ τῶν νεκρῶν) carries the meaning of the divine intention that Jesus' resurrection was God the Father's grant to his Son.

So the stories of the life of Jesus Christ in the four Gospels culminate in the glorious bodily resurrection of Jesus Christ. In fact, the glorious, visible, and bodily resurrection of Jesus Christ is his official coronation ceremony as the King and Lord of the eschatological Kingdom of God, which is granted by God the Father.[24]

Although Jesus directly predicted his death and resurrection three times before his triumphal entry into Jerusalem, his disciples did not understand that Jesus' resurrection was indeed God's grant to his faithful Servant-Son, who obeyed unto his death

---

24. Jesus' bodily resurrection is a visible proclamation and demonstration of Jesus Christ's victory over Satan. The significance of Jesus' bodily resurrection is that it is "proof of Jesus' messiahship, the coronation of the Servant of the Lord to be Christ and Lord, the Prince of Life and Judge," as Bavinck insightfully suggests: "For Scripture, then, everything depends on the *physical* resurrection of Christ. The *that* is integral to the *how*: if Christ did not arise physically, then death, then sin, then he who had the power of death has not been defeated. In that case, actually, not Christ but Satan came out the victor. According to Scripture, therefore, the significance of the physical resurrection of Christ is inexhaustibly rich. Briefly summarized, that resurrection is (1) proof of Jesus' messiahship, the coronation of the Servant of the Lord to be Christ and Lord, the Prince of life and Judge (Acts 2:36; 3:13–15; 5:31; 10:42; etc.); (2) a seal of his eternal divine sonship (Acts 13:33; Rom. 1:3); (3) a divine endorsement of his mediatorial work, a declaration of the power and value of his death, the 'Amen!' of the Father upon the 'It is finished!' of the Son (Acts 2:23–24; 4:11; 5:31; Rom. 6:4, 10; etc); (4) the inauguration of the exaltation he accomplished by his forgiveness and justification (Acts 5:31; Rom. 4:25); (6) the fountain of numerous spiritual blessings: the gift of the Spirit (Acts 2:33). Repentance (Acts 5:31), spiritual eternal life (Rom. 6:4f.), salvation in its totality (Acts 4:12); (7) the principle and pledge of our blessed and glorious resurrection (Acts 4:2; Rom. 8:11; 1 Cor. 6:14; etc.); (8) the foundation of apostolic Christianity (1 Cor. 15:12ff.)." Bavinck, *Reformed Dogmatics*, 3:442.

The New Covenant and the Kingdom of God

as the mediator of the New Covenant. However, after they witnessed Jesus' death, resurrection, ascension, and the Pentecost event, they fully realized that Jesus' resurrection was indeed God's grant to Jesus.

The Pentecost event was the coming of the Holy Spirit through the ministry of the *exalted* Jesus Christ (Acts 2:1–13). Being filled with the promised Holy Spirit, Peter, standing with the eleven apostles, began to preach the good news of the gospel to the Jews (Acts 2:1–41). He proclaimed that Jesus' suffering, death, and resurrection were the result of God's redemptive plan which was "the definitive plan and foreknowledge of God." Yet he proclaimed human responsibility for Jesus' crucifixion, for the Jews crucified and killed Jesus by the hands of pagan men, the officials and soldiers of the Roman Empire. Nevertheless, *God raised up* Jesus from the tomb, as the patriarch David had prophesied about the resurrection of Messiah in Psalm 16:8–11:

> 22 "Men of Israel, hear these words: Jesus of Nazareth, a man attested to you by God with mighty works and wonders and signs that God did through him in your midst, as you yourselves know-23 this Jesus, delivered up according to the definite plan and foreknowledge of God, you crucified and killed by the hands of lawless men. 24 *God raised him up, loosing the pangs of death, because it was not possible for him to be held by it* [ὃν ὁ θεὸς ἀνέστησεν λύσας τὰς ὠδῖνας τοῦ θανάτου, καθότι οὐκ ἦν δυνατὸν κρατεῖσθαι αὐτὸν ὑπ' αὐτοῦ.]. 25 For David says concerning him, "' I saw the Lord always before me, for he is at my right hand that I may not be shaken; 26 therefore my heart was glad, and my tongue rejoiced; my flesh also will dwell in hope. 27 For you will not abandon my soul to Hades, or let your Holy One see corruption. 28 You have made known to me the paths of life; you will make me full of gladness with your presence.' 29 "Brothers, I may say to you with confidence about the patriarch David that he both died and was buried, and his tomb is with us to this day. 30 Being therefore a prophet, and knowing that God had sworn with an oath to him that he would set one of his descendants on his throne, 31 he foresaw and spoke about the resurrection of the Christ, that he was not abandoned to Hades, nor did his flesh see corruption. 32 *This Jesus God raised up, and of that we all are witnesses*[τοῦτον τὸν Ἰησοῦν ἀνέστησεν ὁ θεός, οὗ πάντες ἡμεῖς ἐσμεν μάρτυρες·]. 33 Being therefore exalted at the right hand of God, and having received from the Father the promise of the Holy Spirit, he has poured out this that you yourselves are seeing and hearing. 34 For David did not ascend into the heavens, but he himself says, "' The Lord said to my Lord, Sit at my right hand, 35 until I make your enemies your footstool.' 36 *Let all the house of Israel therefore know for certain that God has made him both Lord and Christ, this Jesus whom you crucified* [ἀσφαλῶς οὖν γινωσκέτω πᾶς οἶκος Ἰσραὴλ ὅτι καὶ κύριον αὐτὸν καὶ χριστὸν ἐποίησεν ὁ θεός, τοῦτον τὸν Ἰησοῦν ὃν ὑμεῖς ἐσταυρώσατε.]." (Acts 2:22–36)

Here, Peter used the language of grant, saying "God raised up"(ὁ θεὸς ἀνέστησεν) when he proclaimed the glory of Jesus' bodily resurrection in verses 24 and 32. God's grant to his faithful Servant-Son did not end with his resurrection. It extended to enthronement at the right hand of God, receiving and pouring out "from the Father the promise of the Holy Spirit." So the coming of the Holy Spirit at Pentecost was the ministry of the exalted Jesus, because he poured out the Holy Spirit received from the Father. Furthermore, God granted Jesus to be "both Lord and Christ."

After Pentecost, Peter's Pentecostal sermon, his healing of the lame beggar, and Peter's sermon in the temple square provoked the heart of the leaders of Judaism in Jerusalem (Acts 2:13—3:26). Peter and John were arrested by the Saducean leaders who did not believe in bodily resurrection (Acts 4:1–4). Peter and John stood before the Jewish high court, the Sanhedrin, composed of seventy-one members, including the high priest who presided (Acts 4:5–12). Before the Sanhedrin, Peter proclaimed the central message of the good news of the gospel, namely the death and resurrection of Jesus. Peter boldly proclaimed that although the Jews crucified Jesus, "God raised" Jesus from the dead:

> 5 On the next day their rulers and elders and scribes gathered together in Jerusalem, 6 with Annas the high priest and Caiaphas and John and Alexander, and all who were of the high-priestly family. 7 And when they had set them in the midst, they inquired, "By what power or by what name did you do this?" 8 Then Peter, filled with the Holy Spirit, said to them, "Rulers of the people and elders, 9 if we are being examined today concerning a good deed done to a crippled man, by what means this man has been healed, 10 *let it be known to all of you and to all the people of Israel that by the name of Jesus Christ of Nazareth, whom you crucified, whom God raised from the dead-by him this man is standing before you well* [γνωστὸν ἔστω πᾶσιν ὑμῖν καὶ παντὶ τῷ λαῷ Ἰσραὴλ ὅτι ἐν τῷ ὀνόματι Ἰησοῦ Χριστοῦ τοῦ Ναζωραίου ὃν ὑμεῖς ἐσταυρώσατε, ὃν ὁ θεὸς ἤγειρεν ἐκ νεκρῶν, ἐν τούτῳ οὗτος παρέστηκεν ἐνώπιον ὑμῶν ὑγιής]. 11 This Jesus is the stone that was rejected by you, the builders, which has become the cornerstone. 12 And there is salvation in no one else, for there is no other name under heaven given among men by which we must be saved." (Acts 4:5–12)

Peter's language of "God raised"(ὁ θεὸς ἤγειρεν) is a self-conscious announcement that the resurrection of Jesus was God's reward for his Son who obeyed unto his death as the faithful Servant, fighting against the Kingdom of Satan for the ultimate victory and glory of the Kingdom of God.

Paul as the apostle also recognized that Jesus' bodily resurrection was God's reward to his faithful Son's meritorious obedience. For example, Paul stayed at Antioch in Pisidia during his first missionary journey with Barnabas. On the Sabbath day, they went to the synagogue. Paul proclaimed the good news of the gospel, explaining about Abraham to Jesus in the light of redemptive history (Acts 13:13–41). Specifically, Paul argued that the Jews crucified Jesus. But he insisted and emphasized that "God raised"

The New Covenant and the Kingdom of God

Jesus from the dead. Paul's use of the language of "God raised," like Peter's language, is the language of grant:

> 26 "Brothers, sons of the family of Abraham, and those among you who fear God, to us has been sent the message of this salvation. 27 For those who live in Jerusalem and their rulers, because they did not recognize him nor understand the utterances of the prophets, which are read every Sabbath, fulfilled them by condemning him. 28 And though they found in him no guilt worthy of death, they asked Pilate to have him executed. 29 And when they had carried out all that was written of him, they took him down from the tree and laid him in a tomb. 30 *But God raised him from the dead* [ὁ δὲ θεὸς ἤγειρεν αὐτὸν ἐκ νεκρῶν,], 31 and for many days he appeared to those who had come up with him from Galilee to Jerusalem, who are now his witnesses to the people. 32 And we bring you the good news that what God promised to the fathers, 33 this he has fulfilled to us their children by raising Jesus, as also it is written in the second Psalm, 'You are my Son, today I have begotten you.' 34 And as for the fact that he raised him from the dead, no more to return to corruption, he has spoken in this way, 'I will give you the holy and sure blessings of David.' 35 Therefore he says also in another psalm, 'You will not let your Holy One see corruption.' 36 For David, after he had served the purpose of God in his own generation, fell asleep and was laid with his fathers and saw corruption, 37 *but he whom God raised up did not see corruption* [ὃν δὲ ὁ θεὸς ἤγειρεν, οὐκ εἶδεν διαφθοράν.]. 38 Let it be known to you therefore, brothers, that through this man forgiveness of sins is proclaimed to you, and by him everyone who believes is freed from everything 39 from which you could not be freed by the law of Moses. (Acts 13:26–39)

Likewise, Paul uses the language of grant when explaining Jesus' resurrection. The words "God raised"(ὁ θεὸς ἤγειρεν) signifies that God rewarded Jesus, who faithfully obeyed as the Servant, even unto death, shedding his blood of the New Covenant. Interestingly, Paul quotes Psalm 2:7, saying, "You are my Son, today I have begotten you" in verse 33. This indicates that Jesus came to this world as the descendent and heir of David. In fact, Psalm 2 is a royal psalm. Psalm 2:7 is specifically Yahweh's decree of coronation of the king of Israel. Reflecting on Psalm 2:7, Paul portrays Jesus' resurrection as God's reward, crowning him as the King of the Kingdom of God after he fought against the Kingdom of Satan unto his death on the cross.

God granted Jesus "all authority in heaven and on earth" with his resurrection (Matt 28:18). So, Jesus began to rule the eschatological Kingdom of God as "the King of kings and Lord of lords" because God bestowed and granted him the kingship and lordship with his resurrection (1 Tim 6:15–16).

Before the Damascus Road conversion experience, Paul thought that people could earn righteousness and salvation through the works of the law. However, after he received the good news of the gospel through revelation by the exalted Jesus Christ, he realized that God grants salvation and all the redemptive blessings, including the inheritance of the eternal Kingdom of God, in Jesus Christ who had rendered meritorious obedience through his life and death. So, God unites believers with Jesus Christ in his death and resurrection. In doing so, he bestows all the promised spiritual blessings and the gift of salvation to the elect (Rom 6:1–14).[25]

25. Scholars who are overly saturated with the eschatological Kingdom of God as "already and not yet"—that is, already inaugurated, but not yet consummated—as well as with the Pauline soteriological concept of union with Christ, falsely put the doctrine of justification into the category of already and not yet. This is a grave misinterpretation and misrepresentation of the Pauline soteriology. A sinner's justification before a holy and righteous God is only by faith alone and grace alone and in Christ alone. There is no other way. A sinner's justification by faith alone is God's once-for-all declaration in the heavenly court. Nevertheless, growing numbers of scholars interpret and promote the biblical doctrine of justification as a category of already and not yet, which is not only anti-Reformational but also anti-Pauline. For example, Beale falsely interprets the doctrine of justification as already and not yet: "To understand better the believer's inaugurated vindication, we must also look at how it is related to the very end of the age and their own resurrection. The following represents the 'not yet' aspect of justification of the Christian, which remains to be consummated in the future. I will argue in the remainder of this chapter that there are three aspects of future, end-time justification: 1. Public demonstration of justification/ vindication through the final, bodily resurrection; 2. Justification/ vindication of the saints through public announcement before all the world; 3. Public demonstration to the entire cosmos of believers' justification/ vindication through their good works . . . On the one hand, this vindication is once for all and definitive. It is definitive in the sense that saints are declared from God's perspective not guilty because Christ suffered the penalty of their sin. And, just as definitely, they are also declared righteous because Christ achieved representative righteousness for them in his resurrected person and was completely vindicated from injustice (showing that he had been righteous all along), a vindication with which the saints are also identified. Consequently, they are declared to have the same righteousness (by imputation or attribution) that Christ possessed throughout his life and still possesses . . . On the other hand, there is a sense in which this vindication is not completed, especially in that the world does not recognize God's vindication of his people. Just as happened to Jesus, the ungodly world has judged the saints' faith and obedience to God to be in the wrong, which has been expressed through persecution of God's people. As was the case with Christ, so with his followers: their final resurrection will vindicate the truth of their faith and confirm that their obedience was a necessary outgrowth of this faith. That is, although they had been declared righteous in God's sight when they believed, the world continued to declare them guilty. Their physical resurrection will be undeniable proof of their validity of their faith, which had already declared them righteous in their past life." Beale, *A New Testament Biblical Theology*, 497–98.

The worst form of justification by faith in light of the already and not yet has been found in Dr. Seyoon Kim's writing. He argues that the Pauline soteriology, including justification by faith, should be understood in light of the eschatological Kingdom of God being already and not yet. He is sympathetic to the New Perspectives on Paul. In doing so, he applies E. P. Sanders' covenantal nomism to Pauline soteriology. Kim argues that Sanders' covenantal nomism, which interprets the soteriology of the Second Temple Judaism as a formula of getting in by grace and staying by obedience, can be a proper hermeneutical tool to interpret Pauline soteriology, including justification by faith. Moreover, Kim argues that the Pauline doctrine of justification should be seen in light of the harmony between the forensic and relational understanding of justification. So, he suggests a new alternative between the Roman Catholic view of justification and the Protestant Reformation view.

Kim argues that Paul teaches the doctrine of justification in three stages, past, present, and future. Sinners are initially justified by faith with the forgiveness of sins. After the initial justification, justified believers should live a life of obedience. Otherwise, there is a possibility of losing initial justification and salvation. Believers' final justification, based upon good works led by the Holy Spirit, will take place in the final judgment after Jesus Christ's Second Coming. By saying so, Kim heavily criticizes

The New Covenant and the Kingdom of God

Jesus as the second person of the Trinity exists and reigns eternally with the Father and the Holy Spirit. However, the Father visibly demonstrated and declared Jesus Christ as "the Son of God," and crowned him as the King and Lord of the everlasting Kingdom of God by his resurrection. This remarkable truth has been addressed by Paul in the introduction of the epistle to the Romans:

> 1 Paul, a servant of Christ Jesus, called to be an apostle, set apart for the gospel of God, 2 which he promised beforehand through his prophets in the holy Scriptures, 3 concerning his Son, who was descended from David according to the flesh 4 *and was declared to be the Son of God in power according to the Spirit of holiness by his resurrection from the dead, Jesus Christ our Lord* [τοῦ ὁρισθέντος υἱοῦ θεοῦ ἐν δυνάμει κατὰ πνεῦμα ἁγιωσύνης ἐξ ἀναστάσεως νεκρῶν, Ἰησοῦ Χριστοῦ τοῦ κυρίου ἡμῶν,], 5 through whom we have received grace and apostleship to bring about the obedience of faith for the sake of his name among all the nations, 6 including you who are called to belong to Jesus Christ, 7 To all those in Rome who are loved by God and called to be saints: Grace to you and peace from God our Father and the Lord Jesus Christ. (Rom 1:1–7)

It is true that Paul primarily attributes to God the Father the resurrection of Jesus, using the language of grant as "God raised." Nevertheless, he affirms that the resurrection of Jesus was a miraculous work of the triune God. In fact, Paul notes that the resurrection of Jesus was the work of "the Spirit of Christ," as well as "the Spirit of God." In doing so, Paul identifies that the Holy Spirit is not only the Spirit of God but also the Spirit of Christ. Remarkably, Paul affirms that the Spirit of Christ who "raised Jesus from the dead" now dwells in believers:

> 9 You, however, are not in the flesh but in the Spirit, if in fact the Spirit of God dwells in you. Anyone who does not have the Spirit of Christ does not belong to him [ὑμεῖς δὲ οὐκ ἐστὲ ἐν σαρκὶ ἀλλὰ ἐν πνεύματι, εἴπερ πνεῦμα θεοῦ οἰκεῖ ἐν ὑμῖν. εἰ δέ τις πνεῦμα Χριστοῦ οὐκ ἔχει, οὗτος οὐκ ἔστιν αὐτοῦ]. 10 But if Christ is in you, although the body is dead because of sin, the Spirit is life because of righteousness. 11 If the Spirit of him who raised Jesus from

---

the traditional understanding of the order of salvation (the *ordo salutis*) wherein justification and sanctification are distinguished, recognizing the logical priority of justification over sanctification.

Kim's three-stage interpretation of the Pauline doctrine of justification is a grave misinterpretation and misrepresentation of Pauline soteriology as a whole. Kim's major problem is that he reads Pauline soteriology in light of the historical critical understanding of the Bible. Moreover, he denies the Pauline antithesis between law and gospel in his interpretation of justification by faith, which is foundational for a proper understanding of the Pauline doctrine of justification by faith alone. Kim's other failure is that he does not recognize the meritorious obedience of Jesus Christ in his life and sacrificial death. So, for Kim, there is no room for the imputation of righteousness of Jesus Christ in God's forensic once-for-all declaration of sinners' justification in the heavenly court.

Unfortunately, Kim's three-stage understanding of justification, against his own intention, opens the floodgate to Roman Catholicism, the New Perspectives on Paul, Arminianism, liberalism, among others. Cf. Kim, *Justification and Sanctification*.

the dead dwells in you, he who raised Christ Jesus from the dead will also give life to your mortal bodies through his Spirit who dwells in you. (Rom 8:9–11)

Jesus earned his resurrection from God through his meritorious obedience in his life and death. His resurrection was the visible affirmation of God that he is the Son of God. So, through the resurrection, Jesus officially and visibly inaugurated his kingship and lordship as "the King of kings and the Lord of the lords," reigning over both visible and invisible kingdoms. In that sense, we can identify Jesus' resurrection as a coronation ceremony, occurring after his meritorious obedience in his life and death for the eschatological Kingdom of God. Believers have the privilege to be "sons of God" by the works of "the Spirit of God." Moreover, receiving "the Spirit of adoption," believers can cry "Abba! Father!" as Jesus cried out in his prayer to the Father in Gethsemane before his crucifixion (Mark 14:36). So, believers are also "children of God." And as children of God, believers receive the special blessings of being "heirs of God and fellow heirs with Christ." Paul lays out all the redemptive blessings for believers who are *in Christ*:

> 12 So then, brothers, we are debtors, not to the flesh, to live according to the flesh. 13 For if you live according to the flesh you will die, but if by the Spirit you put to death the deeds of the body, you will live. 14 For all who are led by the Spirit of God are sons of God. 15 For you did not receive the spirit of slavery to fall back into fear, but you have received the Spirit of adoption as sons, by whom we cry, "Abba! Father!" 16 The Spirit himself bears witness with our spirit that we are children of God, 17 and if children, then heirs-heirs of God and fellow heirs with Christ, provided we suffer with him in order that we may also be glorified with him. (Rom 8:12–17)

As a result, Paul boldly proclaims that salvation is "the gift of God" because all the redemptive blessings, given to believers are God's grant for believers who are in Jesus Christ (Eph 2:4–10).

The Signs of the New Covenant

Under the Old Covenant, circumcision and the Passover meal were two sacraments instituted by God. Under the New Covenant, Jesus instituted baptism and the Lord's Supper as two sacraments as the mediator of the New Covenant, replacing the previous two sacraments.

The covenant community of Israel crossed the Red Sea when they came out from the bondage of Egypt (Ex 14:1–31). In the midst of the deep water of the Red Sea, they were baptized by Yahweh. The baptism of the people of Israel in the Red Sea was the sign and symbol of liberation from Egyptian slavery and bondage by Yahweh. Before the imminent coming of the Messiah, God sent John the Baptist to proclaim repentance and the coming of the Kingdom of Heaven:

The New Covenant and the Kingdom of God

1 In those days John the Baptist came preaching in the wilderness of Judea, 2 "Repent, for the kingdom of heaven is at hand" [[καὶ] λέγων· μετανοεῖτε· ἤγγικεν γὰρ ἡ βασιλεία τῶν οὐρανῶν.] 3 For this is he who was spoken of by the prophet Isaiah when he said, "The voice of one crying in the wilderness: Prepare the way of the Lord; make his paths straight." 4 Now John wore a garment of camel's hair and a leather belt around his waist, and his food was locusts and wild honey. 5 Then Jerusalem and all Judea and all the region about the Jordan were going out to him, 6 and they were baptized by him in the river Jordan, confessing their sins. 7 But when he saw many of the Pharisees and Sadducees coming for baptism, he said to them, "You brood of vipers! Who warned you to flee from the wrath to come? 8 Bear fruit in keeping with repentance. 9 And do not presume to say to yourselves, 'We have Abraham as our father,' for I tell you, God is able from these stones to raise up children for Abraham. 10 Even now the axe is laid to the root of the trees. Every tree therefore that does not bear good fruit is cut down and thrown into the fire. 11 *"I baptize you with water for repentance, but he who is coming after me is mightier than I, whose sandals I am not worthy to carry. He will baptize you with the Holy Spirit and with fire* ['Εγὼ μὲν ὑμᾶς βαπτίζω ἐν ὕδατι εἰς μετάνοιαν, ὁ δὲ ὀπίσω μου ἐρχόμενος ἰσχυρότερός μού ἐστιν, οὗ οὐκ εἰμὶ ἱκανὸς τὰ ὑποδήματα βαστάσαι· αὐτὸς ὑμᾶς βαπτίσει ἐν πνεύματι ἁγίῳ καὶ πυρί]. 12 His winnowing fork is in his hand, and he will clear his threshing floor and gather his wheat into the barn, but the chaff he will burn with unquenchable fire." (Matt 3:1–12)[26]

John the Baptist as the messenger, preparing the way before the Messiah, was prophesied long ago in Isaiah 40:3 and Malachi 3:1. His prophetic proclamation, "He will baptize you with the Holy Spirit and with fire" (αὐτὸς ὑμᾶς βαπτίσει ἐν πνεύματι ἁγίῳ καὶ πυρι), was wonderfully fulfilled at the Pentecost event. The Pentecost event was not only the visible and audible coming of the Holy Spirit after Jesus' ascension; it also was the baptism "with the Holy Spirit and Fire" (ἐν πνεύματι ἁγίῳ καὶ πυρι) for the people who were in the Upper Room (Acts 2:1–13). It signified the beginning of the spread of the good news of the gospel of Jesus Christ to all nations, tribes, peoples, and languages. Luke testifies to the coming of the Holy Spirit in the upper room in Jerusalem at the Pentecost event:

---

26. "Locusts and wild honey" were a good source of food for the people who were living in the desert of the Promised Land in the first century A.D.: "10 And he should not sell them anything from his granary or his press, at any price. And his servant and his maidservant: he should not sell them, 11 for they entered the covenant of Abraham with him. *Blank* No-one should defile his soul 12 with any living being or one which creeps, by eating them, from the larvae of bees to every living 13 being which creeps in water. And fish: they should not eat them unless they have been opened up 14 alive, and the[ir blood poured] away. And all the locusts, according to their kind, shall be put into fire or into water 15 while they are still alive, as this is the regulation for their species . . . " Martinez, ed., "Damascus Document," XII.14–15, 43.

> 1 When the day of Pentecost arrived, they were all together in one place. 2 And suddenly there came from heaven a sound like a mighty rushing wind, and it filled the entire house where they were sitting. 3 And divided tongues as of fire appeared to them and rested on each one of them. 4 *And they were all filled with the Holy Spirit and began to speak in other tongues as the Spirit gave them utterance* [καὶ ἐπλήσθησαν πάντες πνεύματος ἁγίου καὶ ἤρξαντο λαλεῖν ἑτέραις γλώσσαις καθὼς τὸ πνεῦμα ἐδίδου ἀποφθέγγεσθαι αὐτοῖς.]. (Acts 2:1–4)

In particular, verses 3 and 4 signify that the people at Pentecost experienced the baptism of "the Holy Spirit with fire." In many ways, Pentecost was a turning point in redemptive history, especially in that the good news of the gospel began to spread from Jerusalem to all nations, tribes, peoples, and languages. When they were filled with the Holy Spirit, they began to speak in "other tongues (ἑτέραις γλώσσαις)," which were *foreign languages* that they had never learned before. Jewish pilgrims and other foreigners who had come to participate in the annual harvest feast of Pentecost were surprised and amazed when they heard people speaking in "other tongues," which were in fact their own native languages (Acts 2:5–13).[27]

The apostle Peter, as an eyewitness of Jesus' death, resurrection and ascension, experienced the Pentecost event and was baptized "by the Holy Spirit with fire." Thereby, he was able to interpret baptism in light of redemptive history. As Peter explains in

---

27. At Pentecost, "other tongues" (ἑτέραις γλώσσαις) were foreign languages. However, "tongues" (γλώσσαις) afterwards in Acts 10:46 and 19:6, and in 1 Corinthians 14 were not foreign languages. This suggests that the Pentecost event was unique event which cannot be repeated because it was a redemptive historical event which marked the beginning of the spreading of the good news of the gospel from Jerusalem unto the end of the world: "In the early period this outpouring of the Holy Spirit was accompanied in the life of Christ's disciples by a range of extraordinary forces and workings. The moment they were filled with the Holy Spirit on the day of Pentecost, they began to speak in other languages as the Spirit enabled them (Acts 2:4). According to Luke's description, we are dealing here not with a miracle of hearing but with a miracle of speaking or language. Luke was a coworker of Paul and entirely familiar with the phenomenon of glossolalia as this occurred, for example, in the church of Corinth. He himself also speaks of it in Acts 10:46–47 and 19:6. Undoubtedly, the phenomenon that occurred on the day of Pentecost was related to glossolalia, for otherwise Peter could not have said that Cornelius and his household had received the Holy Spirit 'just as we have' (Acts 10:47; cf. 11:17; 15:8). Yet there was a difference. For in 1 Corinthians 14, as also in Acts 10:46 and 19:6, there is mention of tongues or languages without the adjective 'foreign' . . . but Acts 2:4 expressly speaks of 'other' languages. When the members of the church of Corinth speak in tongues, they are not understood unless someone interprets (1 Cor. 14:2ff.). But at Jerusalem the disciples already spoke in other languages before the crowd came running and heard them, so that a hearing miracle is excluded (Acts 2:4). And when the crowd heard them, they understood what was said, for everyone heard them speak in his or her native language (Acts 2:6, 8). The other languages of which verse 4 speaks are therefore undoubtedly the same as those that in verse 6 are called the native languages of those who heard them (cf. also v. 8). Accordingly, they were not unintelligible sounds that the disciples uttered, but other languages, 'new' languages, as they are called in Mark 16:17, languages that unlearned Galileans were not expected to speak (Acts 2:7). And in those languages they proclaimed God's mighty works, especially those that he had done in the last days in the resurrection and ascension of Christ (Acts 2:4, 14ff.)." Bavinck, *Reformed Dogmatics*, 3:501–2.

his first letter, Noah's eight family members, as a covenant community in the original world, were saved at the time of the universal Flood judgment in the midst of Yahweh's redemptive judgment (Gen 6:8—8:19). Water was the means of death for the non-covenant community who were outside of the Ark, which was the symbol of the heavenly Kingdom of God. Meanwhile, water was the symbol of life for the covenant community who entered into the Ark by God's grace. So, in the light of redemptive history, the water baptism of the Noahic covenant community in the Flood judgment is the historical origin of water baptism. Peter uses this redemptive historical background to connect baptism with the salvation of the Noahic covenant community in the midst of a catastrophic redemptive judgment:

> 18 For Christ also suffered once for sins, the righteous for the unrighteous, that he might bring us to God, being put to death in the flesh but made alive in the spirit, 19 in which he went and proclaimed to the spirits in prison, 20 because they formerly did not obey, when God's patience waited in the days of Noah, while the ark was being prepared, in which a few, that is, eight persons, were brought safely through water. 21 Baptism, which corresponds to this, now saves you, not as a removal of dirt from the body but as an appeal to God for a good conscience, through the resurrection of Jesus Christ, 22 who has gone into heaven and is at the right hand of God, with angels, authorities, and powers having been subjected to him. (1 Pet 3:18–22)

Likewise, Peter connects the Noahic Flood judgment itself with baptism, which is a redemptive historical understanding of baptism. Nevertheless, Noah and his family were inside the Ark while God executed his redemptive judgment against the original sinful world. So the Noahic covenant community did not get wet, although they were baptized by God in the midst of the Flood judgment because they were inside the Ark while there was redemptive judgment outside of the Ark. This suggests that the mode of water baptism should not be restricted to the immersion of the entire body with water.[28]

Paul, one of the great persecutors of the church, had a life-changing conversion experience while he was on the way to Damascus. He encountered the crucified and risen Jesus Christ through revelation, and received the good news of the gospel directly from the risen Jesus Christ. "A light from heaven flashed around him," and it was so powerful that he fell to the ground. In light of spiritual baptism, this signifies that Paul

---

28. Baptists insist that the immersion of the entire body with water and coming back up is the only legitimate mode of water baptism under the New Covenant. They argue that the sprinkling and pouring of water on the body is not an acceptable mode of water baptism. This line of thought by Baptists results from their lack of understanding of the mode of water baptism from the perspective of redemptive history. For example, Wayne Grudem, taking a Baptist position, argues that immersing under water and coming back up is the only legitimate mode of water baptism in the New Testament: "The practice of baptism in the New Testament was carried out in one way: the person being baptized was *immersed* or put completely under the water and then brought back up again. Baptism *by immersion* is therefore the 'mode' of baptism or the way in which baptism was carried out in the New Testament." Grudem, *Systematic Theology*, 967.

was baptized "by the Holy Spirit and fire." So Paul was blinded for three days because the "light from heaven" was so powerful. Afterwards, his vision was recovered when Ananias layed hands on him. And Paul was filled with the Holy Spirit (Acts 9:1–19).

After Paul experienced baptism "by the Holy Spirit with fire" during his conversion experience, he became not only an apostle, appointed by the risen Jesus Christ, but also a redemptive historical theologian. Afterwards, he relates the Red Sea crossing of the people of Israel to water baptism:

> 1 I want you to know, brothers, that our fathers were all under the cloud, and all passed through the sea, 2 *and all were baptized into Moses in the cloud and in the sea* [καὶ πάντες εἰς τὸν Μωϋσῆν ἐβαπτίσθησαν ἐν τῇ νεφέλῃ καὶ ἐν τῇ θαλάσσῃ], 3 and all ate the same spiritual food, 4 and all drank the same spiritual drink. For they drank from the spiritual Rock that followed them, and the Rock was Christ. 5 Nevertheless, with most of them God was not pleased, for they were overthrown in the wilderness. (1 Cor 10:1–5)

It is noteworthy to see Paul's redemptive historical reading of water baptism, connecting the Red Sea crossing of Israel with baptism. In particular, we need to pay attention to verse 2 of "and all were baptized into Moses in the cloud and in the sea."[29] In fact, Yahweh orchestrated the Red Sea to be the grand theatre of redemptive judgment, separating the covenant community and non-covenant community. He made a visible distinction between the people of Israel and the Egyptian idol worshippers who pursued the people of Israel for slaughter. Yahweh used the Red Sea as a redemptive theatre to have a holy war between the Kingdom of God and the Kingdom of Satan. The people of Israel represented the Kingdom of God, while the Egyptian soldiers represented the Kingdom of Satan. In this redemptive theatre of holy war between the Kingdom of God and the Kingdom of Satan, Moses not only conducted holy war but also redemptive judgment through baptism. So, Moses with his staff, as the mediator between Yahweh and the people of Israel, conducted baptism while they were crossing the Red Sea. In that sense, Moses became not only the agent of baptism but also the agent of execution of redemptive judgment. Thereby, all the Egyptian forces pursuing the people of Israel faced the judgment of death in the Red Sea by Yahweh's holy war:

> 21 Then Moses stretched out his hand over the sea, and the LORD drove the sea back by a strong east wind all night and made the sea dry land, and the waters were divided. 22 *And the people of Israel went into the midst of the sea on dry ground, the waters being a wall to them on their right hand and on their left.* 23 The Egyptians pursued and went in after them into the midst of the sea, all Pharaoh's horses, his chariots, and his horsemen. 24 And in the morning watch the LORD in the pillar of fire and of cloud looked down on the Egyptian forces and threw the Egyptian forces into a panic, 25 clogging their chariot

---

29. I translate "εἰς τὸν Μωϋσῆν" as "by Moses." This translation effectively carries the meaning that the human conductor of baptism in the Red Sea was Moses.

wheels so that they drove heavily. And the Egyptians said, "Let us flee from before Israel, for the LORD fights for them against the Egyptians." 26 Then the LORD said to Moses, "Stretch out your hand over the sea, that the water may come back upon the Egyptians, upon their chariots, and upon their horsemen." 27 So Moses stretched out his hand over the sea, and the sea returned to its normal course when the morning appeared. And as the Egyptians fled into it, the LORD threw the Egyptians into the midst of the sea. 28 The waters returned and covered the chariots and the horsemen; of all the host of Pharaoh that had followed them into the sea, not one of them remained. 29 *But the people of Israel walked on dry ground through the sea, the waters being a wall to them on their right hand and on their left.* 30 Thus the LORD saved Israel that day from the hand of the Egyptians, and Israel saw the Egyptians dead on the seashore. 31 Israel saw the great power that the LORD used against the Egyptians, so the people feared the LORD, and they believed in the LORD and in his servant Moses. (Ex 14:21–31)[30]

Verse 29, "But the people of Israel walked on dry ground through the sea, the waters being a wall to them on their right hand and on their left" is significant because it testifies that the people of Israel crossed the Red Sea and walked "on dry ground through the sea." This signifies that the people of Israel did not get wet while they were baptized in the Red Sea. The historical episode of Israel's baptism in the Red Sea suggests that the mode of baptism may be diverse including sprinkling, pouring,

---

30. Jonathan Edwards interprets Israel's crossing the Red Sea from the perspective of a Christocentric and eschatological interpretation: "The people of Israel went out with a high hand, and Christ went before them in a pillar of cloud and fire. There was a glorious triumph over earth and hell in that deliverance. And when Pharaoh and his hosts, and Satan by them, pursued the people, Christ overthrew them in the Red Sea; the Lord triumphed gloriously; the horse and his rider he cast into the sea, and there they slept their last sleep, and never followed the children of Israel anymore; as all Christ's enemies are overthrown in his blood, which by its abundant sufficiency, and the greatness of the sufferings with which it was shed, may well be represented by a sea. The Red Sea did represent Christ's blood, as is evident, because the apostle compares the children of Israel's passage through the Red Sea to baptism, 1 Cor. x. 1, 2. But we all know that the water of baptism represents Christ's blood.

"Thus Christ, the angel of God's presence, in his love and his pity, redeemed his people, and carried them in the days of old as on eagles' wings, so that none of their proud and spiteful enemies, neither Egyptians nor devils, could touch them." Edwards, *A History of Work of Redemption*, 70.

However, von Rad interprets Israel's crossing of the Red Sea from the historical-critical perspective, and denies the historicity of that event, identifying it as "Israel's confession of faith": "To start with, they may have gone there while seeking change of pasture-ground, but afterwards, as a less-privileged section of the population, they were conscripted by the Egyptians for forced labour on large-scale building operations. They sought to escape from this—perhaps they simply fled (Ex. XIV. 5). They were pursued, but the chariot division which followed them was drowned while crossing a 'sea.' In this event, quite insignificant by the standards of secular history, those who were delivered experienced something which in its significance far transcended the personal fate of those who at the time shared in it. The deliverance from Egypt and the rescue at the Red Sea found their way into Israel's confession of faith—indeed, they actually became Israel's earliest confession, around which the whole Hexateuchal history was in the end ranged." Von Rad, *Old Testament Theology*, 1:12–13.

and immersion.[31] Moreover, "the people of Israel" who were baptized in the Red Sea included infants. So it is proper to conclude that the baptism of infants in the Red Sea is the origin of infant baptism, when we look at baptism from a redemptive historical perspective.[32] In that sense, in light of redemptive historical continuity between the Old and New Covenants, infant baptism should be warranted and encouraged.[33]

Jesus Christ as the mediator of the New Covenant instituted the Lord's Supper as one of the two sacraments before his arrest and crucifixion. While Jesus was keeping the Passover feast with his disciples, he ate the Passover meal with his disciples in a large upper room of a house in the city of Jerusalem (Matt 26:17–25; Luke 22:7–16).

---

31. Commenting on 1 Corinthians 10:1–2, Michael Horton rightly notes that "the church's historical acceptance of immersion, sprinkling, and pouring" should be justified "as valid modes of baptism" under the New Covenant: "Immersion does seem more suggestive of being buried and raised with Christ and of being drawn out of God's waters of judgment alive. At the same time, those who 'passed through the sea and . . . were baptized into Moses in the cloud and in the sea' in the exodus from Egypt (1 Co 10:1–2) actually escaped immersion in the waters. In view of the varied examples and precedents for ritual purification, the church's historical acceptance of immersion, sprinking, and pouring as valid modes of baptism seems entirely justified. Partisans on all sides should be aware of rejecting the validity of one's baptism on the basis of the amount of water administered." Horton, *The Christian Faith*, 792–93.

32. Traditionally, Baptists have argued that infant baptism is not biblical because the baptismal pattern in the New Testament demonstrates only believers' baptism. For example, Wayne Grudem insists that the evidence of baptism patterned in the New Testament only warrants believers' baptism: "The pattern revealed at several places in the New Testament is that only those who give a believable profession of faith should be baptized. This view is often called 'believers' baptism,' since it holds that only those who have themselves believed in Christ (or, more precisely, those who have given reasonable evidence of believing in Christ) should be baptized. This is because baptism, which is a *symbol of beginning the Christian life*, should only be given to those who have *in fact* begun the Christian life." Grudem, *Systematic Theology*, 970. However, Grudem's rejection of infant baptism, defining baptism as "a symbol of beginning the Christian life" is due to the lack of a redemptive historical understanding of baptism. The proper understanding of baptism, in the light of baptism in the Noahic Flood judgment and the Red Sea, is as a symbol of covenant community.

33. Interpreting Jeremiah 31:29–34, the prophecy of the New Covenant, Gentry and Wellum argue incorrectly that children should be excluded as members of the covenant community under the New Covenant. Their exclusion of children as members of the covenant community is due to their misinterpretation of how the concept of membership in the covenant community changed between the Old and New Covenants, in the light of redemptive historical continuity: "What verse 34 is saying, however, in contrast to verse 29–30, is that in the old covenant, people became members of the covenant community simply by being born into that community. As they grew up, some became believers in Yahweh and others did not. This resulted in a situation within the covenant community where some *members* could urge other *members* to know the Lord. In the new covenant community, however, one does not become a member by physical birth but rather by the new birth, which requires faith on the part of every person. Thus only believers are members of the new community: all *members are believers*, and *only* believers are members. Therefore in the new covenant community there will no longer be a situation where some members urge other members to know the Lord. There will be no such thing as an unregenerate member of the new covenant community. All are believers, all know the Lord, because all have experienced the forgiveness of sins . . . Jeremiah 31:34 is important since it shows that the Presbyterian understanding is flawed. There are no covenant members who are not believers. This challenge to the Presbyterians must be given in humility since, by and large, they have had a much better grasp of the meaning and role of the covenants than Baptists." Gentry and Wellum, *Kingdom through Covenant*, 512.

Jesus instituted the Lord's Supper as he was eating the Passover meal with his disciples. He used the Passover feast as a historical theater to institute the Lord's Supper:

> 26 Now as they were eating, Jesus took bread, and after blessing it broke it and gave it to the disciples, and said, "Take, eat; this is my body." 27 And he took a cup, and when he had given thanks he gave it to them, saying, "Drink of it, all of you, 28 for this is my blood of the covenant, which is poured out for many for the forgiveness of sins. 29 I tell you I will not drink again of this fruit of the vine until that day when I drink it new with you in my Father's kingdom." (Matt 26:26–29)

As Jesus instituted the Lord's Supper, he prophetically anticipated that he would shed his own blood as the sacrificial blood of the New Covenant. In doing so, God sealed his New Covenant with his elect.

Under the Old Covenant, the covenant community participated in the Passover feast and ate the Lord's Passover meal. They remembered Yahweh's mighty works at his Passover, saving the lives of Israel's firstborn sons and the firstborn of the livestock while he executed the judgment of death against all the firstborn sons and the firstborn of the livestock of the Egyptians. In fact, Yahweh used his Passover event as a historical event, which separated the people of Israel and the people of Egypt right before the Exodus. Yahweh executed his judgment of death against all the firstborn sons of Egypt along with all the firstborn of the livestock, while he passed over the doors of the houses of Israel where the blood of the Passover lambs was marked on the lintel and the doorposts (Ex 12:1–32). After the event of the Exodus, Yahweh formally instituted the Passover for the covenant community of Israel to uphold:

> 43 And the LORD said to Moses and Aaron, "This is the statute of the Passover: no foreigner shall eat of it, 44 but every slave that is bought for money may eat of it after you have circumcised him. 45 No foreigner or hired servant may eat of it. 46 It shall be eaten in one house; you shall not take any of the flesh outside the house, and you shall not break any of its bones. 47 All the congregation of Israel shall keep it. 48 If a stranger shall sojourn with you and would keep the Passover to the LORD, let all his males be circumcised. Then he may come near and keep it; he shall be as a native of the land. But no uncircumcised person shall eat of it. 49 There shall be one law for the native and for the stranger who sojourns among you." 50 All the people of Israel did just as the LORD commanded Moses and Aaron. 51 And on that very day the LORD brought the people of Israel out of the land of Egypt by their hosts. (Ex 12:43–51)

So whenever the people of Israel kept the Passover feast, they slaughtered lambs and ate them together. In doing so, they remembered the miraculous past historical event of the original Passover, when Yahweh passed over the houses of Israel, seeing the blood of lambs in their door posts while he executed redemptive judgment against the houses of Egypt. At the same time, they anticipated the coming of the final

Passover lamb's once-for-all sacrifice as the Redeemer (1 Cor 5:6–8). So the covenant community under the New Covenant has covenantal obligation to proclaim the sacrificial death of Jesus Christ, participating in the Lord's Supper until he comes back again (1 Cor 11:23–26).

Israel's Disobedience and the Fall of Jerusalem

Yahweh confirmed the inauguration of the Davidic Kingdom through the Davidic covenant (2 Sam 7:1–14). Although the establishment of the Davidic Kingdom was God's grant to the people of Israel in the Promised Land, the *continuation* of the Davidic Kingdom was dependent upon the Israelites' obedience to the Mosaic law. As we know, Jesus came as the fulfillment of the Messianic prophecy of the Old Testament, which began in the proclamation of the primitive gospel in Genesis 3:15. However, the majority of Israelites rejected Jesus as the Messiah and the Son of God. The Israelites' rejection and unbelief was the culmination of their disobedience to the Mosaic law, because the heart of the Mosaic law typified and foreshadowed the coming Messiah. This is also the historical background explaining why Jesus Christ pronounced the destruction of the temple in Jerusalem, which was the symbolic place of the presence of God. In the beginning of the Olivet Discourse on the Mount of Olives, Jesus prophesied the destruction of the temple in Jerusalem:

> 1 Jesus left the temple and was going away, when his disciples came to point out to him the buildings of the temple. 2 But he answered them, 'You see all these, do you not? Truly, I say to you, there will not be left here one stone upon another that will not be thrown down.' (Matt 24:1–2; cf. Mark 13:1–2; Luke 21:5–9)

Along with the destruction of the temple in Jerusalem, Jesus prophesied the fall of Jerusalem. The city of Jerusalem was the heart of the Promised Land. Moreover, it was the heart of the Davidic Kingdom, which was the theocratic kingdom, typified in the everlasting Kingdom of God on earth. After Jesus' triumphant entry into Jerusalem, before his crucifixion he prophesied the destruction of the Temple and the fall of Jerusalem:

> 20 "But when you see Jerusalem surrounded by armies, then know that its desolation has come near. 21 Then let those who are in Judea flee to the mountains, and let those who are inside the city depart, and let not those who are out in the country enter it, 22 for these are days of vengeance, to fulfill all that is written. 23 Alas for women who are pregnant and for those who are nursing infants in those days! For there will be great distress upon the earth and wrath against this people. 24 They will fall by the edge of the sword and be led captive among all nations, and Jerusalem will be trampled underfoot by the Gentiles, until the times of the Gentiles are fulfilled. (Luke 21:20–24)

The New Covenant and the Kingdom of God

Jesus' prophecy of the destruction of the temple and the fall of Jerusalem was exactly fulfilled in 70 A.D. God used the Roman Empire to prosecute his covenant lawsuit against the disobedient Israelites who constantly violated the Mosaic covenant of law. At last, the Roman soldiers under the leadership of Titus, son of the emperor Vespasian, attacked and destroyed the city of Jerusalem as well as the temple from 66 to 70 A.D. In that sense, we can say that the fall of Jerusalem and the destruction of the temple were a redemptive historical event, because it was the historical mark of the termination of the Old Covenant order. Furthermore, it was the historical mark of the termination of the theocratic kingdom of Israel in the Promised Land as God's covenant lawsuit against the people of Israel who constantly broke the Old Covenant, inaugurated in Exodus 19—24.[34]

Israel as the theocratic kingdom was terminated in 70 A.D. However, Israel as the Jewish descendents of Abraham, Isaac, and Jacob are still valid until the Second Coming of Jesus Christ.

The majority of ethnic Israel rejected Jesus as the Messiah and the Son of God, ultimately crucifying him. They also rejected the good news of the gospel, persecuting the Apostles and Christians. Nevertheless, the apostle Paul in Romans gave a prophetic message that "all Israel will be saved." Paul's prophetic message provides us with a comprehensive picture of ethnic Israel:

> 25 Lest you be wise in your own conceits, I want you to understand this mystery, brothers: a partial hardening has come upon Israel, until the fullness of the Gentiles has come in. 26 *And in this way all Israel will be saved, as it is written, "The Deliverer will come from Zion, he will banish ungodliness from Jacob"* [καὶ οὕτως πᾶς Ἰσραὴλ σωθήσεται, καθὼς γέγραπται· ἥξει ἐκ Σιὼν ὁ ῥυόμενος, ἀποστρέψει ἀσεβείας ἀπὸ Ἰακώβ]; 27 "and this will be my covenant with them when I take away their sins." 28 As regards the gospel, they are enemies of God for your sake. But as regards election, they are beloved for the sake of their forefathers. 29 For the gifts and the calling of God are irrevocable. 30 Just as you were at one time disobedient to God but now have received mercy because of their disobedience, 31 so they too have now been disobedient in order that by the mercy shown to you they also may now receive mercy. (Rom 11:25–31)

Paul discusses how God is faithful to save ethnic Israel, even as he is faithful to save the elect among the Gentiles in Romans 9:1—11:36. This truth provides the background for Paul to say, "And in this way all Israel will be saved" (καὶ οὕτως πᾶς Ἰσραὴλ

---

34. The nation of Israel was restored in the area of Palestine in 1948. However, that was not the restoration of the theocratic Kingdom of Israel, which typified the everlasting Kingdom of Heaven. The current nation of Israel should be considered as one of many nations under the blessings of God's common grace, such as the United States of America, Bolivia, Brazil, China, Japan, Kenya, Korea, Russia, and etc.

σωθήσεται).³⁵ This suggests that the remnant and the elect among the ethnic Israel will be saved by God's grace in Jesus Christ, even though the theocratic kingdom of Israel was terminated by God's covenant lawsuit against Israel due to their disobedience to the Mosaic law and the rejection of Jesus Christ in 70 A.D.

Herman Bavinck rightly interprets Romans 9—11 in light of redemptive history, suggesting that "a remnant chosen by grace" in Israel has always been saved. Likewise, "all Israel" in 11:26 is not the national conversion of "the people of Israel" at the end of time as chiliasts or *dispensationalists* falsely insist. Rather, "all Israel" is "the elect from Israel" who will be saved throughout time until the Second Coming of Christ:

> "All Israel" (πᾶς Ἰσραὴλ, *pas Israel*) in 11:26 is not, therefore, the people of Israel that at the end of time will be converted en masse. Nor is it the church of the Jews and the Gentiles together. But it is the *pleroma* that in the course of

---

35. Dispensational theologians, in general, interpret "all Israel will be saved" as promising that all the people of the nation of Israel will be saved someday in the future. Representatively, Chafer anticipates and promotes "the national salvation of Israel" when he interprets Romans 11:25-27: "The Scriptures bear testimony to the fact that Israel as a nation is to be saved from her sin and delivered from her enemies by the Messiah when He shall return to the earth. It is true that, in this age, the present offers of divine grace are extended to individual Jews as they are to individual Gentiles (Rom. 10:12), and that, without reference to Jehovah's unchangeable covenants with Israel, which covenants are in abeyance (Matt. 23:38-39; Luke 21:24; Acts 15:15-18; Rom. 11:25-27), the individual Jew is now divinely reckoned to be as much in need of salvation as the individual Gentile (Rom. 3:9). These facts, related as they are to the present age-purpose—the calling out of the Church from both Jews and Gentiles alike (Eph. 3:6)—have no bearing upon the divine purpose for the coming kingdom age when, according to covenant promise, Israel will be saved and dwell safely in her own land (Deut. 30:3-6; Jer. 28:5-6; 33:15-17) . . . The complete regathering of Israel to her own land, which is accomplished at the time of her salvation and in connection with her Messiah's return (Deut. 30:3), is anticipated in prophecy as one of the greatest miracles in the entire history of the earth. In Jeremiah 23:7-8, the regathering of that people is said to surpass, as a divine undertaking, even the crossing of the Red Sea. In like manner, it is stated in Matthew 24:31 that this regathering shall be wrought through the ministration of angels . . . The anticipation of such blessings for Israel is the theme of all the prophets, and such, indeed, is the salvation which awaits that people; but God is righteously free to act in behalf of sinners only on the ground of the fact that the Lamb of God has taken away their sins. A major objective in the death of Christ is, therefore, the national salvation of Israel." Chafer, *Systematic Theology*, 3:105-09.

In a similar manner, Wayne House argues as follows: "However, 'all' in verse 26 means that the entire nation of Israel will come to faith in Jesus at a time in the future. There is no reason to say that 'all' means just a part of the nation, the group of individuals who come to faith in Jesus as Messiah throughout history. Even though Paul did sometimes use 'all' to indicate many or all types rather than every individual (e.g., 1 Tim. 2:4), clearly the majority of Jews throughout history have rejected Jesus, and it makes little sense to say that 'all Israel' means 'all types of Israel.' Thus 'all Israel' of Romans 11:26 can only mean the entire nation of Israel will be saved at some point. As that has not yet happened, this passage must refer to the future, rather than the present." House, "The Future of National Israel," 480.

Robertson provides an alternative view, suggesting that "all Israel" include "the entire body of God's elect from among both Jews and Gentiles" in his interpretation of Romans 11: "It is in this context that 'all Israel' in Romans 11:26 reaches its final definition. According to Paul, 'Hardness has happened to part of Israel until the full number of the Gentiles has come in[to Israel], and in this manner all Israel shall be saved.' The full number that are the product of God's electing grace, coming from both the Jewish and the Gentile communities, will constitute the final Israel of God. 'All Israel,' then consists of the entire body of God's elect from among both Jews and Gentiles." Robertson, *The Israel of God*, 188.

centuries will be brought in from Israel. Israel will continue to exist as a people alongside the Gentiles, predicts Paul. It will not expire or disappear from the earth. It will remain to the end of the ages, produce its *pleroma* for the Kingdom of God as well as the Gentiles, and keep its special task and place for that kingdom. The church of God will be gathered out of all peoples and nations and tongues. Paul does not calculate how large that *pleroma* from Israel will be. It is very possible that in the last days the number of the elect from Israel will be much greater than it was in Paul's time or later in our time. There is not a single reason from denying this. The spread of the gospel among all peoples rather prompts us to expect that both from Israel and from the Gentiles are ever-increasing numbers will be saved. But that is not what Paul intends to say: he does not count, but weighs. A full *pleroma* will come from the Gentile world, as well as from Israel, and that *pleroma* will be all Israel (*pas Israel*). In that *pleroma* all Israel is saved, just as in the church as a whole of humanity is being saved.[36]

When we view the ancient history of Israel in light of redemptive history, God chose Israel as a chosen nation and people under the Old Covenant. Nevertheless, it suggests that not all the people of Israel were saved, but only "a remnant chosen by grace." So, Paul in his statement that "all Israel will be saved" provides a glimpse into Israel. In doing so, he suggests that "a remnant chosen by grace," or all the elect among the Jews, will be saved under the New Covenant until the Second Coming of Christ.

The Conquest of Canaan under the Old Covenant and Global Mission under the New Covenant

Yahweh commanded the covenant community of Israel to fight holy war when they conquered the Promised Land. To accomplish that mission, he ordered total destruction in the process of conquering the Promised Land. On the other hand, Jesus

---

36. Bavinck, *Reformed Dogmatics*, 4:670–71. Again, as Bavinck indicates, dispensationalists interpret "all Israel will be saved" as a national conversion of Israel in the future. Countering the dispensational interpretation, Bavinck correctly argues that it is not a national conversion of Israel but of "a remnant chosen by grace" from among all Jews: "It is also the case that a conversion of Israel other than the one indicated by Paul is hard to conceive. For that matter, just what is a national conversion, and how and when will it take place in the case of Israel? One cannot of course have the least objection—the continued existence of the people of Israel in the light of prophecy rather argues for it—to the fact that from Israel as well a very large number of people are still being brought to faith in Christ. But however large this number may be, it remains a remnant chosen by grace (Rom. 11:5). Certainly not even the most fervent chiliast thinks that at some point in the future all Jews without exception will be converted. And even if he did believe this, thinking that in that way alone Rom. 11:26 would be completely fulfilled, then such an end-time national conversion would still not help the millions of Jews who, throughout the ages and right up until the end, died in unbelief and hardness of heart . . . Always, throughout all the ages, also in the days when Israel as a nation was the people of God, it was never more than a small segment of the people who truly served and feared God. And this is how it is, not only in the case of the Jews but also in the case of the Gentiles. It is always 'a remnant chosen by grace' that, from within Christian nations, obtains salvation in Christ." Ibid., 671.

commanded his disciples to love even their enemies, enduring persecution even unto death. To properly understand this apparent contradictory command, it is necessary to examine the episodes from redemptive historical and eschatological perspectives.

The Old Covenant and The Conquest of Canaan

God promised through the Abrahamic covenant that the theocratic kingdom would be established in the Promised Land. Yahweh made a covenant on Mount Sinai with the promised descendents of Abraham through Moses, the mediator of the covenant (Ex 19—24). Surprisingly, within the historical context of the Mosaic covenant, Yahweh issued a very cruel command to the covenant community of Israel that would cross the Jordan River and enter the land of Canaan. His command was to destroy the seven tribes of Canaan that had lived peacefully in the land ever since their ancestors had permanently settled there. How could God give such a brutal command to the covenant people as the God of love? When Yahweh made the Mosaic covenant with the covenant community of Israel, the conquest of Canaan was surely promised and commanded. Yahweh promised that the enemies of Israel would be blotted out from the land of Canaan little by little, until Israel possessed the Promised Land:

> 20 "Behold, I send an angel before you to guard you on the way and to bring you to the place that I have prepared. 21 Pay careful attention to him and obey his voice; do not rebel against him, for he will not pardon your transgression, for my name is in him. 22 "But if you carefully obey his voice and do all that I say, then I will be an enemy to your enemies and an adversary to your adversaries. 23 "When my angel goes before you and brings you to the Amorites and the Hittites and the Perizzites and the Canaanites, the Hivites and the Jebusites, and I blot them out, 24 you shall not bow down to their gods nor serve them, nor do as they do, but you shall utterly overthrow them and break their pillars in pieces. 25 You shall serve the LORD your God, and he will bless your bread and your water, and I will take sickness away from among you. 26 None shall miscarry or be barren in your land; I will fulfill the number of your days. 27 I will send my terror before you and will throw into confusion all the people against whom you shall come, and I will make all your enemies turn their backs to you. 28 And I will send hornets before you, which shall drive out the Hivites, the Canaanites, and the Hittites from before you. 29 I will not drive them out from before you in one year, lest the land become desolate and the wild beasts multiply against you. 30 Little by little I will drive them out from before you, until you have increased and possess the land. 31 And I will set your border from the Red Sea to the Sea of the Philistines, and from the wilderness to the Euphrates, for I will give the inhabitants of the land into your hand, and you shall drive them out before you. 32 You shall make no covenant with them and their gods. 33 They shall not dwell in your land, lest they make

you sin against me; for if you serve their gods, it will surely be a snare to you." (Ex 23:20–33; cf. 34:10–16)

Yahweh renewed the Mosaic covenant with Israel when they reached the plain of Moab after forty years in the wilderness. In the process of the covenantal renewal, he reminded them again to fight the holy war (*cherem*) when they conquered the Promised Land. It is important to note that the word, 'total destruction' (*cherem*), was used for the first time in the historical context of the Mosaic covenant renewal:

> 1 "When the LORD your God brings you into the land that you are entering to take possession of it, and clears away many nations before you, the Hittites, the Girgashites, the Amorites, the Canaanites, the Perizzites, the Hivites, and the Jebusites, seven nations more numerous and mightier than yourselves, 2 *and when the LORD your God gives them over to you, and you defeat them, then you must devote them to complete destruction. You shall make no covenant with them and show no mercy to them.* 3 You shall not intermarry with them, giving your daughters to their sons or taking their daughters for your sons, 4 for they would turn away your sons from following me, to serve other gods. Then the anger of the LORD would be kindled against you, and he would destroy you quickly. 5 But thus shall you deal with them: you shall break down their altars and dash in pieces their pillars and chop down their Asherim and burn their carved images with fire. 6 "For you are a people holy to the LORD your God. The LORD your God has chosen you to be a people for his treasured possession, out of all the peoples who are on the face of the earth. (Deut 7:1–6; cf. 20:16–18)

We need to *eschatologically* interpret and understand Yahweh's command of total destruction by the covenant community of Israel in the process of the conquest of Canaan.[37] Remarkably, Yahweh demonstrated the vivid picture of the day of final judg-

---

37. The command and practice of total destruction (*cherem*) in the conquest of the Promised Land should be understood in light of eschatology and final judgment. Kline pioneered the eschatological interpretation of the conquest of the Promised Land in many ways as he interprets and demonstrates his insight as follows: "During its Joshuan phase the role of the priests continued to identify the campaign against Canaan as a holy war. The high priest Eleazar was associated with Joshua as the medium of oracular directions from the Lord (Num 27:15–23; Josh 14:1; 19:51). And the priests with the ark of the covenant were positioned in front of the Israelite army at the crossing of the Jordan and again, with the sacred silver trumpets, at the demolition of Jericho. Another indication that the Joshuan campaign did not fall under the category of just war but rather of holy war is the intrusion of the principle of final judgment. Israel's taking the territory of Canaan away from the long-time occupants of the land, overriding the common grace conventions and anticipating the eschatological day of the Lord, is indeed the paramount example of intrusion ethics. Instances of the intrusion principle are also found in various episodes within the program of conquest as a whole. For example, there was Rahab's divinely approved deception of the Jericho authorities to whom she would normally owe her allegiance (Joshua 2). And underlying the case of the Gibeonites' deception (Joshua 9) was the prohibition against the Israelites' making covenants with the occupants of the land—contrary to normal common grace policy attested in the practice of the patriarchs (cf., e.g., Gen 14:13). The Joshuan holy war against Canaan, with its intrusion of the ethics of final judgment, was a prototype of the final battle of Har Magedon on the last great day of the Lord." Kline, *God, Heaven and Har Magedon*, 135–36.

ment through the conquest of Canaan typologically and symbolically. In fact, God will execute his final judgment by the means of total destruction when the Parousia comes. No one can escape the final judgment. Only the elect alone in Jesus Christ will enter the fully realized Kingdom of Heaven and have full access to the new heaven and the new earth. In that sense, the final judgment will be glorious and a victorious one for the elect. However, it will be the day of fiery judgment for the reprobate, who are not in Jesus Christ, because they will be thrown into everlasting hell. The glorified elect with the bodily resurrection will fully realize the everlasting Kingdom of God under the reign of the exalted heavenly king, Jesus Christ.

The New Covenant and Global Mission

Between his resurrection and his ascension to heaven, Jesus Christ gave the Great Commission to his beloved disciples. This was an eschatological commission to the disciples, directing them to go out and spread the good news of the gospel of the Kingdom of God from the Promised Land to all nations, embracing Jews and Gentiles without prejudice:

> 16 Now the eleven disciples went to Galilee, to the mountain to which Jesus had directed them. 17 And when they saw him they worshiped him, but some doubted. 18 And Jesus came and said to them, "All authority in heaven and on earth has been given to me. 19 Go therefore and make disciples of all nations, baptizing them in the name of the Father and of the Son and of the Holy Spirit, 20 teaching them to observe all that I have commanded you. And behold, I am with you always, to the end of the age." (Matt 28:16–20)[38]

Jesus Christ decisively proclaimed the victory of the Kingdom of God against the power of the Kingdom of Satan through his life, death, and resurrection. After his death and resurrection, he affirmed to his disciples that "All authority in heaven and

---

38. God commanded the people of Israel under the Old Covenant to wage a holy war with total destruction (*cherem*) when they conquered the Promised Land. However, Jesus commanded his disciples to preach the good news of the gospel of the Kingdom of God to all nations, destroying barriers between Jews and Gentiles. In that sense, the Great Commission may be identified as "the New Covenant commission," compared to the Old Covenant commission, as Kline suggests: "Proceeding to his sovereign charge, Jesus issued the New Covenant commission (Matt 28:19, 20a), the central section of this covenantal formulation, after which the whole is usually named 'the great commission.' While this section corresponds formally to the commandments section of the Mosaic covenants, it differs functionally from the latter as the gospel of grace and truth that came by Jesus differs from the law given through Moses (John 1:17). Israel's obedience to the stipulations of the works arrangement mediated by Moses would be accepted as the legal ground of their continued possession of the typological kingdom. But Jesus does not summon the church to earn the eternal kingdom by obedience to the demands of the new covenant. Rather, it is as the one who, obedient unto the death of the Cross, has himself already merited salvation and the kingdom of glory for his church that Jesus commissions his disciples to go and disciple and baptize, gathering believers to the Lord of Har Magedon, to engage with him in the building of his eternal Glory-temple." Kline, *God, Heaven and Har Magedon*, 163–64.

on earth has been given to me." Before his enthronement in the heavenly Kingdom of God after his ascension, Jesus ordered the Great Commission, the mission to "all nations," embracing both Jews and Gentiles. Going and making "disciples of all nations" was the central focus of the Great Commission. In pronouncing these marching orders, Jesus sealed them with the Trinitarian formula, saying, "in the name of the Father and of the Son and of the Holy Spirit." In addition, Jesus' Great Commission envisioned the mission to all nations, the global mission under the guidance and outworking of the triune God. This is the reason why he gave the command in the name of the Trinitarian God. In that sense, Jesus' Great Commission to his disciples was not only the eschatological vision of mission to all nations under the New Covenant but was also a self-identification of his deity, as one with the triune God.

When Jesus gave an order to his disciples to go out from the Promised Land, he indirectly indicated that the theocratic kingdom in Canaan was coming to an end. It is a redemptive historical reversal. When the covenant community of Israel entered and conquered the Promised Land, the theocratic kingdom of Israel was visibly shaped and realized. It was the earthly vision of the Abrahamic covenant. But the theocratic kingdom of Israel was only a shadow of the Kingdom of Heaven in Jesus. So, Jesus' Great Commission to his disciples to go out from the Promised Land, spreading the gospel to all nations, meant that the theocratic kingdom of Israel was eventually coming to an end. History proved this redemptive historical reversal. The theocratic kingdom of Israel ended in 70 A.D. when Jerusalem fell under the attack of the Roman Empire. At the same time, this signaled that the period between the first and Second Coming of Jesus Christ would be identified as the last days, in which the gospel should be proclaimed and spread to all nations beyond the Promised Land, expanding the spiritual Kingdom of God globally.

Yahweh ordered the waging of holy war, employing total destruction, annihilating idol-worshipping pagan Gentiles in Canaan when the covenant community of Israel under the Old Covenant marched into and conquered the Promised Land. At that time the 'law of retaliation' (*lex talionis*) was the governing principle of the covenant community of Israel in the maintenance of justice and prevention of social evil under the Old Covenant:

> 15 A single witness shall not suffice against a person for any crime or for any wrong in connection with any offense that he has committed. Only on the evidence of two witnesses or of three witnesses shall a charge be established. 16 If a malicious witness arises to accuse a person of wrongdoing, 17 then both parties to the dispute shall appear before the LORD, before the priests and the judges who are in office in those days. 18 The judges shall inquire diligently, and if the witness is a false witness and has accused his brother falsely, 19 then you shall do to him as he had meant to do to his brother. So you shall purge the evil from your midst. 20 And the rest shall hear and fear, and shall never again

commit any such evil among you. 21 Your eye shall not pity. It shall be life for life, eye for eye, tooth for tooth, hand for hand, foot for foot. (Deut 19:15–21)

However, Jesus did not order total destruction when he commanded his disciples under the New Covenant to go out from the Promised Land and spread the gospel to all nations. Rather, he ordered them not to fight and retaliate even against persecutors and enemies, but to embrace, pray, forgive, and love them unto death, fighting not a military war but a spiritual war. Strikingly, this teaching was given to his disciples not after his resurrection when he gave the Great Commission but in the early stage of his earthly ministry, after Jesus chose his original twelve disciples, as we read from the Sermon on the Mount:

> 38 You have heard that it was said, 'An eye for an eye and a tooth for a tooth.' 39 But I say to you, Do not resist the one who is evil. But if anyone slaps you on the right cheek, turn to him the other also. 40 And if anyone would sue you and take your tunic, let him have your cloak as well. 41 And if anyone forces you to go one mile, go with him two miles. 42 Give to the one who begs from you, and do not refuse the one who would borrow from you. 43 *"You have heard that it was said, 'You shall love your neighbor and hate your enemy.' 44 But I say to you, Love your enemies and pray for those who persecute you, 45 so that you may be sons of your Father who is in heaven. For he makes his sun rise on the evil and on the good, and sends rain on the just and on the unjust. 46 For if you love those who love you, what reward do you have? Do not even the tax collectors do the same? 47 And if you greet only your brothers, what more are you doing than others? Do not even the Gentiles do the same? 48 You therefore must be perfect, as your heavenly Father is perfect.* (Matt 5:38–48)

Likewise, the covenant community under the New Covenant should love God and their neighbors and expand the horizon of love, praying and loving their persecutors and enemies even unto death. From the perspective of the Kingdom of God, Jesus' Sermon on the Mount is the proclamation of the coming of the eschatological Kingdom of God.[39] Remarkably, it arrived and was inaugurated with Jesus' incarnation, life, death, resurrection, ascension, and enthronement at the right hand of God in heaven. The vision of the coming eschatological Kingdom of God was proclaimed and taught by Jesus to his disciples and others, although even his disciples did not comprehend its meaning at that moment. In short, Jesus' teaching provided an eschatological kingdom lifestyle under the New Covenant. It is God's will to spread the gospel to

---

39. Based upon a false presupposition of the existence of "the Sayings Gospel Q," James Robinson reexamines Jesus' Sermon on the Mount. In doing so, he denies its historical reality: "Actually, the sayings of Jesus at issue here are what has been known down through history as the core of Jesus' teaching—what we are familiar with under the title Sermon on the Mount. This is Matthew's enlargement of the Sermon in Q, which is actually not a speech Jesus ever made on a given occasion, but a very early collection of his key sayings. Indeed, it may have been formulated as a well-organized whole even before the Sayings Gospel Q itself was composed." Robinson, *The Gospel of Jesus*, 210.

the global community, saving the elect along with expanding his eschatological and spiritual Kingdom of God to all nations through believers' evangelism and mission.

Summary

The prophecy of the New Covenant of Jeremiah 31:31–34 was beautifully fulfilled through Jesus' incarnation, life, death, and resurrection. Making "a new covenant with the house of Israel and the house of Judah" is a prophetic declaration that through the mediator Jesus Christ God will make the New Covenant with the elect, which includes both Jews and Gentiles. In that sense, "the house of Israel and the house of Judah" in Jeremiah's prophecy of the New Covenant is the representative expression of the elect.

The proper understanding of the decree of seventy weeks in Daniel 9:24–27 is significant because it unpacks the future redemptive history at the time of the prophet Daniel. In fact, the decree of seventy weeks revealed that God would "bring in everlasting righteousness" in the Messiah's life, death, and resurrection. Yahweh revealed a future redemptive historical period of seven weeks and sixty-two weeks, stretching from the rebuilding of Jerusalem to the first coming of the Messiah. The first part of Daniel 9:27, stating that "he shall make a strong covenant with many for one week, and for half of the week he shall put an end to sacrifice and offering," discloses the entire redemptive history from the Messiah's crucifixion to the Second Coming of Christ. In this respect, the decree of seventy weeks was the comprehensive summary of future redemptive history after the completion of the seventy years of Babylonian captivity.

After his baptism, Jesus Christ began his public ministry. In doing so, he began to fight a spiritual holy war against the power of Satan and the demons. At the same time, he preached the good news of the gospel of the Kingdom of God to the people while he was training his twelve disciples. As the mediator of the New Covenant, Jesus won a spiritual battle, fighting a holy war against the series of challenges of Satan and demons. And God ratified the New Covenant. In this regard, the New Covenant is a covenant of royal grant. The visible ceremony of the ratification of the New Covenant was realized through the crucifixion and death of Jesus Christ. Paradoxically, from the perspective of spiritual war, Jesus' crucifixion and death on the cross as the mediator of the New Covenant was the culmination and victory of spiritual holy war.

Jesus' words "my blood of the covenant" in the ceremony of the Last Supper to his disciples indicates that the mediator of the New Covenant shed his blood as the means of ratifying the covenant (Matt 26:28). Remarkably, the blood of the New Covenant is efficacious not only to the elect under the New Covenant but also to the elect under the Mosaic covenant, as well as the elect in the period of patriarchal age, even including Adam and Eve.

Jesus' bodily resurrection from the grave was the visible sign of the Father's grant of the eschatological Kingdom of God to his obedient Son, who was able to accomplish his redemptive work through his life and sacrificial death. The Father's grant to his faithful Servant-Son did not end with the resurrection, but extended to enthronement at the right hand of God. Furthermore, the coming of the Holy Spirit at Pentecost was the ministry of the exalted Son who poured out the Holy Spirit, received from the Father. So Jesus began to rule the eschatological Kingdom of God as "the King of kings and Lord of lords" because God bestowed and granted him the kingship and lordship with his bodily resurrection (1 Tim 6:15–16).

Under the New Covenant, Jesus instituted baptism and the Lord's Supper as two new sacraments, replacing the previous two sacraments of the Old Covenant of circumcision and Passover. In light of redemptive history, the water baptism of the Noahic covenant community in the Flood judgment is the origin of water baptism. It is in this redemptive historical background that Peter connects the salvation of the Noahic covenant community in the midst of catastrophic redemptive judgment with baptism (1 Pet 3:18–22). Remarkably, the Noahic covenant community did not get wet at all, although they were baptized by God in the midst of the Flood judgment because they were inside the sealed Ark when God poured out his wrath, executing redemptive judgment outside of the Ark by deluge. The redemptive historical reading of water baptism suggests that the mode of water baptism should not be restricted to the immersion of the entire body into water. Similarly, Paul associated the Red Sea crossing of the people of Israel with water baptism (1 Cor 10:1–5). The people of Israel did not get wet at all when they were baptized in the Red Sea. The historical episode of Israel's baptism in the Red Sea suggests that the mode of baptism may be diverse, including sprinkling, pouring, and immersion. "The people of Israel" baptized in the Red Sea included the infants of the covenant community. In that sense, it is proper to see that the baptism of infants in the Red Sea is the origin of infant baptism, when we look at baptism from a redemptive historical perspective.

The destruction of the temple and the fall of Jerusalem in 70 A.D. was God's covenant lawsuit against Israel's disobedience, which culminated in the persecution and crucifixion of Jesus Christ. It was a redemptive historical event because it was the historical mark of the termination of the Old Covenant order. Moreover, it was the historical mark of the termination of the theocratic kingdom of Israel in the Promised Land. However, although the theocratic kingdom of Israel was terminated in 70 A.D., the ethnic Jews as the descendents of Abraham, Isaac, and Jacob are continuously effective until the Second Coming of Christ. So Paul's prophetic message that "all Israel will be saved" in Romans 11:26a suggests that all the remnant and the elect among ethnic Israel will be saved by God's grace until the Second Coming of Jesus Christ.

We need to eschatologically interpret and understand Yahweh's command of total destruction in the process of Israel's conquest of Canaan under the Old Covenant. God will execute his final judgment through total destruction when the Parousia comes, separating the elect and the reprobate. Strikingly, God typologically displayed the vivid paradigm of the day of the final judgment through the conquest of Canaan in the ancient history of Israel.

However, Jesus as the mediator of the New Covenant did not order total destruction when he commanded his disciples to go out from the Promised Land and spread the gospel to all nations. Rather he commanded his disciples not to fight and retaliate against persecutors and enemies, but to pray, forgive, and love them unto death, fighting not militarily but spiritually. Surprisingly, this eschatological message was proclaimed to his disciples, not after his resurrection when he gave the Great Commission (Matt 28:18–20), but in the early stage of his earthly and public ministry (Matt 5:38–48). So, from the perspective of the Kingdom of God, Jesus' Sermon on the Mount is the proclamation of the coming and the inauguration of the eschatological Kingdom of God through the Messiah's incarnation, life, death, resurrection, ascension, and enthronement in heaven. It is God's glorious will to spread the gospel of the Kingdom of God to all nations under the New Covenant, saving the elect through believers' evangelism, mission, hardships, and persecution, sometimes even experiencing martyrdom until the day of the Lord comes. When Jesus comes back again, he will not return as a suffering Servant but as a glorious Consummator and Judge. And the eschatological Kingdom of God will be consummated and granted to the elect in Jesus Christ along with the new heaven and new earth.

Conclusion

By God's grace, we live in the eschatological age under the blessings of the New Covenant. In fact, the New Covenant is the culmination of the divine covenants, which began in the covenant of creation since the creation of the heavens and earth in the very beginning. It is noteworthy that believers in the Global Mission Age, scattered and dispersed in the Global community, enjoy the blessings of God's covenantal promises made in the Abrahamic covenant.

In fact, believers under the New Covenant are covenant pilgrims in the present world. God in his providence scattered his people after he inaugurated the New Covenant through Jesus Christ's death and resurrection. In particular, the Pentecost event became a redemptive historical turning point for spreading the good news of the gospel to all nations and tribes beyond the Promised Land. The constant formation of covenant pilgrims after the Pentecost event under the New Covenant is the powerful work and demonstration of the Holy Spirit. The Holy Spirit is a leading, invisible, and powerful figure for the Great Commission while he calls and mobilizes the people of God. God is absolutely sovereign, as seen in not only world history but also in redemptive history. The mission to all nations and tribes is initiated and fulfilled not by believers, but by the Holy Spirit who has constantly applied the redemptive work accomplished by Jesus Christ the mediator of the New Covenant.

The visible church under the New Covenant is a covenant diaspora community. God in his providence has scattered and dispersed his people, using diverse means such as persecution, immigration, famine, natural disaster, war, the development of technology, and science. Believers under the New Covenant must be aware that the earthly church is a covenant diaspora community, formed and developed by the work of the Holy Spirit. For example, after the Pentecost event, the Jerusalem church went through great persecution, and the people of God began to scatter as a covenant diaspora community. This is the historical background of the introduction of Peter's epistle:

> 1*Peter, an apostle of Jesus Christ, To those who are elect exiles of the dispersion in Pontus, Galatia, Cappadocia, Asia, and Bithynia* [Πέτρος ἀπόστολος Ἰησοῦ Χριστοῦ ἐκλεκτοῖς παρεπιδήμοις διασπορᾶς Πόντου, Γαλατίας, Καππαδοκίας,

Ἀσίας καὶ Βιθυνίας,], 2 according to the foreknowledge of God the Father, in the sanctification of the Spirit, for obedience to Jesus Christ and for sprinkling with his blood: May grace and peace be multiplied to you. (1 Pet 1:1 –2)

Peter notes that believers, scattered in the regions of Pontus, Galatia, Cappadocia, Asia, and Bithynia, are "elect exiles of the diaspora" (ἐκλεκτοῖς παρεπιδήμοις διασπορᾶς). Certainly, Peter's identification of believers as "elect exiles of the diaspora" has significant meaning and implication. The scattering of God's people is according to divine wisdom and providence. So believers in the Global Mission Age should understand that the earthly church in the last days is a covenant diaspora community which spreads and preaches the gospel to all nations and tribes until the Second Coming of Jesus Christ. As Peter inspirationally explains, believers under the New Covenant are "elect exiles of the diaspora," who are the eschatological colony in the present world. God's goal with the covenant diaspora community is to accomplish the Great Commission before the Second Coming of Jesus Christ.

Although Abraham and his covenant descendents lived their lives as pilgrims on this earth, they focused their hope on the everlasting Kingdom of God, which is the ultimate fulfillment of the promises of the Abrahamic covenant. For this reason, the author of Hebrews identifies the covenant descendents of Abraham as pilgrims on the earth:

> 8 By faith Abraham obeyed when he was called to go out to a place that he was to receive as an inheritance. And he went out, not knowing where he was going. *9 By faith he went to live in the land of promise, as in a foreign land, living in tents with Isaac and Jacob, heirs with him of the same promise. 10 For he was looking forward to the city that has foundations, whose designer and builder is God.* 11 By faith Sarah herself received power to conceive, even when she was past the age, since she considered him faithful who had promised. 12 Therefore from one man, and him as good as dead, were born descendents as many as the stars of heaven and as many as the innumerable grains of sand by the seashore. *13 These all died in faith, not having received the things promised, but having seen them and greeted them from afar, and having acknowledged that they were strangers and exiles on the earth. 14 For people who speak thus make it clear that they are seeking a homeland. 15 If they had been thinking of that land from which they had gone out, they would have had opportunity to return. 16 But as it is, they desire a better country, that is, a heavenly one. Therefore God is not ashamed to be called their God, for he has prepared for them a city.* (Heb 11:8–16)

Abraham and his covenant descendents were yearning to see "a better country, that is, a heavenly one" while they lived in the Promised Land as pilgrims. Similar to the Abrahamic covenant community and their descendents, believers under the New Covenant are pilgrims in the last days in the present world. Although Abraham and his covenant descendents arrived and lived in tents "in a land of promise," they realized by faith that their ultimate homeland was not the earthly land of promise, but the heavenly homeland, granted by God in the Messiah. And they acknowledged that *"they were strangers and exiles on the earth"* (v. 13c). Just as Abraham and his covenant descendents were "strangers and exiles on the earth," believers in the Global Mission Age are strangers and exiles in the present world. God made us strangers and exiles in the present world to preach and spread the good news of the gospel to the ends of the earth. Through the means of evangelism and mission by the covenant diaspora community, God will sovereignly execute his plan to save all the elect before the Second Coming of his Son throughout the Global Mission Field.

As Vos insightfully notes, believers are "colonists, living in the dispersion in the present world." Nevertheless, believers are spiritually "in vital connection with the heavenly world" because God unites us with Jesus Christ in his death and resurrection:

> This same idea is expressed in still another way in 12:22, where the author states that Chistians have come to Mount Zion, the city of the living God, the heavenly Jerusalem. We miss the writer's meaning of this if we regard this as a mere metaphor. Christians are really in vital connection with the heavenly world. It projects into their lives as a headland projects out into the ocean. This is a somewhat peculiar representation, but it is not confined to the Epistle to the Hebrews, for it is also found in Paul's writings. For example, in Phil. 3:20 Paul states "We have our commonwealth in heaven." Christians therefore are colonists, living in the dispersion in the present world. The same idea is set forth still more strongly in Eph. 2:6, "made us sit with him in the heavenly places," and also in Gal. 1:4, "that he might deliver us out of this present evil world." The Christian therefore is a peculiar chronological phenomenon. In Rom. 12:2 the apostle Paul draws the practical inference from this fact: Christians should be fashioned according to the world to come. To Paul, the death and resurrection of Christ are the beginning of the world to come, and of the eschatological process. This conclusion followed necessarily from his teaching on the resurrection and the judgment, both of which began with Christ's death and resurrection.[1]

In the epilogue of Revelation, Jesus promised "Surely I am coming soon." In fact, he will be coming soon to lead his elect to the everlasting Kingdom of God after the final redemptive judgment:

> 12 "Behold, I am coming soon, bringing my recompense with me, to repay everyone for what he has done. 13 I am the Alpha and the Omega, the first and the last, the beginning and the end." 14 Blessed are those who wash their robes, so that they may have the right to the tree of life and that they may enter the city by the gates. 15 Outside are the dogs and sorcerers and the sexually immoral and murderers and idolaters, and everyone who loves and practices falsehood. 16 "I, Jesus, have sent my angel to testify to you about these things for the churches. I am the root and the descendant of David, the bright morning star." 17 The Spirit and the Bride say, "Come." And let the one who hears

---

1. Vos, *The Teaching of the Epistle to the Hebrews*, 51.

> say, "Come." And let the one who is thirsty come; let the one who desires take the water of life without price. 18 I warn everyone who hears the words of the prophecy of this book: if anyone adds to them, God will add to him the plagues described in this book, 19 and if anyone takes away from the words of the book of this prophecy, God will take away his share in the tree of life and in the holy city, which are described in this book. 20 He who testifies to these things says, "Surely I am coming soon." Amen. Come, Lord Jesus! 21 The grace of the Lord Jesus be with all. Amen. (Rev 22:12–21)

The exalted Jesus' proclamation, "I am the Alpha and the Omega, the first and the last, the beginning and the end" (v. 13), signifies that he is not only the Creator and the Redeemer, but also the Consummator. Therefore, he will come as the Consummator in his Second Coming. Moreover, the exalted Jesus' self-identification as "the root and the descendent of David, the bright morning star" (v. 16b) suggests that his Second Coming will consummate the glorious Kingdom of God, which was the heart of the promises of the Davidic covenant. The church in the Global Mission Age will face great persecution. So we do not have to be surprised by great persecution. God will constantly scatter and disperse not only his people but non-Christians globally through persecution, migration, the development of technology, transportation, and other means. In doing so, God will accomplish the Great Commission before the Second Coming of Christ through the powerful works of the Holy Spirit. Believers, as the covenant diaspora community, should continue evangelism and mission until the end of world history, which will happen as God's supernatural intervention with his Son's Second Coming. When the exalted Jesus shouts "Surely I am coming soon" (v. 20b), we as the members of the covenant diaspora community reverently and boldly should shout "Amen. Come, Lord Jesus!" (v. 20c).

The glorious and comprehensive picture of the consummation of the Kingdom of God has been well summarized by Herman Bavinck:

> The renewal of creation follows the final judgment. According to Scripture the present world will neither continue forever nor will it be destroyed and replaced by a totally new one. Instead it will be cleansed of sin and re-created, reborn, renewed, made whole. While the Kingdom of God is first planted spiritually in human hearts, the future blessedness is not to be spiritualized. Biblical hope, rooted in incarnation and resurrection, is creational, this-worldly, visible, physical, bodily hope. The rebirth of human beings is completed in the glorious rebirth of all creation, the new Jerusalem, whose architect and builder is God himself. The salvation of the Kingdom of God, including communion with God as well as the communion of the saints, is both a present blessing and a future, consummated, rich glory. The Kingdom of God has come and is coming.[2]

---

2. Bavinck, *Reformed Dogmatics*, 4:715.

When the Day of the Lord comes, the glorified believers with the bodily resurrection will be surprised by joy, beauty, gladness, glory, happiness, and holiness due to the realization and fullness of the Kingdom of God, granted by God the Father in his Son. Undoubtedly, the glorified eschatological Kingdom of God will be fully realized in the new heaven and new earth. Thereby, the beauty and glory of the glorified believers' communion with the triune God along with angelic hosts will be consummated as the beauty and glory of the triune God will be fully manifested. To be sure, at the same time, the Kingdom of Satan through God's final redemptive judgment will be perfected with eternal torment and punishment, completely separated from the beauty and glory of the eschatological Kingdom of God.

Appendix A

Covenant Theology and Old Testament Ethics
Meredith G. Kline's Intrusion Ethics

KLINE'S 'INTRUSION ETHICS' IS certainly startling and innovative. He published his first landmark article on the subject in 1953.[1] However, there has not been much subsequent discussion on this important issue since then. Greg Bahnsen, a Reformed theonomist, provides a brief but severe criticism of Kline's intrusion ethics.[2] But his criticism fails to penetrate and understand the exact nature of Kline's thought on this relatively complicated issue. Despite Bahnsen's criticism, Elmer Smick indicates that Kline's intrusion ethics is one of the most innovative aspects of his biblical theology. "Kline has written one of his most creative essays on the ethics of consummation in contrast to the ethics of common grace. He wisely warns about the danger of our assuming the prerogative of God to abrogate the principle of common grace."[3] Recognizing disparate opinions, it is the present writer's hope to explain and evaluate Kline's biblical theological rationale for his notion of 'intrusion ethics' as revealed in Old Testament history.[4]

---

1. Kline, "The Intrusion and the Decalogue," 1–22. This important article can also be found, with minor modifications, in *The Structure of Biblical Authority*, 154–71. For a comprehensive and critical analysis of Kline's biblico-covenant theology in the light of modern criticism and the historical development of covenant theology as a whole, see Jeon, *Covenant Theology*. The book is a slight revision of my 1998 Ph.D. dissertation at Westminster Theological Seminary, Philadelphia, Pennsylvania. For a brief summary of Kline's contribution to Reformed systematic theology from a Klinean perspective, see Irons, "Redefining Merit: An Examination of Medieval Presuppositions in Covenant Theology," 253–68; Karlberg, "Reformed Theology as the Theology of the Covenants," ibid., 235–52. Mark Karlberg presents provocative arguments and statements on relevant issues of covenant theology against revisionist and radical revisionist background in his recent book, *Covenant Theology in Reformed Perspective*.

2. Bahnsen, *Theonomy in Christian Ethics*, 571–84. A constructive criticism of theonomy from a Reformed perspective can be found in Barker and Godfrey, *Theonomy; a Reformed Critique*; Kline, "Comments on an Old-New Error," 173–89.

3. Smick, "The Psalms as Response to God's Covenant Love: Theological Observations," 83.

4. Old Testament history covers the postlapsarian history of the Old Testament, thus eliminating the prelapsarian state.

Appendix A

I will argue that Kline's 'intrusion ethics' is the proper way of understanding Old Testament ethics, which is based on *redemptive historical hermeneutics*. Examining Kline's intrusion ethics, we will let Kline speak in his own words, adding some clarifications alongside the critical evaluative interaction.

The Eschatological Kingdom and the Idea of Intrusion

Kline's baseline presupposition in interpreting the complicated nature of Old Testament religion and ethics lies in the idea that God's ultimate design for redemptive history is the consummation and bestowal of the *eschatological kingdom*. The means of attaining the eschatological glorious kingdom in the prelapsarian state was 'the covenant of works' (*foedus operum*), while in the postlapsarian state it is 'the covenant of grace' (*foedus gratiae*). In a sense, eschatological vision moves back to creation, and the first Adam stood under "a covenant of works," which was the door to reach eschatological blessing. Due to the entrance of sin, the attaining of the original eschatological vision through Adam's perfect obedience to the law was canceled. The fall, however, did not delay "the consummation" because "the prospective consummation was either/or" according to the conditions prescribed in the covenant of creation. "It was either eternal glory by covenantal confirmation of original righteousness or eternal perdition by covenant-breaking repudiation of it." A realization of the curse of the covenant might have followed the fall. A gracious God, however, introduced the antithetical way to the eschatological blessing, which is the redemptive covenant in which we find the biblical rationale for the delay of judgment. "The delay was due rather to the principle and purpose of divine compassion by which a new way of arriving at the consummation was introduced, the way of redemptive covenant with common grace as its historical corollary."[5]

It is important to recognize in Kline's biblico-covenant hermeneutics that the role of common grace is extremely crucial to the right understanding of the complicated nature of redemptive history after the fall. In other words, a distinction between the covenants of works and grace, and common grace and special grace, are closely connected to the unfolding mystery of the eschatological kingdom which is the ultimate goal of history. In this sense, we may identify Kline's biblical hermeneutics as *covenantal eschatological kingdom hermeneutics*.

One of the most distinctive contributions of Reformed theology and hermeneutics for the community of Christ's church is the bold recognition that there is a distinction between common grace and saving grace. In his presuppositional apologetics, Cornelius Van Til applied this crucial distinction as one of the essential ingredients of the Christian worldview. However Van Til was not clear whether common grace was *covenantally arranged after the fall*. As a student of Van Til, Kline, correcting and advancing his view

---

5. Kline, *Biblical Authority*, 154–55.

on the issue, presented the distinction between the covenants of common grace and saving grace as one of the key biblical hermeneutical tools. Kline addresses and captures the importance of common grace in his analysis of redemptive history, especially with respect to the proper understanding of the covenant and the eschatological kingdom. He notices that after the fall a gracious God introduced the common grace covenant (Gen 3:16–19) along with the redemptive covenant (Gen 3:15). The consummated blessings of the eternal kingdom and the curse of an eternal hell are *delayed* by the principle of common grace introduced after the fall. In this sense, "the delay and common grace are coterminous." Certainly, there is "the positive contribution of common grace" to the redemptive eschatological program. Common grace as God's mercy and grace provides "the field of operation for redemptive grace, and its material too." The delay in relation to common grace provides a solid historical ground for "a consummation involving an extensive revelation of the divine perfections, a glorified paradise as well as a lake of fire." Therefore, the delay is not only "the delay of mere postponement but the delay of gestation." Kline sees the common grace order within redemptive history, and it will be terminated when the ultimate judgment comes. In that respect common grace is "the antithesis of the consummation, and as such it epitomizes this world-age as one during which the consummation is abeyant."[6]

According to Kline, from the perspective of eschatology, common grace is the means of its delay, while from the vantage point of history common grace provides an important background for the continuation of human history as well as the application of salvation to the elect. Thus, the ultimate goal of redemptive history is the execution of divine judgment represented by the dual sanctions of the eschatological blessing and curse. Its delay, due to the divine introduction of common grace as the historical playground of the application of redemption, is the biblical theological background of Kline's 'intrusion ethics.'

From this concrete biblical-theological concept of the eschatological kingdom, Kline begins to elucidate the general picture of an eschatological intrusion phenomena in redemptive history, tracing it to the Old Testament. "The Covenant of Redemption all along the line of its administration, more profoundly in the New Testament but already in the Old Testament is a coming of the Spirit, an intrusion of the power, principles, and reality of the consummation into the period of delay."[7] Kline shows that the intrusion phenomena of eschatological blessing and curse under the Old Testament is vividly manifested in types and shadows. In short, it is the manifestation of eschatological realism, typologically pictured in the history of the Old Testament, especially under the Old Covenant. This intrusion of the eternal kingdom blessing and cursing was an intrusion into the realm of common grace, which is the divine means of delay of the coming of eschatological judgment through blessing and curse.

---

6. Ibid., 155. Cf. Jeon, *Covenant Theology*, 217–19; Kline, *Kingdom Prologue*, 153–211, 244–62; Van Til, *Common Grace and the Gospel*; Van Til, *The Defense of the Faith*, 151–78.

7. Kline, *Biblical Authority*, 156.

Appendix A

> Breaking through first of all in the Old Testament period, the Intrusion finds itself in an age which is by the divine disposition of history, or, more specifically, by the divine administration of the Covenant of Redemption, an age of preparation for a later age of fulfillment and finality. Its appearing, therefore, is amid earthly forms which at once suggest, yet veil, the ultimate glory. Not to be obscured is the fact that within this temporary shell of the Intrusion there is a permanent core. *The pattern of things earthly embodies realized eschatology, an actual projection of the heavenly reality. It is the consummation which, intruding into the time of delay, anticipates itself.*[8]

The eschatological kingdom which is the ultimate goal of redemptive history is pervasive in the Old Testament. Indeed, Kline's eschatological understanding of the Old Testament is nothing but a flowering and maturing of the covenant hermeneutics developed and adopted in the Reformed covenant tradition under the rubric of the distinction between the covenant of works and covenant of grace (spanning creation, fall, redemption, and consummation, as already indicated).[9]

Alluding to Hebrews 9:23–24, Kline argues that the role of typology is essential to the proper understanding of the eschatology of the Old Testament. There are two stages in the fulfillment of the types of the Old Testament. One stage was fulfilled at the first coming of Christ, and another will be fulfilled and fully realized in the Parousia. Kline notes that the New Covenant church is still under pilgrimage, which depicts the semi-eschatological stage. So, "the apocalypse of Jesus Christ and his kingdom is still in the category of Intrusion rather than perfect consummation." This becomes clearer when we see that "the present age is still characterized by common grace," which may be identified as "the epitome of the delay." We are living in the semi-eschatological stage because we are still waiting for the coming of the exalted Son of Man. Old Testament types such as "the sacrifice of the Passover lamb" were fulfilled by the first coming of Christ. The visible possession of the Promised Land by the covenant people as the antitype of Old Testament type, however, will be realized only in the age to come. Kline observes that the theocratic kingdom of Israel is, in a limited sense, closer to the reality of eschatological kingdom than the church under the New Covenant. "While, therefore, the Old Testament is an earlier edition of the final reality than is the present age of the new covenant, and not so intensive, it is on its own level a more extensive

---

8. Ibid., emphasis mine.

9. I have argued against the background of Kline's critiques that Kline is a true successor and consummator of Geerhardus Vos's biblico-covenant theology, although I would require a minor revision of his thought. In fact, Vos's biblical theology is carefully enshrined and guided by hermeneutical principles such as the distinction between law and gospel along with the antithesis between the covenants of works and grace, which Kline has defended and promoted through his entire career and writings. As such, we cannot promote Vosian biblical theology without these concrete hermeneutical reference points. In other words, if we want to promote the Vosian eschatological kingdom vision in redemptive history, the above-mentioned hermeneutical principles must be presupposed. Cf. Jeon, *Covenant Theology*, 79–102, 279–334.

edition, especially when considered in its own most fully developed form, viz., the Israelite theocracy."[10]

The Garden of Eden, according to Kline, was an earthly projection of the heavenly kingdom and the eschatological kingdom was *offered* as the reward of a successful probation by the first Adam. On the other hand, Kline notices that God revealed the concrete reality of eternal heaven and hell in the postlapsarian state, and that this is shown through *types and shadows*. *The typological kingdom* in the form of Noah's Ark was a most vivid and visual manifestation of the eschatological kingdom in pre-Consummation history, along with the typological kingdom of Israel, shaped and maintained in the Promised Land. In this respect, that the theocratic kingdom of Israel intruded into a common grace world is a vital element in comprehending intrusion ethics. Kline elaborates that the theocratic kingdom of Israel was the intrusion of the eschatological heavenly kingdom in a typological manner.

> Eschatological intrusion was a feature of premessianic times as well as of the present new covenant days, even though the advent of Christ inaugurated a distinctive epoch in the whole development. There was indeed under the old covenant a comprehensive (partly realistic, partly symbolic) projection of the heavenly-eschatological domain into earth history in kingdom form in the theocratic kingdom of Israel. Heaven came to earth in supernatural realism in the phenomenon of the Glory-Spirit revealed in the sanctuary in Israel's midst. The eternal cosmic realm received symbolic expression in the land of Canaan. As is shown by the sharp distinction between this holy, theocratic, Sabbath-sanctified kingdom of Israel and the kingdoms of the common grace world around it, the special Israelite manifestation of the kingdom of heaven was indeed an intrusive phenomenon in the common grace order. Appropriately, in connection with the symbolic kingdom-intrusion under the old covenant there were also inbreakings of the power of eschatological restoration in the physical realm and anticipatory applications of the principle of final redemptive judgment in the conduct of the political life of Israel, notably in the deliverance from Egypt, the conquest of Canaan, and the restoration from exile, though also throughout the governmental-judicial provisions of the Mosaic laws.[11]

Bahnsen's most serious critique of Kline's intrusion ethics necessitates interacting with him and others particularly on the issues of theocracy and covenantal continuity and discontinuity, which are crucial for interpreting Old Testament eschatology and intrusion ethics. William Barker and W. Robert Godfrey summarize succinctly the heart of the problem of theonomist hermeneutics in the following manner: "Particularly, we believe it [theonomy] overemphasizes the continuities and neglects many of the discontinuities between the Old Testament and our time."[12] In short, it fails to

---

10. Kline, *Biblical Authority*, 157.
11. Kline, *Kingdom Prologue*, 158.
12. Barker and Godfrey, *Theonomy: A Reformed Critique*, 11.

provide a hermeneutical balance between the continuity and discontinuity in relation to the Old and New Covenants, exclusively emphasizing the continuity. However, the brilliance of classic covenant hermeneutics, as developed in the Reformed tradition, has endeavored to maintain a comprehensive balance between the continuity and discontinuity of the Old and New Covenants. As a result, covenant theologians have found the reality of the eschatological kingdom one of the most concrete reference points both for the Old and New Testaments throughout redemptive history.[13]

Both Kline and Bahnsen claim the influence of Geerhardus Vos and Cornelius Van Til.[14] Bahnsen appeals to Vos and others to emphasize the covenantal continuity without considering the covenantal discontinuity. Certainly, Vos emphasized covenantal continuity in respect to the unique way of salvation as the covenant of grace in the postlapsarian state, including the Old Covenant. Vos, however, put the emphasis on the covenantal discontinuity between the Old and New Covenants. This covenantal discontinuity was crucial to Vos's covenant hermeneutics in expounding the Old Covenant eschatology. Vos argued that the theocratic kingdom of Israel was governed and maintained by the principle of the law, administering blessing and curse, which points to the eternal heavenly blessing and hellish curse. The obedience

---

13. Jeon, *Covenant Theology*, 1–102.

14. Kline dedicated *The Structure of Biblical Authority* to Van Til in the preface to the 1971 version: "Cornelius Van Til stands as the prince of twentieth-century Christian apologetics. He has had by far the most profound impact on my own thinking of all my teachers. His theological insight and prophetic witness have been a conscience, if not canon, and his warmly human and gracious godliness has been an inspiration for the life which is in Christ Jesus" (Kline, *Biblical Authority*, 15). In addition, Kline indicates that his biblical theology is an expansion and development of Vos's biblical theology in his *magnum opus*, *Kingdom Prologue*, 7: "More, specifically, biblical theology in the classic tradition of Geerhardus Vos has as its distinctive feature a concern with the historical progress of special revelation as disclosed in the Bible . . . For Vos, then, delineating the progress of special revelation is broadly the same as expounding the contents of the several divine covenants . . . What is in Vos's *Biblical Theology* the infrastructure, the particular historical pattern in which the periodicity principle gets applied, becomes here the surface structure." Meanwhile, Bahnsen recognizes the influence of Vos and Van Til in his thought: "Past authors such as Calvin and Fairbairn, as well as current writers like Kevan, H. Ridderbos, Cornelius Van Til, and especially John Murray, have been of great instructional value to me along the way to authoring this study" (Bahnsen, *Theonomy*, xxxiii). Bahnsen identifies with Vos when he emphasizes exclusively covenantal continuity between the Old and New Covenants (ibid., 56–7, 86, 121–22, 218–20). But I have endeavored to prove that there is a balance of continuity and discontinuity between the Old and New Covenants in Vos's biblical theology (cf. Jeon, *Covenant Theology*, 85–91). When Bahnsen provides biblical theological analysis and discussion, in general he is not reliable, because he is not clear on the issues of the law and gospel and covenantal continuity and discontinuity. Paradoxically, as a presuppositional apologist, he shows a comprehensive understanding of philosophical and apologetical issues as he lays it out in his *magnum opus*, *Van Til's Apologetic*. This inconsistency may create a continuing confusion to Bahnsen's followers. In this sense, it is fair to say that Bahnsen as a theonomist does not follow *the classic covenant tradition* of Vos, who maintained a comprehensive balance of continuity and discontinuity between the Old and New Covenants, but *a revisionist covenant tradition*, represented by Murray, exclusively emphasizing a covenantal continuity. To be sure, Murray was not a theonomist as Bahnsen correctly recognizes. So, pushing himself in a theonomic direction, Bahnsen provides a critique of Murray's position that "the penal sanctions of the Older Testament law have been abrogated in this age" (Bahnsen, *Theonomy*, 458).

of Israel was not *meritorious* because it was applied to the continuation of symbolico-typical national blessings and curses. Meanwhile, Kline locates Israel's corporate obedience to the covenant of law under the Old Covenant, applied to the typological theocratic kingdom blessing and curse as *meritorious*. This is the difference between Vos and Kline. I think Vos's approach is more suitable to the understanding of biblical revelation because the obedience of Israel at its best was never perfect. Thus I limit *meritorious obedience* to the sinless obedience of the two Adams, though it was not performed by the first Adam due to the entrance of sin. The balanced understanding of the covenantal continuity and discontinuity in Vos's biblical theology was picked up by Van Til. Van Til applied this principle to Christian theistic ethics, as T. David Gordon correctly argues.[15]

Vos identifies the organization of Israel under the Old Covenant as a theocracy. He emphasizes that the purpose of the theocratic kingdom of Israel was not to teach ideal government in the world but to teach an absolute ideal of heavenly religion and kingdom: "The chief end for which Israel had been created was not to teach the world lessons in political economy, but in the midst of a world of paganism to teach true religion, even at the sacrifice of much secular propaganda and advantage."[16]

The divine intention for the theocratic kingdom of Israel was to typify the eschatological kingdom of Heaven which will be consummated in Christ. In this respect, Vos develops *Old Covenant eschatology* in relation to the typological kingdom of Israel:

> Nor was it merely a question of teaching religion for the present world. A missionary institution the theocracy never was intended to be in its Old Testament state. *The significance of the unique organization of Israel can be rightly measured only by remembering that the theocracy typified nothing short of the perfected kingdom of God, the consummate state of Heaven* [emphasis mine]. In this ideal state there will be no longer any place for the distinction between church and state. The former will have absorbed the latter . . . The fusion between the two spheres of secular and religious life is strikingly expressed by the divine promise that Israel will be made 'a kingdom of priests and an holy nation' [Ex. 19:6]. As priests they are in, nay, constitute the kingdom.[17]

Van Til, following the footsteps of Vos's biblical theology, recognizes the typological and temporal nature of the theocratic kingdom of Israel. The presence of the theocratic kingdom of Israel, argues Van Til, justifies the eschatological interpretation of the Old Covenant. The theocratic kingdom of Israel is not a model for earthly nations, but a type of the eschatological heavenly kingdom.

---

15. Gordon, "Van Til and Theonomic Ethics," 274: "Vos's discussion of the distinctive or particular contribution of each redemptive/revelatory era introduces an element of general *discontinuity or development* between the eras. For Van Til, it is this aspect of development which is critical for interpreting the Old Testament ethic correctly."

16. Vos, *Biblical Theology*, 125.

17. Ibid., 125–26.

> Furthermore, if the severities of the Old Testament but establish the absoluteness of its ethical ideal, its concessions do not compromise it. In order to understand the nature of these concessions we must call to mind the distinction we have drawn between the ultimate and the more immediate goal that God has set before his people. *The theocracy itself is only a stepping stone to a higher theocracy* [emphasis mine]. Even if it had been fully realized, according to the ordinances of God given for it, it would have had, in the whole history of redemption, only a temporary significance. By that we do not mean an unimportant significance. We mean the significance that childhood has for maturity.[18]

Van Til's recognition of the typological character of the theocratic kingdom of Israel led him to read Old Testament theistic ethics with redemptive historical sensitivity and development.

> What we do actually find then in the Old Testament corresponds to what we expect to find. We actually find that there is a gradual development in the clarity with which the final or ultimate ethical ideal is seen. There is a gradual development in the realization that the ethical ideal is absolutely comprehensive and that its final accomplishment lies in the far distant future . . . God treats his children in an infinitely wise way. He sets before them at the early stages of the revelation of himself immediate objectives, without intimating clearly that they are but *stepping stones to a higher and even to an ultimate ideal* [emphasis mine]. This is a pedagogical measure only. If it were not a *pedagogical measure only* there would be a flat contradiction in Old Testament ethics.[19]

However, this redemptive historical understanding of the theocratic kingdom of Israel is generally lacking in theonomy, and in particular in Greg Bahnsen's thought. Bahnsen fails to read eschatology under the Old Covenant because he sees only continuity between the Old and New Covenants. This similar problem has been seen in Murray's biblico-systematic theology. John Murray tried to apply Vosian biblical theology to his systematic theology. However, he tried to revise the classic covenant theology in respect to the original covenant of works and the Mosaic covenant. His rejection of the covenant of works (replacing it with an "Adamic administration") and the exclusive emphasis on the covenantal continuity between the Old and New Covenants have resulted in great confusion for his followers.[20]

---

18. Van Til, *In Defense of the Faith*, 98.

19. Ibid., 93–94.

20. I have evaluated John Murray as a revisionist covenant theologian over against classic covenant theology, which firmly maintains the original covenant of works, and a balance of continuity and discontinuity between the Old and New Covenants. Murray, however, as an orthodox Reformed theologian, maintains the temporal and logical order of *law and gospel, and law and grace not vice versa*, which are the crucial hermeneutical tools for the proper understanding of the *historia salutis and ordo salutis*. Furthermore, the distinction between law and gospel or grace has been a vitally important hermeneutical key for the doctrines of justification by faith alone, the substitutionary view of atonement, sovereign grace in divine election, and the covenant of grace (cf. Jeon, *Covenant Theology*, 103–90).

In this way, Bahnsen's theonomic vision is not compatible with Vos and Van Til, as Gordon correctly realizes.[21] Bahnsen's understanding of theocracy does not grasp eschatology under the Old Covenant because he does not see the uniqueness of theocracy, which is radically different from nations under the common grace realm. In essence then, he misses an important concept of redemptive historical understanding in respect to the typological kingdom of Israel.

> In this prosperity that the gospel has been assured by God's sovereign word there is the indication that the Older Testament 'theocracy' is now a 'Christocracy' intended to become world-wide in its scope ... In its simplest form, a 'theo-cracy' would be the rule of God in a particular country that is, the *moral* rule of God (for in the sense of God's *sovereign*, providential government of whatsoever comes to pass in history *everything* would be 'theocratic,' and it would serve no useful distinction to use the word). Hence a 'Christocracy' would be the moral (i.e., *Messianic*, in distinction from sovereign or providential) rule of Jesus Christ. In this sense the Great Commission (Matt. 28:18–20) intends for the nations to become a Christocracy.[22]

Unlike Murray, it is evident that Bahnsen moves in a radical revisionist direction in his view of law and gospel. Bahnsen's covenantal unity obscures the historical or temporal order of *law and gospel* as the means of eschatological blessing from creation to fall to redemption. What is important to him is 'persevering obedience' in all the divine covenants including the prelapsarian covenant: "Continued blessing for Adam in paradise, Israel in the promised land, and the Christian in the kingdom has been seen to be dependent upon persevering obedience to God's will as expressed in His law. There is complete covenantal *unity* with reference to the law of God as the standard of moral obligation throughout the *diverse* ages of human history" (Bahnsen, *Theonomy in Christian Ethics*, 203). Exegeting 1 Timothy 1:5–10, Bahnsen erroneously stresses that the law and the gospel are completely harmonious: "Paul urges Timothy to demonstrate that there is a complete agreement between the law and the gospel which he has taught" (Ibid., 196). "In Biblical perspective, grace and promise are not antithetical to law and demand. The law and the gospel both aim at the same thing" (Ibid., 183). Meanwhile, interpreting Galatians 3:10–21, Bahnsen appears to maintain that grace and law are antithetical in relation to the way of salvation: "Although the law is not against the promise of God (3:21)since they both aim at the same thing the fulfillment of the promise cannot be made dependent upon obedience to the law, for in redemptive history the law came after the promise (3:15–22). Grace (the promise) and law (the demand) cannot be mixed together as ways of salvation; the man who is saved by grace cannot have anything added to his salvation by law. The promise *grants* what the law could only aim at: righteousness and salvation" (Ibid., 132–33).

21. Gordon, "Van Til and Theonomic Ethics," 275: "It is this emphasis on the typological character of theocratic Israel, on her temporary character, that we perceive a difference in the way Vos influenced Van Til and the way he influenced Bahnsen. That the purpose of Israel was 'not to teach the world lessons about political economy' seems to us incongruent with the perception of theocratic Israel espoused in the Theonomic view. For Theonomy, the civil precepts of the Old Testament 'are a *model* of perfect social justice for all cultures, even in the punishment of criminals,' a '*model* to be emulated by *non-covenantal* nations as well.' For Vos and Van Til, the theocracy and the theocratic legislation are viewed in terms of being 'stepping stones to a higher and even to an ultimate ideal.' The theocracy is a 'model' of the perfect Kingdom in glory; for Theonomy, the theocracy is a 'model' for all other earthly governments. This difference influences the respective ethical programs of Van Til and Theonomy."

22. Bahnsen, *Theonomy*, 427–28.

Appendix A

Likewise, Bahnsen fails to understand the unique typological character of the kingdom of Israel in redemptive history, which points to the eternal ideal kingdom. This hinders him from reading eschatology under the Old Covenant, which is crucial for a proper understanding of Old Testament ethics. In Bahnsen, the Old Testament theocracy becomes "a Christocracy with international boundaries" in the New Testament. Thus the theocracy of Israel does not prevent "the application of God's law to the civil magistrate today."[23] Bahnsen's theonomic and postmillennial visions are the hermeneutical barriers, not adopting *adequate typology*, which is so crucial to redemptive historical hermeneutics represented in classic covenant theology and amillennialism. Although Bahnsen does not specify it, he is critical of the covenantal and amillennial hermeneutics, categorizing it as "the typologist."[24] It is, however, the present writer's estimation that the most profound understanding of covenantal redemptive history has been demonstrated in classic covenant theology and amillennialism, avoiding legalism through the proper adaptation of typology. Likewise, the sound recognition of the typological nature of the theocratic kingdom of Israel is a hermeneutical key to a better understanding of Old Testament ethics. In this regard, I agree with Gordon's analysis that Kline matures and advances Vos's biblical theology and Van Til's theistic ethics.[25]

Advancing Vosian biblical theology, Kline defines theocracy as a *visible and external holy kingdom realm* which is composed of King, land and holy people. As such, theocracy applies to "an external realm," and it does not describe "a spiritual reign of God in the hearts of his people by itself, but includes the geopolitical dimension."[26] In this sense, it is a special and unique kingdom which separates it from common grace nations.

It is important to note that Kline maintains the uniqueness of the theocratic kingdom, because that aspect is vital to an understanding of the typological character of the theocratic kingdom of Israel—a kingdom which foreshadows the eternal, heavenly and cosmic kingdom of God. It is interesting to observe that while Vos identifies the theocratic kingdom of Israel as a fusion between church and state, Kline, avoiding Vosian language, says that it is a unique cultic kingdom.

---

23. Ibid., 432.

24. Ibid., 455–58.

25. Gordon, "Van Til and Theonomic Ethics," 278: "Van Til's ethic is in fact best preserved in the writings of one of Theonomy's most notorious critics, to whom this volume is dedicated. Meredith G. Kline had advanced the position of Vos and Van Til not only in the realm of ethics but in the realm of biblical theology more generally considered. In the writings of Meredith G. Kline, one finds not only agreement with Vos and Van Til regarding the Theocracy, but one finds this agreement to be programmatically significant. For those interested in knowing what Vos and Van Til would have written in the areas of biblical theology and ethics had they each lived another generation, we can think of no better recommendation than a reading of Kline."

26. Kline, *Kingdom Prologue*, 49.

> As seen in the original form of the kingdom of God in Eden, a theocracy is a cultic kingdom through and through. God is King of the entire realm; all of it has the character of a holy house of God. A theocratic kingdom is a holy nation, a kingdom of priests. Membership in the kingdom involves participation in the sanctuary of God, for the kingdom is God's sanctuary. To break covenant by unfaithfulness to the God of the sanctuary is to be cut off from the kingdom, for God is the King of the kingdom. It is this sanctuary identity of the theocratic kingdom that sets it apart in holy uniqueness from all the other kingdoms found in the postlapsarian world . . . *Theocracy is not a combination of church and state institutions. It is a simple unique institution*, a structure *sui generis*. It is the kingdom realm whose great king is the Lord, where all activity is performed in the name of the God-King enthroned, confessed, and worshipped in the cultic epicenter, whence theocratic holiness radiates outward, permeating all, so that the whole realm, land and people, is a sanctuary of the Creator-Lord.[27]

Having defined and understood Israel under the Old Covenant as a theocracy, Kline rightly identifies the theocratic kingdom of Israel as an intrusion which is a type of the eternal heavenly kingdom realm which will be consummated in Christ. Kline's intrusion ethics stands or falls together with the typological character of the theocratic kingdom of Israel. Indeed, *Old Covenant eschatology* is summed up in this typological kingdom through dual sanctions such as blessing and curse which were the pointers to the eternal heaven and hell. This eschatological motif under the Old Covenant was governed by the principle of the law which can be described as 'the covenant of law' (the *foedus legale*) in Kline's biblical theology. He notices that the reality of the eschatological kingdom blessing and curse intruded into Old Testament history through typological modes. This concrete historical reality is the presupposition and biblical-theological background for the discussion and development of intrusion ethics. "Perez makes the breach in the Old Testament; that is, the consummation intrudes itself there. This Intrusion has realized eschatology as its core, while its symbolic surface (the sacramental aspect thereof excepted) forms a typical picture of eschatology not yet realized."[28] Thus, Kline establishes the biblical notion of the intrusion of the eschatological blessing and curse into the common grace realm throughout Old Testament history after the fall. Having defined and explained the intrusive phenomena into the realm of common grace, Kline guides us in a discussion of the relationship between eschatology and ethics.

---

27. Ibid., 50–51, emphasis mine.

28. Kline, *Biblical Authority*, 158. Likewise, a proper application of typology in relation to the exposition of the development of the eschatological kingdom motif through redemptive history is crucial as well. The brilliance of covenant hermeneutics developed in the Reformed tradition lies in the fact that covenant theologians carefully applied typology in their understanding of the eschatological kingdom idea especially under the Old Covenant. For the significance of typology in biblical and systematic theology, see Jeon, *Covenant Theology*, 6–8.

APPENDIX A

The Intrusion and Its Implication for Ethics

Kline finds apparent problems when he surveys Old Testament history in respect to God's law and its application by divine sanction to many situations. It appears that a divinely sanctioned action is not "consonant with the customary application of the law of God according to the principle of common grace"[29] on many occasions. This apparent discrepancy can be resolved, Kline suggests, by the application of the concept of the eschatological intrusion.

Having evaluated Charles Hodge's classification of the biblical laws,[30] Kline further states that biblical laws, including the Ten Commandments, have "multiple aspects of one law which may then have both a mutable and immutable aspect." As an illustration, Kline notices that "laws five through ten in the Decalogue" have both mutable and immutable aspects. Kline explains this double aspect as follows: "For they simply apply to specific cases the grand principle that man must reflect the moral glory of God on a finite scale. This principle is immutable because it concerns the relationship of man to God. On the other hand, the relations governed by this immutable principle are themselves mutable."[31] Likewise, Kline suggests that the application of the law as a whole has both immutable and mutable aspects which are the reflection of redemptive historical sensitivity in its applications.

For an example, Kline proceeds to discuss the definition of our neighbors for the application of the fifth to the tenth commandments. According to Kline, the concept of *neighbor* must be viewed and understood from the vantage point of redemptive history, especially in reference to the eschatological kingdom. Under the New Covenant, according to the principle of commandments five through ten, we must "love our neighbor as ourselves." "The unbeliever is the believer's neighbor today; but the reprobate is not the neighbor of the redeemed hereafter" because God will set a great chasm between them. God, who hates evil according to his immutable nature, "withdrawing all favor from the reprobate," will himself hate unbelievers when the Parousia comes. Glorified believers, following the pattern of God's attitude to unbelievers, will change "their attitude toward the unbeliever from one of neighborly love to one of perfect

---

29. Kline, *Biblical Authority*, 158.

30. Charles Hodge categorizes biblical laws into four areas. (1) The laws based "on the nature of God" belong to "the command to love God supremely." These laws bind "all rational creatures, angels as well as men." The principle of these laws is "absolutely immutable and indispensable." (2) The laws based on "the permanent relations of men in their present state of existence." These laws concern "property, marriage, and the duties of parents and children, or superiors and inferiors." (3) The laws founded upon "certain temporary relations of men, or conditions of society, and are enforced by the authority of God." Many of "the judicial or civil laws of the ancient theocracy" belong to this category. (4) These are the positive laws which come from "the explicit command of God" such as "external rites and ceremonies, as circumcision, sacrifices, and the distinction between clean and unclean meats, and between months, days, and years." Hodge argues that the laws in categories 2, 3, and 4 are mutable, while the laws in category 1 are immutable. Hodge, *Systematic Theology*, 3:265–70.

31. Kline, *Biblical Authority*, 159.

hatred, which is a holy, not malicious passion." Because "the grand principle" of "laws five through ten is immutable," the implication of these laws has to be changed according to "the changes in the intracreational relationships for which they legislate."[32]

Thus, Kline suggests that the definition of *neighbor* must be determined by redemptive historical sensitivity. The grand principle of the laws is immutable in the sense that it is *the imitation of God principle* while the application of the laws is mutable in terms of the intracreational relationship. The glory of God is "a *terminus ad quem*" (an ultimate goal) of the laws.

Having clarified both mutable and immutable aspects of the law, Kline argues that the presence of the eschatological Kingdom in the Old Testament must be understood as the intrusive phenomena into a common grace world. And it anticipates the eschatological judgment characterized as eternal blessing and curse.

> Now it appears that there was introduced in the Old Testament age a pattern of conduct akin to that found in prophetic portrayals of the kingdom of God beyond the present age of common grace. Our thesis is that this Old Testament ethical pattern is an aspect of the Intrusion. Included in it are both anticipations of God's judgment curse on the reprobate and of his saving grace in blessing his elect.[33]

Having explained the relationship between the idea of intrusion and its ethical application in redemptive history, Kline guides us into some specific examples. These examples are divided into the two categories of eschatological blessing and curse under the principle of the dual sanctions. Let us examine Kline's redemptive historical analysis of the examples of intrusion ethics in Old Testament history.

Intrusion of Eschatological Curse

The covenant community of the Israelites entered into the land promised to Abraham by the oath of God (Gen 15). In the process of the conquest of Canaan, however, there was an ethical problem which puzzles average readers of the episode. Kline asks a question: How can we justify "the Israelite dispossession and extermination of the Canaanites over against the sixth and eighth words of the Decalogue?" To resolve this

---

32. Ibid., 159–60.

33. Kline, *Biblical Authority*, 160. Recognizing a possible misunderstanding of intrusion ethics, Kline emphasizes several points to consider carefully. (1) The demands of intrusion ethics in the Old Testament cannot be "a lower or laxer order." (2) The concept of intrusion ethics is not "prejudicial to the permanent validity" of Mosaic moral law. The distinction is not "one of different standards but of the application of a constant standard under significantly different conditions. It is evident that such a distinction must be made between the period of common grace in general and the age of consummation." So, there was "an anticipatory abrogation of the principle of common grace during the Old Testament age." (3) The presence of intrusion ethics in the Old Testament does not interrupt "the unity of the Covenant of Redemption" revealed and begun in Genesis 3:15, which has been known as the *protevangelium* (Ibid.).

ethical problem, Kline suggests that we have to distinguish between normal or common grace war and holy war. Kline describes common grace war as follows.

> The function of the ordinary state when, acting through its officers against criminals or through its military forces against offending nations, it destroys life and exacts reparations. The proper performance of this function is not a violation but a fulfillment of the provisions of common grace. For in God's dealing with mankind in common grace he has authorized the state as 'an avenger for wrath to him that doeth evil.'[34]

However, the common grace war justified by God in international relationships, Kline argues, cannot explain the total destruction involved in the war between the Israelites and Canaanites during the conquest. The conquest of Canaan by the Israelites "before an assembly of nations acting according to the provisions of common grace" would not be justified as "an unprovoked aggression." Furthermore, the conquest violated the basic requirement to show mercy "even in the proper execution of justice."[35]

Thus, Kline argues that the conquest of Canaan was not a common grace war but a holy war, which is an anticipation of eschatological judgment. God's command to the Israelites was clear: they were not to make covenant with the Canaanites or show mercy to them during the conquest (cf. Ex 23:22–33; 34:10–16; Deut 7:1–10; 20:10–18). The holy war was the war of "total destruction" (*cherem*). Achan, who preserved some of "devoted things" against God's command, provoked God, and the Israelites could not defeat Ai until Achan and all the devoted things were destroyed (Josh 7—8). When the covenant community showed mercy, making covenant with Canaanites in the midst of conquest, God rebuked them, pouring out covenant curses upon them (Jdg 2).

It is clear that the conquest of Canaan was a type of eternal judgment which is a vivid manifestation of the eschatological curse. In short, there was an eschatological realism presented in the history of Israel. From the redemptive historical point of view, we must recognize, argues Kline, that the requirements of ordinary ethics were abrogated temporarily and "the ethical principles of the last judgment" were introduced such that God's promises and commands to the covenant community of Israel in respect to Canaan and the Canaanites became their own. Kline goes on to say: "Only so can the conquest be justified and seen as it was in truth not murder, but the hosts of the Almighty visiting upon the rebels against his righteous throne their just deserts—not robbery, but the meek inheriting the earth."[36]

Kline further shows that the dispossession of the Canaanites by the Israelites during the conquest (also involving the temporary abrogation of the eighth commandment) was also related to the tenth commandment. According to Kline, the violation

---

34. Ibid., 162–63.

35. Ibid., 163.

36. Kline, *Biblical Authority*, 163. For a fine discussion of the divine warrior motif in holy war throughout redemptive history from an evangelical perspective, see Longman and Reid, *God Is a Warrior*.

of the eighth and tenth commandments through the conquest was not sin because the neighbor concept under common grace was abrogated by God's command, intruding the neighbor concept of eschatological judgment.

> Must we not, then, also regard the Hebrew man of faith engaged in the conquest as coveting the land of the Canaanites, at least to the degree that he was obeying God's battle charge from his heart and with understanding? Though that would ordinarily be to sin against one who was his neighbor, this was one of the instances where the neighbor concept operative under common grace was abrogated by divine ordering in favor of the neighbor concept of the final judgment and beyond, according to which God's enemies are not the elect's neighbors.[37]

The apparent violation of the tenth commandment by the covenant community through God's command, Kline argues, was an intrusion principle which had the divine purpose of establishing and maintaining the theocratic kingdom as a type of the eternal kingdom: "When the Old Testament believer, at the Lord's command, took his typical stand beyond common grace, to covet the property of the unbeliever was to be in harmony with God's purpose to perfect his kingdom."[38]

Kline traces the Psalms and finds imprecations in Psalms 7, 35, 55, 59, 69, 79, 109 and 137. The imprecations spoken by covenant people such as David and Asaph are troublesome for many readers who encounter elements of cruelty in these prayers and songs directed against their enemies in the name of God. In the Sermon on the Mount, Jesus summarizes the attitude that the covenant community had toward their neighbor and enemy under the Old Covenant by saying, "love your neighbor and hate your enemy" (Matt 5:43; cf. Lev 19:18 and Deut 23:6). However, he proclaims a radical new approach to his followers under the New Covenant, commanding them to "love your enemies and pray for those who persecute you" (Matt 5:44; cf. Lk 6:27–38). This apparent contradiction creates difficulty for Bible readers and interpreters. Kline argues that the best solution to this problem is to understand the imprecations in the Psalms from the perspective of redemptive history and eschatology.

> Normally the believer's attitudes toward the unbeliever are conditioned by the principle of common grace. During the historical process of differentiation which common grace makes possible, before the secret election of God is unmistakably manifested at the great white throne, the servants of Christ are bound by his charge to pray for the good of those who despitefully use and persecute them. Our Lord rebuked the Boanerges when they contemplated consuming the Samaritans with fire from heaven (Luke 9:54; cf. Mark 3:17). We may not seek to destroy those for whom, perchance, Christ has died.
>
> But in the final judgment the Lord will not rebuke James and John if they make similar requests. Then it will be altogether becoming for the saint to

---

37. Kline, *Biblical Authority*, 166.
38. Ibid., 166.

desire God's wrath to descend upon his unbelieving enemy. No longer will there be the possibility that the enemy of the saint is the elect of God. Then the grain harvest will be ripe for the gathering of the Son of Man and the clusters of the vine will be fully ripe for the great winepress of the wrath of God.[39]

As such, Kline understands the imprecations in the Psalms as the intrusive phenomena of the ethics of eschatological consummation, which is sharply different from regular ethics under the principle of common grace. He suggests that we have to distinguish the consummation ethics from common grace ethics because "the imprecations in the Psalms" are the unusual pattern of ethical conduct which informs "the ethics of the consummation." The intrusion by divine inspiration constitutes "a divine abrogation, within a limited sphere, of the ethical requirements normally in force during the course of common grace."[40]

Furthermore, Kline argues that the imprecations in the Psalms inspired by the Spirit of God were conducted within the typological kingdom of Israel, which is the type and intrusion of the eternal kingdom. Therefore redemptive historical interpretation of the imprecations is a concrete hermeneutical principle which ought to be applied.[41]

Kline argues that ethical anticipation of the eschatological judgment of the reprobate is seen in the examples of Old Testament history "involving all the rest of commandments five through ten, excepting the seventh." The seventh commandment could not be altered in redemptive history. The reason, argues Kline, is explained by Paul in 1 Corinthians 6:12–20. It is especially because "every sin that a man doeth is without the body; but he that committeth fornication sinneth against his own body"(1 Cor 6:18).[42]

Under the principle of the common grace realm, Kline suggests that Rahab had a duty to obey "the civil authorities of Jericho." The civilian duty to the civil authorities is well taken and explained by Paul under normal circumstances (Rom 13:1–7). But, Kline argues, Rahab was not in a normal circumstance when she encountered the spies and her own civil authority figures. Rather she participated in the shaping of

---

39. Kline, *Biblical Authority*, 161–62. According to Kline, the covenant is "the Psalter's sphere of existence" since the temple was the central place for the religious and sacramental life of Israel and the psalms have a cultic orientation in general. "The psalms of praise" were "a continual resounding of Israel's 'Amen' of covenant ratification" as a means of "private and public devotion." Psalms such as 78, 105–106, 135–136 rehearsing "the course of covenant history" were "confessional responses of acknowledgment to the surveys of Yahweh's mighty acts" on behalf of Israel. So, when the covenant community of Israel used psalms extolling God's law, Israel made a new commitment "to the stipulations of the covenant." Furthermore, "plaint and penitential psalms" are closely tied to "interaction with the prophetic indictment of Israel in the process of the covenant lawsuit." It is quite natural then that the Psalter begins with an image of "the treaty blessings and curses and the declaration that judgment hinges on man's attitude towards the law of the covenant" (Ibid., 62–64). Likewise Kline suggests that we have to interpret the psalms from the perspective of the Old Covenant and its relation to the eschatological kingdom in redemptive history. Elmer Smick briefly summarizes and analyzes Psalms from the perspective of Kline's approach; see Smick, "The Psalms as Response to God's Covenant Love: Theological Observations," 77–86.

40. Kline, *Biblical Authority*, 162.

41. Ibid.

42. Ibid., 164.

the theocratic kingdom as a Gentile and became an agent of the judgment which was the type of the eschatological judgment. In addition, the inspired authors of Hebrews and James approve Rahab's action as faithful because biblical authors read her episode from a redemptive historical perspective.

> When information was requested of her concerning the enemy spies, it was, according to ordinary ethics, her duty to supply it. Nevertheless, by faith she united herself to the cause of the theocracy and so played her part as an agent of the judgment-conquest which was typical of the final judgment, denying to the obstinate foes of God that respect for their authority which was their due under common grace. For so doing, Rahab receives inspired approbation (Heb. 11:31; Jas. 2:25).[43]

Thus, Kline directs us to think that Rahab's deception of her civil authority figures should be understood in light of the eschatological judgment. Certainly, at surface level, her deception was a violation of the ninth commandment. But at a deeper level, her deception should be justified because it was done for the benefit of the theocratic kingdom and the glory of God. When the Parousia comes, there will be ultimate judgment for those who have hostile intentions against the eternal theocratic kingdom. Although Rahab's deception was involved with the mutable principle of the ninth commandment, she was not violating the immutable principles of the first three laws.

> The enemies of the theocracy lost the ordinary right to hear the truth as that is guaranteed by the ninth commandment. Insofar, therefore, as the theocratic agent did not deny God (or, to put it differently, did not violate the immutable principles of the first three laws of the Decalogue), he might with perfect ethical propriety deceive such as had hostile intent against the theocracy.[44]

Thus, Kline suggests that God approved Rahab's deception against the civil authority which displayed a hostile intention against the theocratic kingdom at that specific moment in redemptive history. This same understanding may be applied to the episode of the Hebrew midwives' deception against Pharaoh (Ex 1:15–21) and Samuel's deception against Saul (1 Sam 16:2).[45]

The penal sanctions regulated under the Old Covenant have been the object of serious debate between Bahnsen and Kline. For example, Bahnsen insists that the death penalty against the violators of the first four, fifth, sixth, and seventh commandments under the Old Covenant must be applied under the current state. Bahnsen's penology is a result of the lack of redemptive historical understanding on the penal sanctions and covenantal discontinuity.[46]

43. Ibid.
44. Ibid., 164–65.
45. Ibid., 165.
46. Bahnsen argues that the justification of "theonomic punishment" is based on "the principle of *equity*, no crime receives a penalty which it does not warrant." Therefore, penal sanctions under the

Appendix A

Kline suggests that the intrusion principle was applied against the members of the covenant community under the Mosaic or Old Covenant. The death penalty was applied to the violators of the first four commandments: "In the area of penal sanctions against offending covenant members, the Intrusion principle again manifests itself. It is especially significant that among the offenses for which the death penalty was prescribed are violations of the first four laws of the Decalogue (see, e.g., Ex 31:14ff.; 35:2 [cf. Num 15:32ff.]; Lev 24:16; Deut 13:5ff.; 17:2ff.)."[47] Why do we have to see this ethical principle as an intrusive phenomena? That is the question Kline himself asks and he answers it. It is because such a violation cannot be a capital crime under the New Covenant age either by the state or the church. Rather, it should be the subject matter of church discipline: "In the present age such violations are subject to ecclesiastical discipline, but the sword may not be wielded by either church or state in punishment of such offenders, according to the principle of common grace."[48] In this respect, capital punishment against the violators of the first four commandments under the theocracy of the Old Testament was the intrusion of the final judgment against those who violated these laws from their heart.

> In the consummation, however, the portion of those who do not obey these laws from the heart will be 'the second death.' It is then consummation justice that was intruded when death was prescribed for religious offenses in Israel, the kingdom where the consummation was typically anticipated. The Intrusion appears most vividly in those instances where the infliction of death was not the act of a theocratic official but of God (see, e.g., Num. 11:1f.; 16:31ff.; 2 Kings 2:24).[49]

So far, we have traced Kline's biblical-theological logic on the intrusion of eschatological curse. Now, we move on to some episodes of the intrusion of eschatological blessing in relation to Old Testament ethics.

---

old covenant must be directly applied to contemporary civil law: "This comes to expression in the civil realm as *just recompense* (Heb. 2:2), as in the *lex talionis* (Ex. 21:23–25; Lev. 24:19–20; Deut. 19:21). Consequently the death penalty is to be viewed as the appropriate response of the magistrate to violations against the purity of the God-man relation (e.g., idolatry, witchcraft, etc.), the sanctity of life and its sources (e.g., murder, adultery) or authority (e.g., striking one's parents). In the areas of theft and property damage, then, full restitution or compensation is the standard of punishment (e.g., Ex. 21:22; Lev. 24:21) . . . Knowing that God's standard of righteousness (which includes temporal, social relations) is as immutable as the character of God Himself, we should conclude that crimes which warrant capital punishment in the *Older* testament continue to deserve the death penalty today" (Bahnsen, *Theonomy in Christian Ethics*, 437, 439, 442).

47. Kline, *Biblical Authority*, 166.
48. Ibid., 166–67.
49. Ibid., 167.

Intrusion of Eschatological Blessing

Kline argues that God's command to Abraham to sacrifice Isaac confronted him with "a contradiction of previous revelation concerning human life, revelation later formulated in the sixth word of the Decalogue." It is "the Creator's prerogative" to designate such importance "to his creatures as he will," and it is man's responsibility "to accept the divine interpretation." "The more unaccountable to man" God's interpretation may be, "the better calculated" it is to highlight in man's heart "the necessity of thinking and living covenantally, that is, in the obedience of personal devotion to his God."[50]

Even though Abraham was faced with this striking command which was apparently contradictory to the sixth commandment, Kline suggests that "Abraham must not make an abstract idol out of the customary prohibition against human sacrifice but must listen to his Father's voice."[51]

Here, Kline suggests typology: Isaac was the type of Christ who was sacrificed by his Father as a substitute in the place of sinners. In that sense, God's command to sacrifice Isaac was "the ethics of the Cross, itself an intrusion of final judgment into mid-history, that was intruded into the Old Testament age in the divine command to sacrifice Isaac." However, "the provision of the sacrificial substitute" teaches us "the inadequacy of sinful human life for making atonement" after Abraham had demonstrated "the obedience of faith." God did not identify "Isaac's life as the life that was actually to be sacrificed as an atonement for sin." Meanwhile, Abraham's obedience to "the Intrusion's demand" demonstrated that he was the father of believers living by every word which came from the mouth of God.[52]

Kline interprets Exodus through Malachi under the rubric of the Old Covenant, which is patterned by the standing and falling of the theocratic kingdom of Israel. Under the theocratic kingdom, Kline argues that there was not a fusion between state and church but *sui generis*. However, Kline suggests that the present church age is radically different from the covenant community under the Old Covenant. In that sense, we have to distinguish carefully between church and state. And it is an adequate implication of the fifth commandment under the New Covenant.

> Apropos of the fifth word, it is in this New Testament age not a legitimate function of a civil government to endorse and support religious establishments. This principle applies equally to the Christian church; for though its invisible government is theocratic with Christ sitting on David's throne in the heavens and ruling over it, yet its visible organization, in particular as it is related to civil powers, is so designed that it takes a place of only common privilege along with other religious institutions within the framework of common grace.[53]

---

50. Ibid., 168.
51. Ibid., 169.
52. Ibid.
53. Ibid., 167.

However, at the consummation, the common grace order, and with it the common grace institution of the state, will be terminated and all things will be under the authority of the visible reigning of Christ. Likewise, the theocratic kingdom of Israel was the type of the eternal Kingdom.

> It is quite otherwise in the consummation. Then every dominion and power in heaven, on earth, and under the earth, must do obeisance to the Christ of God. Moreover, it is this ultimate state of affairs that is found intruded into the Old Testament dispensation in connection with the Israelite theocracy, which typified the perfected kingdom of God.[54]

The intrusion of Christ's universal reign over the eternal kingdom was manifested in the famous cylinder of Cyrus king of Persia (2 Chr 36:22–23; Ezra 1:1–11).

> While this typical kingdom of heaven was in existence, the other nations on earth stood in a peculiar relation to it. We are informed, for example, that 'the Lord stirred up the spirit of Cyrus, king of Persia, so that he made a proclamation throughout his kingdom' in which he professed to have received a charge from the Lord God of heaven to build him a house in Jerusalem (Ezra 1:1ff).[55]

Furthermore, Kline adds that later a Persian king supported the rebuilding and maintaining of the temple. Moreover, they contributed "from government funds for its ritual." The famous Cyrus cylinder instigated by God reveals that Cyrus as a pagan king actively supported the theocratic kingdom of Israel. This process, argues Kline, "is obviously not normative for civil governments in the New Testament dispensation." This is an example of "Intrusion ethics in connection with the Israelite theocracy as a type of the heavenly kingdom into which 'the kings of earth do bring their glory and honor,'" as that is revealed in Revelation 21:24.[56]

Kline evaluates the prophet Hosea's marriage with the harlot Gomer (Hos 1:3) within the historical reality of the Old Covenant, which was directly applied to the covenant community of Israel.[57] Accordingly, Kline argues that the Mosaic law prohibited prostitution, which was a violation of the seventh commandment that resulted in expulsion from "the theocratic congregation"(Lev 19:29; Deut 23:17). In that sense, the marriage episode of Hosea, Kline suggests, is not an episode under the circumstances of common grace but an intrusion of the ethical principle of God's eschatological saving of sinners. "It was certainly implied in this that a harlot might not

---

54. Ibid.
55. Ibid.
56. Ibid., 168.

57. Hosea's marriage to Gomer as an illustration of intrusion ethics, according to Kline, depends on whether Gomer was a harlot when Hosea married her. Recently, Kline has moved away from his previous position that Gomer was a harlot before marriage. As a result, Kline does not consider Hosea's marriage any longer as an example of intrusion ethics. However, I am tracing Kline's biblical theological explanation if we consider that Gomer was a harlot at the moment of her marriage.

be espoused by a covenant member. Nevertheless, in contradiction of this ordinary requirement, the Lord commanded Hosea to marry the harlot, Gomer. In so doing, God was again anticipating an ethical principle entailed in his saving of the elect."[58]

Following the redemptive historical logic, Kline argues that Hosea's marriage must be understood in light of "the eschatological context of divine revelation." Thus it fits the pattern of intrusion ethics. Hosea's marriage is a type of the eschatological marriage between Christ and a church-bride that will include a multitude of forgiven sinners (Matt 25:1–13; Eph 5:22–33; Rev 19:6–9). The glory of the eschatological kingdom marriage was vividly manifested in the episode. So Hosea as the prophet of Israel was not offended by God's striking command to accept Gomer as his wife, anticipating himself "in the great marriage celebration" of the eschatological kingdom Lamb. Likewise, the episode of Hosea's marriage provides the eschatological outlook that "the consummation of God's grace" will be realized when Christ as heavenly bridegroom welcomes "a church-bride composed of a multitude of defiled sinners to be his own."[59]

Conclusion

As we have traced and explained Kline's intrusion ethics, we have seen that it is simply an adequate application of covenant theology to the area of the Old Testament ethics. In fact, Kline as a classic covenant theologian flowers and matures covenant theology, developed and adopted in the Reformed tradition, applying its rich insights to the area of Old Testament ethics. Thus, Kline's intrusion ethics is an important contribution to our understanding of the application of covenant and eschatological kingdom ideas in resolution of some of the most difficult ethical issues revealed in Old Testament history. In conclusion, I may identify Kline's intrusion ethics as *covenantal eschatological kingdom ethics*, based on redemptive historical hermeneutics. I hope that scholars will further develop Kline's intrusion ethics through more discussion and research.

---

58. Kline, *Biblical Authority*, 170. Kline's approach to the prophetical books is quite profound. He suggests that the prophets be read in light of the Old Covenant and eschatological kingdom. The motif of covenant lawsuit is a vital part of the prophetic message based upon the Mosaic Covenant and was constantly applied throughout the history of Israel. The message of judgment characterized in dual sanctions such as blessing and curse is thoroughly reflected. "The peculiarly prophetic task was the elaboration and application of the ancient covenant sanctions. In actual practice that meant that their diplomatic mission to Israel was by and large one of prosecuting Yahweh's patient covenant lawsuit with his incurably wayward vassal people. The documentary legacy of their mission reveals them confronting Israel with judgment . . . Manifestly, then, these writings of the prophets are extensions of the covenantal documents of Moses. They summon Israel to remember the law covenant of Moses commanded at Horeb (Mal. 4:4) and to behold the eschatological future whose outlines were already sketched in the Mosaic curse and blessing sanctions, particularly in the covenant renewal in Moab (Deut. 28ff.) . . . While relating the prophetic office to covenants in general, all such literary and technical parallels pointing to the political sphere of suzerain-vassal relationship as the formal background for the prophetic office serve also as another link, even if indirect, connecting the prophets with the covenants of Moses, inasmuch as the form of the latter, too, derives from that very same background of covenantal statecraft" (Ibid., 57–62).

59. Ibid., 170.

Appendix B

Redemptive Historical Poems
Jeong Koo Jeon

Glory in the Midst of Darkness

In the beginning,
The Light of Glory—
Hovering over deep darkness . . .

In the hopeless wilderness,
The Light of Glory—
In the midst of Israel
Leading day and night . . .

At the tabernacle in the wilderness,
At the temple on Mt. Zion,
Spectacular form penetrated darkness:
Heaven's Glory In-Dwelling.

In the land of Bethlehem Judah
When gloomy darkness filled the world,
A star of Glory appeared
In the sky over a manger;
A little Lamb, abandoning the Glory of Heaven,
Was born here:
The Glory of Light—
The Holy Light of Heaven shining.

In the midst of darkness
Heaven was singing;
Heavenly host and angel sang
Sang the Song of Glory!
Now the victorious little Lamb
Rules the Kingdom of Glory;
(Ah! through faith)
Beyond the Kingdom of Darkness
Receiving the Kingdom of Glory as gift,
We begin to sing.

Until the return of the little Lamb of Glory,
We will sing;
In the dark wilderness
Pondering the invisible Glory
In our midst,
We will sing the Song of Heaven.

When the little Lamb comes again
Passing through the dark world,
We will see the Glory of judgment—the last Glory—
And face eternal Glory.

With heavenly host and angel
We will sing and dance;
In the midst of everlasting Glory
We will sing an endless Song!

The Garden of Eden

In the vast universe,
The original earth was formed.
It was good.
In its midst,
The Garden of Eden was projected
As the earthly form of the eternal Garden.

Appendix B

Adam and Eve walked and lived under the beautiful Glory
Clothed with righteousness, holiness, and wisdom
As the *imago Dei*.
Oh! How beautiful they were after the Beauty!
The Glory over their head protected and guided them.
The Shekinah Glory was dwelling
In the midst of the paradise Garden.
Adam and Eve were ruling and protecting the holy Garden
However, the best had not yet come.
It was upon the shoulder of the first Adam.
He had to accomplish his mission
Perfectly obeying the covenant.

The Sabbath day was commanded and observed
As a holy day
With the glorious anticipation of the eternal Sabbath.

In the midst of the Garden
The tree of life
And the tree of the knowledge of good and evil.
The tree of life was the sign of eternal blessing
While the latter tree was forbidden
As the sign of eternal curse.

When the serpent intruded in the midst of the holy Garden
Adam and Eve failed to curse and expel him from the paradise land.
Instead, they ate the forbidden fruit.
Oh! They sinned and lost
The original righteousness, holiness, and wisdom.

When the Glory appeared to the fallen Adam and Eve,
They were terrified
For it was the day of the Lord,
The day of Judgment, Primeval Parousia.
They hid from the Glory.

But the glimmer of hope was announced
In the woman's offspring.
The holy war between the Kingdom of Darkness and Glory
Was pronounced.

Although the fallen Adam and Eve expelled from the holy Garden,
They were clothed by the righteous garment,
The coming second Adam's righteousness.
Outside of the Garden of Eden
They began their pilgrimage
Yearning for the coming Glory.

Bibliography

Alexander, T. Desmond, Brian S. Rosner, D. A. Carson, and Graeme Goldsworthy, eds. *New Dictionary of Biblical Theology.* Downers Grove, IL: InterVarsity, 2000.

Allis, Oswald T. *The Five Books of Moses.* Phillipsburg, NJ: P&R, 1949.

———. *Prophecy & the Church.* Phillipsburg, NJ: P&R, 1947.

Arnold, Bill T., and Bryan E. Beyer, eds. *Readings from the Ancient Near East.* Grand Rapids: Baker Academic, 2002.

Bahnsen, Greg L. *Theonomy in Christian Ethics: Expanded Edition with Replies to Critics.* Phillipsburg, NJ: P&R, 1984.

———. *Van Til's Apologetic: Readings and Analysis.* Phillipsburg, NJ: P&R, 1998.

Barker, William S., and W. Robert Godfrey, eds. *Theonomy: A Reformed Critique.* Grand Rapids: Academic Books, 1990.

Barth, Karl. *Church Dogmatics.* 5 vols. Edited by G. W. Bromiley and T. F. Torrance. Translated by G. W. Bromiley. Peabody, MA: Hendrickson, 2010.

———. "Gospel and Law," God, Grace, and Gospel. Translated by J. S. McNab. Scottish Journal of Theology Occasional Papers, No. 8. London: Oliver Boyd, 1959, 1–28.

———. *The Theology of Calvin.* Translated by Geoffrey W. Bromiley. Grand Rapids: Eerdmans, 1995.

Bartholomew, Craig G. "Covenant and Creation: Covenant Overload or Covenantal Deconstruction." *Calvin Theological Journal* 30 (1995)11–33.

Bartsch, Hans Werner, ed. *Kerygma and Myth: A Theological Debate.* Translated by Reginald H. Fuller. New York: Harper & Row, 1961.

Bateman, Herbert W. IV, ed. *Three Central Issues in Contemporary Dispensationalism: A Comparison of Traditional and Progressive Views.* Grand Rapids: Kregel Publications, 1999.

Bauckham, Richard. *The Theology of the Book of Revelation.* Eugene, OR: Wipf & Stock, 2005.

Baugh, S. M. *A First John Reader.* Phillipsburg, NJ: P&R, 1999.

———. *A New Testament Greek Primer.* 3rd ed. Phillipsburg, NJ: P&R, 2012.

Bavinck, Herman. *Reformed Dogmatics.* 4 vols. Edited by John Bolt. Translated by John Vriend. Grand Rapids: Baker Academic, 2003–2008.

Beale, G. K. *The Book of Revelation.* In *The International Greek Testament Commentary.* Edited by I. Howard Marshall and Donald A. Hagner. Grand Rapids: Eerdmans, 1999.

———. *Handbook on the New Testament Use of the Old Testament: Exegesis and Interpretation.* Grand Rapids: Baker Academic, 2012.

———. *A New Testament Biblical Theology: The Unfolding of the Old Testament in the New.* Grand Rapids: Baker Academic, 2011.

Beale, G. K., and Benjamin L. Gladd. *Hidden But Now Revealed: A Biblical Theology of Mystery.* Downers Grove, IL: IVP Academic, 2014.

Berkhof, Louis. *Introduction to Systematic Theology.* Grand Rapids: Baker Book House, 1988.

Blaising, Craig A., and Darrell L. Bock, eds. *Dispensationalism, Israel and the Church: The Search for Definition.* Grand Rapids: Zondervan, 1992.

———. *Progressive Dispensationalism.* Grand Rapids: Baker Books, 2000.

Bock, Darrell L., ed. *Three Views on the Millennium and Beyond.* Grand Rapids: Zondervan, 1999.

Brenton, Sir Lancelot C. L. *Septuagint with Apocrypha: Greek and English.* Peabody, MA: Hendrickson, 2015.

Brown, Raymond E. *An Introduction to the New Testament.* New Haven and London: Yale University Press, 2010.

Bruce, F. F. *Paul: Apostle of the Heart Set Free.* Grand Rapids: Eerdmans, 1984.

Brunner, Emil, and Karl Barth. *Natural Theology: Comprising "Nature and Grace" by Professor Emil Brunner and the Reply "No" by Dr. Karl Barth.* Translated by Peter Fraenkel. Eugene, OR: Wipf & Stock, 2002..

Bultmann, Rudolf. *History and Eschatology: The Presence of Eternity.* New York: Harper & Row, 1962.

———. *History of the Synoptic Tradition.* Translated by John Marsh. New York: Harper & Row, 1976.

———. *Jesus and the Word.* Translated by Louise P. Smith and Erminie H. Lantero. New York: Charles Scribner, 1958.

———. *New Testament & Mythology and Other Basic.* Edited and translated by Schubert M. Ogden. Philadelphia: Fortress, 1984.

———. *Theology of the New Testament.* Translated by Kendrick Grobel. New York: Charles Scribner, 1955.

Calvin, John. *Calvin's Commentaries.* 22 vols. Various translators. Edinburgh: Calvin Translation Society, 1863. Reprint, Grand Rapids: Baker, 1996.

———. *Institutes of the Christian Religion.* Edited by John T. McNeill, translated by Ford Lewis Battles. In *The Library of Christian Classics,* vols. XX–XXI. Philadelphia: Westminster, 1975.

Carlson, Richard F., and Tremper Longman III. *Science, Creation and the Bible: Reconciling Rival Theories of Origins.* IVP Academic, 2010.

Carson, D. A. "Evangelicals, Ecumenism, and the Church." In *Evangelical Affirmations,* edited by Kenneth S. Kantzer and Carl F. H. Henry. Grand Rapids: Zondervan, 1990.

Chafer, Lewis Sperry. "Dispensationalism." *Bibliotheca Sacra* 93 (1936) 390–449.

———. Dispensationalism. Dallas: Dallas Seminary Press, 1951.

———. *Systematic Theology.* 8 vols. Dallas: Dallas Seminary Press, 1948.

Charlesworth, James H., ed. *The Old Testament Pseudepigrapha: Apocalyptic Literature &Testaments.* Vol. 1. New York, NY: Doubleday, 1983.

———, ed. *The Old Testament Pseudepigrapha: Expansions of the "Old Testament" and Legends, Wisdom and Philosophical Literature, Prayers, Psalms and Odes, Fragments of Lost Judeo-Hellenistic Works.* Vol. 2. New York: Doubleday, 1985.

Childs, Brevard S. *Biblical Theology of the Old and New Testaments.* Minneapolis: Fortress, 1992.

———. *Old Testament Theology in a Canonical Context.* Philadelphia: Fortress, 1989.

Clouse, Robert G., ed. *The Meaning of the Millennium: Four Views.* Downers Grove, IL: InterVarsity, 1977.

Collins, C. John. "Adam and Eve as Historical People, and Why It Matters." *Perspectives on Science and Christian Faith* 62(2010), 147–65.

———. *Did Adam and Eve Really Exist?: Who They Were and Why Should Care.* Wheaton, IL: Crossway, 2011.

———. *Genesis 1—4: A Linguistic, Literary, and Theological Commentary.* Phillipsburg, NJ: P&R, 2006.

Collins, John J. *Introduction to the Hebrew Bible.* Minneapolis: Fortress, 2004.

Cross, Frank Moore. *From Epic to Canon: History and Literature in Ancient Israel.* Baltimore: Johns Hopkins University Press, 1998.

Darby, John Nelson. *Notes on the Book of the Revelation: To Assist Enquirers in Searching into that Book.* Middletown, DE: Forgotten Books, 2007.

———. *Synopsis of the Books of the Bible.* Middletown, DE: BiblioLife, 2015.

Darwin, Charles. *The Origin of Species: By Means of Natural Selection of the Preservation of Favoured Races in the Struggle for Life.* New York: Penguin Books, 2003.

Dennis, Lane T., ed. *ESV Study Bible: English Standard Version.* Wheaton, IL: Crossway Bibles, 2008.

Dennison, James T. Jr. "Merit or 'Entitlement' in Reformed Covenant Theology: A Review." *Kerux* 24/3 (2009) 3–152.

DeRouchie, Jason S., Jason Gile, and Kenneth J. Turner, eds. *For Our Good Always: Studies on the Message and Influence of Deuteronomy in Honor of Daniel I. Block.* Winona Lake, IN: Eisenbrauns, 2013.

Dillard, Raymond, and Tremper Longman III. *An Introduction to the Old Testament.* Grand Rapids: Zondervan, 1994.

Dumbrell, William J. *Covenant and Creation: A Theology of Old Testament Covenants.* Eugene, OR: Wipf & Stock, 1984.

Dunn, James D. G. "The Incident at Antioch (Gal. 2:11–18)." *Journal for the Study of the New Testament* 18 (1983) 3–57.

———. *Jesus, Paul, and the Law: Studies in Mark and Galatians.* Louisville: Westminster, 1990.

———. "The Justice of God: A Renewed Perspective on Justification by Faith." *Journal of Theological Studies* 43 (1992) 1–22.

———. *A New Perspective on Jesus: What the Quest for the Historical Jesus Missed.* Grand Rapids: Baker Academic, 2006.

———. "The New Perspective on Paul." *Bulletin of the John Rylands University Library of Manchester* 65 (1983) 95–122.

———. *The New Perspective on Paul.* Grand Rapids: Eerdmans, 2008.

———. *New Testament Theology: An Introduction.* Nashville: Abingdon, 2009.

———. "Works of the Law and the Curse of the Law (Galatians 3:10–14)." *New Testament Studies* 31 (1985) 523–42.

———. "Yet Once More—'The Works of the Law': A Response." *Journal for the Study of the New Testament* 46 (1992) 99–117.

Durham, John I. *Exodus.* In *Word Biblical Commentary,* vol. 3. Waco, TX: Word Books, 1987.

Edwards, David L., and John Stott. *Evangelical Essentials: A Liberal-Evangelical Dialogue.* London: Hodder and Stoughton, 1988.

Edwards, Jonathan. *A History of Redemption: Containing the Outlines of a Body of Divinity.* Lexington: Hard, 2011.

Eichrodt, Walther. *Theology of the Old Testament.* Translated by J. A. Baker. Vol. 1. In *The Old Testament Library.* London: SCM, 1964.

———. *Theology of the Old Testament.* Translated by J. A. Baker. Vol. 2. In *The Old Testament Library.* Philadelphia, PA: Westminster, 1967.

Elam, Andrew M., Robert C. Van Kooten, and Randall A. Bergquist. *Merit and Moses: A Critique of the Klinean Doctrine of Republication.* Eugene, OR: Wipf & Stock, 2014.

Elliger, Karl, and Wilhelm Rudolph, eds. *Biblia Hebraica Stuttgartensia.* 5th ed. Stuttgart: Deutsche Bibelgesellschaft, 1997.

Enns, Peter. *The Evolution of Adam: What the Bible Does and Doesn't Say about Human Origins.* Grand Rapids: Brazos, 2012.

———. *Inspiration and Incarnation: Evangelicals and Problem of the Old Testament.* Grand Rapids: Baker Academic, 2005.

———. "Preliminary Observations on an Incarnational Model of Scripture: Its Validity and Usefulness." *Calvin Theological Journal* 42/2 (2007) 219–36.

Estelle, Bryan D., J. V. Fesko, and David VanDrunen, eds., *The Law Is Not of Faith: Essays on Works and Grace in the Mosaic Covenant.* Phillipsburg, NJ: P&R, 2009.

Ferguson, Everett. *Backgrounds of Early Christianity.* 3rd ed. Grand Rapids: Eerdmans, 2003.

Ferry, Brenton C. "Cross-Examining Moses' Defense: An Answer to Ramsey's Critique of Kline and Karlberg." *Westminster Theological Journal* 67 (2005) 163–68.

———. 'Works in the Mosaic Covenant: A Reformed Texamony." In *The Law Is Not of Faith*, edited by Bryan D. Estelle, J. V. Fesko, and David VanDrunen, 76–103. Phillipsburg, NJ: P&R, 2009.

Fesko, J. V. "Calvin and the Witsius on the Mosaic Covenant." In *The Law Is Not of Faith*, Bryan D. Estelle, J. V. Fesko, and David VanDrunen, 25–43. Phillipsburg, NJ: P&R, 2009.

———. "The Republication of the Covenant of Works." *The Confessional Presbyterian* 8 (2012) 197–212.

———. *The Theology of the Westminster Standards: Historical Context and Theological Insights.* Wheaton, IL: Crossway, 2014.

Funk, Robert W. *Honest to Jesus: Jesus for a New Millennium.* New York: HarperCollins, 1996.

Funk, Robert W., Roy W. Hoover, and The Jesus Seminar. *The Five Gospels: The Search for the Authentic Words of Jesus.* New York: Harper, 1997.

Fuller, Daniel P. *Gospel and Law: Contrast or Continuum? The Hermeneutics of Dispensationalism and Covenant Theology.* Grand Rapids: Eerdmans, 1980.

———. "The Hermeneutics of Dispensationalism." Th.D. diss., Northern Baptist Theological Seminary, Chicago, 1957.

———. "A Response on the Subjects of Works and Grace." *Presbyterion* 9 (1983) 72–79.

Futato, Mark D. "Because It Had Rained: A Study of Genesis 2:5–7 with Implications for Gen. 2:4–25 and Gen. 1:1—2:3." *Westminster Theological Journal* 60 (1998) 1–21.

Gaffin, Jr., Richard B. "Biblical Theology and the Westminster Standards." In *The Practical Calvinists: An Introduction to the Presbyterian and Reformed Heritage: In Honor of D. Clair Davis' Thirty Years at Westminster Theological Seminary*, edited by Peter A. Lillback, 425–42. Great Britain: Christian Focus, 2002.

———. "Biblical Theology and the Westminster Standards." *Westminster Theological Journal* 65 (2003) 165–79.

———. *The Centrality of the Resurrection: A Study in Paul's Soteriology.* Grand Rapids: Baker Book House, 1978.

———. "The Holy Spirit." *Westminster Theological Journal* 43 (1980) 58–78.

———. *Perspectives on Pentecost: Studies in New Testament Teaching on the Gifts of the Holy Spirit.* Grand Rapids: Baker Book House, 1979.

———. *Resurrection and Redemption: A Study in Pauline Soteriology.* Th.D. diss., Westminster Theological Seminary, 1969.

———. *Resurrection and Redemption: A Study in Paul's Soteriology.* Phillipsburg, NJ: P&R, 1987.

———. "Review Essay: Paul the Theologian." *Westminster Theological Journal* 62 (2000) 121–41.

———. "Systematic Theology and Biblical Theology." In *The New Testament Student and Theology,* vol.3. edited by John H. Skilton, 32–50. Philadelphia: P&R, 1976.

———. "The Vitality of Reformed Dogmatics." In *The Vitality of Reformed Theology: Proceedings of the International Theological Congress June 20–24th 1994, Noordwijkerhout, The Netherlands.* Edited by J.M. Batteau, J.W. Maris, and K. Veling, 16–50. Kampen: Uitgeverij Kok, 1994.

Gage, Warren A. *The Gospel of Genesis: Studies in Protology and Eschatology.* Winona Lake: Carpenter, 1984.

Garlington, D. B. "The Obedience of Faith in the Letter to the Romans; Part I: The Meaning of *hupakoen pisteos* (Rom 1:5; 16:26)." *Westminster Theological Journal* 52 (1990) 201–24.

———. "The Obedience of Faith in the Letter to the Romans; Part II: The Obedience of Faith and Judgment by Works." *Westminster Theological Journal* 53 (1991) 47–72.

Garrett, Duane A. "Type, Typology." In *Evangelical Dictionary of Biblical Theology*, edited by Walter A. Elwell, 785–7. Grand Rapids: Baker Book House, 1996.

Gentry, Peter J., and Stephen J. Wellum. *Kingdom through Covenant: A Biblical Theological Understanding of the Covenants.* Wheaton, IL: Crossway, 2012.

Golding, Peter. *Covenant Theology: The Key of Theology in Reformed Thought and Tradition.* Geanies House, Scotland: Christian Focus Publications, 2004.

Goldsworthy, Graeme. *According to Plan: The Unfolding Revelation of God in the Bible.* Downers Grove, IL: InterVarsity, 1991.

———. *Christ-Centered Biblical Theology: Hermeneutical Foundations and Principles.* Downers Grove, IL: InterVarsity, 2012.

Gordon, T. David. "Van Til and Theonomic Ethics." In *Creator, Redeemer, Consummator: A Festschrift For Meredith G. Kline,* edited by Howard Griffith and John H. Muether, 271–78. Greenville, SC: Reformed Academic, 2000.

Greidanus, Sidney. *Preaching Christ from the Old Testament: A Contemporary Hermeneutical Method.* Grand Rapids: Eerdmans, 1999.

Griffith, Howard, and John R. Muether, eds. *Creator, Redeemer, Consummator: A Festschirift For Meredith G. Kline.* Greenville, SC: Reformed Academic, 2000.

Grudem, Wayne. *Systematic Theology: An Introduction to Biblical Doctrine.* Grand Rapids: Zondervan, 2000.

Gundry, Robert H. *A Survey of the New Testament.* 5th ed. Grand Rapids: Zondervan, 2012.

Hagopian, David G., ed. *The Genesis Debate: Three Views on the Days of Creation.* Mission Viejo, CA: Crux, 2001.

Hahn, Scott W. *Kinship by Covenant: A Canonical Approach to the Fulfillment of God's Saving Promises.* New Haven: Yale University Press, 2009.

Harris, Stephen L. *Understanding the Bible.* Palo Alto: Mayfield, 1985.
Harrison, Ronald K. *Introduction to the Old Testament.* Grand Rapids: Eerdmans, 1988.
Hart, D. G. "Princeton and the Law: Enlightened and Reformed." In *The Law Is Not of Faith*, edited by Bryan D. Estelle, J. V. Fesko, and David VanDrunen, 44–75. Phillipsburg, NJ: P&R, 2009.
Hegel, G. W. F. *The Phenomenology of the Spirit.* Translated by A. V. Miller. Oxford University Press, 1977.
———. *The Philosophy of History.* Translated by J. Sibree. Mineola, NY: Dover Publications, 2004.
Hegg, Timothy J. *The Abrahamic Covenant and the Covenant of Grant in the Ancient Near East.* Northwest Baptist Seminary, 1980.
Heidel, Alexander. *The Babylonian Genesis: The Story of Creation.* Chicago: University of Chicago Press, 1963.
———. *The Gilgamesh Epic and Old Testament Parallels.* Chicago: University of Chicago Press, 1963.
Hendrickson, William. *More Than Conquers: An Interpretation of the Book of Revelation.* Grand Rapids: Baker Books, 1998.
Hillers, Delbert R. *Covenant: The History of a Biblical Idea.* Baltimore: Johns Hopkins University Press, 1969.
Hodge, Charles. *1 & 2 Corinthians.* In *The Geneva Series of Commentaries.* Carlisle, PA: Banner of Truth, 1978.
———. *The Epistle to the Romans: A Commentary on Romans.* Reprint, Carlisle, PA: Banner of Truth, 1975.
———. *Systematic Theology.* 3 vols. Grand Rapids: Eerdsmans, 1995.
Hoekema, Anthony A. *The Bible and the Future.* Grand Rapids: Eerdmans, 1994.
Horton, Michael. *The Christian Faith: A Systematic Theology for Pilgrims on the Way.* Grand Rapids: Zondervan, 2011.
———. *Introducing Covenant Theology.* Grand Rapids: Baker Books, 2006.
House, H. Wayne. "The Future of National Israel." *Bibliotheca Sacra* 166 (2009) 463–81.
Hughes, Philip E. *The True Image: The Origin and Destiny of Man in Christ.* Grand Rapids: Eerdmans, 1989.
Irons, Lee. "Redefining Merit: An Examination of Medieval Presuppositions in Covenant Theology." In *Creator, Redeemer, Consummator: A Festschrift For Meredith G. Kline*, edited by Howard Griffith and John H. Muether, 253–68. Greenville, SC: Reformed Academic, 2000.
Jeon, Jeong Koo. "The Abrahamic Covenant and the Kingdom of God." *The Confessional Presbyterian* 7 (2011) 123–38, 249–50.
———. *Calvin and the Federal Vision: Calvin's Covenant Theology in Light of Contemporary Discussion.* Eugene, OR: Wipf & Stock, 2009.
———. "Calvin and the Two Kingdoms: Calvin's Political Philosophy in Light of Contemporary Discussion." *Westminster Theological Journal* 72/2 (2010) 299–320.
———. "The Covenant of Creation and the Kingdom of God." *The Confessional Presbyterian* 9 (2013) 123–42.
———. *Covenant Theology: John Murray's and Meredith G. Kline's Response to the Historical Development of Federal Theology in Reformed Thought.* Lanham: University Press of America, 2004.

———. *Covenant Theology and Justification by Faith: The Shepherd Controversy and Its Impacts*. Eugene, OR: Wipf & Stock, 2006.

———. "Covenant Theology and Old Testament Ethics: Meredith G. Kline's Intrusion Ethics." *Kerux* (2002) 3–33.

———. "The Noahic Covenants and the Kingdom of God." *Mid-America Journal of Theology* 22 (2013) 179–209.

Johnson, Dennis E. *Triumph of the Lamb: A Commentary on Revelation*. Phillipsburg, NJ: P&R, 2001.

Jones, G. H. "'Holy War' or 'Yahweh War'?" *Vetus Testamentum* 25 (1975) 642–58.

———. "The Concept of Holy War." In *The World of the Old Testament*, 299–322. Edited by R. E. Clements. Cambridge: Cambridge University Press, 1989.

Josephus, Flavius. *Josephus: The Complete Works*. Translated by William Whiston. Nashville, TN: Thomas Nelson, 1998.

Kaiser, Walter C. Jr. *The Promise-Plan of God: A Biblical Theology of the Old and New Testaments*. Grand Rapids: Zondervan, 2008.

———. *Toward an Old Testament Theology*. Grand Rapids: Zondervan, 1981.

Kang, Sa-Moon. *Divine War in the Old Testament and in the Ancient Near East*. New York: Walter de Gruyter, 1989.

Karlberg, Mark W. *Covenant Theology in Reformed Perspective*. Eugene, OR: Wipf & Stock, 2000.

———. "Reformed Theology as the Theology of the Covenants: The Contributions of Meredith G. Kline to Reformed Systematics." In *Creator, Redeemer, Consummator: A Festschrift For Meredith G. Kline*, edited by Howard Griffith and John H. Muether, 235–52. Greenville, SC: Reformed Academic, 2000

Kim, Seyoon. *Justification and Sanctification: What Is Justification and Sanctification?* Seoul: Duranno, 2015.

———. *The Origin of Paul's Gospel*. 2nd ed. Tübingen: J. C. B. Mohr (Paul Siebeck), 1984.

———. *Paul and the New Perspective: Second Thoughts on the Origin of Paul's Gospel*. Grand Rapids: Eerdmans, 2002.

Kline, Meredith G. "Because It Had Not Rained." *Westminster Theological Journal* 20/2 (1958) 146–157.

———. *By Oath Consigned: A Reinterpretation of the Covenant Signs of Circumcision and Baptism*. Grand Rapids: Eerdmans, 1968.

———. "Comments on an Old-New Error." Review of Greg L. Bahnsen's *Theonomy in Christian Ethics*. *Westminster Theological Journal* (1978/ 1979) 173–89.

———. "Gospel until the Law: Romans 5:13–14 and the Old Covenant." *Journal of the Evangelical Theological Society* 34/4 (1991) 433–46.

———. *Glory in Our Midst: A Biblical-Theological Reading of Zechariah's Night Visions*. Overland Park, KS: Two Age, 2001.

———. *Images of the Spirit*. Eugene, OR: Wipf & Stock, 1998.

———. "The Intrusion and the Decalogue." *Westminster Theological Journal* 16/1 (1953) 1–22.

———. *Kingdom Prologue: Genesis Foundations for a Covenantal Worldview*. Overland Park, KS: Two Age, 2000.

———. "Space and Time in the Genesis Cosmogony," *Perspective on Science and the Christian Faith* 48/1 (1996) 2–15.

———. *The Structure of Biblical Authority*. Eugene, OR: Wipf & Stock, 1997.

———. *Treaty of the Great King: The Covenant Structure of Deuteronomy: Studies and Commentary.* Eugene, OR: Wipf & Stock, 2012.
Köstenberger, Andreas J., and Richard D. Patterson. *Biblical Interpretation: Exploring the Hermeneutical Triad of History, Literature, and Theology.* Grand Rapids: Kregel Academic, 2011.
Kugel, James L. *The Bible As It Was.* Cambridge: Harvard University Press, 1997.
———. *The Great Poems of the Bible: A Reader's Companion with New Translations.* New York: Free Press, 1999.
———. *How to Read the Bible: A Guide to Scripture, Then and Now.* New York: Free Press, 2008.
———. *The Idea of Biblical Poetry.* New Haven: Yale University Press, 1981.
Ladd, George Eldon. *A Commentary on the Revelation of John.* Grand Rapids: Eerdmans, 1979.
———. *A Theology of the New Testament.* Grand Rapids: Eerdmans, 1993.
LaRondelle, Hans K. *Our Creator Redeemer: An Introduction to Biblical Covenant Theology.* Berrien Springs, MI: Andrews University Press, 2005.
Letham, Robert. "'Not a Covenant of Works in Disguise' (Herman Bavinck) The Place of the Mosaic Covenant in Redemptive History." *Mid-America Journal of Theology* 24 (2013) 143–77.
Lillback, Peter A., ed. *Seeing Christ in All of Scripture: Hermeneutics at Westminster Theological Seminary.* Philadelphia: Westminster Seminary Press, 2016.
Lillback, Peter A., and Richard B. Gaffin Jr., eds. *Thy Word Is Still Truth: Essential Writings on the Doctrine of Scripture from the Reformation to Today.* Phillipsburg, NJ: P&R, 2013.
Longman III, Tremper, and Daniel G. Reid. *God Is a Warrior.* Grand Rapids: Zondervan, 1995.
Lunn, Nicholas P. "Patterns in the Old Testament Metanarrative: Human Attempts to Fulfill Divine Promises." *Westminster Theological Journal* 72/2 (2010) 237–49.
Machen, J. Gresham. *Christianity & Liberalism.* Grand Rapids: Eerdmans, 2009.
———. *The New Testament: An Introduction to Its Literature and History.* Edited by W. John Cook. Edinburgh: The Banner of Truth Trust, 1997.
———. *The Origin of Paul's Religion.* Grand Rapids: Eerdmans, 1976.
Marshall, I. Howard. *New Testament Theology.* Downers Grove, IL: InterVarsity, 2004.
Martinez, Florentino Garcia, ed. *The Dead Sea Scrolls Translated: The Qumran Texts in English.* Translated by Wilfred G. E. Watson. Grand Rapids: Eerdmans, 1996.
Marx, Karl, and Friedrich Engels. *The Communist Manifesto.* New York: International, 2016.
McCarthy, Dennis J. *Old Testament Covenant: A Survey of Current Opinions.* Richmond, VA: John Knox, 1972.
McComiskey, Thomas E. *The Covenant of Promise: A Theology of the Old Testament Covenants.* Grand Rapids: Baker, 1985.
Mendenhall, George E. "Ancient Oriental and Biblical Law." *The Biblical Archaeologist* 17/2 (1954) 26–46.
———. "Covenant Forms in Israelite Tradition." *The Biblical Archaeologist* 17/3 (1954) 50–76.
———. *Law and Covenant in Israel and the Ancient Near East.* Pittsburgh: The Biblical Colloquium, 1955.
Meyer, Marvin, ed. *The Nag Hammadi Scriptures: The Revised and Updated Translation.* New York: HarperCollins, 2007.

BIBLIOGRAPHY

Middleton, J. Richard. *A New Heaven and a New Earth: Reclaiming Biblical Eschatology.* Grand Rapids: Baker Academic, 2014.

Millard, A. R. "A New Babylonian Genesis Story." *Tyndale Bulletin* 18 (1967) 3–18.

Morgan, Christopher W., and Robert A. Peterson, eds. *Hell under Fire: Modern Scholarship Reinvents Eternal Punishment.* Grand Rapids: Zondervan, 2004.

Murray, John. *The Covenant of Grace: A Biblico-Theological Study.* Phillipsburg: P&R, 1988.

Nestle, Eberhard, and Kurt Aland. eds. *Novum Testamentum Graece.* 27th ed. Stuttgart: Deutsche Bibelgesellschaft, 1993.

Niehaus, Jeffrey J. "Covenant and Narrative, God and Time." *Journal of the Evangelical Theological Society* 53/3 (2010) 535–59.

Noth, Martin. *Exodus: A Commentary.* Translated by J. S. Bowden. In *The Old Testament Library.* Philadelphia: Westminster, 1962.

———. *The History of Israel.* Translated by P. R. Ackroyd. New York: Harper & Row, 1960.

———. *The Laws in the Pentateuch and Other Studies.* Translated by D. R. Ap-Thomas. London: SCM, 1984.

Olinger, Danny E., ed. *A Geerhardus Vos Anthology: Biblical and Theological Insights Alphabetically Arranged.* Phillipsburg, NJ: P&R, 2005.

Owen, John. *Biblical Theology: The History of Theology from Adam to Christ.* Translated by Stephen P. Westcott. Pittsburg: Soli Deo Gloria, 2007.

Peterson, Robert A. *Hell on Trial: The Case for Eternal Punishment.* Phillipsburg, NJ: P&R, 1995.

Philo. *The Works of Philo: New Updated Edition.* Translated by C. D. Yonge. Peabody, MA: Hendrickson, 2011.

Pink, Arthur W. *The Divine Covenants.* Grand Rapids: Baker, 1975.

Pinnock, Clark. "The Destruction of the Finally Impenitent." *Criswell Theological Review* 4/2 (1990) 243–59.

Poythress, Vern S. *God Centered Biblical Interpretation.* Phillipsburg, NJ: P&R, 1999.

———. *The Returning King: A Guide to the Book of Revelation.* Phillipsburg, NJ: P&R, 2000.

———. *Understanding Dispensationalists.* Phillipsburg, NJ: P&R, 1993.

Pritchard, James B., ed. *The Ancient Near East: An Anthology of Texts & Pictures.* Princeton: Princeton University Press, 2011.

Rahlfs, Alfred, and Robert Hanhart, eds. *Septuaginta.* Stuttgart: Deutsche Bibelgesellschaft, 2006.

Ramm, Bernard L. *The Christian View of Science and Scripture.* Grand Rapids: Eerdmans, 1979.

Ramsey, D. Patrick. "In Defense of Moses: A Confessional Critique of Kline and Karlberg." *Westminster Theological Journal* 66 (2004) 373–400.

Reymond, Robert L. *A New Systematic Theology of the Christian Faith.* Nashville: Thomas Nelson, 1998.

Riddlebarger, Kim. *A Case for Amillennialism: Understanding the End Times.* Grand Rapids: Baker Books, 2003.

Ridderbos, Herman N. *The Coming of the Kingdom.* Translated by H. de Jongste. Edited by Raymond O. Zorn. Phillipsburg, NJ: P&R, 1962.

———. *Paul: An Outline of His Theology.* Translated by John Richard De Witt. Grand Rapids: Eerdmans, 1990.

———. *Paul and Jesus.* Translated by David H. Freeman. Phillipsburg, NJ: P&R, 2002.

---. *When the Time Had Fully Come: Studies in New Testament Theology.* Grand Rapids: Eerdmans, 1982.

Ritschl, Albrecht. *Three Essays.* Translated by Philip Hefner. Eugene, OR: Wipf & Stock, 2005.

Robertson, O. Palmer. *The Christ of the Covenants.* Phillipsburg, NJ: P&R, 1980.

---. "Genesis 15:6: New Covenant Expositions of an Old Covenant Text." *Westminster Theological Journal* 42 (1980) 259–89.

---. *The Israel of God: Yesterday, Today, and Tomorrow.* Phillipsburg, NJ: P&R, 2000.

Robinson, James M. *The Gospel of Jesus: A Historical Search for the Original Good News.* New York: HarperCollins, 2005.

---. *Jesus: According to the Earliest Witness.* Minneapolis, MN: Fortress, 2007.

Russell, James Stuart. *The Parousia: The New Testament Doctrine of Christ's Second Coming.* Bradford, PA: International Preterist Association, 2003.

Ryrie, Charles C. *Basic Theology: A Popular Systematic Guide to Understanding Biblical Truth.* Chicago: Moody, 1999.

---. *Dispensationalism.* Chicago: Moody, 2007.

---. *The Ryrie Study Bible: ESV.* Chicago: Moody, 2011.

Sanders, E. P. "The Covenant as a Soteriological Category and the Nature of Salvation in Palestinian and Hellenistic Judaism." In *Jews, Greeks and Christians: Religious Cultures in Late Antiquity,* edited by Robert Hamerton-Kelly and Robin Scroggs, 11–44. Leiden, 1976.

---. *Jesus and Judaism.* Philadelphia: Fortress, 1985.

---. *Jewish Law from Jesus to the Mishnah: Five Studies.* London: SCM /Philadelphia: Trinity, 1990.

---. *Paul.* Oxford / New York: Oxford University Press, 1992.

---. *Paul and Palestinian Judaism.* Philadelphia: Fortress, 1977.

---. *Paul, the Law and the Jewish People.* Philadelphia: Fortress, 1983.

Saucy, Robert L. *The Case for Progressive Dispensationalism: The Interface between Dispensational & Non-dispensational Theology.* Grand Rapids: Zondervan, 1993.

Schweitzer, Albert. *The Mystery of the Kingdom of God: The Secret of Jesus' Messiahship and Passion.* Translated by Walter Lowrie. New York: Dodd, Mead, 1914.

---. *The Quest of the Historical Jesus.* Translated by W. Montgomery. Mineola, NY: Dover, 2005.

Scofield, Cyrus I., ed. *The New Scofield Reference Bible. The Holy Bible Containing the Old and New Testaments. Authorized King James Version,* edited by E. Schuyler English. New York: Oxford, 1967.

---, ed. *The Scofield Reference Bible. The Holy Bible Containing the Old and New Testaments. Authorized Version.* New York: Oxford, 1917.

Smick, Elmer B. "The Psalms as Response to God's Covenant Love: Theological Observations." In *Creator, Redeemer, Consummator: A Festschrift For Meredith G. Kline,* edited by Howard Griffith and John H. Muether, 77–86. Greenville, SC: Reformed Academic, 2000.

Sohn, Seock-Tae. *The Divine Election of Israel.* Grand Rapids: Eerdmans, 1991.

---. *YHWH, The Husband of Israel: The Metaphor of Marriage between YHWH and Israel.* Eugene, OR: Wipf & Stock, 2002.

Stek, John. "'Covenant' Overload in Reformed Theology." *Calvin Theological Seminary* 29 (1994)12–41.

BIBLIOGRAPHY

Turretin, Francis. *Institutes of Elenctic Theology.* 3 vols. Translated by George Musgrave Giger and edited by James T. Dennison Jr. Phillipsburg, NJ: P&R, 1992–1997.

VanDrunen, David. *A Biblical Case for Natural Law.* In *Studies in Christian Social Ethics and Economic.* No. 1. Grand Rapids: Action Institute, 2006.

Vangemeren, Willem. *The Progress of Redemption: The Story of Salvation from Creation to the New Jerusalem.* Grand Rapids: Baker Books, 1995.

Van Til, Cornelius. *Common Grace and the Gospel.* Phillipsburg, NJ: P&R, 1972.

———. *The Defense of the Faith.* Phillipsburg, NJ: P&R, 1967.

———. *In Defense of the Faith: Christian Theistic Ethics.* Vol. 3. Phillipsburg, NJ: P&R, 1980.

Venema, Cornelis P. "The Law of Moses: Not a Disguised Covenant of Works." *The Confessional Presbyterian* 8 (2012) 212–27.

———. "The Mosaic Covenant: A Republication of the Covenant of Works?" *Mid-America Journal of Theology* 21 (2010) 35–101.

von Rad, Gerhard. *Genesis: A Commentary.* In *The Old Testament Library.* Philadelphia: Westminster, 1972.

———. *Holy War in Ancient Israel.* Translated and edited by Marva J. Dawn. Grand Rapids:Eerdmans, 1991.

———. *Theologie Des Alten Testaments.* Band I and II. München: Chr. Kaiser Verlag,1958 & 1965.

———. *Old Testament Theology.* 2 vols. Translated by D. M. G. Stalker. New York: Harper & Row, 1962, 1965.

Vos, Geerhardus. *Biblical Theology: Old and New Testaments.* Grand Rapids: Eerdmans, 1988.

———. *The Eschatology of the Old Testament.* Edited by James T. Dennison Jr. Phillipsburg, NJ: P&R, 2001.

———. *Grace and Glory: Sermons Preached in the Chapel of Princeton Theological Seminary.* Carlisle, PA: The Banner of Truth Trust, 1994.

———. *The Pauline Eschatology.* Phillipsburg: P&R, 1994.

———. *Redemptive History and Biblical Interpretation.* Edited by Richard B. Gaffin, Jr. Phillipsburg: P&R, 1980.

———. *Reformed Dogmatics: Theology Proper.* Vol. 1. Translated and edited by Richard B. Gaffin, Jr. Bellingham, WA: Lexham, 2014.

———. *The Teaching of the Epistle to the Hebrews.* Edited by Johannes G. Vos. Phillipsburg, NJ: P&R, 1956.

———. *The Teaching of Jesus: Concerning the Kingdom of God and the Church.* Eugene, OR: Wipf & Stock, 1998.

Waltke, Bruce K. *An Old Testament Theology: An Exegetical, Canonical, and Thematic Approach.* Grand Rapids: Zondervan, 2007.

Weinfeld, Moshe. "The Covenant of Grant in the Old Testament and in the Ancient Near East." *Journal of the American Oriental Society* 90 (1970) 184–203.

Wellhausen, Julius. *Prolegomena to the History of Israel: With a Reprint of the Article Israel from the "Encyclopedia Britannica."* Translated by J. Sutherland Black and Allan Menzies. Edinburgh: Adam & Charles Black, 1885.

———. *Deuteronomy and the Deuteronomic School.* Oxford University Press, 1972.

Wenham, Gordon J. *Genesis* 1—15. In *Word Biblical Commentary*, vol. 1. Waco:Word, 1987.

———. *Genesis* 16—50. In *Word Biblical Commentary*, vol. 2. Waco: Word, 1994.

Wenham, John. *Facing Hell: An Autobiography* 1913–1995. Paternoster, 1998.

Bibliography

Westerholm, Stephen. *Israel's Law and the Church's Faith: Paul and the Recent Interpreters.* Grand Rapids: Eerdmans, 1988.

———. *Perspectives Old and New on Paul: The "Lutheran" Paul and His Critics.* Grand Rapids: Eerdmans, 2004.

Whitcomb, John C. Jr., and Henry M. Morris. *The Genesis Flood: The Biblical Record and Its Scientific Implications.* Grand Rapids: Baker, 1979.

Williams, Michael D. *Far as the Curse Is Found: The Covenant Story of Redemption.* Phillipsburg, NJ: P&R, 2005.

Wright, N. Thomas. *The Climax of the Covenant: Christ and the Law in Pauline Theology.* Minneapolis, MN: Fortress, 1991.

———. "The Paul of History and the Apostle of Faith." *Tyndale Bulletin* 29 (1978) 61–88.

———. *Surprised by Hope: Rethinking Heaven, the Resurrection, and the Mission of the Church.* New York: HarperOne, 2008.

———. *What Saint Paul Really Said.* Grand Rapids: Eerdmans , 1997.

Young, Davis A. *The Biblical Flood: A Case Study of the Church's Response to Extrabiblical Evidence.* Grand Rapids: Paternoster, 1995.

Young, Edward. J. *Genesis 3: A Devotional and Expository Study.* Edinburgh / Carlisle: The Banner of Truth Trust, 1983.

———. *Studies in Genesis One.* Phillipsburg, NJ: P&R, 1964.

———. *The Study of Old Testament Theology.* London: James Clark, 1958.

———. *Thy Word Is Truth: Some Thoughts on the Biblical Doctrine of Inspiration.* Carlisle, PA: The Banner of Truth Trust, 1991.

Names Index

Allis, Oswald T., xxn15, 112n23
Arnold, Bill T., 3n4, 31n27, 36n6, 68n10, 69n12

Bahnsen, Greg L., 225, 229–30, 232–34, 241, 242n46
Barker, William S., 225n2, 229
Barth, Karl, xiiin1, xvii–xviii, 14n13
Bartholomew, Craig G., 13n11
Bartsch, Hans Werner, xviiin12, xixn13
Bateman, Herbert W., xxn15
Bavinck, Herman, xi, xiii, xiv, xvi, xviin8, 96n13, 164, 172n1, 173n2, 194n24, 202n27, 210, 211n36, 223
Beale, G. K., 14n12, 26n25, 169n30, 198n25
Bergquist, Randall A., 96n13
Berkhof, Louis, xiiin1
Beyer, Brian E., 3n4, 31n27, 36n6, 68n10, 69n12
Blaising, Craig A., xxn15
Bock, Darrell L., xxn15
Bruce, F. F., 66n7
Brunner, Emil, xiiin1
Bultmann, Rudolf, xvii–xix, 79n24, 182n13, 191n22
Busenitz, Irvin A., 33n2

Calvin, John, xx–xxi, 1n1, 3n3, 5n7, 8, 31n28, 36n7, 49–50, 50n17, 67n9, 71n17, 90n7, 96–97, 129, 191n21, 230n14
Carlson, Richard F., 18n18
Carson, D. A., 189n18
Chafer, Lewis Sperry, 210n35
Collins, C. John, 1n1, 14, 18n18
Collins, John J., 1n1, 33n2, 58n1, 65, 85n1, 125n30, 131n1, 133n3, 138n8, 142n13, 172n1, 178n7

Darby, John Nelson, xix
Darwin, Charles, xvii, 18n18

Dennison, James T., 96n13
Dillard, Raymond, 112n24
Dumbrell, William J., 1n1, 33n2, 58n1, 103n20, 131n1, 172n1
Durham, John I., 85n1

Edwards, David, 41n10
Edwards, Jonathan, xi, xxin19, 1n1, 33n2, 40–41, 58n1, 76n20, 85n1, 131n1, 140n10, 160n22, 180n8, 184n16, 205n30
Eichrodt, Walther, 124n28
Elam, Andrew, 96n13
Engels, Friedrich, xvii
Enns, Peter, 18

Ferry, Brenton C., 96n13
Fesko, J. V., 96n13, 98n16
Funk, Robert W., 181n11
Futato, Mark D., 3n2

Gaffin, Richard B., xivn4
Gage, Warren A., 39n8
Gentry, Peter J., 85n1, 88n5, 138n7, 173, 206n33
Godfrey, W. Robert, 225n2, 229
Golding, Peter, 1n1, 85n1, 131n1, 172n1
Goldsworthy, Graeme, 103n20
Gordon, T. David, 231, 233–34
Grudem, Wayne xix, 14n12, 168n29, 203n28, 206n32

Hagopian, David G., 3n2
Hahn, Scott W., 85n1, 90n6, 132n1, 133n3, 139n9, 141n11, 151n15, 172n1, 190n20
Harris, Stephen L., 6n8
Harrison, Ronald K., 37n7
Hart, D. G., 96n13, 98n17
Hegel, G. W. F., xvii
Hegg, Timothy J., 12n10

Names Index

Heidel, Alexander, 3n4
Hillers, Delbert R., 12n10, 68n11
Hodge, Charles, xi, 98–99, 109–10, 129, 236
Hoekema, Anthony A., 165, 166n26, 166n27
Horton, Michael, 1n1, 33n2, 43n11, 71n16, 85n1, 132n1, 172n1, 182n12, 206n31
House, H. Wayne, 210n35
Hughes, Philip E., 41n10

Irons, Lee, 225n1

Jeon, Jeong Koo, ix–x, xxn15, xxn17, xxin21, 12n10, 67n9, 71n17, 96n13, 98n16, 98n17, 225n1, 227n6, 228n9, 230n13, 230n14, 232n20, 235n28
Johnson, Dennis E., 165n24
Jones, G. H., 79n23
Josephus, Flavius, 179n7

Kaiser, Walter C., 125n29
Kang, Sa-Moon, 79n23
Kant, Emmanuel, xvii
Karlberg, Mark W., 96n13, 225n1
Kim, Seyoon, 198n25
Kline, Meredith G., xi–xii, xv, xxi, 1n1, 3n2, 5n6, 13n10, 14n12, 21n20, 22, 23n23, 28n26, 33n2, 35–36, 43n11, 45n12, 47n14, 48n15, 52n20, 54n21, 58n1, 60n4, 68n11, 71n15–17, 75n19, 80n25, 83n27, 85n1, 88n5, 96n12, 96n13, 105n21, 112n23, 112n24, 118n25, 119n27, 132n1, 138, 143n14, 151, 172n1, 179n8, 180, 213n37, 214n38, 225–45
Kugel, James L., 94n11, 135n4, 141n12, 174n4

Ladd, George E., 167n28
LaRondelle, Hans K., 33n2, 172n1
Letham, Robert, 96n13
Lillback, Peter A., xiv
Longman, Tremper, 18n18, 79n23, 112n24, 238n36
Lunn, Nicholas P., 33n2, 58n1

Martinez, Florentino Garcia, 201n26
Marx, Karl, xvii
McCarthy, Dennis J., 13n10, 68n11, 88n5, 132n1
Mendenhall, George E., 13n10, 68n11
Meyer, Marvin, 181n11
Middleton, J. Richard, 167n28, 169
Millard, A. R., 3n4
Morgan, Christopher W., 41n10
Morris, Henry M., 37n7
Murray, John, 1n1, 33n2, 58n1, 71n17, 85n1, 132n1, 172n1, 230n14, 232

Niehaus, Jeffrey J., 58, 71n16
Noth, Martin, 85n1, 93n10, 111n23, 119n26

Olinger, Danny E., xxin20
Owen, John, xi, xxin19, 37n7

Peterson, Robert A., 41n10
Philo, 6n8, 94n11
Pinnock, Clark, 41n10
Poythress, Vern S., xxn15, xxii–xiii
Pritchard, James B., 3n4, 36n6, 68n10

Ramm, Bernard, 37n7
Ramsey, D. Patrick, 96n13
Reid, Daniel, 79n23, 238n36
Reimarus, Hermann, 182n11
Reymond, Robert L., 14n12
Ridderbos, Herman, 79n24, 172n1, 189n19, 230n14
Robertson, O. Palmer, 1n1, 20–21, 33, 45n12, 54n21, 58n1, 70n14, 85–86, 88n5, 132n1, 138n6, 153–54, 172n1, 210n35
Robinson, James M., 181n10, 216n39
Ryrie, Charles C., xx, 132, 155n18, 156n19, 159n21, 160, 175n5, 176n6

Sanders, E. P., 198n25
Saucy, Robert L., xx
Schweitzer, Albert, xvi, 158n20, 183n14, 187n17
Scofield, Cyrus I., xix
Smick, Elmer B., 225, 240n39
Stek, John, 13n11
Stott, John, 41n10

Turretin, Francis, xi, 14–15, 85n1, 86–87, 132n1, 172n1

VanDrunen, David, 43n11
Vangemeren, Willem, 58n1
Van Til, Cornelius, 96n13, 226–27, 230–34
Venema, Cornelis, 96n13
von Rad, Gerhard, 26n24, 45n12, 79n23, 125n29, 131n1, 205n30
Vos, Geerhardus, ix, xi, xxi–xiii, 1n1, 16–17, 27n26, 34n2, 58n1, 66n8, 72n18, 75n19, 85n1, 172n1, 222, 228n9, 230–34

Waltke, Bruce K., 1n1, 3n3, 3n4, 14n12, 18n18, 33n2, 36n5–7, 43n11, 46, 49n16, 54n21, 85n1, 88n5, 92n9, 111n23, 132n1, 172n1, 184n15
Warfield, Benjamin B., 98
Weinfeld, Moshe, 13n10, 71n16, 133n3
Wellhausen, Julius, 18n18

Names Index

Wellum, Stephen J., 85n1, 88n5, 138n7, 173, 206n33
Wenham, Gordon J., 1n1, 34n2, 50, 58n1
Wenham, John, 41n10
Whitcomb, John C., Jr., 37n7

Williams, Michael D., 1n1, 34n2, 45n12, 58n1, 63n5, 86n1, 132n1, 172n1
Wright, N. Thomas, 14, 41n10

Young, Davis A., 37n7
Young, Edward J., xiv, 23n22, 26, 112n23

Subject Index

Aaron, 100, 103–4, 110, 207
Abel, 163
    and Cain, 28–29, 52
Abraham (patriarch), 58, 77, 79, 81, 85, 93, 111, 114–16, 121, 128, 133, 153, 196–97, 209, 221–22
    believers as sons of, 60, 62–66, 82, 221, 243
    call of, xv, 58, 60–63
    called Abram, 60n3
    covenant with, *see* Abrahamic Covenant
    Jesus as Son/offspring of, 61–62, 64, 82, 166, 171, 190n20
    justification by faith of, 59, 62–67, 84, 182n12
    offspring/descendants of, 10, 11, 59–65, 71–73, 81, 84, 85, 93, 111, 128, 131, 133, 140, 175, 197, 201, 209, 212, 218, 221
    promises to, 59–66, 71–75, 77, 81–84, 85, 88, 92, 99, 105n21, 114, 117, 119, 121, 124, 133, 160, 190, 212, 220–21, 237
    sacrifice of Isaac, 59, 73, 79–84, 243
    type of Christ, 81–84
    as warrior, 71, 186
Abrahamic Covenant, xxiii, 12, 45, 58–84, 99, 103n20
    as blessing to all nations, 61–62, 63n5, 81–83, 190n20, 220
    community of, 65, 85, 121
    contrasted with Mosaic Covenant, 70–71, 86–88, 90n6, 105n21, 107–8, 114, 128, 150, 212
    as covenant of grace, 45, 59, 63, 71, 75, 83, 86–87, 108, 120, 130, 153, 170
    as covenant of royal grant, 12, 59, 67–73, 83, 105n21, 119–20, 124, 132–33, 138, 140, 170, 172, 181–82, 190
    and Davidic Covenant, 12, 132–33, 138, 140, 150–52, 170–72, 181–82, 190
    everlasting, 74–75, 100, 151–52, 170
    fulfilled in conquest, 77, 212, 215, 218
    fulfilled in Jesus Christ, 61–65, 82
    fulfilled in offspring, 73, 81
    fulfilled ultimately, 60–61, 77, 84, 170, 221
    and God's oath, 59, 60, 72–74, 83, 87–88, 92, 114–16, 120, 128, 153, 190, 237
    and land, 65–66, 71–72, 110, 116–17, 119, 121, 124, 128, 130, 131, 151, 160, 170, 237
    and Messiah, 59–65, 81–82, 84, 105n21, 151
    and New Covenant, 12, 174, 181–82, 221
    and Noahic Covenant, 12, 76, 170, 172, 181–82
    ratification ceremony of, 70n14, 71–74, 83, 87–89
    sealed with circumcision, 45, 66–67, 74–75, 107–8, 121–22
    and Sodom and Gomorrah, 59, 76–79, 84
    and theocratic kingdom, 60–61, 65, 72, 81, 150, 170–71, 212, 215, 218
Achan, 126, 238
Adam:
    contrasted with Christ, 14, 18–20, 36, 83n27, 98, 180, 182, 231
    covenantal head, 1, 13–15, 17, 32, 35, 180, 182
    historical, 18–20
    mature at creation, 8
    obedience of, 15–16, 36, 226, 229, 231, 248
    see also Adam and Eve; Adamic covenant of works
Adam and Eve:
    clothed by God, 25–26, 40
    commanded, 10–12, 17
    creation of, 2, 15
    cursed, 27–28
    dominion of, 103

267

Adam and Eve (*continued*)
    expulsion, 1–2, 17, 27–28, 33, 40, 52,
        248–49
    fall of, xv, xix, xxiii, 1–2, 9, 13–14, 16–17,
        19–20, 23–24, 26–29, 32, 34–36, 59–60,
        77, 90, 98–99, 103n20, 226–28, 233n20,
        235, 248–49
    God's grace towards, 25–26, 32, 40
    gospel proclaimed to, 63, 99
    in garden, 2, 9, 48, 247–48
    keeping Sabbath, 10–12
    priestly duty of, 21, 27
    saved by Christ, 188, 217, 249
    viceregency of, 2, 26
Adamic covenant of works, 1, 2, 12–15, 17, 20–
    21, 25, 28, 32, 85n2, 86n4, 98, 105, 140,
    143n14, 226, 229, 232, 233n20, 248
ancient Near East, xv
    battle bow, 45
    cosmogony, 3n4
    texts of, xxi, 31n27, 36, 58, 67–69
    treaties of, 12, 32, 34, 58–59, 67–69, 71–72,
        83, 86–87, 88, 112n24, 119–20, 128, 130
angels, 3, 7, 17, 24, 31n28, 38, 40, 42, 73, 76,
    77, 80, 92, 93, 156, 160n22, 163, 164,
    165, 179n7, 185, 193, 194, 203, 205n30,
    210n35, 212, 222, 224, 236n30, 247
animals/creatures, xxiii, 5, 32, 34, 37, 44, 54,
    75n19, 76, 135
    as clothing, 26, 40
    as food, 48–52, 57
    blood of, 49, 52–53, 70n14
    clean and unclean, 34, 47–52, 57
    man's dominion over, 47, 48, 49n16, 103n20
    on the Ark, 35, 37, 44–45, 48, 50, 168
    as sacrifices, 47, 49, 52, 67, 70n14
apologetics, presuppositional, 226, 230n14
archaeology, 58, 125n30
Ark, Noahic, 24, 30, 34–35, 37, 44, 47–48,
    78–79, 168–69, 218
    as kingdom of God, 35–36, 41–43, 47,
        49n15, 50, 52, 57, 203, 229
    as salvation, 35, 39–40
ark of the Covenant, 95, 121, 124n28, 137–38,
    143–44, 213n37
Arminianism, 199n25
Assyrians, 24, 148–49, 154
    treaties of, 69–70, 112n24
atonement, 25–26, 52–53, 80–81, 178, 180,
    232n20, 243

Babylon, 61, 70, 105n21, 106, 140n10, 147, 150,
    154–55, 175–78, 179n7, 180, 217
    texts of, 3n4, 36n6

baptism, 37n7, 40, 45, 200–206, 218
    of Jesus, 172, 182–85, 217
Baptists, 203n28, 206n32, 206n33
Barth, and neo-orthodoxy, 14n13
belief, xvi, 6, 25, 53, 63, 65–66, 86, 89, 157,
    163–64, 185, 192, 197–98, 205–6; *see
    also* faith
believers (Christian), xiii–xv, xix, xxi, 4, 17, 20,
    27, 39, 46, 51, 55, 57n23, 62, 64, 66–67,
    74, 80n25, 86, 87, 161, 163–67, 173,
    198–200, 206n32, 206n33, 214n38, 217,
    219, 220–24, 236, 243
    Gentile, 54, 66
    Old Covenant, 67, 96–97, 129, 206n33
Bible, ix–x, xii–xxiii, 4, 8n9, 18n18, 23, 33–34,
    41n10, 58–59, 66n8, 76, 87, 135n4, 165,
    167n28, 172, 178n7, 199n25, 230n14,
    239; *see also* Scriptures, Word of God
biblical theology, ix, xix, xxi–xxii, 14n12, 21n20,
    26n25, 34, 43n11, 45n12, 47n14, 48,
    75n19, 83n27, 225, 227, 228n9, 230n14,
    231–32, 234–35, 242, 244n57
blessings:
    common grace/earthly, xxi, 2, 26, 28, 30, 35,
        43–44, 134, 154, 171, 209
    heavenly/redemptive, 2, 13, 16–17, 19–20,
        59, 61–62, 64, 73–74, 81–82, 83n27, 84,
        104, 107–8, 112, 114, 140, 151, 166, 169,
        171, 176, 194, 197–98, 200, 210n35, 220,
        223, 226–27, 233n20, 237, 242–43, 248
    as covenant sanctions, 2, 12, 15, 32, 39, 68,
        87, 88, 90n6, 94–97, 100, 102, 104–5,
        107, 111–13, 117, 120, 129, 141–42,
        149–50, 170, 180n8, 227, 230–31, 235,
        237, 240, 245n58
blood, 12, 54, 75n19, 113, 155
    of animal sacrifices, 49, 67, 89–91, 188, 207
    atoning, 52–53, 90, 188
    of Christ/of New Covenant, 6, 49, 53,
        90–91, 96, 163, 188–89, 197, 205n30,
        207, 217
    menstrual, 107
    on doorposts, 207
    prohibition against consuming, 49, 52–54,
        201n26
    as ratification of covenant, 67, 69, 70n14,
        71, 89–91, 96n12, 188–89, 207, 217
    sprinkling of, 70n14, 90–91, 163

Cain, 30; *see also* Abel: and Cain
Caleb, *see* Joshua.
Canaan, 16, 60–61, 65, 83, 87, 103–4, 140,
    151–52, 170, 215, 229
    and Garden of Eden, 77, 103n20

Subject Index

conquest of, 58, 78–79, 83n27, 93, 97, 103–4, 108, 111, 115–16, 119, 121–28, 130, 131, 133, 152, 211–15, 218–19, 237–40
and intrusion ethics, 237–40
capital punishment, 34, 53, 54–57, 108, 242
Christ Jesus (Jesus, Jesus Christ):
anointed, 184–85
ascension of, xviii, 40, 51, 54, 61, 160–61, 171, 189, 195, 201–2, 214, 216
baptism of, 172, 182–85, 217
before Pilate, 158–59
believers justified by faith in, xxi, 26, 53, 61–62, 66n7, 86, 89, 128, 173, 198–99
blood of, 49, 53, 90–91, 163, 188–89, 197, 205n30, 207, 217
contrasted with Adam, 14, 18–20, 36, 83n27, 98, 180, 182, 231
covenant community "in Christ," ix, xv, 19, 31, 53, 57, 59, 62, 64–65, 74, 79, 81, 84, 91, 97–98, 140, 162–63, 198–200, 208, 222, 226, 239, 245
death of, xviii, 18–20, 39–40, 51, 54, 61, 66n7, 74, 81, 90–92, 96–97, 140, 159–63, 171–73, 180–82, 187, 189, 190n20, 191, 198, 208, 214, 217–18, 220–22
defeat of Satan, 138, 140, 165, 169, 172, 181–87, 193, 194n24, 196–97, 214, 217
disciples of, xviii–xix, 40, 51, 55–56, 82, 157–59, 161, 167n28, 185, 191–95, 202, 206, 214–19, 239–40
earthly ministry of, 40, 55–56, 61, 157–58, 172, 181–88, 191–93, 217
exaltation of, 5, 7, 110, 132, 153–56, 160–66, 171, 189, 195–97, 203, 214–18, 222–23, 228
forgiveness through, xiii, 26, 34, 59, 73, 80, 90–91, 184–85, 188, 189n18, 189n19, 191n22, 194, 197, 198n25, 206n33, 207, 245
fulfilled covenant of works/Mosaic law, 19, 49, 97–98, 101, 129, 140, 173n2, 180–81
fulfilled Scripture, xiv–xv, xxi, 61–64, 79–82, 97, 101, 133, 151, 154, 156, 159, 170–72, 193, 195, 208, 217
gospel of, 5, 18, 36n5, 39, 55, 62, 64, 96, 161, 172, 184, 201, 203, 215, 217, 221
High Priest, 188, 190–91
identity of, 7, 79, 82, 101, 154
incarnation/first coming of, xviii, 20, 101, 132–33, 160, 166n27, 171, 179, 181, 197, 216–17, 223, 228–29
instituted Lord's Supper, 188–89, 200, 206–8, 218
instituted water baptism, 45, 200, 218
involved in creation, 3n3, 5–7, 223
Judge, 169, 179n8, 194n24, 214
King, 132, 138, 156–67, 171, 179n8, 184–85, 194, 199, 214, 233, 243–44
last Adam, 20, 180–82, 249
Lord, 7, 19–20, 25, 53, 57n23, 64, 82, 99, 158–59, 161–62, 164, 166, 171, 175n5, 187, 193–97, 199–200, 218–19, 223–24, 239–40
Mediator, 32, 39, 45, 55, 81, 90–2, 97–98, 162–63, 172, 180, 188–89, 206, 217, 219–20
Messiah, xiv, 44, 59, 61, 73, 79–80, 82, 90, 92, 96n12, 101, 125, 129, 133, 151, 153–59, 160–64, 171, 172, 174, 179–80, 183n14, 184, 186–88, 194n24, 200–1, 208–9, 210n35, 217, 219, 222
obedience of, 19–20, 36, 39, 81, 83, 189, 193, 196–200, 214n38, 231, 248
pre-incarnation of, 205n30
prophet, 78, 183n13, 184n16, 187, 191–95, 208–9
rejected by the Jews, xiv, 5, 61–62, 64, 157–58, 172–73, 186, 191–92, 195–97, 208–10, 218
resurrection of, 18, 20, 39–40, 51, 54, 61, 66n7, 159–63, 171–73, 181, 189, 191–204, 214–22
revelation of, xiii–xv, 5, 7, 14n13, 24, 63–64, 164, 197, 203
righteousness of, 26, 39–40, 140, 180, 182n12, 203, 249
sacrifice of, 44, 49, 53, 59, 73, 80–1, 84, 92, 96–97, 99, 162, 179n8, 189–91, 199n25, 207–8, 218, 228, 243
salvation through, 20, 32, 53, 61–62, 74, 81, 84, 97, 100, 140, 179, 182n12, 198–200, 210–11, 214, 218–19
Second Coming of/return of/Parousia, 24–25, 41–42, 46, 59–61, 75, 78, 110, 125n29, 125n30, 130, 132–33, 155n18, 160–61, 164–67, 169, 171, 176n6, 179–80, 198n25, 208–11, 214–24
sinlessness of, 36, 39, 79, 81, 83n27, 180, 189
Son, xviii, 4–7, 24, 42, 199, 214–15
son of Abraham, 61–64, 82, 140, 166, 171, 190n20
son of David, 61, 132, 138n7, 140, 153–63, 166–67, 170–71, 182n12, 184–87, 197, 243
Son of God, xv, 5–6, 18, 40, 64, 79–80, 82, 96n12, 156, 158, 162–63, 172, 182–86, 190, 192–97, 199–200, 208–9, 217–18, 222–24

269

Subject Index

Christ Jesus (*continued*)
    Son of Man, 24–25, 42–43, 59, 63, 78–82, 84, 161, 183n14, 192–93, 228, 240
    Spirit of, 39, 199
    sufferings of, 39, 189n19, 195, 203
    teachings of, 24, 42–43, 55–56, 78, 82, 101, 169, 185, 189n19, 191–93, 214–19
    temptation of, 185–87
    triumphal entry of, 157, 172, 186–87, 193–94, 208
    types of, 36, 39–40, 80, 83, 92n8, 96, 99, 130, 133, 138, 140, 153–55, 159, 169–71, 231, 235, 243, 245
    virgin birth of, 156, 172, 181–82
church, 40–41, 85, 92, 192
    Body/Bride of Christ, 6, 164, 245
    discipline, 111, 242
    distinct from Israel, xix–xx, 132n2, 156n19, 173
    early, 5, 53–54, 63–64, 161–62, 164, 180n8, 181n11, 202n27, 203, 222
    ethics, 160
    mission of, 55
    modern, xvi, xix, xxiii
    New Covenant, 51, 55, 160, 180n8, 206, 210–11, 214n38, 220–21, 226, 228, 243
    persecution of, 223
    and state, 56, 60n4, 231, 234–35, 242–43
circumcision, 236n30
    and Abrahamic covenant, 45, 66–67, 74, 107, 121
    in early church times, 53
    at Gilgal, 108, 121–22, 130
    and holy war, 122–23,
    and Mosaic covenant, 107–9, 129, 207
    as sacrament, 45, 200, 218
commandment(s) (laws of God), 16, 49, 51, 53–54, 81–82, 83n27, 91, 101–2, 106–7, 110, 112, 117, 126, 131, 135, 142, 145–46, 148, 151, 155, 214n38, 248
    in garden, 2, 10–12, 17, 22, 25, 27
    see also Ten Commandments
common grace, 9, 28–31, 34, 41, 55–56, 60, 209n34, 213, 225–29, 233–37, 239–42, 244
    covenant of, xv, xxiii, 1–2, 9, 20–21, 27–34, 41, 43–48, 52, 54–57, 60, 75, 226–27
    war of, 59, 78, 93, 116, 124–25, 238–39
conquest of Canaan, *see* Canaan
consummation (final), xv, xix, xxii–xxiii, 12, 19, 59n2, 99, 103n20, 171, 176, 179n8, 180, 223, 225–29, 235, 237n33, 240, 242, 244–45

Covenant(s):
    Abrahamic, xxiii, 12, 45, 58–84, 86–88, 90n6, 92, 99–100, 103n20, 105n21, 107–10, 114–21, 124, 128, 130–33, 138, 140, 150–53, 160, 170–74, 181–82, 190, 212, 215, 218, 220–21, 237
    blood of, 70n14, 90–91, 163, 188, 189n19, 207, 217
    of common grace, xv, xxiii, 1–2, 9, 20–21, 27–34, 41, 43–48, 52, 54–57, 60, 75, 226–27
    in creation, 1–32, 138n7, 220
    Davidic, xxiii, 10, 12, 100, 131–73, 182, 190, 197, 208, 223
    Deuteronomic, 11, 90n6, 118, 119n27
    Edenic covenant of works, 1, 2, 10, 12, 14–16, 20–22, 25, 32, 85n2, 180, 182
    everlasting, 75, 100–1, 129, 142, 151–52, 170, 176
    of grace, xxi, xxiii, 1–2, 14–15, 19, 20–35, 40, 44–46, 57, 58–59, 70n14, 71, 75, 83, 85–87, 89–90, 92–93, 96–99, 104, 107–12, 120, 128–30, 173, 180n8, 188, 190, 226–28, 230
    Mosaic/Sinaitic, xxiii, 11–16, 22–25, 45, 50–53, 68, 70–71, 75, 85–130, 138n7, 140–53, 162, 170–83, 188, 190, 209, 212–13, 214n38, 217, 232, 245n58
    New, xxiii, 12, 36, 39, 45, 49–58, 62, 74–76, 81–83, 87, 90–92, 96–98, 110–11, 132, 151, 162–63, 172–219, 220–21, 228–32, 236, 239, 242–43
    Noahic, 12, 23–24, 30, 33–57, 75–76, 132, 138, 170, 172, 182
    ratification of, 65–74, 83, 87–88, 93, 96n12, 112–14, 117, 119, 128, 150, 179n8, 183, 187–90, 217, 240
    renewal of, 11, 33–34, 57, 68, 75n19, 87, 105n21, 111–15, 118–20, 127, 130, 149–50, 174n4, 213, 245n58
    of royal grant, 12, 34–35, 36n4, 57, 59, 65, 67, 71, 83, 119–20, 124, 130, 132–33, 138, 140–41, 170, 172, 181–82, 187, 190–91, 217
    sanctions of, xv, 2, 12, 15–16, 32, 68, 105n21, 112–13, 120, 141, 142n13, 150, 170, 180n8, 227, 230n14, 235–37, 241–42, 245
    of works, 1–2, 10–22, 25, 28, 32, 59n2, 85–87, 96–99, 105, 129, 138, 140, 143n14, 180, 182, 226, 228, 232
Covenant community:
    Abrahamic, 74, 77–79, 84, 85, 221
    Adamic, 28–30

Subject Index

Church/New Covenant, xviii, xx, 39, 45, 53–55, 74, 79, 162, 173, 189n18, 206n33, 208, 216, 220–23, 243
    Edenic, 10–12, 21
    of Israel, 8–17, 22, 24, 50–53, 65, 70–71, 75, 78–79, 87–97, 100–5, 111–18, 120–21, 124–36, 142–54, 157, 162–63, 170–78, 183, 200, 204, 206n32, 207, 211–15, 237–39, 240n39, 242–44
    Noahic, 23, 30, 34–35, 38–39, 41–45, 50, 79, 168, 203, 218
creation, xiv, xv, xix, xxii–xxiii, 1–21, 59n2, 77, 86n2, 99, 103n20, 164, 169, 188, 226, 228, 233n20
    covenant of, 138n7, 220
    days of, 2–3, 8–9, 11–12, 109
    ex nihilo, 2–4
    New, 168n29, 169n30
    redemption of, 168n28, 223
Creator, xiii–xv, 1–21, 23, 30–32, 34, 38, 43, 46, 47, 48n15, 49, 54, 60n4, 77, 162, 168, 223, 235, 243
crucifixion, xviii, 18, 39, 61, 159, 162, 172, 173, 179, 182, 187, 188, 190n20, 191, 193, 195, 200, 206, 208, 217, 218; *see also* Christ Jesus: death
cultural mandate, 27, 47–49
curses, *see* blessings: as covenant sanctions; judgments of God
Cyrus (king of Persia), 244

Daniel, 82, 176–80, 217
Darwinian evolution, xvii
David (king), 61, 103n20, 154, 170, 197
    anointed, 132–34, 136, 170, 184
    Christ as Son of, 61, 153–58, 160, 162, 166–67, 170–71, 184–87, 197, 199, 222–23, 243
    conquers Jerusalem, 136–38
    and Goliath, 122–23
    as prophet, 157–59, 183n13, 184n16, 190–91, 195
    as psalmist, 9, 151, 157, 159, 170, 190–91, 195, 239
    and temple, 143–44
    as type of Christ, 138, 140
    see also Davidic Covenant; Davidic Kingdom; Davidic Messiah
Davidic Covenant, xxiii, 10, 12, 100, 131–36, 138–46, 151–57, 160, 165–73, 182, 190, 197, 208, 223
Davidic Kingdom, 131–33, 140, 142–43, 145–60, 163, 166–68, 170–71, 208

Davidic Messiah, 153–64, 175–76, 184–87, 197
Day of the Lord, 22–25, 32, 124n28, 213n37, 219, 224, 248
Dead Sea Scrolls, 179n7
Decalogue (Ten Commandments), 11, 17, 75, 88, 91–92, 95, 236, 238–44
demythologization, xviii–xix
Deuteronomic Covenant, 11, 90n6, 118, 119n27
Deuteronomy (Book of), 90n6, 103n20, 111–12, 114, 118, 119n26, 125n30, 130, 135n4, 138n8, 141n12, 142n13, 185–86
diaspora of Christians, 31, 162–63, 220–23
diaspora of Old Covenant community, 148–49, 162
dispensationalism, xix–xx, 58, 86, 132–33, 153–54, 155n18, 156n19, 159n21, 160, 171, 175n5, 176n6, 210, 211n36
divided kingdom of Israel, 24, 146–49, 152–55, 170, 174
Domitian (emperor), 164

earth, age of, 8
Edenic covenant of works, 1, 2, 10, 12, 14–16, 20–22, 25, 32, 85n2, 180, 182
election/elect, 29, 64, 87, 175–76, 206, 209, 232n20, 239
eschatology/eschatological (concerning the end), xiv, xx–xxi, xxiii, 12–13, 15–17, 41–42, 55, 78, 107, 129–30, 135n4, 163, 183n14, 205, 213–19, 220–22, 227–45
    blessings, 13, 16, 20, 107, 226–27, 233n20, 235, 237, 242–45
    judgment/curses, xv, 2, 23, 32, 41, 76, 78, 80n25, 84, 107, 116–17, 213n37, 227, 235, 237–42
    Kingdom of God, xiii, xv, 2, 39, 82, 132–33, 160–71, 184, 194, 197–98, 200, 216–19, 224, 226–45
ethics, 80n25, 160, 232; *see also* intrusion ethics
evangelical(s)/evangelicalism, xix, xx, 3n2, 8n9, 18, 41n10, 51, 55, 110, 167, 238n36
evangelical mission, missionaries, xi, xvi, xix, 31, 55, 161–62, 211, 214–15, 217, 219, 220–23
    God as missionary, 63
    of Paul, 63, 66, 149, 196
evangelism, 63, 161, 217–19, 222–23
existentialism/existential theology, xiiin1, xviii–xix, 182n13, 191n22
Exodus of Israel, , 41, 109, 111, 118, 121, 144, 152, 200, 204–7, 218
Ezekiel (prophet), 175–76, 179n7

Subject Index

faith, xiv–xviii, 4, 16n16, 25–26, 29, 36n5, 37n7, 39, 59–67, 72n18, 80n25, 83n27, 84, 89, 90, 99, 112n23, 125n30, 128, 162–63, 173, 176, 182n12, 198n25, 199, 206n23, 210n35, 211n36, 221, 232n20, 239–43, 247; *see also* belief
fall of man, xv, xix, xxiii, 1–2, 9, 13–14, 16–17, 19–20, 23–24, 26–29, 32, 34–36, 59–60, 77, 90, 98–99, 103n20, 226–28, 233n20, 235, 248–49
Flood:
    as judgment, 8, 23, 30–1, 33–52, 57, 75–76, 78, 79n23, 168–69, 203, 206n32, 218
    myths, 3n4, 36n6
    universal nature of, 23, 34, 36–38, 78, 203
food laws, 51, 54, 100; *see also* blood

Garden of Eden, 1–2, 9–23, 26–29, 32, 33, 36, 40, 48, 49n16, 52, 63, 77, 83n27, 85n2, 103n20, 182, 229, 235, 247–48
Gentile Christians, 53–54, 62–63, 66, 175, 183n13, 209–11, 214–17, 241
Gentiles, 63–64, 66, 84, 149, 184, 193, 208, 241
glory of God, 1, 4–9, 20–23, 31, 41, 42, 47, 60, 62, 65, 72–74, 81–82, 88–89, 93–94, 102, 104, 125n30, 129, 144, 146, 151–52, 158n20, 160n22, 161, 164, 183–84, 196, 214, 223–29, 233, 236–37, 241, 244–45, 246–48
Gnosticism, 181
God the Father:
    and Abrahamic Covenant, 58–84
    and Covenant of Creation, 1–32
    covenant lawsuit of, 13, 16, 51, 70, 104, 122, 142, 147, 150, 153, 173–77, 209–10, 218, 240, 245n58
    Creator, xiii–xv, 1–21, 23, 30–32, 34, 38, 43, 46, 47, 48n15, 49, 54, 60n4, 77, 162, 168, 223, 235, 243
    and Davidic Covenant, 131–71
    and Mosaic Covenant, 85–130
    and New Covenant, 172–219
    and Noahic Covenants, 33–57
    oaths of, 59–60, 67, 72–74, 81, 83, 87–89, 92, 104, 106, 112–17, 120, 128, 138–40, 143, 151n15, 153, 159, 189–91, 195, 237
    in theophany, 4, 9, 21–23, 72–73, 88–89, 93–94, 129, 183
    triunity of, xvi, 1, 4–5, 7, 13, 27, 31, 36n5, 79, 100, 169, 182–83, 199, 215, 224
gospel, xiii, xvii, xx, 2, 5, 14n13, 16, 18, 25, 27, 32, 36n5, 40, 43, 51, 55, 59n2, 62–66, 86, 95–97, 99, 161–62, 165, 166n27, 172, 180n8, 184–85, 189n19, 191n22, 195–97, 199, 201–3, 209, 211, 214–17, 219, 220–22, 228n9, 230n14, 232n20, 233
    primitive gospel (*protoevangelium*), 25–27, 40, 43, 63, 208
Gospels, xviii, 6, 61, 79, 96, 172, 181, 183n13, 193–94; *see also* pseudo-gospels
grace of God/saving grace, xiii–xiv, xix, xxi, 1–2, 6, 14n13, 15–16, 19, 25–28, 32, 34–35, 36n5, 39–40, 53, 55, 60, 63–64, 67, 70, 72–74, 89–90, 92n8, 97, 100, 105n21, 128, 151, 153, 170, 172–73, 179, 189n19, 198n25, 199, 203, 210–11, 214, 218, 220–21, 226, 232n20, 245
grammatical-historical interpretation, xx, xxii
Great Commission 162, 197, 214–16, 219, 220–23, 233

heaven/heavenly (of God's dwelling place), 2, 3, 6–17, 20–29, 35, 38–44, 55–64, 73, 77–83, 91, 94, 107, 110, 114, 117, 118, 129–30, 144, 151, 154, 159, 160n22, 161–71, 182–84, 189–97, 198n25, 202–4, 213–24, 228–31, 234–35, 239, 243–46
heavens (created), 1, 3–4, 6, 8, 9, 11, 12, 30, 34–39, 45n12, 47–49, 51–52, 65, 82, 101, 109, 115, 139, 142, 144, 148, 154–55, 164, 167, 178, 182, 196, 220, 221
Hebrew scriptures, xiv, 19, 45n12, 61, 65, 77n21, 158, 172
Hegel's dialectic, xvii
hell/hellish, 2, 15, 16, 25, 38, 39, 41–43, 76n20, 107, 129, 166, 167n28, 169, 192, 205n30, 214, 217, 229, 230, 235
historical criticism, xvi–xix, xx, xxi, 14n13, 45n12, 69n12, 79n24, 93n10, 111n23, 119n26, 125n30, 135n4, 141n12, 142n13, 158n20, 178n7, 181n10, 181n11, 182n13, 183n14, 187n17, 191n22, 198n25, 205n30
historical Jesus, xvi–xviii, 158n20, 183n14, 187n17
Holy Spirit, xvi, 4–5, 22–24, 31, 39, 53–55, 63–65, 74, 99, 122, 156–57, 159, 161, 166, 173, 182–86, 188–89, 194n24, 195–96, 198n25, 199–204, 214–15, 218, 220–23, 227, 229, 240
holy war (*cherem*), 25, 40, 45–46, 55, 59, 78–79, 84, 93, 108, 115–16, 121–28, 132–33, 135–36, 138, 140, 170, 175, 177, 204, 211, 213, 214n38, 215, 217, 238, 249
homosexuality, 76–77
Hosea, 13–15
    and Gomer, 244–45

Subject Index

image of God/*imago Dei*, 2, 15, 17, 21, 49, 54, 248
incarnation of Christ, xviii, 20, 40, 173n2, 181, 216, 217, 219, 223
    pre-incarnate Son, 5-6
inerrancy of Scripture, xii, xiv, xvii, xxii
inheritance, eternal, xv, 16, 64-65, 83, 91, 164, 182n12, 188-89, 198
    of Canaan, 151-52, 170, 221
intrusion ethics (Kline), 9, 38, 80n25, 213n37, 225-29, 235-45
Isaac:
    binding of, 59, 73, 79-84, 243
    patriarch, 10, 62, 85, 93, 111, 114-17, 119, 128, 133, 151-53, 180, 184, 185, 191, 192, 196-97, 201, 202, 206, 209, 218, 220-21
Isaiah (prophet), 100, 155-56, 168n29, 201
Islam and *jihad*, 79n23
Israel (theocratic nation), xv, 8, 22, 50, 52, 61, 63, 70, 80, 83n27, 85, 88-89, 94-95, 102, 105-11, 117-18, 121, 128, 131, 157, 159-60, 174, 183-84, 195-96, 209-10, 215, 228-29, 231
    Christ as fulfillment of, 101, 130, 154, 156, 159, 163, 172, 176, 188, 215, 217
    circumcision of, 45, 66-67, 74, 107-9, 121-23, 129-30, 200, 207, 218, 236n30
    conquest of Canaan, 58, 78-79, 83n27, 93, 97, 103-4, 108, 111, 115-16, 119, 121-28, 130, 131, 133, 152, 211-15, 218-19, 237-40
    disobedience of, 13, 15-16, 24, 97, 101, 103-6, 111, 114, 126, 147-50, 152, 154, 173-74, 178, 208-9, 218, 230
    distinct from church, xix-xx, 110-11, 132n2, 156n19, 228-29, 243
    divided kingdom of, 24, 146-49, 152-55, 170, 174
    exile of, 105n21, 114, 147-49, 175-78
    Exodus of, 41, 109, 111, 118, 121, 144, 152, 200, 204-7, 218
    foreshadows Christ, xv, 110, 129-30, 154, 157
    foreshadows Kingdom of God, 168, 171-72, 215, 217, 229, 231-34, 240, 242-45
    Judges of, 133
    judgment/curses upon, 11, 13, 16, 24, 51, 71, 86-87, 97, 104-7, 110, 112, 114, 126, 129, 141, 149-50, 152-54, 170, 173, 175, 208-10, 215, 218, 230-31, 242, 245n58
    land of, 66n6
    laws of, 11-12, 15-17, 45, 50-53, 75, 89-92, 96, 100, 107-9, 113-14, 129, 173, 207-8, 215, 230
    mission to the nations of, 63n5
    modern nation of, 209n34
    monarchy of, 106, 122-23, 131-59, 163, 168-70, 174, 184, 197, 208
    obedience of, xxi, 11-12, 16, 70, 74, 87-89, 95-96, 98-104, 107, 110-11, 114, 117-19, 122, 129-31, 134, 138n7, 143, 147, 149-50, 154, 173-74, 208-10, 214n38, 218, 230-31
    rejection of Jesus, xiv, 5, 61-62, 64, 157-58, 172-73, 186, 191-92, 195-97, 208-10, 218
    salvation/blessing of, 16, 63n5, 87, 90, 104, 107, 109-10, 112, 119, 121-22, 129, 141, 149-50, 170-71, 173, 209-11, 230-31
    sworn oaths of, 70, 87-89, 100-1, 113-14, 120-21, 128, 130, 150, 173-74, 190
    tabernacle of, 8-9, 92, 95, 100, 102, 143, 246
    temple of, 8-9, 39n8, 42, 51, 54, 81, 140, 141n12, 143-45, 157, 163-64, 179n7, 179n8, 191-92, 196, 208-9, 214, 218, 240, 244, 246
    under Abrahamic covenant, 128-29, 151-53, 170-71
    under Mosaic covenant, 70n14, 85-130, 140, 145-50, 154, 170, 178, 208-10, 213, 230-31
    wilderness era of, 24, 50, 87, 97, 101-12, 115, 118, 121-22, 130, 133, 152, 204, 213, 246-47

Jeremiah (prophet), 10, 70, 106, 174, 177, 192
    and New Covenant, 75, 96, 173, 174-75, 189n18, 206n33, 217
Jericho, 82, 108, 117, 119, 121-22, 124-25, 127, 213, 240
Jerusalem, 51, 64, 70, 146-47, 149-50, 157, 159, 161, 162-63, 172
    fall to Babylon, 39n8, 41, 100, 106, 174-78
    fall to Rome, 39n8, 51, 54, 100, 111, 129, 164, 173, 179n8, 180, 208-9, 215, 218
    founded by David, 133, 136-38, 139n8, 143, 151n15, 153, 154, 170
    Jesus' entry into, 186-87, 193-94, 208
    New/Heavenly, 17, 42, 154, 163-64, 167, 168n29, 169, 222-23
    rebuilt, 179, 217, 244
    temple in, 8-9, 39n8, 42, 51, 54, 81, 140, 141n12, 143-45, 157, 163-64, 179n7, 179n8, 191-92, 196, 208-9, 214, 218, 240, 244, 246
Jerusalem Council, 53-54
Jesus/Jesus Christ, *see* Christ Jesus

Subject Index

Jewish Christians, 7, 53, 66, 162–63, 175, 210–11, 217
Jews/Judaism, xiv, 5, 6n8, 31n28, 40, 52n19, 55–56, 61–64, 66n6, 79, 83n27, 84, 91, 132, 157–59, 165, 172, 174n4, 176–77, 179, 183n13, 184, 186, 191–92, 195, 196, 198n25, 202, 209, 210n35, 214–15, 218
John the Apostle, 6–7, 17, 29, 52, 81, 85, 161, 164–68, 180n8, 196
John the Baptist, 80, 180n8, 182, 183n14, 184–85, 187n17, 192, 200–1
Jordan River, 108, 111, 113–15, 117–19, 121, 124, 128, 130, 134, 182, 183n14, 185, 201, 212, 213n37
Joshua, 55, 102, 108, 111, 117–31, 213n37
  and Caleb, 103–5
Judaism, *see* Jews/Judaism
Judges, period of, 119n26, 131, 133, 139n8
judgments of God, xxi, xxiii, 11, 13, 22–24, 28, 34, 37–38, 40, 45n12, 56, 106, 124n28, 151–52, 157, 163, 165, 173–75, 184–85, 191n22, 194n24, 206–7, 213–14, 218–19, 226–27, 237, 241, 245n58
  eschatological/ final, xiii, xv, xxiii, 2, 15, 19, 23, 31–32, 38–43, 46, 57, 75–79, 80n25, 84, 103n20, 107, 116–17, 125n30, 135, 166–69, 171, 179, 198n25, 213–14, 218–19, 222–24, 227, 229, 237–43, 247–48
  Flood, 8, 23, 30–1, 33–52, 57, 75–76, 78–79, 168–69, 203, 206n32, 218
  redemptive, 23, 30, 40–41, 59–61, 75–79, 84, 93, 121, 128, 203–4, 207, 218, 222–24, 229
  on Sodom and Gomorrah, 37–38, 46, 59, 76–79, 84
justification:
  and Abrahamic Covenant, 59, 62, 66–7, 84
  in Christ, 19, 26, 194n24, 249
  by faith, xxi, 16n16, 26, 59, 62–7, 84, 198n25, 232n20
  in New Covenant, 176, 194n24, 198n25
  of Old Testament believers, xxi, 26, 62, 66–67, 84, 182n12
  by works, 53, 66–67

kerygma, xviii–xix
Kingdom of God:
  and Abrahamic Covenant, 58–84
  and Covenant of Creation, 1–32
  and Davidic Covenant, 131–71
  eschatological, xiii, xv, 2, 39, 82, 132–33, 160–71, 184, 194, 197–98, 200, 216–19, 224–45
  and Mosaic/Sinaitic Covenant, 85–130

and New Covenant, 172–219
and Noahic Covenants, 33–57
types of, 36, 39, 42, 44, 47, 59–61, 83, 103n20, 105n21, 110, 120, 131–33, 140n14, 143, 155, 159, 169, 171, 208, 209n34, 229, 231–35, 239–40, 242, 244–45
kingdom of heaven, xiv, 101, 103n20, 154, 157–58, 185, 189n19, 200–1, 209n34, 214, 215, 231, 244
Kingdom of Satan, xiii, xv, xxiii, 23–25, 34–35, 40, 43, 135n4, 140, 169, 181, 196–97, 204, 214, 224

law (Mosaic/Sinaitic), xxi, 11–16, 19, 24, 53, 59, 63–67, 70n14, 71, 84–92, 95–102, 105, 108–13, 117, 120, 128–31, 138n5, 139n8, 140–49, 154–55, 170, 173–74, 177–78, 180n8, 182n12, 189n18, 189n19, 190, 197, 207–10, 214n38, 229–30, 234, 236, 240n39, 244
  ceremonial, 25, 49, 51–53, 91–92, 134, 188, 236n30
  food, 51–52, 54, 100; *see also* blood
  given on Mt. Sinai, 17, 22, 71, 85, 92, 94, 102, 105, 108–10, 129, 148, 183, 212
  judicial, 91–92, 98–99, 236n30, 237n33
  moral, 91–92, 98–99, 236n30, 237n33
  Ten Commandments (Decalogue), 11, 17, 75, 88, 91–92, 95, 236, 238–44
liberal theology, xviii

Marxism, xviii
mediator:
  Jesus Christ, 19, 32, 36, 39, 45, 53, 55, 76, 81–82, 83n27, 90–92, 96n12, 97–98, 162–63, 172–74, 176, 180, 181, 187, 188–89, 191n21, 192n23, 194n24, 195, 200, 204, 206, 217, 219, 220
  Joshua, 120, 128
  Moses, 11, 15, 71, 85, 89, 93, 94n11, 110–11, 117, 118n25, 120n27, 183, 212, 214n38
  Noah, 36, 39–40
Melchizedek, 151n15, 157, 191
Messiah, xiv–xv, 25, 27, 44, 56, 73, 76, 157, 179n7
  Creator, 5
  offspring of Abraham, 61, 81
  Son of David, 132–33, 151, 153–59, 160, 162–64, 184, 186–87
  See also Christ Jesus: Messiah
Messianic prophecy, 25, 27, 35, 44, 59, 61, 79–81, 92, 132, 154–57, 176n6, 180, 190–91, 195, 208, 210n35, 217

SUBJECT INDEX

millennium (eschatological), 160, 165n24, 166n22
missionaries, *see* evangelical mission
monarchy period, 106, 122–23, 131–59, 163, 168–70, 174, 184, 197, 208; *see also* David; Davidic Kingdom; Saul
moral law of God, 13, 16, 51, 70, 104, 122, 142, 147, 150, 153, 173–77, 209–10, 218, 240, 245n58; *see also* Ten Commandments
Mosaic/Sinaitic Covenant, xxiii, 11–16, 22–25, 45, 50–53, 68, 70–71, 75, 85–130, 138n7, 140–53, 162, 170–83, 188, 190, 209, 212–13, 214n38, 217, 232, 245n58
    as covenant of grace, 95–93, 96–99, 104, 107–12, 120, 128–30, 173n2, 190
    externally covenant of law, 85n2, 87–89, 94, 96–102, 104–8, 110–14, 119–20, 122, 126, 128–30, 138n7, 140–50, 153, 162, 170–80, 188, 190, 209, 231, 235
    fulfilled by Jesus, 19, 49, 97–98, 101, 129, 140, 173n2, 180–81
    and republication, 87, 96–99, 129
    as suzerainty covenant, 12, 87–88, 112, 128, 130
Moses (leader), 19, 52, 62, 70n14, 72n18, 85, 89–95, 102–5, 107–18, 124, 127–28, 130, 131, 133, 144, 163, 183–84, 189, 204–7, 212, 214n38
    authorship of Pentateuch, xxi, 3, 15–16, 37n7, 49–50, 53–54, 90, 93n10, 96, 99, 111n23, 245n58
    mediator, 11, 15, 71, 85, 89, 93, 94n11, 110–11, 117, 118n25, 120n27, 183, 212, 214n38
    prophet, 62, 85, 93, 111–14, 118, 124, 130, 131, 133, 183
Mount Moriah, 59, 73, 79–84
Mount Sinai, 17, 22, 71, 85, 92, 94, 102, 105, 108–10, 129, 148, 183, 212
Mount Zion, 136, 138, 143–44, 157, 162–63, 187, 209, 222, 246
    as Mount Moriah, 81
    mythology, xviii, 3n4, 36n6, 191n22

Nag Hammadi documents, 181n11
Nathan, 139n8, 141, 142n13, 184n15
Nero (emperor), 164
New Covenant, xxiii, 12, 36, 39, 45, 49–58, 62, 74–76, 81–83, 87, 90–92, 96–98, 110–11, 132, 151, 162–63, 172–219, 220–21, 228–32, 236, 239, 242–43
    community of, xviii, xx, 39, 45, 53–55, 74, 79, 162, 173, 189n18, 206n33, 208, 216, 220–23, 243
    continuity with Old Testament, xx, 90n6, 160, 206, 229–32, 242
    as covenant of royal grant, 12, 132, 181–82, 187, 191, 217
    Jesus as Mediator of, 19, 32, 36, 39, 45, 53, 55, 76, 81–82, 83n27, 90–92, 96n12, 97–98, 162–63, 172–74, 176, 180, 181, 187, 188–89, 191n21, 192n23, 194n24, 195, 200, 204, 206, 217, 219, 220
    mission of, 55, 214–19
    prophesied by Jeremiah, 75, 96, 173, 174–75, 189n18, 206n33, 217
    sacraments as signs of, 45, 200, 203n28, 206, 208, 218
New Heavens and New Earth, 167–70, 214, 219, 224
New Jerusalem, 17, 42, 154, 163–64, 167, 168n29, 169, 222–23
New Perspectives on Paul, 198n25
Noah, 30, 34–57, 58, 60, 75–76, 78–79, 168–69, 178n7, 203, 206n32, 218, 229
    and Ark, 24, 30, 34–44, 47–48, 49n15, 50, 52, 57, 78–79, 168–69, 203, 218, 229
    covenant community of, 23, 30, 34–35, 38–39, 41–45, 50, 79, 168, 203, 218
    and Flood, 8, 23, 30–1, 33–52, 57, 75–76, 78, 79n23, 168–69, 203, 206n32, 218
    obedience of, 36, 39
    as prophet, 39–40
    sacrifices by, 44, 47–49, 52
    as type of Christ, 35–36, 39, 49
Noahic Covenants:
    Prediluvian covenant, 12, 23–24, 30, 33–36, 39–40, 44, 50–51, 57, 132, 138, 170, 172, 182
    Postdiluvian covenant, 30, 33–34, 43–57, 75–76

oaths:
    sworn by Israel, 70, 87–89, 100–1, 113–14, 120–21, 128, 130, 150, 173–74, 190
    sworn by Yahweh, 59–60, 67, 72–74, 81, 83, 87–89, 92, 104, 106, 112–17, 120, 128, 138–40, 143, 151n15, 153, 159, 189–91, 195, 237
obedience, 46, 53, 66, 73, 84, 86n2, 182, 198n25, 199, 221, 233n20
    of Abraham, 66–67, 74, 80n25, 81–83, 151n15, 243
    of Adam, 15–16, 36, 226, 229, 231, 248
    of Christ, 19–20, 36, 39, 81, 83, 189, 193, 196–200, 214n38, 231, 249
    of David, 151n15

SUBJECT INDEX

obedience (*continued*)
   of Israel, xxi, 11–12, 16, 70, 74, 87–89, 95–96, 98–104, 107, 110–11, 114, 117–19, 122, 129–31, 134, 138n7, 143, 147, 149–50, 154, 173–74, 208–10, 214n38, 218, 230–31
   of Noah, 36, 39
Olivet Discourse, 24, 42–43, 208
original sin:
   as the first sin, 1, 19, 21–22, 25–26, 28, 33, 40, 63, 85, 182
   as human condition, 19

pagans, 24, 60, 63, 108–9, 148, 162–63, 173, 195, 215, 231, 244
Parousia, 9, 23n23, 24, 27, 31–32, 41, 43, 46, 54n21, 76, 79, 84, 117, 135, 158, 214, 218, 228, 236, 241, 248; *see also* return of Christ *and* Second Coming
Passover, 158, 191, 200, 206–8, 218, 228
Paul (apostle), 54, 62, 196–97, 202n27, 204
   apostle to Gentiles, 63–66, 84
   conversion of, 5, 19, 24, 62–66, 84, 197, 203–4
   former legalism of, 62–64, 197
   theology of, xiii, 5–6, 16n16, 18–20, 24–25, 26n25, 56–57, 59, 62–67, 79n24, 84–85, 90n6, 98–99, 182n12, 196–200, 198n25, 204, 209–11, 218, 222–23, 240–41
Pentateuch, xxi, 69n12, 85, 93n10, 111n23
   Mosaic authorship of, xxi, 3, 15–16, 37n7, 49–50, 53–54, 90, 93n10, 96, 99, 111n23, 181n10, 245n58
Pentecost, 7, 31, 40, 51, 55, 61–62, 65, 159, 161–62, 184, 195–96, 201–2, 218, 220
Peter, 37n7, 38–40, 51, 53, 57n23, 62–63, 159, 161, 168n29, 184–85, 195–97, 202–3, 218, 220–21
   confession of, 192–93
Plato (Platonism), 181n11
predestination, 29
Presbyterians, 206n33
Promised Land, 16, 50–52, 55–56, 61, 65, 71–72, 77–83, 87, 92–93, 96–97, 100–22, 125n29, 127–30, 131, 133, 140–41, 148, 150, 157, 162–63, 170–74, 176n6, 177–78, 201n26, 208–21, 228–29, 233n21, 237; *see also* Canaan; Zoar
Promises of God, xxi, 14, 17, 19, 32, 59, 61, 65, 81, 86, 91, 98–99, 138n7, 159, 161, 163, 168n28, 168n29, 182n12, 195–99, 210n35, 221–22, 233n20
   to Abraham, 59–66, 71–76, 79–84, 85, 87–88, 90n6, 105n21, 107–8, 111, 114, 117, 121, 123–24, 128, 133, 150–52, 160, 170–71, 190, 212, 220–21
   to Adam and Eve, 25, 28
   to David, 132, 139–40, 141n12, 144–45, 151, 154, 155n18, 156n19, 160, 182n12, 223
   to Israel, 110, 114–15, 119, 125n29, 129, 174–75, 176n6, 188–89, 212, 231, 238
   of Kingdom, 13, 60, 83, 91, 105n21, 150, 188–89, 212
   of land, 16, 50–52, 55–56, 61, 65, 71–72, 77–83, 87, 92–93, 96–97, 100–22, 125n29, 127–30, 131, 133, 140–41, 148, 150, 157, 162–63, 170–74, 176n6, 177–78, 201n26, 208–21, 228–29, 233n21, 237
   to Noah, 33, 44, 46, 76
Prophecy, xix, 23–26, 36–37, 40, 61–62, 73, 80–84, 88, 93, 101, 104, 128, 132, 135n4, 141, 146–50, 174, 177–80, 188, 209, 211n36, 218, 223, 237, 240n39, 245n58
   Messianic, xiv, 25, 59, 62, 79–84, 132, 140n10, 154–59, 172, 180n8, 187, 190–91, 194–95, 201, 208, 210n35, 217
   of New Covenant, 75, 96, 173, 174–75, 189n18, 206n33, 217
Prophets of God, 7, 13, 23, 39–40, 62, 96–97, 101, 134, 146–49, 151–52, 184n15, 184–85, 187, 192, 197, 199, 245n58
   Daniel, 82, 176–80, 217
   David, 157–59, 183n13, 184n16, 190–91, 195
   Ezekiel, 175–76, 179n7
   Hosea, 13–15, 244–45
   Isaiah, 100, 155–56, 168n29, 201
   Jeremiah, 10, 70, 75, 96, 106, 173–75, 177, 189n18, 192, 206n33, 217
   Jesus, 78, 183n13, 184n16, 187, 191–95, 208–9
   Moses, 62, 85, 93, 111–14, 118, 124, 130, 131, 133, 183
   Noah, 39–40
protoevangelium, 25–26; *see also* gospel: primitive gospel
pseudo-gospels, 181n11, 216n39

Rahab, 124, 125n30, 213n37, 240–41
rainbow sign, 45–46, 75
Redeemer, xiii, 1, 5, 7, 9, 99, 207–8, 223
redemption, xiii–xv, xix–xxii, 1–2, 9, 13n11, 19–21, 25, 27, 32–35, 40–45, 52, 57–60, 64, 73, 75n19, 76, 78, 81, 84, 86, 99–100, 103n20, 104, 130, 140n10, 160n22,

166, 167n28, 173n2, 182, 188, 191n22, 193–200, 218, 220, 226–28, 231–32
redemptive history, xv, xix–xxiii, 1–2, 18–20, 25–29, 31, 33–34, 37, 39n8, 40–41, 43, 46–47, 49, 52n19, 55–66, 72–75, 78–79, 83n27, 84, 85, 88, 90n6, 96–99, 103n20, 108, 116, 125n29, 125n30, 128, 133, 140n10, 153–55, 156n19, 159–60, 163–64, 196, 202–4, 206, 209–12, 215–20, 226–34, 235n28, 236–42, 245, 246–48 (poems)
Reformation, Protestant, xi, xx–xxi, 96, 198n25
reprobation, 24, 28–29, 32, 39, 41–43, 46, 79, 214, 218, 236–37, 240
resurrection:
  of believers, 20, 132n2, 163, 165–66, 194n24, 198n25, 214, 222–24
  of Christ, xviii, 6–7, 18, 20, 40, 51, 54–55, 61, 64–65, 66n7, 81, 133, 156n19, 159–66, 171–72, 173n2, 179, 181, 189, 191–203, 214–20, 222
  general, 20, 165–66, 167n28, 169, 196
return of Christ, 60–61, 75, 82, 164, 166n26, 167n28, 175n5, 210n35, 219, 247; *see also* Parousia, Second Coming
revelation, ix–x, xiii–xiv, 7, 16, 23
  general, xiii, 1, 4, 8
  in Jesus, 5–6, 14, 24, 63–64, 78–82, 164, 173n2, 183, 189n19, 193, 197, 203
  progressive, 61, 66n8, 72n18, 164, 230n14, 232
  special, xiii–xv, xxii–xxiii, 1, 3–4, 10–11, 15, 18n18, 25–29, 32–43, 51, 59–60, 65, 70, 74, 75n19, 76–82, 91–93, 99, 107, 109, 115, 128–29, 135n4, 142, 161, 166–69, 172–78, 188, 190, 192, 217, 227, 229, 237n33, 244–45
Roman Catholic Church, 198n25
Roman Empire, 54–56, 100, 157, 163–64, 172–73, 195, 209, 215

Sabbath, 1, 53–54, 100, 119n27, 193, 196–97, 229
  and creation eschatology, 10–12, 248
  as sign of Mosaic Covenant, 75, 108–11, 130
sacraments, 75n19, 235
  baptism, 37n7, 40, 45, 200, 203n28, 205n30, 206n31, 206n32, 218
  circumcision as, 45, 200
  Lord's Supper, 200, 206, 218
  Passover meal as, 200
  tree of life as, 16–17, 27

sacrifice(s), 13, 24–25, 29, 44, 47–54, 69, 89–91, 99, 134, 137, 149, 178–79, 190, 217, 228, 236n30
  of Christ, 44, 49, 53, 59, 73, 80–81, 84, 92, 96–97, 99, 162, 179n8, 189–91, 199n25, 207–8, 218, 228, 243
  of Isaac, 59, 80–82, 83n27, 84, 243
  by Noah, 44, 47–49, 52
salvation:
  by grace through faith, 9, 16, 25, 27, 32, 35, 39–40, 43–45, 53, 62, 67, 73–74, 86–87, 89–90, 96–100, 103n20, 109, 128–29, 172–73, 200, 210–11, 218, 233n20
  of the Jews, 53, 209–11, 218
  in New Covenant, xvi–xvii, xx, 20, 25, 32, 53, 62, 65, 73–74, 82–84, 86–87, 90, 96, 179, 189n19, 190–91, 194n24, 196, 198n25, 200, 203, 210–11, 214, 218, 222–23, 227, 230
  of Noahic covenant community, 30, 35, 37n7, 39, 203, 218
  of Old Testament saints, 39–40, 62–63, 67, 74, 76–78, 84, 87, 89–90, 91n7, 96–100, 104, 109, 112, 124, 128–29, 134, 143, 151, 176, 182n12, 205, 210–11, 230
Samuel (prophet), 62, 134–35, 184n15, 241
Satan, 20–21, 23, 27, 138, 165, 169, 172, 182, 185–87, 193, 194n24, 205n30, 217; *see also* Kingdom of Satan
Saul (first king of Israel), 122–23, 132–36, 141, 142n13, 161–62, 170, 184n15, 241
Scriptures, ix, xiii–xiv, xvi–xvii, xix, xxii, 18–19, 22, 33, 58, 61, 63, 65, 85, 158, 165n24, 172, 192, 194, 199, 210n35, 223; *see also* Bible; Hebrew Scriptures; Word of God
Second Coming, 24, 42, 59, 78, 110, 125n29, 125n30, 130, 132–33, 155n18, 160–61, 164–67, 169, 171, 176n6, 179–80, 198n25, 209–11, 215, 217–18, 221–23; *see also* Christ Jesus: return; Parousia
Second Temple Judaism, 198n25
Septuagint, 34n3, 77n21, 77n22, 81n26
Sermon on the Mount, 46, 55, 74, 101, 169, 216, 219, 239
Seventh Day Adventists, 52n19
Sihon and Og (kings), 115–16
sin(s)/sinners, 7, 12, 15, 18–40, 46, 53, 59, 66, 73–99, 103n20, 104, 111, 120, 126, 147–48, 152–53, 162, 170–88, 189n18, 189n19, 190, 191n22, 194n24, 197–213, 223, 226, 239–45, 248
Sinaitic Covenant, *see* Mosaic Covenant

Subject Index

Sodom and Gomorrah, 31, 37–38, 39n8, 46, 59, 71
    as redemptive judgment, 59, 77–79, 84
    as type of eschatological judgment, 76–79, 84
Solomon, 81, 140–47, 154, 184n15, 184n16
Spirit of God, *see* Holy Spirit
state (political), 28–30, 34, 45n12, 54n21, 55–57, 60, 209n34, 231, 234–35, 238, 241–44, 245n58
Stephen, 161–63
systematic theology, xi–xii, xviii–xxii, 225n1, 232, 235n28

tabernacle, 8–9, 92, 95, 100, 102, 143, 246
temple, 8–9, 39n8, 42, 54, 81, 140, 141n12, 143–45, 157, 163, 191–92, 196, 214, 240, 244, 246
    destruction of, 51, 54, 164, 179n7, 179n8, 208–9, 218
Ten Commandments (Decalogue), 11, 17, 75, 88, 91–92, 95, 236, 238–44
theocracy, 11, 21n20, 29, 34, 47–48, 50, 51–52, 57, 65, 72, 81, 83, 100, 109, 110, 121, 130, 131, 137, 143n14, 150, 170–71, 173, 208–9, 212, 215, 218, 229
theonomy, 225, 229, 230n24, 231n15, 232–34, 242n46
theophany, 4, 9, 21–23, 72–73, 88–89, 93–94, 129, 183
Titus (son of Emperor Vespasian), 209
Tower of Babel, 30–31
treaties:
    ancient Near Eastern, 12, 34, 58–59, 67–71, 83, 85–87, 112, 120
    of royal grant, 12, 59, 67, 71, 83
    suzerainty, 12, 32, 68–70, 72, 87–88, 118n25, 119, 128, 130

tree of knowledge of good and evil, 2, 13, 15–17, 21–22, 23n23, 27, 48n15, 248
tree of life, 2, 15–17, 27, 222–23, 248
triune God, xvi, 1, 4–5, 7, 13, 27, 31, 36n5, 79, 100, 169, 182–83, 199, 215, 224
types/typology:
    of Christ, 19, 35–36, 39, 49, 90, 92n8, 96, 99, 138, 140, 154, 172, 179n8, 182n12, 184n16, 208, 228, 243
    of eschatological judgment, 16, 41–42, 76–78, 84, 87, 107, 117, 125, 129, 168, 213–14, 217–18, 227–28, 238, 241
    of justification/salvation, 26, 35, 40, 47, 91n7, 107, 129, 227
    of Kingdom of God, 36, 39, 42, 44, 47, 59–61, 83, 103n20, 105n21 110, 120, 131–33, 140n14, 143, 155, 159, 169, 171, 208, 209n34, 229, 231–35, 239–40, 242, 244–45
    of Sabbath rest, 10, 130

Westminster Standards, 87, 92n8, 97–99, 129
wilderness generation, 24, 50, 87, 97, 101–12, 115, 118, 121–22, 130, 133, 152, 204, 213, 246–47
Word of God, xii, xiv, xvii, xix, xxii, 110, 185–86; *see also* Bible; Hebrew Scriptures; Scriptures
worldview:
    ancient Near Eastern, 2
    biblical, xv, xxiii, 2, 47, 226
    Greco-Roman, xviii, 4, 6
    Jewish, 40

Zedekiah (king), 70, 106, 149–50
Zion, *see* Jerusalem *and* Mount Zion
Zoar, 38, 77–78, 117

Scripture Index

Genesis

1–2	3n2, 13n11, 18
1–3	1, 9, 32
1:1	2, 3
1:1–2	4
1:1—2:25	1, 32
1:2–23	3
1:2—2:3	2, 3
1:2—2:24	2
1:10	8
1:12	8
1:14–19	5
1:18	8
1:21	8
1:25	8
1:26	5, 31n28
1:26–30	47
1:28	48–49
1:29	48n15
1:29–30	48
1:31	8, 9
2:1–3	11
2:2–3	10
2:4–25	3, 13
2:7–9	15
2:15–17	14
2:16–17	17, 48n15
3	13, 22
3:1–7	21, 182
3:7	26n24, 26n25
3:8	22–24, 32
3:8–13	22
3:14–15	21, 25
3:14–19	20, 21
3:15	1, 2, 25, 27, 32, 35, 40, 43, 59–61, 63, 75, 79, 87, 90, 96, 98, 128, 172–73, 182, 188, 208, 227, 237n33
3:16–19	2, 27, 28, 30, 32, 41–43, 57, 227
3:20–21	25
3:21	26, 49n15
3:21–24	40
3:22	16, 17
3:22–24	17, 27
4:1–7	52
4:1–8	29
4:4	49n15
4:17–22	29–30
6:5–7	34
6:5—8:19	23, 30, 33
6:5—9:17	33
6:8	34, 35
6:8—8:19	203
6:17	36
6:17–22	35
6:18	36
6:22—7:5	39
7:1–3	47
7:1–24	168
7:2	50
7:8	50
7:15–16	42
7:17	36n7
7:17–24	37
7:21–23	41
8:1–12	168
8:13–19	168–69
8:20	50
8:20–22	44, 48, 80
8:20—9:17	30, 33, 43, 75n19
9:1	44
9:1–3	49
9:1–7	47
9:2	49n16
9:3	48n15, 49, 50
9:3–6	54

Genesis (continued)

Reference	Page
9:4	52
9:7	44
9:8–13	44–45
9:8–17	45n12, 75
9:11	76
9:11–15	46
9:15	76
10:1–32	30
11	xv
11:1–9	30–31
11:7	31n28
11:27—25:11	58, 88
12:1–3	60, 63n5
12:3	61, 66n6
12:4	72n18
12:7	72n18
13:10	77
14:13	213n37
14:8–24	71
15	71, 72, 237
15:1	71
15:1–6	65
15:6	59, 65n6, 66–67
15:13	72n18
15:17	72n18, 73, 74
15:17–20	120
15:17–21	72, 88
15:18–21	160, 176n6
17:1	72n18
17:1–2	74
17:1–14	107
17:5	60n3
17:9–14	74–75
17:22–27	66
18:17–19	61
18:22—19:19	38
19:4–5	76–77
19:12–17	77
19:23–25	38
19:23–26	78
22:1–19	92n9
22:8	80
22:9–14	80
22:15–18	73
22:16–18	190n20
22:18	81, 90n6
26:1–5	81–82
26:2f.	83n27
26:5	83n27

Exodus

Reference	Page
1–18	96n12
1:15–21	241
12:1–32	207
12:43–51	207
14:1–31	200
14:5	205n30
14:21–31	204–5
19–24	12, 68, 70, 85, 88, 102, 108, 111, 190, 209, 212
19–40	96n12
19:1–6	109
19:6	231
19:7–10	89
19:8	70, 150
19:16–20	22, 94
19:18	94
20	17
20:2	88
20:3–17	88, 91
20:8–11	11, 75
20:14–19	92
20:22–26	92
21:1—23:9	92
21:22–25	242n46
23:20–33	88, 92, 93, 212–13
23:22–33	238
24	88
24:3	70, 150
24:4–7	89
24:4–8	90
24:7	70, 150
24:8	70n14
24:12	94n11
24:12–14	102
24:15–18	94, 183–84
25:10–22	95
25:16–22	95
31:12–17	11–12
31:12–18	75
31:14–18	109, 242
34:10–16	213, 238
35:2	242
35:30—39:43	102
39:32–43	102
40:1–15	95
40:1–33	95, 102
40:16–33	95
40:34–38	102

Leviticus

1:3–17	80
11:1–47	51
11:40	50
11:46–47	51
12:1–5	107
12:1–47	51
17:10–16	53
18:1–5	16, 100
18:5	109–10
19:18	239
19:29	244
24:5–10	100
24:8	100n19
24:16	242
24:19–21	242n46
27:34	92

Numbers

4:15	138n5
10:11–16	102
11:1–2	242
13:1–24	103
13:25–33	103
13:27	103n20
14:1–4	103
14:5–10	103–4
14:13–19	104
14:20–25	104
14:26–38	104–5
15:32–36	110, 242
16:31ff.	242
19:5	91n7
21:21–35	115
27:15–23	118n25, 213n37

Deuteronomy

1:1–5	112
1:1—34:12	68
1:6—3:29	105
1:6—4:49	112
1:30	125n29
2:14–19	105–6
2:26–35	115–16
2:28—3:22	115
3:1–7	116
3:28	118n25
4:25–31	114
5:1—26:19	112
5:1—26:49	113
5:12–15	11
6:13	185
6:16	185
7:1–5	124, 127
7:1–6	213
7:1–10	238
8:3	185
9:1–6	115
12:10	139n8
13:5ff.	242
14:3–21	51
14:21	50
17:2ff.	242
17:14–20	131, 133
19:15–21	215–16
19:21	242n46
20:10–15	78
20:10–18	238
20:16–18	78, 124, 127, 213
23:6	239
23:14	125n29
23:17	244
26:9	103n20
27:1–26	113
27:1—30:20	112
27:11–26	113
28ff.	245n58
29:9–16	113–14
30:3	210n35
30:3–6	210
30:15–20	117
31:1–8	117
31:1—34:12	112
31:3	118n25
31:7	118n25
32:42	45n12
33:29	71n15
34:1–8	117–18
34:9	118n25
34:9–12	118

Joshua

1:6	125n29
1:9	125n29
2	213n37
3:1–17	119
4:1–24	121
5:2–9	108, 121
5:3–9	122
5:13–15	125n29
6:1–27	124

Joshua (continued)

6:1—12:24	119
6:2	125n29
6:15–21	124
6:17	125n30
6:21	125n30
7:1–9	126
7:10–15	126
7:22–26	126
7–8	238
8:1	125n29
8:1–29	126
8:24–29	126–27
9	213n37
10:8	125n29
10:29–43	127
10:40–43	127
11:1–23	127
11:6	125n29
11:16–20	127–28
13:1–7	119
13:8–33	128
13:8–21:45	119
14:1	213n37
14:1—19:51	128
19:51	213n37
20:1–9	128
21:1–45	128
21:43–45	119
21:44	119n27
23	119n27
23:1	119n27
24	111, 119n27
24:1–33	68, 119, 128, 130
24:2–13	121
24:11–13	121
24:13	123
24:14–25	120

Judges

2	238
3:28	125n29
4:14	125n29
6:3	125n29
7:2ff.	125n29
7:15	125n29

1 Samuel

10:1–27	134
11:1–11	134
11:12–15	134
13:5–15	134–35
13:15ff.	125n29
13:3	125n29
15:1–11	135, 170
16:2	241
16:13	184n16
17:1–58	122
17:24–37	123
17:48–54	123
18:18	125n29
21:6	125n29
25:28	125n29
28:5–6	125n29
30:7–8	125n29

2 Samuel

5	138
5:1–5	133, 136, 170, 184
5:6–7	136, 170
5:17–25	136–37, 170
5:19	125n29
5:22–23	125n29
6	138
6:1–15	137–38
7	138, 139n8
7:1–14	208
7:1–17	133, 138
7:6–8	139n8
7:11–13	143
7:11–17	142
7:12–16	132, 154, 160
7:12–17	141, 170
7:14	141n11, 143n14
7:14–15	138n7, 142n13
7:15–16	151
11:11	125n29

1 Kings

2:1–4	142
3:6	138
5	139n8
6:1–37	143
8:1–11	144
8:22–26	144–45
8:62–66	145

Scripture Index

9:1–9	145
10:23–25	145–46
11:29–40	146
12:16–24	146–47

2 Kings

2:24	242
13:1–7	152–53
13:22–25	153
17:6–23	147–48

1 Chronicles

11:1–3	184
13:1–13	138
15:23–28	138
16:7–43	151
16:14–24	151, 170

2 Chronicles

3:1	81
7:4–10	145
15:8–15	149
36:22–23	244

Ezra

1:1–11	244

Psalms

2:7	197
7	239
7:12–13	45n12
16:8–11	195
18:2	71n15
18:14	45n12
27:1–4	9
33:4–9	4
35	239
55	239
59	239
64:7	45n12
69	239
77:17	45n12
78	240n39
79	239
89	154
89:1–4	139
89:3–4	151, 154–55
89:26–36	141n11
89:27–37	155
89:28–29	151
89:28–37	142–43
89:30–32	143n14
89:33–37	139, 151
96:1–6	9
104:19–30	5
105:1–45	152
105–6	240n39
109	239
110:1	159n21, 160n22
110:1–7	157
110:4	191
132	143
132:10–12	140
132:11–18	143
135–36	240n39
137	239
144:6	45n12

Isaiah

9:2–8	155
9:7	156n18
11	156n18
13:6	24
13:9	24
24:1–6	100–1
24–25	156n18
40:3	201
40:3–5	180n8
40:10	71n15
53:7	80
54	156n18
59:20–21	175n5
60–61	156n18
62:11	71n15
66:22	168n29

Jeremiah

11:1–17	106–7
23:7–8	210n35
25:1	177
25:8–14	177
28:5–6	210
29:10	180

Jeremiah (continued)

31	96, 173, 189n19
31:29–34	206n33
31:30	189n18
31:31–34	76, 174, 175n5, 189n18, 217
32	96
32:31	189n19
32:34	189n19
32:37–40	175n5
32:40	97n14
33:14–26	9
33:15–17	210
33:19–26	10
34:17–21	70
34:17–22	150
34:18–19	72n18
34:19–20	150
46:10	24

Ezekiel

14:14	178n7
14:20	178n7
16:60–63	175n5
28:3	178n7
29:19	71n15
34:20–31	175
34:23–24	140n10
37:20–28	175n5, 176n6

Daniel

1:1–4	177
7:13–14	82
9:1–2	177
9:11–15	177–78
9:24	180
9:24–27	178, 179n7, 217
9:27	180n8, 217

Hosea

1:3	244
6:4–11	13
6:7	14, 15n15

Joel

3:14	24

Amos

5:18–27	23–24

Obadiah

15	24

Habakkuk

3:11	45n12

Zechariah

9:14	45n12

Malachi

3:1	201
4:4	245n58
4:5	24

2 Maccabees

4:23–28	179n7

Matthew

1:1	61
1:16–17	61
3:1–12	201
3:16–17	182
4:1–11	185
4:5–6	180n8
4:23–25	185
5:1—7:29	55, 101
5:5	169
5:13–16	74
5:17–20	101
5:38–48	216, 219
5:43	239
5:43–45	55

5:44	239
5:45	46
8:28–34	186
12:22–28	186
16:13–20	192
16:21–23	192–93
17:22–23	193
20:17–19	193
21:1–11	187
21:2	187n17
22:15–22	56
22:41–46	157
23:35	29
23:38–39	210n35
24:1–2	208
24:31	210n35
24:36–42	42–43
24:36–44	24
25:1–13	245
26:17–25	206
26:26–28	188
26:26–29	207
26:28	189n19, 217
28:1–10	193–94
28:16–20	162, 214
28:18	197
28:18–20	219, 233
28:19–20	214n38

Mark

1:12–13	185
1:19–21	182
3:17	239
5:1–20	186
12:13–17	56n22
12:35–40	157, 158n20
13:1–2	208
14:24	189n19
14:36	200
16:1–8	194
16:17	202n27

Luke

1:26–33	156
1:33	156n18
3:21–22	182
4:1–13	185
6:27–38	239
8:26–39	186
9:54	239

10:26–28	99
17:26–30	78
19:8–10	82
19:11	160
20:20–26	56n22
20:41–44	157
21:5–9	208
21:20–24	208
21:24	210n35
22:7–16	206
22:20	189n19
24:1–12	194

John

1:1–14	6
1:17	85, 214n38
1:29–31	80
2:19–22	192
4:22	83n27
6:42	xviii
14:3	167n28
17:24	164
18:33–40	158
20:1–10	194

Acts

1:9–11	161
2:1–4	202
2:1–13	31, 161, 195, 201
2:1–41	195
2:4	202n27
2:5–13	202
2:6	202n27
2:8	202n27
2:13—3:26	196
2:14ff.	202n27
2:22–36	195
2:23–24	194n24
2:29–36	159
2:33	194n24
2:34	159n21
2:36	194n24
3:13–15	62, 194n24
3:22–25	62
4:1–4	196
4:2	194n24
4:5–12	196
4:11	194n24
4:12	194n24
5:31	194n24

Acts (continued)

7:54–60	161–62
8:1–8	161
9:1–19	204
10:1–48	51
10:9–16	51–52
10:34–43	184–85
10:42	194n24
10:46–47	202n27
11:17	202n27
13:13–41	196
13:26–39	197
13:33	194n24
15:1–5	53
15:1–35	53
15:8	202n27
15:11	53
15:15–18	210n35
15:19–21	53–54
15:27–29	54
19:6	202n27
12:2	222
13:1–5	56–57
13:1–7	240
16:25–27	64

1 Corinthians

5:3–5	25
5:6–8	207–8
6:12–20	240
6:14	194n24
6:18	240
10:1–2	205n30, 206n31
10:1–5	204, 218
11:23–26	208
14	202n27
15:1–58	20
15:12ff.	194n24
15:42–49	20

2 Corinthians

3:6	98

Romans

1:1–7	199
1:3	194n24
1:18–21	xiii
2:12–15	11
2:16	64
3:9	210n35
3:21–31	98
3:28	67
4	98, 182
4:1–25	66
4:25	194n24
5:12–21	14, 18, 19
6:1–14	198
6:4–5	194n24
6:10	194n24
8:9–11	199–200
8:11	194n24
8:12–17	200
8:17–18	164
8:21	164
8:28	164
9–11	209–10
10:1–8	16n16
10:12	210n35
11:5	211n36
11:25–27	210n35
11:25–31	209
11:26	218
11:26–27	175n5, 210n35, 210–11

Galatians

1:4	222
1:11–13	64
1:16–17	64
3	98
3:5–9	63
3:6	65n6
3:6–14	66
3:10–14	16n16
3:10–21	233n20
3:15–16	63
3:15–29	75
3:17	85
4:26	164

Ephesians

1:1–6	64–65
1:11–14	64–65
1:20–22	160n22
2:4–10	200
2:6	222
2:8	36n5
3:6	210n35
5:22–33	245

Philippians

2:13	36n5
3:20	222
3:21	164

Colossians

1:15–20	6
3:4	164

1 Thessalonians

4:13—5:11	25

2 Thessalonians

2:1–4	25

1 Timothy

1:5–10	233n20
2:4	210n35
6:15–16	197, 218

2 Timothy

2:8–10	64
3:15	xvii

Hebrews

1:1–4	7
1:1–14	162
2:2	242n46
6:13–18	73
7:20–28	190
7:26–28	80
8:13	180n8
9:11–15	188
9:15–22	91
9:19	91n7
9:23–24	228
11:1–3	4
11:4	29
11:8–16	221
11:10	164
11:13–16	164
11:31	241
12:1–2	162
12:18–29	162–64
13:14	164

James

2:23	72n18
2:25	241

1 Peter

1:1–2	220–21
2:13–14	57n23
3:18–22	39–40, 203, 218
3:21	37n7

2 Peter

2:4–6	38
2:5	40
3:5–7	38
3:6–13	41
3:10–13	46
3:13	164, 168n29

1 John

3:2	164
3:11–15	29

Jude

7	76n20

Revelation

1:1–3	164
2:7	17
3:12	164
4:8–11	7
5:6–14	81
19:6–9	245
20:1–6	165–66, 171
20:8–9	41
21:1	164, 167

Revelation (*continued*)

21:1–3	168n29	21:24	244
21:1–8	167, 169	21:27	164
21:1—22:21	169n30	22:1–2	17
21:2ff.	164	22:3–4	164
21:22–27	42	22:12–21	222–23
		22:15	169n30

www.ingramcontent.com/pod-product-compliance
Lightning Source LLC
Chambersburg PA
CBHW081416230426
43668CB00016B/2256